# RELIGION AND SCIENCE

## HISTORICAL AND CONTEMPORARY ISSUES

A Revised and Expanded Edition of
*Religion in an Age of Science*

## Ian G. Barbour

HarperSanFrancisco
*An Imprint of* HarperCollins*Publishers*

FIRST HARPERCOLLINS REVISED EDITION PUBLISHED IN 1997
Library of Congress Cataloging-in-Publication Data
Barbour, Ian G.
    Religion and science : historical and contemporary issues / Ian G. Barbour. — 1st Harper-Collins rev. ed.
    p.    cm.
    Rev. ed. of: Religion in an age of science. 1st ed. 1990. Includes bibliographical references and indexes.
    ISBN 0–06–060938–9 (pbk.)
    1. Religion and science. I. Barbour, Ian G.  Religion in an age of science. II. Title.
BL240.2.R367   1997
291.1'75—dc21                                                97-6294

 98 99 00 01 ❖/RRD 10 9 8 7 6 5 4 3

# Contents

94197

PART TWO

# RELIGION AND THE METHODS OF SCIENCE

PART THREE

# RELIGION AND THE THEORIES OF SCIENCE

PART FOUR

# PHILOSOPHICAL AND THEOLOGICAL REFLECTIONS

# Preface

This volume opens with three historical chapters on the interaction between science and religion since the seventeenth century. They are similar to the historical chapters in my earlier book *Issues in Science and Religion* but extensive revisions have been made to take into account the writings of historians in recent years.

The remaining nine chapters are taken with some revisions from my first series of Gifford Lectures given in Scotland and published as *Religion in an Age of Science*. They deal with the contemporary science-religion dialogue concerning the methods and theories of science and their implications for concepts of God and human nature. New sections have been added on "Nature-centered Spirituality" (in chapter 4), "Chaos Theory and Complexity" (in chapter 7), and "God as Determiner of Indeterminacies" and "God as Communicator of Information" (in chapter 12). In discussing both historical and contemporary issues I have made more explicit use of the fourfold typology of chapter 4, and I have explored further the relevance of alternative views in relation to environmental ethics. A Glossary and an Index of Selected Topics have also been added.

Readers who seek a briefer treatment may wish to read the volume somewhat selectively. Some chapters or sections could be skimmed, skipped, or postponed for later reading. Some persons may be more interested in the physical sciences (chapters 1, 7, and 8), others in the life sciences (chapters 3, 9, and 10), although both have been significant in the ongoing interaction of religion and science. Within part two, chapters 4 and 5 on basic questions of methodology are more important than chapter 6, which pursues further the similarities and differences between the two fields of inquiry (the conclusions of part two are given at the end of chapter 6). In part four, chapter 11 on process thought elaborates the philosophical framework that I have found most helpful, but a summary of process theology can be found in the last section of chapter 12.

I am grateful to the Center for Theology and the Natural Sciences in Berkeley, California, and its founder and director, Robert John Russell, for the conferences, seminars, and publications that have been a continuing stimulus to my own thought. Presentations given at workshops sponsored by the John Templeton Foundation as part of its program of awards for new courses in science and religion have provided additional opportunities to discuss many of the ideas in this volume with faculty members from diverse disciplines.

IAN G. BARBOUR
CARLETON COLLEGE
NORTHFIELD, MINNESOTA
Nov. 1, 1996

# Introduction

What is the place of religion in an age of science? How can one believe in God today? What view of God is consistent with the scientific understanding of the world? In what ways should our ideas about human nature be affected by the findings of contemporary science? How can the search for meaning and purpose in life be fulfilled in the kind of world disclosed by science?

A religious tradition is not just a set of intellectual beliefs or abstract ideas. It is a way of life for its members. Every religious community has its distinctive forms of individual experience, communal ritual, and ethical concerns. Above all, religion aims at the transformation of personal life, particularly by liberation from self-centeredness through commitment to a more inclusive center of devotion. Yet each of these patterns of life and practice presupposes a structure of shared beliefs. When the credibility of central religious beliefs is questioned, other aspects of religion are also challenged.

For many centuries in the West, the Christian story of creation and salvation provided a cosmic setting in which individual life had significance. It allowed people to come to terms with guilt, finitude, and death. It provided a total way of life, and it encouraged personal transformation and reorientation. Since the Enlightenment, the Christian story has had diminishing effectiveness for many people, partly because it has seemed inconsistent with the understanding of the world in modern science. Similar changes have been occurring in other cultures.

Much of humanity has turned to science-based technology as a source of fulfillment and hope. Technology has offered power, control, and the prospect of overcoming our helplessness and dependency. However, for all its benefits, technology has not brought the personal fulfillment or social well-being it promised. Indeed, it often seems to be a power beyond our control, endangering social patterns and the environment on a scale previously unimaginable.

Five features of our scientific age set the agenda for this volume:

*1. The Success of the Methods of Science.* The impressive achievements of science are widely known. Scientific research has yielded knowledge of many previously inaccessible domains of nature. The validity of such discoveries receives additional confirmation from the fact that they have led to powerful new technologies. For some people, science seems to be the only reliable path to knowledge. For them, the credibility of religious beliefs has been undermined by the methods as well as by the particular discoveries of science. Other people assert that religion has its own distinctive ways of knowing, quite different from those of science. Yet even they are asked to show how religious understanding can be reliable if it differs from scientific knowledge. Science as a method constitutes the first challenge to religion in a scientific age. It is the topic of part 2.

*2. A New View of Nature.* Many of the sciences show us domains of nature with characteristics radically different from those assumed in previous centuries. What are the implications of the novel features of quantum physics and relativity, such as the indeterminacy of subatomic events and the involvement of the observer in the process of observation? What is the theological significance of the "Big Bang," the initial explosion that started the expansion of the universe 15 billion years ago, according to current theories in astrophysics? How are the scientific accounts of cosmic beginnings and biological evolution related to the doctrine of creation in Christianity? Darwin portrayed the long, slow development of new species, including the human species, from the operation of random variations and natural selection. More recently, molecular biologists have made spectacular discoveries concerning the role of DNA in evolution and in the development and functioning of organisms today. What do these discoveries tell us about the nature of life and mind? Such questions are explored in part 3.

*3. A New Context for Theology.* I hold that the main sources of religious beliefs, as systematized in theology, are the religious experience and the stories and rituals of a religious community. However, two particular areas of theological reflection must take into account the findings of contemporary science: the doctrine of human nature and the doctrine of creation. Instead of reductionism, which holds that all phenomena are determined by the behavior of molecular components, I will develop a relational and multilevel view of reality. In this view, interdependent systems and larger wholes influence the behavior of lower-level parts. Such an interpretation provides an alternative to both the classical dualism of spirit and matter (or mind and body) and the materialism that often replaced it. I will suggest that process theology offers a distinctive answer to the question: How can God act in the world as understood by science today? These issues are taken up in part 4.

*4. Religious Pluralism in a Global Age.* The technologies of communication, travel, and today's global interdependence have brought adherents of differing world religions into increasing contact with each other. In the past, absolutist religions' claims have led to repression, crusades, and religious wars, and they continue to contribute to hostilities in the Middle East, Northern Ireland, the Balkans, and elsewhere. In a world where some future conflict could escalate into a wider war, we must take seriously the problem of religious pluralism. There is also a great diversity of ideas within each tradition. For example, feminist authors have criticized the dominance of patriarchal assumptions in the history of Christian thought, and Third World liberation theologians have pointed to the influence of economic interests in theological interpretation. Religious pluralism calls into question exclusive claims for any one religious tradition or theological viewpoint. This issue arises throughout the book, but especially in chapters 6 and 10. We will focus attention on the Christian tradition, but some discussion of other traditions is included (see Buddhism, Hinduism, Judaism, and Islam in the Index of Selected Topics).

5. *Threats to the Environment.* Ours is a planet in crisis. Deforestation, soil erosion, harmful chemicals, and pollution of land, air, and water, together with population growth, are severely damaging the environment in all parts of the globe. We are losing biodiversity and endangered species at an unprecedented rate. Can religious traditions contribute to a new environmental ethic? The Christian tradition has rightly been criticized for drawing too sharp a line between humanity and other creatures and for viewing humanity and human salvation as the purpose of creation. The tradition has also stressed divine transcendence at the expense of immanence in nature. But contemporary writers are recovering ideas of stewardship, celebration of nature, and the sacred in nature, which can contribute to environmental ethics today. In addition, we must turn to science to understand the evolutionary kinship of all creatures and the ecological interdependence of all life forms as well as the possibility of more sustainable patterns of agriculture, technology, and resource use. Out attitudes toward nature are affected by both religion and science.

I have explored this last theme more fully in another volume, *Ethics in an Age of Technology* (HarperSanFrancisco, 1993). But ethical implications will be evident at many points in the present volume (see Environmental Ethics in the Index of Selected Topics). Views of nature influence the way we treat nature, and views of human nature affect our understanding of human values and goals. This book defends an ecological theology that is supportive of efforts to preserve the environment.

In looking at these five challenges—science as a method, a new view of nature, a new context for theology, religious pluralism, and threats to the environment—my goals are to explore the place of religion in an age of science and to present an interpretation of Christianity that is responsive both to the biblical faith and to contemporary science.

The first three chapters that follow are designed to give some historical background for these contemporary issues. Many historical accounts have portrayed the "warfare" of science and religion. But this metaphor suggests two armies arrayed against each other and neglects the great diversity of responses and the debates within both the scientific and religious communities. Equally dubious are the accounts that assume a basic harmony between science and religion, claiming that any conflicts were merely the product of misunderstandings on one side or the other. The historical evidence is more diverse than either of these accounts, and therefore more illuminating with respect to current issues.

# Part One

## RELIGION AND
## THE HISTORY OF SCIENCE

## CHAPTER 1

# Physics and Metaphysics in the Seventeenth Century

The seventeenth century was a period of such crucial and rapid change in outlook that we may justifiably speak of it as marking the birth of modern science. Two landmarks in the growth of the new science were Galileo's *Dialogue* (1632) and Newton's *Principia* (1687). The lives of these two persons also provide illuminating examples of the interactions between science and religion that are our concern. It was in the physical sciences that the new intellectual climate first captured the human imagination and became the basis for a new world view. To see the extent of the transition wrought, we will start by outlining some assumptions of the Middle Ages that were challenged in the seventeenth century. We look successively at "The Medieval World-Drama," "Galileo's 'Two New Sciences,'" and "The Newtonian World-Machine."

Our objective is to analyze how views of God and human nature were affected by the new methods of inquiry in science and the new scientific understanding of nature. We will indicate briefly the approaches taken by Aquinas, by Galileo, and then by Newton, to the following topics: (1) methods in science, (2) the character of nature, (3) methods in theology, (4) God's relation to nature, and (5) human nature. The final section of the chapter examines the positive contributions of religious thought to the rise of science and the major points of conflict.

In some cases, specific scientific theories, such as the Copernican theory that the sun rather than the earth is the center of the planetary system, seemed to conflict with traditional religious ideas. But science also influenced religious thought indirectly by calling philosophical assumptions into question, especially those in *epistemology* (analysis of methods of inquiry and theories of knowledge) and *metaphysics* (analysis of the most general characteristics of reality; see Glossary for definitions of frequently used specialized terms). We will be considering both direct and indirect influences of the new science on views of nature, God, and humanity.

These chapters of historical background do not try to describe all the complex factors in the growth of modern thought in either science or religion. In each field new ideas were the product, not of isolated individuals, but of communities of inquiry within wider cultural contexts. The social history of both science and religion is as important as an account of "great scientists" or "important theologians." However, the discussion of a few pivotal figures in their social contexts can serve to illuminate the origins of contemporary issues.

## I. THE MEDIEVAL WORLD-DRAMA

Amid the rich diversity of the Middle Ages, Thomas Aquinas (1225–1274) stands out as the most systematic and influential medieval author. His synthesis of Christian theology and Aristotelian philosophy articulated a distinctive approach to both science and religion that dominated Western thought until the seventeenth century. Let us consider his views on each of our five topics.

### 1. METHODS IN SCIENCE: EXPLANATION BY PURPOSES

During the 1950s and 1960s, several widely read books by historians of science portrayed the radical character of the "scientific revolution" of the seventeenth century and claimed that the Middle Ages made no substantial contributions to science.[1] More recently, specialists in the history of medieval science have made detailed studies of particular people and topics. They insist that medieval authors must be examined in the context of their own times and that significant advances were made in medicine, technology, and physics. They point to continuity as well as discontinuity between medieval and early modern science. For example, Galileo's concept of inertial momentum had a precursor in the writings of Jean Buridan and Nicole Oresme at the University of Paris in the fourteenth century, namely their idea of "impetus" as the cause of continuing motion.[2]

Yet even these recent authors acknowledge that medieval science was carried out within an Aristotelian framework with goals very different from those of Galileo and his successors. Medieval writers were primarily interested in the logical relationships among ideas, and only secondarily were they interested in testing hypotheses by experiments. I will argue that modern science really does represent a revolution in methods of inquiry, so that ideas with forerunners in earlier centuries were used in a new way. Greek science was recovered when the writings of Aristotle were translated from Arabic in the thirteenth century. From 1250 to 1650, Aristotle was the core of the curriculum in the universities of western Europe. Science was not an autonomous profession but a branch of philosophy, and Aristotle's *Physics* was widely read and discussed—and challenged, even though its basic assumptions were still accepted.

For what type of explanation of an event should one search? To what sort of questions about nature is it most important to seek answers? Aristotle sought explanations in terms of the true *form* or intelligible *essence* of an object and the *purpose* it fulfills. Why do objects fall? For Aristotle and his followers, motion is explained by the tendency of each thing to seek its own natural resting place. The "natural place" of fire is up, and that of earth is down. The *end* of the motion—in the sense both of *terminus* and of *purpose*—was of more interest than the intervening process. Why does an acorn grow? To become an oak. Why is there rain? To nourish plants. Causality is described by *future goals* ("final causes") and *innate tendencies* ("formal causes"), not just by the effects of past events ("efficient causes") acting on objects in the present ("material causes"). The future goal need not be consciously entertained by an entity (for example, an acorn) but is built into its structure so that by its own nature it achieves the fulfillment of the end appropriate to its kind by the expression of *form* through *matter.*[3]

Attention was directed to the *final end* and not to the detailed process of change from moment to moment. The behavior of each creature follows from its essential nature. If every creature realizes its potentialities, the most illuminating questions are those concerning the uses of things and what they can do. The central feature of all change, in this view, is the transformation of *potentiality* into *actuality.* Logical connections, not simply temporal ones, must be traced. The categories of explanation are essence and potentiality, not mass and motion connected by laws in space and time. In the Middle Ages, this search for purposes was also the result of conceiving every object as having a place in a cosmic hierarchy, the creation of a purposeful God. God's purposes in creating things, though not always discernible, constitute the ultimate explanation of their behavior.[4]

Because of this assumption of the rationality of the universe, both Greek and medieval science were primarily *deductive* (starting from necessary general principles and reasoning to particular exemplifications of those principles) rather than *inductive* (starting from particular observations and generalizing from them). This preference for deductive logic was closely related to the classical idea, particularly prominent in Plato, that knowledge is contemplation of *the perfect forms* of eternal truth rather than observation of their imperfect embodiment in the changing world. The way a thing behaves was also linked with its status in the overall scheme. The goal was not primarily, as in modern science, the description, prediction, and control of a limited phenomenon but rather the understanding and contemplation of the meaning of the part in relation to the whole and to God.

This does not mean that *observation* was absent from Aristotelian and medieval science. Many of Aristotle's conclusions were in conformity with common experience. He had done considerable biological classification, for example, which required careful observation. But the categories of teleology (purpose) did not in general lend themselves to *theories* that could be tested by further *experiment.* We shall see that Galileo deliberately set aside all questions of purpose and "final cause" and introduced a totally different kind of concept tied to measurable relationships between observable phenomena.

## 2. NATURE AS A CREATED HIERARCHY

Aristotelian cosmology and Christian theology were merged to form the *medieval picture of the universe.* Earth was a fixed central sphere surrounded by the concentric spheres of the heavens. The planets, in the Ptolemaic theory, followed circles whose centers were attached to moving spheres; heavenly objects, being perfect and incorruptible, were said to make use only of the perfect form, the circle. This geocentric (earth-centered) scheme was easily visualized and corresponded to the commonsense experience of the solidity of the earth. Here *position* and *destiny* coincided. Humanity was unique and central in both location and importance; the divine was more perfect and comprehensive, separated both geographically and metaphysically from the created order. Within this overall pattern, every entity from greatest to least had its status and purpose in the graded *hierarchy of reality:* God, planets, angels, men, women, animals, and plants. Everything was in its neatly arranged place in an integrated total plan. It was a law-abiding world, but the laws were moral and not mechanical. This was the medieval view of the universe that the new science would call into question.

A wide variety of *attitudes toward nature* was expressed during the Middle Ages. At times spiritual destiny seemed so to outweigh temporal relationships that the world was treated as a great allegory whose essential secret was its religious meaning, not its operation or its causes. Symbolic interpretations of nature were sometimes derived from ancient legends unrelated to any factual observations. At other times, particularly among the common people, nature seemed to be the seat of evil forces and demonic powers, as it had been to most of the late Greek (Hellenistic) world; it was to be a long struggle before science would be free from association with magic, sorcery, and astrology. To some people, the sense of God's creation was overpowering; to St. Francis, for example, nature was a sacrament of the divine. For Aquinas and his followers, the conviction of God's rationality encouraged an affirmative attitude toward nature, which, as we shall see, contributed indirectly to the rise of science.

Medieval thought was in general *realistic* in the sense that it held the world to be real as perceived, experienced, and understood. The rational powers of the intellect were believed to be capable of grasping the true essence of the world. It was said that nature is immediately present to us and clearly intelligible to our minds. Color and warmth, love and purpose were taken as integral characteristics of existing beings. The possibility of knowledge of the external world was not seriously doubted, as it has been in modern philosophy since Descartes.

Note finally that nature was assumed to be essentially *static,* with all its species created in their present forms. It was a completed world in which there could be no fundamental novelty except as God acts in it. However, the life of each creature might include outward change and development as its God-given potentialities unfold. One might say that the basic image of nature was that of a Kingdom—a fixed, hierarchical, ordered society under a sovereign Lord.

## 3. METHODS IN THEOLOGY: REASON AND REVELATION

To understand some of the subsequent interactions of science and religion, we must briefly summarize the sources of authority in medieval theology.

Scholastic thought was based on both *reason* and *revelation,* showing again the characteristic synthesis of elements from Greek philosophy and biblical faith. God is known through both *natural* and *revealed* theology. The natural truths are open to all people by the unaided powers of human reason; the revealed truths were disclosed by God through Christ and the prophets and are transmitted through scripture and tradition as preserved by the church. Since all truth is from God, the two basic sources will be consistent with each other.

In Aquinas's system, *reason* is an important preamble to faith. It can establish some theological truths, including the existence of God. The teleological argument leads from the evidence of design in nature to the idea of an intelligent Designer. The cosmological argument moves from the contingency of the world to its necessary ground, a First Cause of all effects. God has been at least partially disclosed in the universe. But to Aquinas this natural theology remained secondary to revealed theology; it was not the main source of knowledge of God, as it was to be for many thinkers by the eighteenth century.[5]

*Revelation* is necessary, according to Aquinas, because the most important theological truths are not accessible to reason. God's existence is rationally demonstrable, but the trinity and the incarnation are not. The divine plan of salvation was made known through the channels God chose to establish. Even those truths that can be proven philosophically have been made more readily available to the average person through revelation. Faith is thus primarily the acceptance of revealed truths on the authority of the church rather than (as for the Protestant Reformers) an attitude of trust and commitment in direct personal relationship to God as known in Christ. In medieval thought, the church is not only the channel of divine grace, mediated through Christ's death and the efficacy of the sacraments, but also the channel of divine truth, imparted through Christ's teaching and transmitted by the continuing community that was his chosen instrument.

*The Bible* was only one element in this total system of thought, and scripture was considered authoritative only as interpreted by the church. Moreover, the doctrine of "levels of truth" in the Bible allowed some flexibility for allegorical interpretation and poetic meaning. Scripture was thus only one issue in the conflict that arose between Galileo and the Catholic Church. Galileo's defense of Copernican astronomy seemed to threaten an inclusive intellectual scheme that was strongly dependent on Aristotelian assumptions and on an institutional church that asserted its authority to interpret scripture.

## 4. GOD AS CREATOR AND REDEEMER

In Aquinas's conception of God, Aristotle's *Unmoved Mover* and the Bible's *personal Father* had become one. The metaphysical First Cause of Greek philosophy was identified with the dynamic purposeful Creator of biblical theology. Though at times the more abstract philosophical attributes (omniscience, omnipotence, omnipresence, eternity) may seem to have predominated over more personalistic biblical images (father, judge, savior), Aquinas's writing clearly pictures a God who is concerned about human redemption. We must here restrict ourselves to some comments on the Thomistic understanding of God's relation to nature.

Aquinas presents one form of the *cosmological argument:* every event must have a cause, which in turn must be the effect of an earlier cause, and so forth, back to a First Cause. But Aquinas also considers the possibility of an infinite sequence of causes—an idea that is being discussed by some astronomers today. He maintains that the crucial feature of all events in the world, whether in a finite or an infinite series, is their *contingency,* the fact that they might not have occurred. Why is there anything rather than nothing? Every entity in the world is dependent on other entities, and all are sharply distinguished from God, a necessary being whose existence is not dependent on the existence of other beings. Aquinas also defends the argument from design; but the argument did not exclusively determine his concept of God (as it did for many writers in later centuries); for him the intelligent Designer was always the biblical Creator.[6]

Moreover, in contrast with the deism of the eighteenth century, Aquinas portrays God as *continuing ruler of nature* and not just as its original Creator. Divine governance is an active power sustaining and working through the natural order. God is the "primary cause" of every event, but there are "secondary causes" through which God works. Aquinas believed that natural processes can be explained in relative independence of any direct acts of God, and yet their functioning depends on powers not inherent in them but provided by God's sustaining activity. Divine *concurrence* is required for anything to happen. God is also the Supreme Good, the goal of nature. God's activities as creator, ruler, and goal are not divided temporally as past, present, and future, for these functions interpenetrate each other. As the Supreme Good, God draws all things in the present toward their appointed ends. In this sense, Dante can say it is "love that moves the heavens and all the stars," for all things aspire to fulfill God's will.

There are several ways of *accomplishing the divine will* beyond action as Creator and Supreme Good. God works through natural causes, governs the world through angels, and acts directly through miracles to accomplish specific results. God's influence on nature is thus rich and complex, including a number of functions operating at various levels. The new concept of nature that developed with the emerging science was to affect the interpretation of these relationships and the concept of God they imply.

## 5. HUMANITY AS CENTER OF THE COSMIC DRAMA

If God was the supreme member of the hierarchy of being in medieval thought, humanity was *the center of the cosmic drama.* Nature was subordinate to humanity. The functions of creatures lower in the scale were explained mainly by their role in human life, for the world was designed to serve human interests. Nature was primarily the stage setting for the drama of God and humanity. World history was understood to follow a divine plan, whose epochs could be symbolized by five words: *Creation, Covenant, Christ, Church,*

*Consummation.* The fall of the first humans introduced sin into the world. The cosmic drama centers in God's redemptive act for the salvation of humanity: the incarnation of Christ and his atoning death. Our goal is union with God, and salvation lies in aligning our purposes with God's, making use of the means of grace God has appointed.

Human nature, in medieval thought, is a union of mortal body and immortal soul. This *body/soul dualism* was indebted more to Greek than to biblical thought (as I will suggest in chapter 10). We are free and rational beings, whose duty and fulfillment lie in conforming at once to reason and to God's will. Everything else is to be scrutinized for its significance in our pilgrimage and its purpose in the divine plan leading ultimately up to God. Human beings, in this view, differ radically from all other creatures. While the scheme is ultimately theocentric (God centered), its portrayal of the world is *anthropocentric* (human centered). This assumption was to be challenged in very diverse ways, first by Copernican astronomy, then by Darwinian evolution, and more recently by environmentalists who claim that the sharp separation of humanity from nature in classical Christian thought was one of the historical roots of environmentally destructive attitudes in Western culture.

This was the total plan, the coherent pattern into which all things fitted and from which they derived their significance. It was a unified hierarchical order in which every being plays its part. All nature serves humanity, and humanity serves God. The social order, too, was fixed and hierarchical. Science, cosmology, society, history, and theology all expressed the same pattern of meaning. This, in briefest outline, was the medieval world view, which in its main features was not greatly altered by the Reformation in the sixteenth century but which was to be drastically transformed by the impact of modern science.

## II. GALILEO'S "TWO NEW SCIENCES"

Galileo Galilei (1564–1642) has rightly been called the father of modern science, for in his work the distinctive features of the new scientific methodology first found explicit formulation and fruitful practice. His trial and condemnation by the church authorities in Rome was also the first dramatic example of conflict between religion and science in the West.

### 1. METHODS IN SCIENCE: MATHEMATICS AND OBSERVATION

The key feature of the new science was the combination of mathematical reasoning and quantifiable observations. A century before Galileo, the importance of *mathematical simplicity* had already been defended by Copernicus. The Ptolemaic system, in which the sun and planets were assumed to revolve around the earth, had required more and more amendments, by adding wheels within wheels, in order to agree with the astronomical data available; these additions were cumbersome and arbitrary. The Copernican model, in which the planets and the earth revolve around the sun, agreed with the available observations with comparable accuracy and was much simpler mathematically. Copernicus extolled the beauty of a small number of concentric circles, much in the Pythagorean tradition of belief in the harmony of numbers. In the absence of any new data, the support he received was largely philosophical in character; the revival of Platonism was beginning to undermine the authority of Aristotle, who had held the Ptolemaic view.[7]

In the writing of Johannes Kepler early in the seventeenth century, belief in *mathematical harmony* found even more rhapsodic expression. He was able to show that the accurate observational data he inherited from Tycho Brahe were consistent with a modification of the Copernican system, namely the assumption of elliptical rather than circular planetary orbits. Kepler saw "geometrical perfection" itself as the reason why the planets follow mathematically exact orbits. In his belief in "the mystery of number" and "the music of the spheres," as in his conviction that "God ever geometrizes," there were aesthetic and religious as well as scientific motives.[8] Yet in the process of stressing precise observations and the display of mathematical relationships, an important change was occurring: the universe was increasingly seen as a mathematical structure. The significant relationships were quantitative, not qualitative, as they had been for Aristotle. Without the achievements of mathematics, neither the seventeenth-century scientific revolution nor the innovations of twentieth-century physics would have been possible.

Galileo found additional observational evidence to support the Copernican model. In 1610, using the newly invented telescope, he observed the mountains of the moon and saw that the moon is an irregular physical object and not a perfect "celestial sphere." His discovery of Jupiter's moons showed that the earth was not the center of all motions, and his data on the phases of Venus fitted perfectly with Copernican assumptions.

In Galileo's study of motion the use of mathematical equations was combined with an emphasis on *experimentation*. The combination of theory with experiment can be traced, of course, to earlier centuries (scholars in northern Italy in the fifteenth century, Ockhamists at Oxford in the fourteenth century, and such figures as Archimedes in ancient Greece), but it became explicit in Galileo's careful investigations. His description of the discovery of the equations of accelerated motion, using a ball rolling down an inclined plane, is a classic example of reasoning back and forth between theory and experiment. He used concepts such as length, time, and velocity, which could be tied to measurements and expressed in mathematical symbols. He described how he considered a possible mathematical relationship between velocity and distance and then deduced the expected law of motion this would yield—a deduction that turned out to be incompatible with experimental results. He tried other theoretical assumptions, calculated the equations deducible from them, and made experimental tests of these equations. Here were all the characteristics of the new science: the distinctive type of concept, the combination of theory and experiment, and the goal of expressing laws of nature as mathematical relationships among measurable variables.[9]

The *experimental* side of the new science was indeed crucial. It received additional support from various sources, including the improved instruments and the interest in practical problems fostered by developing technologies (such as navigation, metallurgy, and military weaponry). But it is misleading to identify science primarily with observations, as was done in Galileo's day by Sir Francis Bacon—and more recently by David Hume and modern positivism. Bacon believed that science consists of the accumulation and classification of observations. He insisted that induction is the easy road to knowledge: make observations, summarize them, and generalize. Discovery can be a routine and automatic process, he said, carried out "as by machinery"; only patience is needed, not difficult or abstract thought. The Baconian account leaves out the whole theoretical side of science, and above all it omits the role of creative imagination in the formation of new concepts.

As an example of *an imaginative new concept,* consider Galileo's idea of motion without air resistance (which was the key to the principle of inertia). His contribution here was no mere "careful observation" but a conception of the world as we do *not* experience it. He imagined observed motion to arise from two sources, neither of which could be observed alone: a continuing uniform inertial motion and a frictional retarding force. Aristotle's view had been closer to everyday observations; a cart left to itself does come to its "natural" state of rest if there is no horse to keep it moving. Galileo imagined an idealized frictionless case that, left to itself, would continue to move uniformly. Starting from such an "ideal case," he could argue that the cart comes to rest not because of any natural tendency to do so but because friction hinders its uniform motion.

Galileo asked not *why* objects move, but *how* they move. He was content to describe how phenomena progress, and he completely ignored questions about the purposes they serve, which he saw as irrelevant to the problems in which he was interested. The questions that were being asked of nature were fundamentally different from those that had been asked in the Middle Ages. Interest was being directed not to final causes operating toward the future or to formal causes in the essence of the object, but to efficient causes. In all these ways Galileo's work embodied the approach typical of modern science, and it led to a new ideal of what it means to explain something.

## 2. NATURE AS PARTICLES IN MOTION

Several historians and philosophers writing in the 1950s and earlier were interested in the *metaphysical assumptions* of the founders of modern science. They analyzed the distinctive concepts of the new physics and described the mathematization and mechanization of nature.[10] These "internalist" accounts—accounts of changes in ideas within the scientific community—have been criticized more recently by "externalist" historians, who insist on the importance of wider social and cultural forces in the history of science. Some of them have questioned whether a single coherent "scientific revolution" can be discerned amid the variations among periods, nations, and historical periods.[11] I believe that we must take both ideas and social forces into account and that despite the diversity of disciplines and periods, the development of seventeenth-century physics was so influential both on other sciences and on prevailing views of nature that it deserves special attention.

Galileo's writing was notable for its preliminary formulation of a new picture of nature as *matter in motion*. The "corpuscular philosophy" of the seventeenth century was not yet the nineteenth-century "atomic theory," which, after Dalton, was supported by considerable empirical evidence. Yet it was more than a revival of the "atomism" of Democritus in ancient Greece, which had been entirely philosophical and speculative in character. In effect, Galileo extrapolated from his own work; he assumed that the ultimate constituents of nature were exhaustively describable *in the same categories* that he found to be so powerful in analyzing the motion of observable objects.

The categories of *mass, space,* and *time* were relatively unimportant to medieval authors. In Galileo's thought these categories were central because they could be treated mathematically. The world was taken to be composed of particles to which were ascribed only two properties: mass and motion. Change no longer meant transition from potentiality to actuality but the rearrangement of particles in time and space. During the seventeenth century, the quantifiable concepts with which the scientist could deal so successfully were gradually taken to characterize the real world (apart from humanity) without remainder. Galileo never elaborated a mechanistic view of nature, but some of the key assumptions of such a view are evident in his writings.

Galileo called mass and motion "*primary qualities*," characteristic of the objective world independent of the observer, and he distinguished them from "*secondary qualities*," such as color and temperature, which he believed to be purely subjective reactions of the senses to the world. Pain is in me, not in the pin that pricks me; so also heat and sound were said to reside in the mind, not in the object observed. Galileo concluded:

I cannot believe that there exists in external bodies anything, other than their size, shape or motion (slow or rapid), which could excite in us our tastes, sounds, and odors. And indeed I should judge that, if ears, tongues, and noses be taken away, the number, shape, and motion of bodies would remain, but not their tastes, sounds, and odors. . . . And I again judge that heat is altogether subjective.[12]

It was Galileo's contemporary, René Descartes (1596–1650), who gave the most complete philosophical exposition of this distinction between primary and secondary qualities, developed into a radical *dualism of matter and mind*. The external world is self-sufficient matter extended in space. Mind, on the other hand, is unextended "thinking substance." Mathematics, which for Descartes was always the exemplar of the "clear and distinct ideas" of which one could be certain, was the key to understanding nature. The whole range of nonhuman life was put by Descartes on the side of matter; he claimed that all animals are automata, complex machines without intelligence or feeling. Even the human body was to be treated as a machine. Descartes allowed only one exception, the human mind. To mind were relegated all the qualities and aspects of experience with which the new science could not deal. Everything except the human mind consisted of matter in motion.[13] By the next century some philosophers would be denying the exception and defending a metaphysics of materialism.

## 3. METHODS IN THEOLOGY: SCRIPTURE, NATURE, AND THE CHURCH

Galileo's ideas were seen as threats to the authority of Aristotle, the Bible, and the Roman Catholic Church. *Aristotle's authority,* enshrined in the Thomistic synthesis, was vigorously defended in Catholic circles. A Protestant scholasticism had developed also in northern Europe. Luther's follower, Melanchthon, had introduced educational reforms that made extensive use of Aristotle. The philosophical distinctions made by many Protestant theologians on the continent late in the sixteenth century and their practice of citing classical authorities paralleled the practices of Catholic scholars. Thus much of the early opposition to Copernican astronomy was a product of the respect in which Aristotle was held.

Luther, and even Calvin, had been somewhat flexible in *biblical interpretation.* For each of them, the locus of authority was not the verbal text itself but the person of Christ, to whom scripture pointed. Scripture was important as the witness to the redemptive events in which God's love and forgiveness in Christ had been mediated to us. To the early Reformers, scripture is confirmed in human experience by the Holy Spirit. But by the beginning of the seventeenth century, the Bible was seen by some Protestants in northern Europe as a deposit of *inerrant information,* including information about scientific questions, which had been dictated by God. Rather than being a record of events in which God was revealed, scripture itself was viewed as infallible knowledge in propositional form verbally imparted by God. Those holding this view opposed the Copernican theory as contrary to biblical passages implying a geocentric universe. In England there was a greater diversity of views concerning the interpretation of scripture and greater acceptance of Copernican views.[14]

*The Roman church* had reacted defensively to the rise of Protestantism. In the Council of Trent (1545–1563) its doctrines had been more sharply defined over against the ideas of the Reformation. In contrast to Protestantism, it was not scripture itself but scripture as interpreted by the tradition of the church that was said to be the ultimate authority. The Counter-Reformation had also developed a number of authoritarian measures to exclude heretical views, including the Inquisition, censorship to prevent publication, and the *Index of Prohibited Books.* It was this powerful church bureaucracy that Galileo confronted.

In his *Letter to the Grand Duchess Christina* in 1615, Galileo set forth two principles of interpretation to be used when scientific theories seem to conflict with a literal interpretation of scripture.

1. *Independence.* In some passages Galileo claims that science and scripture have different goals and are irrelevant to each other. He cites Augustine's assertion that scripture does not teach us about matters that are not relevant to our salvation, and he continues:

It follows that since the Holy Ghost did not intend to teach us whether heaven moves or stands still . . . so much the less was it intended to settle for us any other conclusion of the same kind. . . . Now if the Holy Spirit has purposely neglected to teach us propositions of this sort as irrelevant to the highest goal (that is, our salvation), how can anyone affirm that it is obligatory to take sides on them?"[15]

Galileo quotes Cardinal Baronius: "The intention of the Holy Ghost is to teach us how one goes to heaven, not how heaven goes." On cosmological questions the writers of the Bible had to "accommodate themselves to the capacity of the common people," using "the common mode of speech" at the time.

This would be a version of what I will call the *Independence* model of the relation of science and religion (chapter 4). In this view, theology is neutral with respect to cosmology; differing scientific theories should be evaluated by scientific criteria alone. If Galileo had adhered to this distinction and the church authorities had accepted it, there would have been *no possibility of conflict.* Scientific theories and religious teachings would have been treated as separate realms of discourse.

2. *Potential Conflict.* In other passages Galileo asserted that a metaphorical interpretation of scripture is acceptable only when a literal interpretation would conflict with a scientific theory that can be *proved with certainty.* Scientific theories that cannot be irrefutably demonstrated should be rejected in favor of a literal interpretation of scripture:

Among physical propositions there are some with regard to which all human science and reason cannot supply more than a plausible opinion and a probable conjecture in place of a sure and demonstrated knowledge; for example, whether the stars are animate. Then there are other propositions of which we have (or may confidently expect) positive assurances through experiments, long observation, and rigorous demonstrations; for example, whether or not the earth and heavens move, and whether or not the heavens are spherical. As to the first sort of propositions, I have not doubt that where human reasoning cannot reach—and where consequently we can have no science but only opinion and faith—it is necessary in piety to comply absolutely with the strict sense of Scripture.[16]

But Galileo overstated the degree of proof he could provide, and there was still considerable disagreement among astronomers. Cardinal Bellarmine had proposed a face-saving compromise: Galileo could present the Copernican model as a convenient calculating device for correlating observations and making predictions, provided he did not defend it as a true representation of reality. Both Pope Urban VIII and Galileo at first accepted this formula for treating the Copernican theory as "hypothetical." But in the *Dialogue on the Two Chief World Systems* (1632), Galileo's own convictions were but thinly veiled. He put the arguments for the Ptolemaic system—including some that had been advanced by the pope—into the mouth of a character called Simplicio, who could not be taken very seriously. The pope was personally affronted. Galileo also used physical evidence (an argument from the earth's tides, which was later shown to be erroneous), in violation of the idea of treating the Copernican system as a mathematical formalism. The debate was further complicated by political factions and personal rivalries within the church hierarchy.[17]

The famous *trial of Galileo* before a panel of cardinals was held in 1633, and he was condemned by a vote of seven to three for violating an injunction sent to him in 1616 requiring him "not to hold, teach, or defend in any way whatsoever that the earth moves." He recanted and spent the rest of his life under house arrest. He was forbidden to publish but managed to get his *Discourses on Two New Sciences* published in Protestant Holland in 1638, four years before his death. The *Dialogues* were not removed from the *Index of Prohibited Books* until 1822. In 1984 a commission appointed by Pope John Paul II to reexamine these events acknowledged that "church officials had erred in condemning Galileo." In 1992 the pope reviewed the commission's findings. He said that there are "two realms of knowledge" and that by failing to distinguish them, theologians had been led "to transpose into the realm of the doctrine of the faith a question that in fact pertained to scientific investigation."[18]

## 4. GOD AS AUTHOR OF NATURE AND SCRIPTURE

Galileo's *concept of God* did not depart significantly from that of classical Christianity. He said that the Book of Nature and the Book of Scripture cannot conflict because they come from the same author. He therefore reinterpreted passages of scripture whose literal interpretation conflicted with Copernican theory. But he still held scripture and its message of redemption in high regard. However, the idea that God is known through the Book of Nature opened the door to a greater reliance on natural theology as science expanded, which in later generations would lead to new views of God's relation to nature.

With final causality dismissed, the idea of God as the Supreme Good toward which all things strive was before long replaced by God as *First Cause*, understood as the initial link in the chain of efficient causes. With Galileo began the development whereby God was to become merely the original creator of the interacting atoms in which resides all subsequent causality. Nature, once created, was considered to be independent and self-sufficient. In medieval as well as Reformation thought, God's concurrence had been viewed as a very direct and active relationship. As attention focused on natural causes, God's role was gradually relegated to that of First Cause.

Even at this early stage, various philosophers tried to reconcile the picture of *a mechanical world* with *belief in God*. In Descartes's case, an extreme dualism of mind and matter provided a realm for the operation of both God and the human soul. Descartes was impressed by the mathematical rather than the experimental side of the new science. For example, he formulated Cartesian geometry and applied it to physical systems. He was a thoroughgoing *rationalist;* only directly intuited "clear and distinct ideas" provide us with certainty, since sense impressions are confused and unreliable. The mind apprehends *a priori* ideas that are not dependent on experience for their vindication. Our idea of God is innate, a primordial apprehension of the divine. Thus for Descartes it is through the participation of the human mind in the realm of ideas that God is known. Descartes did hold, however, that in addition to creating the world, God renews it in each instant; he maintained that time is discontinuous and that but for God's continual recreation the universe would collapse into nothingness. But the sequence of events in the world is determined by the mechanical laws of matter in motion.

The *pantheistic* solution proposed by Benedict Spinoza (1632–1677) went much further in rejecting the traditional concept of God. There is no cosmic purpose, he wrote, for all things occur in accordance with inflexible laws of cause and effect. The world is a mechanical and mathematical order, not in any sense a personal and moral one. Spinoza used the term *God* only to refer to the immutable structure of the impersonal cosmic order; he specifically rejected any idea of God as a purposeful or intelligent being, saying that "neither intellect nor will appertain to God's nature." God is the "infinite substance" of which extension is one attribute, but this substance has no ethical properties since good and evil are entirely relative to human desires. The harmonious perfection of this world-system can itself be the supreme object of human devotion. True wisdom, he suggested, consists in resignation to the power of the universe; we must come to understand and accept the impartial necessity of inexorable law, which governs our lives.[19] But Spinoza's philosophical response to the mechanical view of the world involved too great a departure from prevalent ideas to be influential in his own century, though it was picked up by later thinkers, including Einstein. Most people in the seventeenth century continued to affirm a traditional view of God along with an increasingly mechanical view of nature.

## 5. HUMANITY IN THE NEW COSMOLOGY

Medieval cosmology had set the eternal celestial realm in opposition to the terrestrial scene of change and decay; the graded "hierarchy of being" approached perfection as it approached the divine. The new cosmology obliterated this distinction between the corruptible and the incorruptible; it applied uniform natural categories to the whole universe. The identity of purpose and place was destroyed. In particular, *humanity was demoted* from the center of the universe to a spinning planet orbiting the sun. Human uniqueness and the idea of God's particular concern for human life seemed in danger. Speculation about life on other planets is not a new phenomenon of the space age; the issue was raised by Galileo's opponents, and the implications of a "plurality of worlds" were extensively discussed. Nicholas of Cusa and Giordano Bruno had already encountered vehement opposition to their ideas of the infinity of space. The new cosmology was resisted, then, not only because it challenged the authority of Aristotle, scripture, and the church, but because it threatened the whole medieval scheme of purpose and meaning in which the spatial location of humanity was correlated with status in the cosmic hierarchy.

However, human beings still had a very special status and dignity because of their *rational minds*. The medieval dualism of body and soul was carried over in another form in the Cartesian dualism of matter and mind. Human beings were still the great exception in a world that was increasingly seen as a mechanical system of particles in motion. In Galileo's day the sharp separation of humans from the rest of nature was still accepted by most philosophers and theologians.

## III. THE NEWTONIAN WORLD-MACHINE

Isaac Newton (1642–1727) was born the year Galileo died, and by the end of the century he was the preeminent figure in the scientific revolution. His idea of nature as a law-abiding machine had an enormous influence far beyond science itself. Yet despite some unorthodox theological ideas, Newton himself retained a fairly traditional concept of God. Let us examine his views on the five themes of this chapter.

### 1. METHODS IN SCIENCE: EXPERIMENT AND THEORY

Newton carried further Galileo's use of mathematically expressed *theories* and *experiments*. His invention of calculus was an important contribution, but he was also an ingenious experimenter in mechanics and optics. His method involved the continual interaction of observation and theory. But it should be underscored that there are no rules for discovering the *concepts* through which this may occur fruitfully. New concepts are the product, not of precise observation or of mathematical deduction alone or even of the two together, but of creative imagination.

In the case of *the law of gravity,* his novel insight was the idea that the earth's gravitational pull might extend to the moon—in other words, that the moon might be continually falling toward the earth, as the legendary apple did. Newton had already realized from the laws of motion that what was required to keep the moon in orbit was a centripetal force (toward the earth) not a tangential force (pushing it along the orbit). He had shown that the force necessary for a planet to follow one of Kepler's ellipses would be an attraction toward the sun varying with the inverse square of the distance. Using the prevailing estimates of the distance to the moon, Newton calculated the period of the moon's revolution that would be expected if there were an inverse-square gravitational force toward the earth. The result disagreed by 12 percent from the observed lunar period. Later, when it was found that the estimates of the distance had been in error, he repeated the calculations with the new data and found excellent agreement. The whole incident provides an illuminating example of the interaction of observation, theory, mathematical deduction, and an imaginative new concept.

Newton insisted that the scientist's task is *descriptive* and that premature speculation must be avoided. He was willing to investigate the behavior of objects influenced by gravity while leaving unanswered the question of the nature of gravity; in the absence of experimental evidence, we must simply admit we don't know.[20] When he advanced speculations with less adequate empirical support, as in his corpuscular theory of light, he did so with considerable caution and tentativeness. He may not have been as free from metaphysical assumptions as he thought, but he did clearly recognize that a scientific theory could be useful even when it did not answer all the questions one might ask about a phenomenon.[21] In Newton's day scientific theories were assumed to be representations of objective reality as it is in itself. We will find this epistemological *realism* rejected by Kant and extensively debated by twentieth-century physicists and philosophers.

## 2. NATURE AS A LAW-ABIDING MACHINE

Newton's laws of motion and gravity seemed applicable to all objects, from the smallest particle in the laboratory to the farthest planet. This was still a single harmonious order, as in the Middle Ages, but now it was a structure of forces and masses rather than a hierarchy of purposes. This magnificent synthesis of diverse domains was rightly admired, and the perfection of mathematical law made a great impression on Newton's contemporaries. It suggested an image of *the world as an intricate machine* following immutable laws, with every detail precisely predictable. Here was the basis for the philosophies of determinism and materialism that later generations were to develop. Newton himself believed that the world-machine was designed by an intelligent Creator and expressed God's purposes; to later interpreters, impersonal and blind forces appeared to be entirely self-contained.

The concepts of Newtonian physics, which had been so superbly successful in astronomy and mechanics, were increasingly adopted as the basis of an all-encompassing metaphysics. Newton himself accepted Galileo's view that nature (apart from humanity) is exhaustively describable as *particles in motion*. The properties that could be treated mathematically—mass and motion—were alone considered to be characteristics of the real world; other properties were taken to be purely subjective, having no existence outside the mind. Since "efficient" causes had replaced "final" causes, all causality was assumed to be reducible to forces between particles and all changes reducible to the rearrangement of particles. John Locke wrote, "By the figure, bulk, texture, and motion of these small and insensible corpuscles all the phenomena of bodies may be explained." E. A. Burtt gives this summary:

It was of the greatest consequence for succeeding thought that now the great Newton's authority was squarely behind the view of the cosmos which saw in man a puny, irrelevant spectator of the vast mathematical system whose regular motions according to mechanical principles constituted the world of nature. . . . The world that people had thought themselves living in—a world rich with color and sound, redolent with fragrance, filled with gladness, love, and beauty, speaking everywhere of purposive harmony and creative ideals—was crowded now into minute corners in the brains of scattered organic beings. The really important world outside was a world hard, cold, colorless, silent and dead; a world of quantity, a world of mathematically computable motions in mechanical regularity.[22]

In such a mechanical world, however, Newton himself still found room for both God and the human spirit.

## 3. METHODS IN THEOLOGY: "NATURAL THEOLOGY"

The English authors whom we would call scientists called themselves "natural philosophers" or "virtuosi." They were mainly from Anglican (Church of England) and Puritan (Calvinist) backgrounds. The charter of the Royal Society instructed its fellows to direct their studies "to the glory of God and the benefit of the human race." Robert Boyle (1627–1691) said that science is a *religious task,* "the disclosure of the admirable workmanship which God displayed in the universe." Newton believed the universe bespeaks an all-powerful Creator. Sprat, the historian of the Royal Society, considered science a valuable aid to religion. This view is celebrated in Addison's hymn:

The spacious firmament on high,
With all the blue ethereal sky
And spangled heavens a shining frame,
Their great Original proclaim.

The unwearied sun from day to day,
Does his Creator's power display,
And publishes to every land,
The work of an Almighty hand.

The virtuosi identified themselves with the Christian tradition in which they were nourished, and many of them seem to have experienced a personal response of *reverence* and *awe* toward the marvels they beheld. The psalmist had written, "The heavens declare the glory of God, and the firmament showeth God's handiwork," and the virtuosi felt they could appreciate this handiwork in ways not possible to any previous generation. Expressions of awed surprise and admiration at the skill of the Creator dot the pages of their writings. The sense of the grandeur and wisdom of God was evidently a very positive experience for many of them and not just an abstract intellectual formula or a concession to cultural respectability.

Yet their approach to religion was departing increasingly from traditional Christianity. Many factors contributed to this shift. England had been torn by religious strife and civil war between royalists (mainly Roman Catholic or Anglican) and parliamentarians (mainly Puritan); when the monarchy was restored in 1660, a need was felt for a minimum common basis of reasonable agreement. Contact with other cultures also suggested the value of *religious universality*. A small but influential group of scholars known as the Cambridge Platonists had asserted that reason and revelation are not incompatible; they advocated a philosophical approach to theology (drawing particularly from Platonic idealism) and urged toleration rather than dogmatism. A growing confidence in human reason, a more optimistic view of human capacities, and a desire to provide a rational defense of the essentials of religion are reflected in such treatises as Locke's *The Reasonableness of Christianity.* The virtuosi had a personal stake in defending themselves from the charge of irreligion, and they went to great lengths to show that atomism does not lead to atheism. They had to reply to Hobbes's view that the universe is the product of the chance concourse of particles; they wanted to establish that although they were atomists, they were not materialistic atomists.

The most common form taken by their writing about religion was some variation of *the argument from design*. This passage from Newton's *Optics* is typical:

Whence is it that nature doth nothing in vain; and whence arises all that order and beauty which we see in the world? How came the bodies of animals to be contrived with so much art, and for what ends were their several parts? Was the eye contrived without skill in optics? . . . Does it not appear from phenomena that there is a being incorporeal, living, intelligent?[23]

The eye evoked particular admiration as a triumph of ingenuity and workmanship implying an intelligent Designer, but other illustrations were frequent. The rotation of the earth, the inclination of its axis, the proportions of land and sea all seemed perfectly arranged—the day for work, the night for rest, the seasons for crops, and so forth. Boyle pointed out that lambs are born in the spring when there is fresh grass for them.

The virtuosi, like the medieval scholastics, found *a pattern of divine benevolence* in the design of all things. Because they still saw humans as spiritual beings, as exceptions to the mechanical pattern of the world, they often assumed that the purpose of the rest of nature was human convenience as well as the glory of God to whose wisdom it witnessed. But unlike authors in the Middle Ages, they considered purposes to be entirely external to nature and not immanent in their operation. Nature is a complete and functioning machine that is not itself striving toward any ends, and God is the original First Cause, not the Final Cause. Scientific explanations and descriptions of causal chains must be given strictly *without any reference to purposes*. Boyle, who detected purposes everywhere, was very critical of teleology as an explanation for present behavior. An answer to the ultimate question of "why" is no substitute for an answer to the immediate question of "how," which he said should be given in terms of the "bulk, shape, and motion" of constituent parts. A total explanation of things will go beyond mechanism, but it is not the object of experimental science. He maintained that there are levels of truth, which must be carefully distinguished.[24]

The argument from design assumed, of course, that the world had been instantaneously created *in its present form*. The idea of evolution and change was simply absent from seventeenth-century thought about nature. If one assumed that the world came into existence fully developed, the argument for an intelligent Designer seemed persuasive; it was the only apparent alternative to the view that the world is the product of the chance concourse of atoms. The problem of evil and the existence of catastrophes and cruelty in nature were dismissed by saying that a few parts may have to suffer because of laws beneficial to the whole or by asserting that God has higher purposes that mortal wisdom cannot penetrate. More often, the unpleasant aspects of nature were ignored and the evidence selected to support the benevolent pattern that was assumed.[25]

In addition to the argument from design, the areas of supposed consensus among the religions of the world were cited to support a *"reasonable and universal religious faith"* open to all cultures and not dependent on any particular historical revelation. This common core of belief was said to include three ideas: the existence of a Supreme Being, the immortality of the soul, and the obligation to moral conduct. The virtuosi believed that this common core was also the essence of Christianity, which they thought they were defending; actually it represented a major departure from biblical faith. Religion became less a matter of living experience than of intellectual demonstration. Ethics was reduced to utilitarian prudence and a minimum moral code. Nature, not history, was the clue to the knowledge of God. God as Creator, not God as Redeemer, was increasingly the focus of interest. God's relation to the individual and the experience of forgiveness and reorientation were seldom mentioned. In all these areas the virtuosi moved away from the Christ-centered orientation of the Middle Ages and Reformation. "Rational religion" had been intended as a support for the essentials of Christianity, but by the next century it was to become a substitute for them. Reason, originally a supplement to revelation, began to replace it as the path to knowledge of God. The change did not come about initially by open conflict but by the reinterpretation of Christianity from within.

## 4. GOD AS DIVINE CLOCKMAKER

Nowhere was the impact of scientific on religious thought greater than in the modification of the role of God in relation to nature. God became primarily the Designer of the world-machine, though various attempts were made to find a place for God's continuing activity within a mechanical natural order.

Boyle's favorite analogy for the world was the famous clock at Strasbourg. The analogy served him well in arguing for the divine Clockmaker, for a clock is obviously not the work of chance but of intelligent artifice. But the analogy also makes clear the difficulties in finding any room for present divine activity, for a clock once started runs its own independent mechanical course.

Most of the virtuosi, as least until the end of the century, were willing to make an exception to the rule of law in the case of *biblical miracles*, which they felt to be part of their Christian heritage. God intervenes on rare occasions for special reasons. Some authors felt that miracles and the fulfillment of prophecies were evidence for the validity of revelation; they claimed that miracles were public events observable by the senses and attested by reliable witnesses. Other interpreters showed more ambivalent attitudes; having used the *regularity* of the world as their main argument for God, they did not want to make too much of the *irregularities*. Thus Boyle started by affirming God's freedom to rule the created order but ended by asserting that God's wisdom was displayed primarily in planning things so that no intervention would be needed. God the Cosmic Legislator demonstrated care for the welfare of the creatures in the perfection of the original creative act. Laws are the instruments through which God governs, and violations are "very rare." The rule of law, not miraculous intervention, is the chief evidence of God's wisdom.[26]

There were various attempts to preserve the doctrine of *providence*. Some writings simply affirmed both a mechanical universe and a God who cares about each detail, without trying to reconcile the two assertions. Others equated providence with God's prevision; foreseeing the chain of causes, God could adjust things in advance to secure providential ends without violating the ensuing order. More commonly, providence received a very general interpretation. Not the particular events but the *total design* represented God's benevolence. God set things in motion in a harmonious way, planning the overall structure and order of the world for the welfare of the creatures. Once started, the operation of nature would follow fixed laws, with material causes acting from their own necessity. God's *concurrence* had traditionally been conceived of as an active participation, and some of the virtuosi so interpreted it. Boyle stated that if the Almighty were to discontinue support of the universe it would collapse. Continuing divine involvement is necessary, he said, since a law is not a real power but only a pattern of regularity. But it was the clock analogy that provided the basic interpretive image of the world as a perfect machine, autonomous and self-sufficient. Divine preservation became passive acquiescence rather than active sustenance.

Newton, however, believed that God has a *continuing active role* in the physical world. He said that space is eternal and immutable and is constituted by God's omnipresence. He held that gravitational attraction is not a power inherent in matter; he proposed that God may act either directly, to make bodies attract each other by exact laws, or indirectly, through an ether or a diffusion of very tenuous matter. Newton saw the laws of nature as a continuing expression of God's sovereignty and will, acting in a regular way.

Newton held that God has foreknowledge of events in history as well as nature. He was fascinated by *biblical prophecies,* especially the book of Revelation, and he wrote extensively about the hidden meanings of symbolic references to future events, including the coming of the paradise on earth (the millennium) that was anticipated before the end of the world. Newton's lifelong interest in *alchemy* was motivated by his belief that mechanical action alone cannot account for living organisms; he held that God directs the motion of passive particles through an animating spirit. He rejected the traditional trinitarian view of God and defended Arianism, the fourth-century view that Christ was neither fully God nor fully human but a created being who was God's agent on earth. Because of these unorthodox views, it took a special royal dispensation for him to be a fellow at Cambridge without the Anglican ordination usually required.[27]

Newton also asserted that God has a continuing function in *adjusting the solar system.* He believed that there is no scientific explanation for the pattern of the planets, holding that coplanar orbits with motions in the same direction cannot be accounted for by natural causes. Attraction between planets would cause perturbations that would build up if God did not occasionally step in to correct them, perhaps through the action of comets. In addition, God somehow prevents the stars from collapsing together under gravitational attraction.[28] The scientific inadequacy of Newton's references to divine intervention became obvious in the next century. Laplace's nebular hypothesis was able to account for the coplanar and unidirectional character of planetary motion, and the "irregularities" were shown to be due either to inaccurate observations or to perturbations that would eventually cancel each other out. The "God of the gaps," introduced to explain areas of scientific ignorance, was destined to retreat in the light of new knowledge to become the Retired Architect, the inactive God of deism.

Most of the other virtuosi believed that divine benevolence was expressed in the original act of creation and not in intervention. They wanted to assert the primacy of spirit over matter without compromising the orderliness of the universe. Against Hobbes, they maintained that the universe is the product of intelligent purpose, not of blind chance. Against Leibniz, they maintained that creation was an act of God's will and freedom, not of rational necessity. Against Spinoza, they maintained that God is separate from the world and external to it, not identical with the nexus of inexorable law. Though the *function of God* was drastically reduced, the *conception of God* was still the traditional one of personal intelligence and will, not the pantheistic Absolute.

## 5. HUMAN NATURE: BODY AND MIND

Humanity, we have said, was considered by the virtuosi to be an exception to the rule of mechanical law. The Newtonian universe was still a moral and purposeful order because it was designed by God, and humanity still had dignity because of *human reason*. Though we are quite alone within the vast and complex world-machine, we are not alien to it because the rational order of nature is akin to human reason. Since nature is the product of divine reason, it is beneficent and is comprehensible by human reason. The traditional idea of soul is here identified with "rational spirit" and is taken to guarantee the unique status of humanity.

Locke and his successors hoped that the approach Newton had used so successfully to understand the natural order could be used also to develop *a science of human nature and society*. These early attempts, to be sure, were modeled more after the rational-deductive elements of the new physics than after its observational side. Criticisms of existing institutions in the light of what seemed "natural" and "reasonable" were strongly influenced by cultural traditions and class interests. Locke himself developed a concept of "natural rights" from which he could justify joint rule by a Protestant king and parliament in the constitutional monarchy of 1689. He was a powerful apologist for the great seventeenth-century struggles for civil liberties and religious toleration.

The distinctive *status of mind* was generally defended in this period by a mind/body dualism similar to that of Descartes. Hobbes's view that mind is reducible to the concourse of atoms was strenuously resisted. The human mind, imprisoned in the brain, was believed to have only indirect contact with the world. Since there was no longer a metaphysical continuity in the universe, epistemology had become a problem for philosophy. But the triumph of Newtonian science had helped to increase confidence in human reason, and it laid the groundwork for the Enlightenment view of inevitable progress.

Feminist authors have argued that this elevation of reason over emotion and of mind over body was influenced not only by the new science but also by the *patriarchal assumptions* of a male-dominated culture. The new scientists were as exclusively male as the clergy had been for many centuries. Control and domination of nature express attitudes associated more often with men than with women in Western culture. We will examine these feminist critiques of modern science in chapter 6.

## IV. RELIGION AND THE RISE OF SCIENCE: CONFLICT OR HARMONY?

Can we make any generalization about the interaction of religion and science in the seventeenth century? It is evident that at some points, such as the Galileo case, the growth of science was hindered by religious beliefs and by the institutional church. Such instances of the *conflict* between science and religion were the theme of two influential historical accounts written in the aftermath of the Darwinian controversy, J. W. Draper's *History of the Conflict between Religion and Science* and A. D. White's *A History of the Warfare of Science with Theology in Christendom*. Both of them portrayed a protracted "warfare" in which the conservative forces of theological dogmatism opposed the progressive forces of scientific rationality and were defeated in successive engagements. Both studies gave the Galileo affair as a prime example.[29]

In recent decades this *conflict thesis* has been extensively criticized as a selective and oversimplified historical account. Science and religion were not unified forces opposing each other like armies on a battlefield. Often, as in the case of Newton, scientific and religious ideas interacted in complex ways within the life of the same person. Many of the debates occurred among scientists and among theologians and not just between the groups, as we will see again in the varied responses to Darwin in both communities. There were also significant differences in the way the issues were approached within particular national cultures—in England, France, and Germany, for instance.[30]

At the opposite extreme are accounts that portray an *inherent harmony* between scientific and religious ideas. For example, it has been argued that Puritanism in England contributed significantly to the scientific revolution. The Puritans defended the authority of local congregations and associations against the state-supported Anglican church; such antiestablishment attitudes may have encouraged greater openness to new ideas. In the Puritan Revolution of 1640–1660, parliamentary government replaced the monarchy, and the Anglican church was disestablished. In the Royal Society, founded in 1660, seven out of ten members were Puritans, many of them clergy—a ratio far out of proportion to the population as a whole. Puritan schools put science courses in their curricula. The Presbyterians and Congregationalists, in particular, accepted a Calvinist theology, which, it is claimed, provided strong motivation for scientific work.

The set of attitudes sometimes called "*the Protestant ethic*" was a distinctive viewpoint toward daily work among Calvinists. Calvin, like Luther, had rejected the idea that "religious" vocations are superior to "secular" ones; people should serve God not by withdrawing to a monastic life but by carrying out any honest and useful job with integrity and diligence. We are justified before God by divine grace, not by human works, yet we can respond to God's love by our lives in the world. Calvinism was more activist than Lutheranism in encouraging this-worldly enterprise, holding that work conducted in a rational and orderly way furthers the general welfare and is approved by God. The Christian should glorify God by working with honesty, sobriety, and thrift.

The sociologist Robert Merton has argued that this constellation of values in Puritanism gave strong support to *scientific work*. The study of nature was held to be at once intrinsically fascinating, beneficial to humankind, and religiously acceptable, for it would both reveal God's handiwork and exemplify rational and orderly activity.[31] Bernard Barber summarizes the relevance of Puritan beliefs for science:

The Puritans held the view that man could understand God through understanding Nature, because God revealed himself in the workings of Nature. Therefore science was not antagonistic to religion but rather a firm basis for faith. They felt that since "good works" were a sign, if not a proof, of election to salvation, and that since one could glorify God through social utilitarianism, then science was good because it was an efficient instrument of good works and social improvement. And they valued reason highly because God had chosen man alone to possess it and because it restrained laziness and idolatry.[32]

The *Merton thesis* has been the subject of extensive debate for several decades. Some critics have claimed that the values Merton identified as Puritan were widely shared by other groups, including Anglicans. Moreover, there were divisions within Puritanism, and theological beliefs as well as political loyalties were changing rapidly.[33] But detailed studies by Charles Webster have supported a cautious rendition of the Merton thesis: Puritanism did not cause the development of science in England, but Puritan ideas and the political revolution itself gave strong encouragement to scientific work.[34] I. B. Cohen concludes his introduction to a recent volume devoted to the debate: "Enriched by modifications and qualifications introduced by scholarly critics, the essential Merton thesis has become a conspicuous feature of all expositions of the Scientific Revolution, arguably the most significant event in modern history."[35]

Other scholars have suggested a connection between the Calvinist emphasis on *the sovereignty of God* and the virtuosi's belief in *the passivity of matter.* According to Aristotle and medieval writers, material objects actively fulfill their purposes. Renaissance alchemists held that esoteric forces and invisible powers are present in matter; some of them defended pantheistic views in which God was identified with nature. Astrologers claimed that planets and human destinies are linked by higher influences or correspondences. But the virtuosi insisted that matter has no inherent powers or active internal principles. It is inert, lifeless, and obedient to God's will. External laws are imposed on it by God. In this light, the "mechanical philosophy" was not a rejection of religious convictions but a way of defending Calvinist ideas against some of its rivals.[36]

But in acknowledging the role of Puritans, we should not neglect *the contributions of Anglicans.* They had controlled Oxford and Cambridge and were well represented in the active core of the Royal Society, founded in 1660, the year the monarchy and the Anglican church were restored to power. Many Anglican scientists advocated religious toleration but used the new science to defend their royalist political views. The rule of law in nature, they said, is analogous to the rule of law in society. The analogy was used to support the monarchy, established church, and market economy against the threat to social stability posed by the more radical reformers and separatists. Science was increasingly valued for its technological applications and as a source of power over nature—and thus as a source of economic and political power in society. Political and ideological as well as religious convictions interacted with scientific ideas in complex ways.[37]

In short, neither the *conflict* thesis nor the *harmony* thesis concerning science and religion fits all the evidence. A more accurate account will have to reflect the *diversity* of interactions during this crucial century.

Let us ask a final broader question—so broad, in fact, that any answer is bound to be speculative and difficult to support with historical evidence. Why was it in *Western civilization* alone, among all the cultures of the world, that science in its modern form developed? Arabic science was more advanced than Western science in the thirteenth century, especially in astronomy, optics, and medicine, but it fell far behind in subsequent centuries. One recent study suggests that a major factor in the decline of science in the Islamic world was the tight control by religious authorities over higher education. Aristotle and Greek science were banned from institutions of higher learning because they challenged the authority of the religious tradition; science could be studied only in separate libraries and astronomical observatories. By contrast, Aristotle's natural philosophy was at the core of the required curriculum in Western universities, as we have seen, and it was extensively debated, preparing the way for its eventual overthrow. The Thomistic synthesis sought to Christianize Aristotle rather than to exclude him. The West had greater confidence in human reason, and its universities allowed considerable freedom of inquiry as long as basic theological doctrines were not rejected. China, the other region of the world where science might have developed, made impressive advances in practical technology but not in theoretical science; higher education was controlled by state officials and was based on the authority of the humanistic classics, which said little about science.[38]

*The rise of modern science* was, of course, a complex social phenomenon covering several centuries and influenced by numerous factors. There were economic forces, such as the growth of trade and commerce and the availability of wealth and leisure. Technological interest was encouraged by practical problems in metallurgy, navigation, the trades, and military weaponry. Skilled craftsmen and artisans were learning to make tools and scientific instruments. The founding of such institutions as the Royal Society, regional scientific societies, and the circulation of letters and journals aided the new enterprise.[39] Our concern, however, lies with *the intellectual presuppositions* underlying the rise of science.

Interest in nature for its own sake was in part a *reaction against medieval thought*. Rejecting otherworldliness, scholars of the Renaissance in the fourteenth century had begun looking with new excitement to the potentialities of life in this world. At first interest had been directed to the classical cultures of antiquity, to art and literature, and to secular but nonscientific learning. But the creative genius of Leonardo da Vinci, for example, was expressed in areas as varied as art, engineering, and anatomy. Exploration of geographical frontiers and natural phenomena evoked the curiosity of the adventurous. With the rejection of the authority of the church in the Reformation, greater diversity of thought prevailed in northern Europe and a more important role was assigned to the individual in the pursuit of truth.

But the medieval legacy also included presuppositions about nature that were congenial to the scientific enterprise. First, the conviction of *the intelligibility of nature* contributed to the rational or theoretical component of science. The medieval scholastics, like the Greek philosophers, did have great confidence in human rationality. Moreover, they combined the Greek view of the orderliness and regularity of the universe with the biblical view of God as Lawgiver. Monotheism implies the universality of order and coherence (though in the prescientific era this was not conceived primarily in terms of laws of cause and effect).

Second, the doctrine of creation implies that *the details of nature can be known only by observing them.* For if the world is the product of God's free act, it did not have to be made as it was made, and we can understand it only by actual observation. The universe, in other words, is contingent on God's will, not a necessary consequence of first principles. The world is both orderly and contingent, for God is both rational and free. By contrast, Greek thought had taken a predominantly deductive approach; it held that, starting from general principles, one should be able to infer how all the details of the world are ordered. Every specific element of the cosmos, said Socrates, flows by necessity from God's nature. In addition, the Platonic tradition viewed matter as an inferior embodiment of pure rational forms; the eternal forms can be grasped in their essence by intuitive reason, not by examining finite objects that imperfectly illustrate them. It is perhaps not surprising that the rational side of Greek thought (for example, mathematics and geometry) was stronger than its experimental side.[40]

Third, *an affirmative attitude toward nature* is dominant in the Bible. The goodness of the world is a corollary of the doctrine of creation. God's purposes involve the created order and the sphere of time and history. To be sure, there were world-denying themes in medieval thought (partly derived from the Greek and Hellenistic worlds), but the extremes of gnosticism and Manichaeism, in which matter is inherently evil, were repudiated. Undoubtedly considerable fear of the demonic in nature continued to haunt the popular imagination and perhaps hindered the rise of science. But in figures such as St. Benedict, St. Francis, and St. Thomas, we can see the goodness of creation affirmed in several modes—practical, spiritual, and intellectual. Yet biblical religion had never deified natural forces or the vitalities of organic life; the world was not an object of worship, and thus it could become an object of study.

But if the biblical view of creation, along with the Greek emphasis on rationality, eventually helped to foster science, why was *scientific development in the Middle Ages* relatively meager, even though practical technologies were impressive? Perhaps the answer lies partly in the weight of Aristotle's authority and the excessive rationalism of the scholastics, partly in the dominance of the institutional church against which both Renaissance and Reformation rebelled—and of course partly in the social and economic factors mentioned earlier. The scientific revolution happened only once in human history, and one can but speculate as to why it did not occur at another time or place.

Nevertheless, many historians of science have acknowledged the importance of the Western religious tradition in molding assumptions about nature that were congenial to the scientific enterprise.

## V. SUMMARY

In this chapter we have sketched five topics in their development from the medieval "World-Drama" to the Newtonian "World-Machine." From this account we can summarize some themes and distinguish the issues that were the product of short-lived circumstances from those that were of continuing importance.

### 1. Methods in Science

Considering in turn the Middle Ages, Galileo, and Newton, we moved from "Explanation by Purposes" to "Mathematics and Observation" and "Experiment and Theory." Preoccupation with purposes had for centuries diverted attention from mechanical causes and hindered the growth of the approach characteristic of modern science. In the seventeenth century, remarkable success was achieved by concentrating on physical explanations and "efficient" rather than "formal" or "final" causes. Theory and experiment were linked by imaginative new concepts; these have remained the basic elements of scientific methodology. Theories were assumed to provide a literal representation of reality (realism)—a viewpoint we will find rejected by many contemporary philosophers of science who, in the light of twentieth-century physics, stress the selective and abstractive character of scientific concepts, models, and theories.

The virtuosi believed there were divine purposes in nature but held that they should play no role in the scientific account. Some scientists in later generations were to conclude that mechanical explanation eliminates all theological meaning; the issue was to become acute again during the evolution controversy. I shall maintain, however, that when correctly expressed, analysis in theological terms is not displaced by analysis in scientific terms, since science and theology ask fundamentally different sorts of questions, even if they interact at some points. In an age dominated by religion, it was necessary to assert the independence of science, as Galileo tried to do. Today, in an age dominated by science, it may sometimes be necessary to assert the independence of religion. The dominance of either science or religion and the assumption that one must exclude the other have been in part products of the failure to analyze adequately the characteristics of diverse ways of knowing. What are the functions of differing types of explanations, and what are the appropriate processes of inquiry? What are the strengths and limitations of the methods of science? These will be the subjects of part 2.

### 2. The Character of Nature

The natural world was viewed successively as "A Created Hierarchy," "Particles in Motion," and "A Law-Abiding Machine." In the development of an atomistic and mechanistic worldview, a particular set of scientific concepts was extended into a metaphysical system purporting to account for everything in the world except humanity. The mathematical ideal was used as the criterion for selecting those quantifiable characteristics that were attributed to the external world as objective "primary qualities." The success of the categories of physics produced the confidence that everything could be explained in terms of those categories.

During the ensuing century, the mechanistic interpretation of nature was to be developed further in the deterministic, materialistic, and atheistic philosophies of the French Enlightenment, but it was attacked in the romantic reaction toward the close of the century. We shall see later that twentieth-century physics entailed a major change in basic concepts and assumptions; Thomas Kuhn presents it as an example of what he calls a "paradigm shift." Modern physics casts doubt on the deterministic and mechanistic assumptions of the Newtonian world view. A closely related problem is *reductionism*, the attribution of reality exclusively to the smallest constituents of the world and the attempt to interpret higher levels of organization in terms of lower levels. To this problem we will return in part 3 in examining contemporary views of nature.

## 3. Methods in Theology

For the three periods considered we used the headings "Reason and Revelation," "Scripture, Nature, and the Church," and "Natural Theology." Biblical theology had been so merged with Aristotelianism in the Middle Ages that church leaders reacted to criticisms of Aristotle's cosmology as if they were attacks on Christianity. This was a major source of conflict in Galileo's time but diminished in importance in subsequent centuries. Yet it reflects a perennial problem: How can theologians make use of the best philosophy and science of their day, as Aquinas made use of Aristotle, and yet avoid distorting the essential Christian message by making an inflexible system that hinders response to new intellectual currents?

Biblical literalism contributed to the condemnation of Galileo by the Catholic Church. Such literalism was also present in Protestant scholasticism but was on the wane in northern Europe by the end of the century, and it was never as common on the English scene. The same sort of conflict was to arise again, however, between biblical literalists and proponents of evolution. The basic issue here is whether biblical revelation is to be understood as infallible propositional information capable of dictating scientific conclusions. In a later chapter I will defend a view of revelation in human experience and historical events that tries to avoid both appeal to a literal inerrant text, on the one hand, and the complete dismissal of revelation as a source of religious understanding, on the other.

In the Middle Ages and subsequent Catholicism, the argument from design and other forms of natural theology were only a preamble to revealed theology; the most important religious truths were to be found only in the tradition of the church. Among the early Reformers, natural theology played a minor role, for to them the basis of religious knowledge was God's redemptive act in Christ, confirmed in the acceptance of God's forgiveness. The English virtuosi gave a greater role to natural theology. They thought they were defending Christianity, but they often turned from history and religious experience to nature as the chief clue to knowledge of God. It was but one more step for writers in the next century to defend natural theology and reject Christianity; some skeptics went further, abandoning even the idea of an intelligent Designer.

Natural theology includes the three types of argument from nature that we have encountered in this chapter and will meet again. (a) *Particular gaps in the scientific account* are said to require God's intervention (for example, Newton's belief that God has to readjust the planets or the nineteenth-century belief in the special creation of humanity in evolutionary history). Such arguments have often been undermined when the alleged "gaps" were closed. (b) *The design of particular features of organisms* is attributed to God. Such arguments were widely used in the next century. They appeared dubious after Darwin, though God could still be viewed as the Designer of the evolutionary process. (c) *The orderliness, intelligibility, creativity, and contingency of nature* are general properties not dependent on particular gaps in the scientific account. This type of argument is less vulnerable to the advance of science and is defended by some scientists and theologians today.

## 4. God and Nature

Three concepts of God were described: "Creator and Redeemer," "Author of Nature and Scripture," and "The Divine Clockmaker." The virtuosi tried to preserve a continuing function for God in the cosmic machine, and many of them were devout Christians. But they prepared the way for the God of deism, the God who started the machine and left it to run by itself. Today we must still grapple with the problem faced by the virtuosi: What are the modes of God's activity in relation to the natural order beyond the establishment of its laws? How can God act in a law-abiding world?

The God of deism turned out to be too remote to inspire religious commitment. In the Middle Ages, the sense of God's reality pervaded all aspects of culture. Philosophy and cosmology, art and literature, the church and its sacraments all conspired to make God seem near at hand. For the Reformers, God's presence in Christ and in the experience of forgiveness was always relevant to the life of the individual and the community. Nineteenth-century liberalism stressed the idea of divine immanence in nature, with God actively involved in the life of the world. What concepts of God are consistent with both religious needs and scientific understanding today?

## 5. Human Nature

The status of humanity was traced from the "Center of the Cosmic Drama" to "Humanity in the New Cosmology" to "Human Nature: Body and Mind." The displacement of human beings from a central geographical position had been widely accepted by the end of the seventeenth century. But the defensive reaction to Copernican astronomy was not unlike the reaction to the threat to human dignity in evolution or to recent speculation about intelligent life on other planets. In each case human uniqueness was cast in doubt.

In the seventeenth century, human dignity seemed to rest in the power of reason and in the mind/body dualism, which was widely assumed. The realm of mind was taken to be the one exception to the rule of mechanical law. Humanity was not yet absorbed into nature or metaphysically continuous with natural processes, as many nineteenth-century authors were to assume. The status of mind and the relation of humanity to the rest of nature have been central issues in philosophy and theology ever since.

Thus some of the causes of conflict between science and religion in this earliest phase were short-lived—for example, the respect in which Aristotle was held. Other problems remained acute in the following centuries and are still encountered today—for example, the tendency for theologians to make uninformed pronouncements about scientific theories or for scientists to turn their technical concepts into all-inclusive metaphysical systems. Other questions from this early period continue to be of crucial importance today. What are the similarities and differences between the methods of science and the methods of religion? How can God act in a world of scientific law? Which aspects of the traditional view of human nature can be retained, and which must be revised in the light of scientific knowledge?

## CHAPTER 2

# Nature and God
# in the Eighteenth Century

None of the scientific discoveries of the eighteenth century had philosophical or theological repercussions comparable to those of Newton's work. In physics the century saw the further development of mechanics by Lagrange, d'Alembert, Laplace, and others. The experiments of Priestley and Lavoisier with combustion and the identification of oxygen were the beginning of modern chemistry. In biology Linnaeus formulated a comprehensive system of classification for plants, and Buffon performed a similar service for animal forms. By the end of the century the technological applications of science were starting to have an impact on society, especially in the early phases of the Industrial Revolution in England. But the main change in the outlook of the age came not from any particular new discovery but from the spreading influence of the idea of science itself. This was a period of intellectual transition in which a characteristically modern temper emerged. We will look at these changes as they affected the interaction of scientific and religious ideas.

Section I, "The Age of Reason," gives some examples of the movement to extend to other areas of thought the ideal of rationality that had been so impressively demonstrated in Newtonian physics. The new view of nature was deterministic and reductionistic. Deistic views of God were common, but an increasing group of skeptics rejected all concepts of God and defended atheistic and materialistic philosophies. The new view of human nature was optimistic; the age was confident of human perfectibility through reason and of inevitable social progress through science.

Section II, "The Romantic Reaction," indicates the reaction against these ideas that occurred late in the century. Poets and novelists of the romantic movement defended human freedom, imagination, and intuition; to them, nature was not an impersonal machine but a living companion, permeated by beauty, vitality, and an underlying spiritual reality. Such movements as Pietism and Methodism brought a revitalization of personal religion and a repudiation of the rationalism of the Enlightenment.

Section III, "Philosophical Responses," outlines the understanding of science and religion set forth by two philosophers who greatly influenced subsequent thought. Hume claimed that sensory experience is the only source of knowledge; he was an agnostic concerning religion. Kant, on the other hand, defended the sphere of religion and morality, which he distinguished from the sphere of scientific inquiry. His system of thought provided a new and distinctive way of reconciling the claims of science and religion by assigning them to separate realms of discourse.

## I. THE AGE OF REASON

The eighteenth century saw itself as the Age of Reason in which the ideal of rationality manifest in science would permeate all human activities. The Enlightenment, as the new intellectual movement was called, was a diverse phenomenon, varying among countries and among individual thinkers, yet it displayed typical attitudes differing from those of any previous century. Its most articulate and extreme spokesmen were the French intellectuals of the midcentury, but its spirit permeated Germany, England, and the American colonies and influenced the subsequent climate of thought throughout the modern world. From among the many ideas of the Enlightenment, we select three that are relevant to this volume. Nature was viewed as a self-sufficient deterministic mechanism whose operation could be explained by natural forces. God became a debatable hypothesis, defended by some as a reasonable assumption, rejected by others as the dubious dogma of a reactionary church. Finally, the dominant mood was confidence in human perfectibility and the achievement of the ideal society by the application of reason to human affairs.

### 1. NATURE AS A DETERMINISTIC MECHANISM

The generations following Newton held him in a high esteem that approached adulation. Alexander Pope, whose precise literary style voiced the spirit of the new age, exulted:

Nature and Nature's laws lay hid in night:
God said, Let Newton be! and all was Light.[1]

Pierre Laplace (1749–1827) wrote that Newton was not only the greatest genius who ever lived but also the most fortunate, since there is only one universe and it can be the lot of but one person in history to be the interpreter of its laws. Newtonian mechanics became the prototype for scientific work; it supplied the guiding image for the kind of question that should be asked and the type of concept that should be used. Above all, the Newtonian paradigm established a new idea of what counts as a satisfactory explanation in science—and, by extrapolation, in any field.

Laplace himself carried further the mathematical analysis of *the mechanics of planetary motion*. He showed that the small irregularities caused by the mutual attraction of the planets, which Newton thought would be cumulative unless God stepped in to correct them, would instead automatically cancel each other out over a long time span. His nebular hypothesis, which proposed that the solar system was formed from the cooling and condensing of nebular gases, could account for the coplanar orbits of the planets without invoking God's intervention. Thus when Napoleon said to him, "M. Laplace, they tell me you have written this large book on the system of the universe, and have never even mentioned its Creator," Laplace could give his famous reply, "I had no need of that hypothesis."[2]

Laplace was an articulate spokesman for the new view of nature as *a self-sufficient and impersonal mechanism*. The world was no longer seen as the purposeful drama of the Middle Ages or even as the continuing object of providential supervision, as for Newton, but as a set of interacting natural forces. If events are wholly governed by natural causes, any remaining gaps in the scientific account should be filled, not by introducing a *deus ex machina*, but by further search for physical explanations. Though many scientists continued to believe in the existence of God, no reference to such beliefs was considered appropriate within scientific treatises. The secularization of knowledge in science, as in other fields, meant that theological ideas, whatever their role elsewhere, were to be excluded from the study of the world.

Laplace also explicitly formulated the *determinism* implicit in the view of reality as matter in motion. The laws of mechanics, which were assumed to govern the motion of all objects from the smallest particle to the largest star, would in principle allow the prediction of the path of every particle from the forces acting on it:

We ought then to regard the present state of the universe as the effect of its anterior state and as the cause of the one which is to follow. Given for one instant an intelligence which could comprehend all the forces by which nature is animated and the respective situation of the beings who compose it—an intelligence sufficiently vast to submit these data to analysis—it would embrace in the same foundation the movements of the greatest bodies of the universe and those of the lightest atom; for it, nothing would be uncertain and the future, as the past, would be present to its eyes.[3]

Nature was here assumed to be a complete mechanical system of inflexible cause and effect, governed by exact and absolute laws, so that all future events are inexorably determined.

Moreover, Laplace's view was explicitly *reductionistic*. Epistemological reductionism was expressed in the conviction that all phenomena will ultimately be explained by physical laws; metaphysical reductionism is evident in his conviction that reality is constituted by its smallest components, particles in motion. One of the links between these two ideas was the belief that causal efficacy resides in the external impact of one particle on another, so that all explanations of cause and effect can be given in terms of mechanical forces between moving bodies. Descartes had envisioned a mechanical world with the exception of the human mind. Now Diderot, along with many of the writers of the French *Encyclopédie*, defended a metaphysics of materialism, which claimed to account for humanity, too. In *Man the Machine*, La Mettrie maintained that consciousness is an illusory by-product of atomic motions. It is perhaps understandable that the concepts of mechanics, which had proved so fruitful, were deemed capable of giving an exhaustive analysis of all events. William Dampier suggests that this was "a natural exaggeration of the power of the new knowledge which had impressed the minds of men with its range and scope, before they realized its necessary limits."[4]

## 2. THE GOD OF DEISM

There were of course many people in eighteenth-century Europe who continued to accept traditional religious ideas. But the distinctive new viewpoint characteristic of the intellectual leaders of the Enlightenment was the "rational religion" whose origins, growth, and decline we may trace in three overlapping stages.[5]

In the first stage, which was a continuation of the views of the virtuosi described in the previous chapter, *rational religion* and *the Christian tradition* were regarded as alternative routes to the same basic truths. This common core of universal beliefs was said to include the ideas of God, moral conduct, and immortality. These beliefs were also taken to be the essence of Christianity, which was "one form of the religion of reason whose principles are discoverable by all people in all ages." The argument from design was often used in this period. John Ray, the founder of modern botany, had written *The Wisdom of God Manifested in the Works of Creation* (1691), extolling the perfection of design in the world of plants and animals, and his book was widely quoted. Matthew Tindal's *Christianity as Old as Creation* (1730) stated that the Bible was a republication of these universal ideas and not a unique revelation. Here was a supposedly clear path "through Nature to Nature's God."

The *existence of evil* in the world was minimized by these exponents of natural theology. A favorite argument employed to justify the presence of destructive animals or insects was the idea that God had not wanted to deny existence to any possible kind of being. It was asserted that there is an ascending ladder of creatures from worm to angel, "a great chain of being."[6] The advantages of creating a "full" universe, with all niches occupied, outweighed any disadvantages from the presence of less desirable types of being. The optimism of the age is seen in the assertion that this is "the best of all possible worlds"; in Pope's words, "Whatever is, is right." The universe is complete and perfect, for the status quo is God's intention. Here was a "cosmic Toryism," which glorified things as they are and rejected the traditional conviction (linked to the doctrine of the fall) that there is something radically wrong with the whole created world. Despite such modifications of tradition, the defenders of natural theology in this first stage were friendly to Christianity and believed that reason confirms its central tenets.[7]

The second stage, *the heyday of deism,* saw natural theology used as a substitute for revelation. The sufficiency of reason was confidently affirmed, and scripture was assigned a subordinate role. Revealed theology was on the defensive, as in Bishop Butler's *Analogy of Religion, Natural and Revealed*

(1736). It is symptomatic of his times that Butler tried to vindicate revelation by its analogy to natural theology. The evidence from nature is by no means clear and simple, he suggested; it is not a realm of pure order and reason but of ambiguities and perplexities. Nor is scripture always obscure, as its critics claim. Instead, we confront in both cases a mixture of clarity and obscurity; if nature is accepted as evidence of God, said Butler, then scripture should be equally acceptable. But the net effect of his argument was to cast doubt on natural theology rather than to strengthen the case for revelation.[8]

The third stage, *the waning of deism,* can be attributed primarily to its own inherent weaknesses. The Cosmic Designer, who started the world-machine and left it to run on its own, seemed impersonal and remote—not a God who cares for individuals and is actively related to human life or a Being to whom prayer would be appropriate. It is not surprising that such a do-nothing God, irrelevant to daily life, became a hypothesis for the origin of the world or a verbal formula that before long could be dispensed with completely. In deism, God was a rational inference from the impersonal structures of nature, unrelated to personal experience. The arguments of natural theology did not move people to the kind of commitment and personal involvement that an active religious life requires.[9]

The deists also attacked the institutional church; traditional Christianity was pictured as the enemy of the religion of reason. Miracles were rejected as primitive superstitions, and instances of cruelty and immorality in the biblical record were cited. Any creed, dogma, or ritual was suspect as out of keeping with the new temper. Explorers and scholars were becoming more familiar with other world religions, and many of them accepted a cultural relativism that rejected exclusive claims for any one religious tradition. In England the attacks on traditional beliefs were moderate and restrained; in France they were often vehement and bitter, provoked by the church's unbending orthodoxy and repressive measures. Voltaire applied his wit to the ridicule of Christianity, though to his death he remained a deist. In America, Thomas Paine's *Age of Reason* found contradictions in the Bible and celebrated the victory of reason over superstition but defended the idea of God and the moral law. Jefferson, Franklin, and others among the "founding fathers" defended more moderate versions of deism.[10]

The "enlightened" of the first generation supported both natural and revealed religion; those of the second adhered to natural religion but rejected revelation. By the third generation there were skeptical voices calling for *rejection of all forms of religion.* Baron d'Holbach denied God, freedom, and immortality and proclaimed that matter is self-existent. Nature alone is worthy of worship: "O Nature! Sovereign of all beings! And you, her adorable daughters, virtue, reason, and truth! Be ever our only Divinities."[11] Diderot's materialistic philosophy expressed a more militant atheism reflecting the anticlericalism that was later to erupt so violently in the French Revolution. Hostility toward the church centered in its authoritarianism (in alliance with the monarchy) and its social conservatism, which were taken to be enemies of freedom and progress.

## 3. HUMANITY AS PERFECTIBLE BY REASON

Enlightenment authors were confident of *the power of reason* not only in science but in all human affairs. A Newton of the social sciences was eagerly anticipated; with the discovery of social laws it would soon be possible to understand society and regulate human activities accordingly. As some interpreters saw it, once we know what is "natural" we can remove the artificial constraints imposed by governments; in economics the laws of supply and demand would automatically ensure the welfare of society. The "natural" was equated with the good and the rational. Here Nature (usually capitalized) was considered an ally of human progress; we can feel at home in an orderly and harmonious world. Nature and Reason were to be the benign guides to humanity's ascent; and if their dictates seem to have varied considerably according to the liberal or conservative proclivities of particular authors, we must recall that "natural" and "reasonable" were at best rather vague concepts. Neither the detailed empirical data nor the systematic theoretical constructs of the later social sciences were yet present.[12]

Such *optimism about human nature* in many eighteenth-century writings was a major departure from the Christian tradition. It was asserted that human beings are not born sinful but are born good and then corrupted by society. According to Rousseau, people are naturally virtuous; evil arises from social institutions. We can protect the inherent goodness of children by allowing them to grow without external restraints. If ignorance rather than sin limits human achievement, education and the spread of reason will accomplish the liberation of humanity. Condorcet wrote, "The result of my work will show by reasoning and facts that there is no limit set to the perfection of the powers of man, that human perfectibility is in reality indefinite."[13]

*Expectations of human progress* often knew no bounds. Awareness of the possibility of deliberate and far-reaching institutional change, which has been part of Western thought since the Enlightenment, was coupled with a utopian anticipation of the perfection of society. It was assumed that science and material progress would automatically bring virtue and happiness. Heaven on earth would be a social achievement. Soon war would be looked on as a crime. Here was a new philosophy of history in which a state of perfection would come in this life by human efforts alone, and science was to be the source of salvation. This was, as Carl Becker puts it, a "secular eschatology," a new vision of the heavenly city on earth.[14] This was the future hope, which made individual effort significant; the human race in its coming perfection should be the object of our devotion and loyalty.

Among many Enlightenment authors, especially in France, there was great confidence in "*social engineering*" and the technical control of society, with little recognition of the dangers that accompany the power of some people over other people. Science was to be the great liberator—not the enslaver, as in such recent novels as George Orwell's *1984* or Aldous Huxley's *Brave New World*. It was expected that humanity would rise to unprecedented heights and all evils would vanish if individuals and societies would follow the principles of reason. Far from being an age of skepticism, this was an age of great faith—in human capacities. Nature, God, and humanity were all approached in the same rationalistic spirit.

If some features of the Enlightenment deserve criticism, its *positive contributions* deserve acknowledgment also. It was one of the forces in the spread of religious toleration. There had been earlier voices on behalf of religious liberty in England—Baptists and Congregationalists upholding the principle of voluntary association, and Quakers defending individual conscience, for example. The Enlightenment now added its defense of freedom of expression and its opposition to all forms of dogmatism and particularism. Again, the new outlook was a liberating force for human creativity, for the dignity of the individual, and for the legitimate autonomy of inquiry, which is a valid aspect of secularization. At its best the eighteenth century showed a passion for social justice and humanitarian reform that can be admired even by those who do not share its utopian confidence in human perfectibility.

## II. THE ROMANTIC REACTION

Romanticism was the rebellious child of the Enlightenment; it rejected a number of its parent's ideas, even while accepting without question many of the assumptions it inherited. The reaction against the Age of Reason is evident in many areas of thought during the last half of the eighteenth century (and continuing into the nineteenth), though the form it took and the date of its occurrence varied from country to country. In political theory there was a revival of conservatism and concern for the values of earlier traditions—sometimes, as in the case of Edmund Burke, inspired in part by revulsion at the excesses of the French Revolution. There were new forms of nationalism and new philosophies of history as the unfolding of culture and spirit (for example, Hegel, Fichte, and others, in Germany). We can note only two expressions of this protest that touch on science and religion. First, the romantic movement in literature pointed to the limitations of science and tried to deal with aspects of experience that had been neglected in the intellectualism of the Age of Reason. Imagination and intuition, it was now proclaimed, are as important as reason; the poet was said to respond to the beauty and inner life of nature, which escape scientific analysis. Second, the Pietist and Methodist movements recovered the transforming power of personal religious experience, which had been lost among the abstract arguments of deism.

### 1. ROMANTICISM IN LITERATURE

The rejection of many of the ideals of the Enlightenment is both implicit and explicit in the literature of the romantic movement. The Age of Reason had concerned itself with a restricted range of human interests and experiences. "It was no accident," writes J. H. Randall, "that the scientific age of the Enlightenment produced little that can rank with the world's greatest art and poetry."[15] For it had neglected *emotion* and *imagination* in concentrating on reason alone. The romantic protest turned to the richness, concreteness, and immediacy of living experience, which is not known through the artificial abstractions of scientific inquiry. The hero of Goethe's *Faust,* for example, had mastered all scientific knowledge but found it empty and sought fullness of life through immersion in the vitality of experience. Such writers as Shelley and Byron celebrated the creative individual, the romantic hero seeking love, friendship, and fulfillment.

Romanticism exalted *freedom, individuality,* and *wholeness.* Against the determinism of the Enlightenment, human freedom and creativity were proclaimed. In contrast to preoccupation with unchanging laws, there was new interest in growth and development, in dynamic and historical processes—an orientation that helped to prepare the climate of thought in which the idea of the historicity of nature and its evolution could later be formulated. In contrast to concern for the universal and the general, the new emphasis centered on uniqueness, individuality, and self-expression. Against the abstractness of rational principles, the concreteness of human experience as lived was sought. Against the atomism and reductionism of former decades, it was now said that organic wholes are more than the sum of their separate parts and that they must be grasped in their dynamic unity. And against the expectation that technology and reason would bring human happiness, it now seemed that the human misery that accompanied the Industrial Revolution (and, in a very different form, the French Revolution) was evidence of the limitations of science and social engineering as sources of salvation.[16]

A number of writers defended the importance of *imagination* in human understanding. Thus Coleridge suggested that the creative poet, by fusing metaphors and images into new wholes, communicates from the depth of personal experience and evokes the reader's response. We never know other persons by general concepts but rather by acts of intuition and imagination, which grasp their inner lives. Coleridge wrote extensively about existential questions of selfhood, remorse, and moral conscience. To him religious faith was not intellectual argumentation but fidelity, commitment, and decision. We are creatures of feeling and emotion as well as reason, he said, of heart and soul as well as mind.[17]

The *poet's vision of nature* portrayed much that the scientist had ignored. Romanticism carried on the Enlightenment's interest in nature but saw it in very different terms—not as an impersonal machine but as a living companion, a source of warmth, vitality, and joy, of healing and restoring power. The poet's intuition can respond to the beauty of nature, which eludes the cold abstractions of science. To Wordsworth a flower is far more than what the botanist can study:

Our meddling intellect
Mis-shapes the beauteous forms of things
We murder to dissect.[18]

And I have felt
A presence that disturbs me with the joy
Of elevated thoughts, a sense sublime
Of something far more deeply interfused,
Whose dwelling is the light of setting suns,
And the round ocean and the living air,
And the blue sky and in the mind of man;
A motion and a spirit that impels
All thinking things, all objects of all thought,
And rolls through all things.[19]

God is not the external creator of an impersonal machine but a spirit pervading nature and known in human experience. The divine indwelling, God's immanence in the world and in the human soul, which had been lost in deism, was reasserted by the romantic poets. They held that the beauty of nature and its deeper spiritual reality, linking all beings together, are known in personal response, not in scientific analysis.

## 2. PIETISM AND METHODISM

In contrast to the rationalism of the deists, the upsurge of personal religion in the second half of the eighteenth century brought a powerful revitalization of traditional Christianity. The new evangelical fervor and recovery of experiential religion occurred across national and denominational lines. *Pietism* in Germany early in the century was a reaction against Lutheran scholasticism. Francke led the movement to gather within the church small groups that could cultivate the devotional life and the inner experience of the soul. In other cases separate communities were formed, such as the Moravian Brethren, who resolved to practice a more rigorous pattern of Christian life and morality. These groups spoke of the experience of the Holy Spirit and the new life in Christ and urged a return to the simplicity of the gospel and its transforming power. Not dogmas or reasoned arguments but personal experience of God's presence and the regeneration of individual life were taken as primary. Kant, whom we shall consider shortly, acknowledged the influence of his pietistic upbringing and defended the importance of the realm of inner experience—especially moral conscience—as the basis of religion.

*The Methodist movement* brought a similar religious renewal to England. John Wesley, in the decades following his conversion in 1738, preached a message of personal evangelical faith. His theology did differ at some points from his Anglican heritage, but the main difference was his message of Christian commitment and conversion—"spiritual rebirth" in response to Christ as personal savior—which gained many followers from the middle and working classes. Wesley held that self-centeredness is overcome not by rational argument but by a radical transformation and reorientation of the self. Love and ethical concern are fruits of the new life in Christ and the power of the Spirit in personal experience. Wesley also emphasized individual moral exertion and an ethic of pure living and Christian discipleship at a time when moral laxity was widespread.

Wesley had considerable interest in science, which is reflected in his reading, in the curriculum of the schools he established, and in the books he published, several of which included long selections from scientists. His book on medicine consisted mainly of popular home remedies, and it went through thirty-two editions. Another book on electricity drew from Benjamin Franklin's writings and included purported medical applications of electricity. His *Survey of the Wisdom of God in Creation* (five volumes in its final form) was a veritable encyclopedia of current science in a variety of fields. But his interest lay in practical applications and in the use of science to demonstrate God's wisdom; he distrusted what he saw as grandiose claims for systematic theories. He had no difficulty accepting Copernican astronomy but expressed doubts about Newtonianism, partly because of its association with deism. The *Principia* was in his recommended school curriculum—but so was a book by Hutchinson, a critic of Newton's theories. Wesley criticized both Newton and Hutchinson for claiming to know more about God's designs than mortals can expect to know.[20]

In America, the great *religious revivals* of the early nineteenth century swept westward with the frontier; the deism that had been common at the time of the nation's founding had virtually disappeared. The message of repentance, acceptance of Christ, and practical morality was preached by camp-meeting orator, circuit rider, and rural pastor. From both Europe and America the expanding missionary movement took the gospel to the corners of the world. The theology of all these groups was traditional, and they justified their beliefs by biblical quotations, but they emphasized personal religion rather than theological creeds.

## III. PHILOSOPHICAL RESPONSES

The two greatest philosophers of the eighteenth century were profoundly indebted to the growth of science, and both wrote extensively about religion, though they differed in their conclusions. Hume, emphasizing the observational side of science, held that all knowledge is derived from sense impressions; scientific theories and laws are summaries of observations. Judged by these standards, the evidence for religious beliefs appeared unconvincing, and Hume gave detailed replies to the arguments of natural theology. Kant's view of science, on the other hand, gave prominence to the role of the human mind in the interpreting of data. He said that religion must be grounded in practical life and moral conscience. These two very different ways of relating science and religion had far-reaching influences on subsequent thought.

## 1. SCIENTIFIC EMPIRICISM AND RELIGIOUS AGNOSTICISM (HUME)

Descartes, Leibniz, and Spinoza in the seventeenth century had been impressed by the rational, theoretical, mathematical side of the early physics. For them, mathematics was the prototype of knowledge, for its reasoning is certain, universal, and *a priori*—that is, deducible from self-evident truths or the relationships among ideas. Locke, by contrast, had been impressed by the observational side of Newtonian science. He had given the first systematic formulation of *empiricism*, the claim that sensory experience is the only source of knowledge and the primary authority for the truth of propositions. He insisted that the mind is a *tabula rasa*, a blank tablet, on which the senses write. Ideas are not innate but empirical in origin, built up from the particular impressions of the five senses.

Like Locke, David Hume (1711–1776) held that the only reliable human knowledge is based on *sense impressions*. Ideas are memory-images of perceptions, and their validity must be tested by tracing them back to the sense data from which they arose. Hume says that if an idea is ambiguous a person should always "have recourse to the impressions which render it clear and precise."[21] Hume thought of experience as a succession of separate and disconnected perceptions; he held that we have no knowledge of the relations among impressions. The human self is not a continuing entity with an enduring unity but a stream of such isolated impressions. The mind merely records, rearranges, and compares sense data. Hume was thus led to assert that a scientific theory or law is simply a convenient summary and correlation of individual observations—a view we will find echoed by Hume's intellectual descendants, the logical positivists of the twentieth century.

Among the concepts to which Hume applies this theory of knowledge is the idea of *causality*. Traditionally causality had been understood as necessary connection; if a cause occurs, then its effect must occur. But, says Hume, we cannot observe necessary connection or any kind of compulsion or power that one event has over another. We observe only repeated temporal succession among sense impressions. This constant conjunction leads to a habit of association. The connection is only psychological, an expectancy or anticipation formed in our minds by force of habit. The terms *cause* and *effect* do not correspond to any observable attributes but only to our customary way of looking at events that repeatedly follow each other. Thus "laws of nature" are not prescriptions of what has to happen, and scientific knowledge is never universal or certain. Laws are only human expectations based on previous experience.[22]

If causality is only a habit of expectation, Hume argues, then *the argument for God as First Cause* is undermined. For expectations can arise only from the repetition of sequences. We have indeed seen people making clocks, and thus when we find a clock we assume it was made by a clockmaker. But we have not observed a Creator creating other universes, and we cannot generalize from experience concerning the production of worlds. From similar effects we postulate similar causes, but there are no analogies for the universe as a whole. Science asks only about limited sequences, not about the total process or the origin of the order and structure of events; any statement beyond science is speculation.[23]

Hume also attacked *the argument from design.* If there is order in the world, the organizing force might be within nature rather than external to it; the world appears less like a clock or machine than like a plant or animal with an internal principle of life. Why not stop with the assertion that there is some principle of order within the world or perhaps a generative force or a blind vitality instead of going on to postulate a Creator? The phenomena of the universe are too varied for us to pick any one of its aspects as the basis for an analogy. There is so much pain and suffering that we would have to assume either two world powers, one working for good and the other for evil, or else a single morally neutral Creator. From a finite world one could at best infer only a finite God. We need postulate only a degree of power and intelligence sufficient to account for the properties of the world rather than ascribing infinite attributes and absolute perfections to God.

Hume rejects the Enlightenment's confidence in the power of reason. He claims that no universal laws can be derived from particular observations. He argues that necessity can be attributed only to logical relations. But Hume says that when he steps out of his study he has to put aside his doubts (for example, about the existence of objects, selves, and causal connections) and fall back on "*common sense*" and "*natural belief.*" Life would be impossible on the basis of "unmitigated skepticism."[24] We cannot avoid the conviction that events are caused, but this is a "natural sentiment" based on feeling and instinct, even though it is not demonstrable on the basis of reason. Custom, common sense, and moral sentiment are reliable enough for practical purposes.

There are some passages in Hume's writings in which he seems to allow for similar "*natural beliefs*" in religion, a kind of implicit faith that has its own validity quite apart from the dubious reasoning of natural theology. In the conclusion of the *Dialogues on Natural Religion,* Philo, the skeptical character, confesses to "a deeper sense of religion impressed on the mind." He concedes that the presence of design strikes him "with irresistible force," even though the arguments for it are logically unconvincing, and he postulates a divine intelligence "bearing some remote analogy to the human mind." Other passages, such as his discussion of the insignificance of mind in the universe or his suggestion that the principle of order may be entirely internal to the world, seem to endorse a metaphysics of naturalism. But his most frequent assertions, which are supported by his own theory of knowledge, are neither theistic nor atheistic but *agnostic.* God's existence can be neither proved nor disproved, and in the absence of dependable evidence it is best to reserve judgment about such ultimate questions.[25]

Whatever his own positive beliefs may have been, Hume's main religious impact stemmed from his attack on deism and natural theology. In future chapters we will scrutinize several presuppositions underlying his attack. We will find his extreme *empiricism* inadequate as a description of science, for it neglects the crucial role of creative imagination in the invention of concepts and theories by which the data are interpreted. We will reject his view of experience as a series of disconnected sense impressions and will stress the contextual character of understanding and the apprehension of relations and wholes as well as parts. Again, the form of the *teleological argument* that Hume attacked assumed the initial Designer of a static mechanical world. More recent reformulations of the argument are in certain respects less vulnerable to his critique, for they acknowledge an evolutionary universe with immanent principles of order—more analogous to an organism than to a machine—and they ask about the ultimate source of such built-in orderliness. Finally, we will find that many contemporary theologians agree with Hume in rejecting *natural theology* but that they do so primarily on other grounds; they hold that religion is not based on rational argument but on historical revelation or on moral and religious experience.

## 2. SCIENCE AND RELIGION AS SEPARATE REALMS (KANT)

Immanuel Kant (1724–1804) provided a new approach in which no conflict can occur between science and religion. He was familiar with eighteenth-century science and proposed (before Laplace) a nebular hypothesis for the formation of the planets in the early solar system. But he held that there are limitations in the methods of science that leave room for religious beliefs. Let us examine first his analysis of science, in which elements of *empiricism* and *rationalism* are combined in a novel synthesis. Kant agreed with Hume that there is no knowledge apart from experience. But he was convinced that the mind does not simply receive sense data passively but organizes it actively in accordance with its own interpretive principles. The mind brings to the confused flux of fragmentary impressions a distinctive way of structuring and relating them; the categories of human thought are imposed on the raw materials of the senses. Knowledge is thus the joint product of sensory material and the structure of consciousness, which actively organizes and interprets by its own forms of understanding.[26]

Among the forms of understanding imposed by the mind are *space* and *time*. We organize experience, Kant says, by spatial and temporal relations, and we cannot imagine a world without them, even though space and time cannot be directly perceived. They are forms of thought that determine the way we both perceive and conceive of things. *Causality* is also a category of understanding that is brought to the interpretation of sense data rather than being derived from it. The idea that "every event has a cause" is not an empirical observation or a generalization from experience but an indispensable presupposition of human thought. Causality is a general form by means of which the mind unifies the chaos of discrete data. The human mind provides the most general categories for interpreting the relationships among impressions.

Kant agrees with Hume in criticizing the classical argument for *God as First Cause*. He, too, holds that the idea of causality can be applied only to perceptual experience, but he says the idea originates in the built-in categories of human understanding rather than in habits of association. We can have no experience of the world-as-a-whole to which a causal interpretation might properly apply; the concept of cause can be used only for terms within a temporal series, not for the entire series.[27]

For Kant the starting point of religion lies in an entirely different realm, our *sense of moral obligation*. Not theoretical problems of metaphysics but practical problems of ethics require God as a postulate. We experience value as well as fact; we ask not only what is, but what we ought to do. Kant gives as one formulation of the moral law the injunction to act in such a fashion that the principle of your action could be adopted by all people; that is, you should apply to yourself only rules that could be applied universally. This is a "categorical imperative," independent of particular circumstances or individual inclinations. Ethics for Kant consists in the duty to follow the universal law, the principle of unlimited generalization.[28]

Kant goes on to suggest that God is a *postulate of the moral order*. When we act from response to duty we implicitly affirm that the world is a moral order. The presence of moral law presupposes a lawgiver who is its source and guarantor. Moral endeavor also requires some sort of correlation between virtue and ultimate happiness; we are led to postulate a God who will bring about justice by ensuring that virtue is rewarded in the next life. Similarly, Kant holds that recognition of ethical imperatives implies the existence of human freedom. Determinism does indeed reign in the realm of phenomena studied by science, for causality is an inescapable category in the interpretation of events in space and time. But the acknowledgment of "ought" in daily life presupposes alternatives of choice. Hence practical reason affirms both God and freedom, even though theoretical reason cannot prove their existence.[29]

Kant was able to fit both *science* and *religion* into his theory of knowledge. He had great respect for Newtonian science and insisted that claims of knowledge must be restricted to empirically based relations among natural phenomena. Yet, in keeping with the biblical tradition and his own pietistic background, Kant attached great importance to moral choice, good and evil, sin and judgment; he departed from that tradition in making ethics primary and central and theology secondary and derivative. As a child of the Age of Reason, he interpreted ethics as obedience to universal rational principles, but he went beyond that age in recognizing the limitations of "theoretical reason" and in using "practical reason" as the basis of religion. To him, both the natural and the moral order were rational, but they constituted independent realms.[30]

Kant thus offered a new way of *reconciling science and religion* by a division of labor. Each has its own realm and function, and they do not compete with each other. This is a distinctive version of what I will call the *Independence* thesis. Religion does not have to defend itself by pointing to the ever-diminishing gaps in the scientific account or to purported evidences of design. In the realm of natural phenomena, science is exhaustively competent. The function of religious beliefs is not to extend scientific explanations, but to clarify and support moral life by relating it to the character of ultimate reality. As E. A. Burtt puts it:

For Kant, science and religion occupy entirely different spheres and are given distinct functions which are so adjusted that they need never conflict. The realm of possible knowledge belongs to science, and science has complete freedom to explore that realm by its own method. The task of religion is to enlighten our moral devotion and give it cosmic serenity.[31]

The *influence of Kant* is evident in much of nineteenth-century philosophy and theology. In philosophical idealism (Hegel and his successors) the rationalist elements in Kant's thought were developed at the expense of his empiricist convictions; the structures of consciousness were taken to be the pattern of reality, and God was interpreted as Absolute Mind. In Protestant liberalism (Ritschl and his successors) Kant's emphasis on the moral life was combined with loyalty to the theological framework of biblical ethics. Existentialists (Kierkegaard and his successors) rejected Kant's rationalism, but they agreed that the context of religion is the activity of selves in decision— and that science and religion are separate realms of discourse. The ghost of Kant still hovers over those who say that science deals with facts and religion deals with values.

## IV. SUMMARY

In this chapter we have seen the development of new patterns of thought during the eighteenth century concerning several of our topics.

### 1. Methods in Science

Many thinkers of the Enlightenment wanted to extend to all problems the methods that had been so successful in physics. Newtonian physics was taken as the model not only for other natural sciences but also for scientific solutions to the problems of society. Hume dwelt on the empirical side of science and concluded that any idea that cannot be traced to sense data is without significance; for him, as for recent positivists, empirical verification is the criterion for all knowledge. Kant, on the other hand, maintained that the human mind supplies crucial conceptual categories in the interpretation of sense data. The relation between the observable and the conceptual components of science has been a continuing issue in philosophical reflections on science.

### 2. God and Nature

Laplace's writing was taken as representative of the deterministic and reductionistic view of nature as a self-sufficient machine in which all future events are inexorably determined by the laws of matter in motion. Some thinkers portrayed God as the remote and impersonal clockmaker, the cosmic Architect of deism. Others, such as the materialists of the French Enlightenment, rejected all concepts of God. The romantic movement went to the opposite extreme, picturing nature as creative, spontaneous, and growing, permeated by beauty and an underlying spiritual reality. Here God's immanence in nature and in the human soul was reasserted. Methodism, Pietism, and the evangelical revivals recovered the biblical view of a personal God actively related to humanity but had little to say about God's relationship to nature.

### 3. Methods in Theology

Three basic approaches to religious knowledge were represented.

(a) *Revelation.* During the Enlightenment the idea of historical revelation came under increasing attack. But Methodism and Pietism later recovered the convictions of the Reformation concerning the centrality of scripture in religious life.

(b) *Natural Theology.* The early part of the century saw extensive development of the arguments for a First Cause and an intelligent Designer. Despite the criticisms of Hume and Kant, the argument from design was widely used in the first half of the nineteenth century until it was reformulated in the period after Darwin.

(c) *Moral and Religious Experience.* A third source of religious knowledge, distinct from both revealed and natural theology, came into prominence late in the century. The romantic movement defended intuition, imagination, and the immediacy of experience. The Methodist revival, though traditional in its doctrines, encouraged experiential religion and personal reorientation. Kant found the basis for religion in the experience of moral obligation. In each of these cases there was a sphere for religion that did not compete with the sphere of science. These attempts to justify religious beliefs in terms of moral and religious experience were developed further in the nineteenth century and contributed to Protestant liberalism.

### 4. Human Nature

Most authors of the Enlightenment held an optimistic view of humanity, deriving primarily from their confidence in human reason. Not sin but ignorance is the basic human problem, they said, and better education and social planning are the answers. Even the French authors who extended a mechanistic metaphysics to include human beings believed in the inevitability of progress. The romantic movement was more ambivalent about human capacities, and it looked to intuition and imagination rather than reason for human fulfillment. It extolled the creativity and freedom of the individual and asserted the goodness of human nature uncorrupted by society. The religious revivals late in the century returned to the traditional idea of human sinfulness and the need for conversion. This diversity of appraisals carried over into the nineteenth century.

## CHAPTER 3

# Biology and Theology
# in the Nineteenth Century

During the nineteenth century physics expanded dramatically with theories of light, electricity, and thermodynamics. Chemistry in its modern form grew from its foundation in Dalton's atomic theory early in the century to Mendeleev's formulation of the periodic table and the rise of organic chemistry by its close. A flourishing practical technology based on these physical sciences was contributing to the Industrial Revolution, which changed the face of Western society. Our discussion must be limited to biology, for it was in this area that the scientific development occurred that undoubtedly had the most far-reaching impact on human thought, constituting one of the major revolutions in intellectual history.

Charles Darwin (1809–1882) occupies a place in biology not unlike that of Newton in physics. Each proposed a set of theoretical concepts that was able to encompass, within a single unified scheme, vast reaches of data from many types of phenomena—animate and inanimate, respectively. The scientific ideas of each greatly influenced other fields of thought. Each person's work served as the point of departure for the elaboration of a distinctive world view—summed up in the image of nature as a mechanism, in Newton's case, and as a dynamic process, in Darwin's. The argument from design, so common in the writings of Newton and his age, was one of the ideas most seriously called into question by the theory of evolution.

In the first section below, the contributions of Darwin and his forerunners at the scientific level are summarized. In section II, "Theological Issues in Evolution," the central problems behind the ensuing controversy are analyzed: the authority of the Bible, the challenge to purpose and design, the threat to the status of humanity, and attempts to derive ethical norms from evolution. Section III, "Diverging Currents in Theology," considers some of the varied theological responses, from traditionalist to modernist, that occurred in Protestant and Catholic circles, and some forms of evolutionary naturalism are described.

## I. DARWIN AND NATURAL SELECTION

The component elements of the theory of evolution had been separately proposed long before the publication of *On the Origin of Species* in 1859. It needed Darwin's genius and persistence to fit these ideas together into a unified theory and to collect an impressive array of evidence in its support. Let us look at his work as a scientist and the view of nature implied by his theory.

### 1. FORERUNNERS OF DARWIN

Charles Lyell's *Principles of Geology* (1830) marked a turning point in modern geology. Up to that time, the prevailing geological theory had been *catastrophism,* which postulated a sequence of great cataclysms (Noah's flood being the most recent), between which God had created new species. Such a series of acts of divine creation bore some resemblance to the Genesis account and yet could allow for the differing fossils discovered in successive rock strata. By 1801 Georges Cuvier had reconstructed from fossil bones some twenty-three species now extinct, including the giant mastodon, but he held that such creatures were produced by divine intervention amid great world upheavals unlike any present-day events. As early as 1795 James Hutton had defended the opposing uniformitarian view, which assumed the operation of natural causes such as vulcanism, sedimentation, and erosion through great spans of time. Lyell carried *uniformitarianism* much further and gave for a wide variety of geological phenomena the first detailed and systematic explanation assuming that regular laws "within the existing order of nature" had acted throughout the past. Lyell's portrayal of the long, slow working of natural processes was acknowledged by Darwin as a formative influence on his own thought.[1]

The new geology did not, however, alter the prevailing assumption of biologists concerning *the fixity of species.* In the previous century, Carl Linnaeus had worked out the first comprehensive system of botanical classification; he held that the distinction of species depends on the existence of separate lineages that do not change. The usefulness of his classificatory scheme helped to perpetuate the conviction that there are permanent differences among species. To be sure, Comte de Buffon had pointed out the natural variability of species and had suggested that the extinction of some types might be related to the struggle for survival. And in 1802 Jean Baptiste Lamarck (1744–1829) had defended unlimited organic change, maintaining that an animal's organs develop through habitual use and that these acquired modifications are inherited. For example, the short-necked ancestors of the giraffe in successive generations would have gradually developed longer necks by reaching for leaves. But Lamarck's view found few supporters during his lifetime. The advocates of the stability of species prevailed, less because of opposition to science on the part of the church than because of ingrained habits of thought on the part of biologists themselves.[2] As the history of science often demonstrates, scientists are part of a larger culture whose thought patterns influence the questions they ask, the concepts they use to interpret data, and the assumptions made in the formulation of theories.

Belief in *the stability of biological forms,* which for so long dominated Western thought, had several sources. It was in part a corollary of the conviction that each type of being was created by God in its present form, as depicted in Genesis. It was in some measure a legacy of the Aristotelian doctrine that all individual beings are embodiments of eternal forms or unchanging essences. Classically the goals of each organism and the "final causes" of its activity were taken as the primary explanation of its structures. Thus Darwin can be said to have dealt the death blow to Aristotelian biology, as Newton did to Aristotelian physics.

In the period before Darwin, some theologians saw in the new geology a threat to *biblical authority,* but most did not. Biblical literalism had long since been questioned. After Galileo's day, biblical references to the sun's motion were usually regarded as metaphorical; the six days of Genesis could also be viewed metaphorically or taken to refer to six epochs. Moreover, none of the basic biblical affirmations were challenged by geology. The status of humanity was not diminished by a longer time span. If each species was endowed with its present form at the time it was created, and if humankind was a special creation by God, human uniqueness was protected. As Charles Gillispie points out, geology did not even undermine the argument from design.[3]

*The argument from design,* in fact, still enjoyed great popularity despite the criticisms by Hume and Kant. Exponents of natural theology in the early nineteenth century were confident in their ability to discover the beneficent plan of God's wisdom within the biological order. Many volumes were written in this period tracing the providential adaptation of creatures to their goals. These works were aided by, and in turn contributed to, the accumulation of careful anatomical observations. William Paley's *Natural Theology* (1802) was a required text in Darwin's university education. As one example, the book describes the eye's complex structure coordinated to the one aim of vision. Paley argued that a person on a desert island, finding a watch whose parts are integrated in the accomplishment of a single purpose, infers the existence of a watchmaker; similarly, the coordinated structures in natural organisms lead us to infer the existence of an intelligent Designer.[4]

The *Bridgewater Treatises* popularized other biological discoveries in which was displayed "the benevolent contrivance of means to ends." Books entitled *Physico-Theology, Insect-Theology,* and *Water-Theology* extolled the workmanship and foresight of the Creator as revealed by new scientific findings. The gradations of complexity among living forms, which were coming to light in great profusion, were understood not as clues to historical and developmental relationships, but as steps in the ordained hierarchy of life, the immutable "chain of being," of which humankind was the highest step and final end. Natural theology was here cast in a form that was to prove particularly vulnerable to the concept of evolution.[5]

## 2. DARWIN'S SCIENTIFIC WORK

In 1832 the young Charles Darwin was naturalist on the HMS *Beagle* as it started a five-year voyage around the world. The second volume of Lyell's book on geology reached him while he was observing flora and fauna in South America. The critical experience of the trip was his study of *slight variations among species,* especially variations found among the islands in the remote Galapagos chain. On each island a species lived in isolation from neighboring islands with similar environmental conditions. Six years later, reading Thomas Malthus on the effects of human population pressure and competition, Darwin found the clue for a theory by which to interpret the data collected on the voyage. As he later recorded:

[B]eing well-prepared to appreciate the struggle for existence which everywhere goes on, from long-continued observation of the habits of animals and plants, it at once struck me that under these circumstances favorable variations would tend to be preserved and unfavorable ones to be destroyed. The result of this would be the formation of new species. Here, then, I had at last got a theory by which to work.[6]

His theory of natural selection combined several ideas: (a) *Random variations.* Darwin had ample evidence of the occurrence and inheritability of small variations among the individual members of a species. He could only conjecture about the causes of these differences, but he recognized that his theory did not in itself require an explanation for them. (b) *The struggle for survival.* In general, more young organisms are born than can survive to parenthood. Some variations confer a slight advantage in the intense competition for existence that occurs among members of a species and among different species in a given environment. (c) *The survival of the fittest.* The individuals having such an advantage will on average live longer, have more progeny, and hence multiply slightly more rapidly. Over a long period of time this would result in the *natural selection* of such variations and the corresponding reduction of other less favorable variations, so that the gradual transformation of the species would occur. Darwin held that natural selection is the main though not the exclusive factor that determines the direction of evolutionary change.

Darwin's work exhibits clearly the characteristic method of science described in chapter 1: the fruitful interplay of *observation* and *theory*. No amount of data constitutes a scientific theory unless it is unified by the creative invention of an imaginative hypothesis; but no theory is of use in science unless it can be tested against individual observations and can guide the further collection of data. Before he finally published *Origin* in 1859, Darwin had spent twenty-seven years amassing from many fields an amazing array of facts on the variation of species. He studied in detail the breeding of domesticated animals, such as dogs, in which the owner selects from among a given species the variations he wants to favor and thereby, after many generations of selection, produces new types never previously existing. In those cases, human choice was the agent of selection among the small variations whose cumulative effects added up to major modifications. Darwin studied problems as diverse as hybridization of plants, comparative structures of embryos, "vestigial" or rudimentary organs, and the geographical distribution of animal and plant forms, both living and extinct. The sheer range and magnitude of the data he brought into correlation with his theory is staggering.

In subsequent editions of *Origin* Darwin responded to the problems raised by his critics. In the conclusion of the last edition (1872) he wrote:

Species have been modified, during a long course of descent, . . . chiefly through the natural succession of successive, slight, favourable variations; aided in an important manner by the inherited effects of the use and disuse of parts; and in an unimportant manner, that is in relation to adaptive structures, whether past or present, by the direct action of external conditions, and by variations which seem to us in our ignorance to arise spontaneously. It appears that I formerly underrated the frequency and value of these latter forms of variation, as leading to permanent modifications of structure independently of natural selection.[7]

Here he assigned an "important" but still subordinate role to Lamarckian ideas ("the inherited effects of the use and disuse of the parts").

In *Origin* Darwin avoided mention of humanity, but a dozen years later he gave a thorough discussion of human origins in *The Descent of Man* (1871). He tried to show how all human characteristics might be accounted for in terms of the gradual modification of anthropoid ancestors by the process of natural selection. The close resemblance of humans and gorillas in anatomical structure had already been widely noted; Darwin indicated how upright posture, larger brain size, and other distinctive changes might have been produced. He insisted that human moral and mental faculties differ in degree rather than in kind from the capacities of animals, among which there are rudimentary forms of feeling and communication. Human existence, hitherto considered sacrosanct, was thus brought within the sphere of natural law and was analyzed in the same categories applied to other forms of life.

## 3. ALTERNATIVE THEORIES OF EVOLUTION

The *reception of Darwin's ideas among scientists* varied greatly both within and among nations. The evidence for a long evolutionary history of descent from common ancestors and simpler life forms was widely accepted, but many scientists rejected the claim that natural selection was the chief agent of change. In England, Thomas Huxley and later George Romanes were strong advocates of natural selection. Alfred Russel Wallace had discovered the principle of natural selection independently of Darwin but thought it could not explain human intelligence. But Lyell held that Darwin had overemphasized selection, and such distinguished scientists as Richard Owen, Adam Sedgwick, and Lord Kelvin rejected it. Herbert Spencer, who was a powerful voice in the popularization and defense of evolution, was a Lamarckian.

In America, the Harvard naturalist Asa Gray was a strong defender of selection, though he thought variations might be guided by providential design. But E. D. Cope was a leading exponent of neo-Lamarckianism and was influential as editor of *The American Naturalist*. Louis Agassiz at Harvard was a vocal anti-Darwinian; he adhered to a form of philosophical idealism that assumed a mind behind creation. A comparative study of scientific responses to Darwin concludes that "by the end of the century there were probably more neo-Lamarckians than Darwinians in American science."[8] In France, Darwin was at first not well received by biologists, but later he gained support from the anticlerical movement. As in other countries where church authorities criticized Darwin, some scientists defended him partly to assert as a newly emerging professional group their independence from clerical interference. In Germany, Ernst Haeckel combined a Lamarckian viewpoint with advocacy of a philosophy of materialism.[9]

Let us define *Darwinism* as the belief that natural selection of variations is the main (though not exclusive) source of evolutionary change. Why did many biologists at the end of the century defend alternatives to Darwinism?

First, *at the scientific level*, there were unsolved problems in Darwinism. Some physiological structures seemed to have no useful function, and the early stages of some evolutionary changes did not appear to be adaptive. The absence of any detailed theory concerning the generation and inheritance of variations was a continuing issue, and many scientists looked for alternative hypotheses. But Lamarckians had no success in forming a testable theory of inheritance that would explain how physiological changes during an organism's life could be passed on to its descendants. Some developmental biologists held that the growth of the embryo of an individual organism (ontogeny) recapitulates the history of the species (phylogeny). The growing organism was said to embody a kind of residual memory of the stages its ancestors had gone through. But this was a vague analogy and not a testable theory.

Second, many developmental biologists assumed that the growth of an organism is the unfolding of *an internally programmed plan*. This was often coupled with the idea that the evolution of differing species occurs along parallel paths because of forces originating within organisms themselves (orthogenesis). Looking for order in nature, biologists found linear trends, which they ascribed to the internal predisposition of the organism to change in a particular direction—even if the trend went too far and resulted in nonadaptive features (or extinction), which they believed selection could not explain. Biologists adopting these views had usually been influenced by philosophical idealism, which had been strong in England and even stronger in Germany. Idealism is the belief that basic organizational plans or archetypes underlie all structures in the material world. For some idealists, basic forms were said to be ideas in the mind of God, but not all idealists were theists.[10]

Third, the *philosophical implications* of Lamarckism seemed more acceptable than those of Darwinism. In place of a ruthless process of competitive struggle, or the external selection of organisms by the environment, Lamarckians held that internal forces and the creativity of organisms played a part in their evolutionary history (either by their mental activity or by positive physiological responses to the environment). For many Lamarkians, belief in the directional and progressive character of evolution could be maintained, in contrast to the unpredictability of variations and the opportunistic character of selection in Darwinian theory. A sense of purpose could be preserved even by those without specifically theistic beliefs. Internal tendencies might express patterns among forms or specific divine intentions. In either case, Lamarckism was a less radical break with earlier philosophical and religious assumptions than was Darwinism.

Fourth, the *social implications* of Lamarckism were more optimistic than those of Darwinism. If human behavioral choices can affect our heritable evolutionary future, the possibility of a rapid improvement of humanity offered a hopeful prospect for social change. (It was this feature that led Soviet authorities to give their blessing to Lysenko in his revival of Lamarckism in the 1940s.) Of course, Lamarckism offered little guidance concerning the kinds of biological change that should be sought or the cultural changes that might accompany them. Spencer was a vehement advocate of free-enterprise capitalism, while Haeckel supported socialism. The differences between biological and cultural evolution were not critically analyzed.

Attempts to verify Lamarckism in laboratory experiments early in the twentieth century turned out to be dubious or ambiguous, and Darwinian explanations of the data could often be offered. The distinction between genetic constitution (genotype) and physical appearance (phenotype) was only gradually accepted, and the one-way flow of information from genes to growing organisms was acknowledged. At the scientific level the Darwinian revolution was not really completed in the nineteenth century and had to await Mendelian genetics, which did provide a testable theory of the inheritance of variations. Evolution was eventually seen as a change in the relative frequency of genes in populations, but "population thinking" represented a major shift in conceptual frameworks, one that took place only slowly. The synthesis of population genetics and evolutionary theory did not occur until the 1930s. With the discovery of DNA in the 1950s and subsequent developments in molecular biology, evolutionary theory has been expanded and modified beyond Darwin's ideas (see chapter 9).

## 4. NATURE AS DYNAMIC PROCESS

Let us consider the impact of the theory of evolution on the prevailing view of nature. First, the *importance of change* had already been suggested by earlier theories such as uniformitarianism in geology and the discovery of extinct species in paleontology, but it took Darwin's work to suggest that all of nature is in a state of flux. It is difficult for us today to imagine the revolution in thought that occurred when the world was no longer seen as an essentially static structure of immutable forms but as characterized throughout by development and change. Stability had been only an illusion produced by our limited time scale. Over an immensely long span of time, nature itself has a history. With the "unfreezing" of the patterns of life, the world was transformed from a fixed hierarchical order into a dynamic process.

Second, nature became a complex of *interacting forces in organic interdependence*. The interaction of the individual with the environment assumed much greater significance. To be sure, the idea of struggle and the picture of "nature red in tooth and claw" seem in retrospect to have been carried to excess by Darwin's successors, perhaps in part because of the influence of the reigning social philosophy of competitive individualism. Today greater attention is given to the sources of coordination and organization within the body and the structures of internal stability and harmony, which were neglected by Darwin himself. Moreover, the cooperative aspects of nature, such as symbiosis between species or the social behavior of insects and animals, have been found to be as important for survival as are the competitive aspects. Nevertheless, the interactive character of "the web of life" and the importance of the environmental context have, since Darwin, been permanent features of our view of nature, and they prepared the way for modern ecology.

Third, evolution entailed the extension of *the rule of law* to new areas of nature. At first sight, the role of *chance* in Darwin's theory might seem to have constituted a restriction of the domain of lawfulness. Variations arise accidentally, but they are preserved lawfully according to the advantage they confer. Though both law and chance thus contribute to change, attention was directed primarily to the lawlike aspects. The ratio of individuals with differing characteristics was taken to be in principle a quantitative question, calculable by the mathematics of probability; here was a new kind of law that incorporated chance, namely a statistical law. Some of Darwin's defenders were explicit advocates of determinism. Huxley, the most vocal British champion of evolution, held that chance is but the operation of natural laws not yet known; he argued that from primeval conditions all subsequent events could in principle have been predicted. Only at the turn of the century was the role of chance welcomed as a release from the determinism of inexorable law; for Peirce, James, and Bergson, chance was an indication of spontaneity, novelty, and creativity, a source of the genuinely new and unpredictable in the history of nature.

Fourth, nature was now understood to include *human beings*. This was taken to imply that human culture could also be analyzed in categories derived from biology. Social scientists, eager to exploit the prestige of the new science, turned to biology for interpretive analogies, as in the previous century they had turned to physics. A society was said to be an organism, and social adaptation amid group struggle was the key to its survival. In more general terms, evolution stimulated social scientists' interest in the processes of change and development. Critical methods of historical research were already in use, thanks in part to the romantic movement with its concern for origins and growth. These trends combined to encourage a historical approach in which ideas, institutions, cultures, and religions were seen as evolving.

## II. THEOLOGICAL ISSUES IN EVOLUTION

Four topics were central in the theological debate that followed the publication of Darwin's *Origin*. We will consider in turn: (1) the challenge to scripture; (2) the challenge to design; (3) the challenge to the status of humanity; and (4) evolutionary ethics and social Darwinism.

### 1. METHODS IN THEOLOGY: THE CHALLENGE TO SCRIPTURE

Long before Darwin, *biblical literalism* had been cast in doubt by scientific theories—from Copernican astronomy to the new geology. Moreover, the scholarly analysis of biblical texts—the historical and literary research known as "higher criticism"—had already contested the inerrancy of scripture. It appears surprising, therefore, that some people rejected evolution in order to defend biblical authority. One reason was that other historic Christian beliefs—the purposefulness of the world, human dignity, and the drama of creation and the fall—seemed to be threatened. Many people knew only one way to defend these religious convictions, namely to assert biblical infallibility.

Moreover, some of the leading scientists had linked evolution with their own *atheistic viewpoints*, and conservative churchmen opposed both indiscriminately. Such a liaison between a scientific theory and a sweeping attack on religion had occurred previously among the French skeptics, but it was a less familiar phenomenon in England and America. Darwin himself was cautious in his criticism of religion, but some of his defenders—most notably Huxley—went on the offensive against Christianity, partly in order to defend the independence of science as a new profession from the influence of the established church, which had been so strong in universities and in cultural leadership in England. Conservative religious leaders reacted defensively. Both sides in these debates failed to distinguish between evolution as a scientific theory and evolutionary naturalism as an interpretive philosophy.

For the literalists there could be no compromise with evolution. Genesis describes the once-for-all creation of species in their present form. Philip Gosse proposed that God had put all those fossils in a plausibly misleading pattern in order to test our faith. From the ages of Adam's descendants, Archbishop Ussher had calculated that creation must have occurred in 4004 B.C.E. There was abundant opportunity for appeal to prejudice—or to satire, as when Bishop Wilberforce asked Huxley whether he traced his descent from an ape on his grandfather's side or his grandmother's.[11]

But there were many others whose view of scripture allowed *the acceptance of evolution*. The majority of Protestant authors distinguished between the religious ideas of Genesis and the ancient cosmology in which those ideas were expressed. They interpreted the biblical account as a symbolic and poetic rendition of affirmations about the dependence of the world on God—affirmations that are compatible with acceptance of evolution as God's way of creating. The modernists went further; for them the Bible was a purely human document, a record of evolving religious insights. The evolutionary view of nature molded the modernist understanding of God; the divine was now an immanent force at work within the process, an indwelling spirit manifest in the creative advance of life to ever higher levels. Most Catholic thinkers avoided the extremes of both literalism and modernism. Though Rome was at first reluctant to accept evolution, a position was gradually defined that acknowledged the development of the human body from animal ancestry but insisted on the special creation of each human soul. We will later examine some of these diverse responses in greater detail.

## 2. GOD AND NATURE: THE CHALLENGE TO DESIGN

Paley's version of the argument from design was particularly vulnerable, for it had started from the observed *adaptation of organic structures to useful functions*. Such adaptation could now be accounted for by the impersonal process of natural selection without invoking any preconceived plan. Adaptations are present today because they were useful in the past, not because their present usefulness was anticipated in the past. The species now living are here because they have survived while thousands of others lost out in the competitive struggle. Moreover, some of the facts that had always created difficulties for the advocates of design, such as useless rudimentary organs and traces of limbs, could now be readily explained.

In the twenty-three years between the return of the *Beagle* and the publication of *Origin* in 1859, Darwin moved from the traditional religious beliefs in which he had been brought up to a tentative and minimal deism. He rejected miracles, revelation, and special creation, and he objected on moral grounds to the idea of hell. He said that the suffering in nature, which he had seen so frequently, was inconsistent with the notion of a beneficent God. He argued that detailed providential design would have resulted in perfect adaptation, but he saw evidence only of differential adaptation, which was all that was required for natural selection to be effective.[12]

Even though he rejected particular providence in the design of specific features of organisms, he referred repeatedly in *Origin* and subsequent writings to a general providence in *the design of the laws* through which evolution occurs. In *Origin* he quoted a letter from Charles Kingsley holding that the creation of simple forms capable of self-development implies as noble a conception of God as a creation needing further creative acts. Darwin held that a world "so marvelously ordered," however imperfect in the details, could not be the result of blind chance. God as designer of laws must have provided the overarching pattern and progressive direction. In a letter to the Harvard naturalist Asa Gray he wrote: "I am inclined to look at everything as resulting from designed laws, with the details left to the working out of what we may call chance."[13] In other passages he spoke of natural laws as the "secondary means" by which God created.

Later in life, however, Darwin was more uncertain of even this very broad interpretation of design. In a letter three years before his death he described himself as *agnostic:* "In my most extreme fluctuations I have never been an Atheist in the sense of denying the existence of God. I think that generally (and more and more as I grow older), but not always, that an Agnostic would be the more correct description."[14] His agnosticism was partly the product of his recognition that his own theory assigned a lowly origin to the human mind. In his *Autobiography* (written in 1879) he recalled

the extreme difficulty, or rather the impossibility, of conceiving this immense and wonderful universe, including man with his capacity for looking far backwards and far into futurity, as the result of blind chance or necessity. When thus reflecting I feel compelled to look to a First Cause having an intelligent mind in some degree analogous to that of man: and I deserve to be called a Theist. . . . But then arises the doubt, can the mind of man, which has, as I fully believe, been developed from a mind as low as that possessed by the lowest animals, be trusted when it draws such grand conclusions?[15]

In a more personal vein, he laments the loss of his former enjoyment of natural scenery, poetry, and literature and says that he has become "a kind of machine for grinding general laws out of a large collection of facts." He says that he used to love music but "my soul is too dried up to appreciate it as in old days. . . . I am a withered leaf for every subject except Science. It sometimes makes me hate Science."[16]

Asa Gray, on the other hand, continued to defend *a broad concept of design.* He maintained that the overall history of nature can be understood in purposeful terms, despite the occurrence of waste and struggle. "Emergence is design by wholesale, the direction of the process by which mind and moral personality arose, which are not explainable by matter in random motion." Gray presented the idea of a Creator working through evolution to produce a gradually unfolding design; he also implied that God providentially supplies the variations in the right direction. Other scientists held that God does not intervene at all but has built design into the very structure of the processes through which higher forms of life and eventually humanity could come into being.[17]

## 3. HUMAN NATURE: THE CHALLENGE TO THE STATUS OF HUMANITY

In the Western tradition, *humanity was set apart* from all other creatures. Humans alone are rational beings; human reason was considered totally different in kind from whatever intelligence animals have. It was held that human beings alone possess an immortal soul, which defines their true nature and relationship to God. This uniqueness of status now appeared to be denied by the theory of evolution. Distinctions between human and animal characteristics were indeed minimized by Darwin and his followers.

Surviving primitive tribes, as Darwin presented them, almost closed the gap between humans and animals. Huxley claimed that there is less difference between humans and the highest apes than between higher and lower apes. Humanity, absorbed into nature, seemed to be the product of accidental variations and the struggle for survival, a child of blind chance and law.

*The human moral sense* had always been considered a distinctive capacity, but Darwin claimed that it too had originated by selection. In early human history a tribe whose members had strong social instincts, such as fidelity and self-sacrifice for the common good, would have had an advantage over other tribes. If morality conferred survival value, standards of conscience would have tended to rise. In the extinction of savage races in conflict with more civilized ones Darwin saw further evidence of built-in ethical advance. In a similar fashion he traced each human emotional and intellectual characteristic back to origins in the earlier stages of human and subhuman development.

Other biologists, however, gave greater emphasis to *distinctive human characteristics*. Wallace insisted that the presence of the human brain radically altered the character of evolution; with the development of intellect, bodily specialization and changes in other physical organs were less important. Wallace also recognized that the gap in intellect between humans and apes was far greater than Darwin had acknowledged; nor could primitive tribes fill the gap, for their inherent mental capacities are actually as great as those of civilized peoples. Wallace saw the distinctiveness of language as symbolic communication, where Darwin had seen little difference between animal signals and human speech. At each of these points, subsequent investigation has tended to vindicate Wallace's contributions.

In his later writing, Wallace went further and claimed that natural selection cannot account for *the higher human faculties*. He pointed out that the brain size in primitive tribes, which is comparable to that in highly civilized groups, actually provides a mental capacity far beyond the simple needs of their aboriginal patterns of life, for which a much smaller brain would have sufficed. "Natural selection could only have endowed savage man with a brain a little superior to that of an ape, whereas he actually possesses one very little inferior to that of a philosopher."[18] And how can one explain musical, artistic, or ethical capacities that contribute nothing to survival? Wallace felt that such "latent powers" possessed in advance of the need to employ them indicate that "some higher intelligence may have directed the process by which the human race was developed." More recent opinion has not supported Wallace's idea of "latent powers," but it has tended to agree with him in holding that human evolution involved distinctive processes that had been neglected by Darwin.

It is perhaps understandable that Darwin overemphasized *the continuity of humans and animals*. The earlier tradition had portrayed such an absolute discontinuity that to establish human rootedness in nature Darwin looked for all the similarities he could find, overlooking the differences. The tremendous scope of the theory of evolution had been amply demonstrated, and it was easy to assume that all human phenomena could be exhaustively interpreted in essentially biological terms. It is also understandable that some scientists and theologians, in reaction to such claims, insisted that natural selection could not account for human beings. Today we can see that in the long history of the world, the emergence of humanity marks a genuinely new chapter—one not disconnected from previous chapters and yet one that involves factors not previously present. Something radically different takes place when culture rather than the genes becomes the principal means by which the past is transmitted to the future and when conscious choice alters that future.

Moreover, both opponents and proponents of evolution often seem to have made the implicit assumption that *our ancestry determines our nature.* Much of the emotion accompanying the rejection of the idea that "we have apes in our family tree" can be traced to this notion that source fixes meaning. Human origins were too readily taken by both sides to be the chief clue to human significance; a subhuman past somehow came to imply a less than fully human present. This is a temporal form of reductionism, which finds the significance of an entity not in its smallest parts, as in eighteenth-century materialism, but in its most primitive beginning; it is a philosophical assumption equally destructive to human dignity and equally unwarranted as a conclusion from the data. These issues are pursued further in chapter 10.

## 4. EVOLUTIONARY ETHICS AND SOCIAL DARWINISM

Darwin and his defenders believed that the theory of evolution undermined the classical argument from design and the traditional status of humanity, but their attitudes toward the future were not pessimistic. Amid the optimism of the late nineteenth century the evolutionary pattern seemed to convey a hopeful message. In the climate of the Victorian era the idea of *evolutionary progress* became a secular substitute for providence. Not blind fate but a beneficent cosmic process governs our future and guarantees the final fruition of history and even human perfectibility. Faith in progress replaced the doctrines of creation and providence as assurance that the universe is not really purposeless. Neither uniform law nor accidental chance is any threat if it leads to inevitable advance and if nature is a coherent and intelligible system. The Harvard philosopher John Fiske wrote that human dignity is reinstated because "evolution shows us distinctly, for the first time, how the creation and perfection of man is the goal toward which nature's work has been tending from the first." The Enlightenment faith in social progress had been expanded to confidence in a progressive universe.

Was this *concept of progress* an inference from the scientific data? Darwin himself was evidently aware of the ambiguity at this point. He recognized that in speaking of "the fittest to survive," a biologist is not rendering a moral judgment but only referring to adaptations conferring a reproductive advantage. The "improvement" of a species means only an advantage in competition in a given environment; it might appear to be "retrogression" in a different environment or when viewed against the whole pattern of organic development. If Darwin and his supporters nevertheless often used "progress" in a way that implied a value judgment, they did so, says J. C. Greene,

because in their heart of hearts they believed that the processes of nature operated, however slowly and sporadically, to produce ever higher forms of existence. As naturalists they tried to define "improvement," "fitness," "highness," and the like in biological terms, but their use of the terms was subtly colored by the indomitable optimism of their age. The nineteenth century believed in progress, but it was not very careful to define what it meant by progress.[19]

The problem of *the relation of ethical norms to evolution* is significant if conscious human choice now influences future evolution. In some passages, Darwin implied that anything humans do is an expression of natural selection and that if progress is inherent in the process no human decision can hinder it. In other passages, he urged readers to choose deliberately the pattern that the rest of nature exemplifies. He warned that future progress would be hindered by sentimental policies that protect weaker individuals, such as the sick or maimed, who would be eliminated under more competitive conditions. "There should be open competition for all men; and the most able should not be prevented by laws or customs from succeeding best and rearing the largest number of offspring." But Darwin was not altogether consistent, Greene suggests, for there was "deep in his character a warm humanitarianism and a strong holdover of the Christian ethic in which he had been trained."[20] He recognized "a higher morality," which would encourage respect and love toward all persons, including the weak, but such a morality would lessen the competitive struggle and thus undermine what he had taken to be the source of progress.

The belief that *competition promotes progress* fitted in well, however, with the individualistic social philosophy common in this period. Biological and political ideas merged in what has been called *social Darwinism*.[21] Even before he read Darwin, Herbert Spencer (1820–1903) had tried to show that laissez-faire private enterprise was in keeping with the stern disciplines of nature that produce biological improvement. He found in the evolutionary struggle as Darwin described it a justification for his claim that economic competition unhampered by government regulation fosters human welfare. The survival of the fittest was to be the instrument for the evolution of society also; rugged individualism would bring beneficial results. Competition among groups and the conflict of races had been valuable historically, "a continuous overrunning of the less powerful or less adapted by the more powerful or more adapted, a driving of inferior varieties into undesirable habitats, and, occasionally, an extermination of inferior varieties." British colonialism could be justified on such grounds. Spencer's writings were popular in America, partly because they could be used to defend the competitive struggle of free-enterprise capitalism. But Spencer, like Darwin, faced difficulties in his attempt to derive ethical norms from evolution. Having made biological survival his criterion of progress, he could provide no satisfactory basis for rejecting an appeal to arms, such as that of Prussian militarism, which would try to prove a nation's fitness on the battlefield.

Huxley, taking issue with both Darwin and Spencer, held that valid *ethical norms cannot be derived from evolution*. Standards appropriate for human conduct simply cannot be obtained by examining natural selection or copying the law of the jungle: "Let us understand, once for all, that the ethical progress of society depends not on imitating the cosmic process, still less in running away from it, but in combating it."[22] Huxley asserted:

The practice of that which is ethically best—what we call goodness or virtue— involves a course of conduct which in all respects is opposed to that which leads to success in the cosmic struggle for existence. In place of ruthless self-assertion, it demands self-restraint; in place of thrusting aside or treading down all competitors, it requires that the individual shall not merely respect, but shall help his fellows; its influence is directed, not so much to the survival of the fittest, as to the fitting of as many as possible to survive. It repudiates the gladiatorial theory of existence.[23]

Having rejected both evolutionary ethics and revealed religion, Huxley fell back on a sort of moral intuitionism as the source of ethical norms, though the goals he actually defended seem principally to reflect his religious upbringing and surrounding culture. We will find this discussion of the relation between evolution and ethics continuing vigorously today, especially in the new field of sociobiology, which studies the evolutionary origins of human social behavior.

## III. DIVERGING CURRENTS IN THEOLOGY

We have seen that the theory of evolution raised questions about the authority of scripture, the argument from design, the status of humanity, and the basis of ethics. The reactions of particular religious groups varied from vehement repudiation of evolution to enthusiastic welcome. We will outline first some traditionalist interpretations among conservative Protestants and in Roman Catholic circles. The modernist movement, by contrast, modified traditional doctrines to accommodate evolution. Liberal theology was intermediate between traditionalism and modernism; it accepted historical research on biblical texts and justified its ideas by appeal to religious and moral experience. Finally, some examples of interpretations of evolution in naturalistic and atheistic philosophies are given.

The inadequacy of historical accounts portraying only the "conflict" or "warfare" of science and religion was pointed out in chapter 1. Similar observations could be made about the nineteenth century. To be sure, conflict was experienced by some adherents of traditionalism and naturalism, but many other options were also being explored. Moreover, debates about evolution were occurring *within* the scientific community, as noted earlier, which further undermines the metaphor of "warfare" between two unified armies arrayed against each other.[24]

## 1. TRADITIONALIST RESPONSES TO EVOLUTION

Among *conservative Protestants* there was considerable reluctance to acknowledge either evolution or historical scholarship on the Bible, though most such groups eventually made at least some adjustment to both. One of the leading American conservatives was Charles Hodge of Princeton Seminary. His view of scripture would not in itself have prevented assent to evolution. He held that the truths that biblical authors "intended to teach" (in which they were inspired to act as infallible spokesmen for God) must be distinguished from additional ideas that they "happened to believe" (in which they were often mistaken). This distinction allowed Hodge to defend Copernican astronomy, for the writers of the Bible "may have believed that the sun moves round the earth, but they do not so teach"; they shared with their country-men "the views then prevalent as to the mechanism of the universe."[25] Hodge rejected evolution, not in the name of scriptural inerrancy, but in the name of the biblical understanding of human nature and destiny. Although he granted that there may have been widespread changes in the past history of animals, he insisted that "man is not a developed ape." He also understood natural selection to imply the denial of God's design of the world and continuing relationship to it.

There were other Protestants, however, who combined an *orthodox theology* with an *acceptance of evolution*. We have already noted some examples among the scientists. Asa Gray, for instance, was a Congregationalist with moderate Calvinist views. Among theologians, James McCosh, president of Princeton University and an influential Presbyterian, suggested that God not only established the initial design of the whole evolutionary process but continues to work through what appear to us as "spontaneous" changes. The "chance" variations, for which Darwin could give no explanation, may have been caused by "the supernatural choices of an intervening Designer" who directs apparently accidental variations to effect particular purposes. Evolution was the way in which the creative activity of God was expressed in time. But McCosh speculated that in the case of human origins it might be necessary to assume some additional divine action if the unique spiritual features of humanity are to be accounted for. In contrast to the optimism of Spencer, he was keenly aware—as were both Calvin and Darwin—of the struggle and tragedy of existence. His views of God, Christ, and human nature were close to those of traditional Christianity, but he urged the churches to recognize the evidence for evolution.[26]

A recent study by James Moore points out that some Calvinists such as Gray and McCosh agreed with Darwin in emphasizing *natural selection*. They differed from the modernists, who were strong advocates of evolution but usually favored Lamarckian alternatives and defended Spencer's optimism concerning inevitable progress. Moore suggests that Calvinists who believed in God's sovereignty could more readily accept natural selection as a lawful process. Providence and predestination were said to act through the laws of nature; all events occur according to God's will. The Calvinist supporters of Darwin gave a subordinate role to Lamarckian drives and internal directive forces that might mediate between a transcendent God and mechanical processes.[27]

Conservative responses in the decades following Darwin should be distinguished from the later American movement known as *fundamentalism.* The name originated in a series of pamphlets entitled *The Fundamentals,* starting in 1909; they were a conscious and defensive reaction against the modernism that seemed to have sacrificed all distinctive Christian beliefs in accommodation to evolutionary philosophies. Fundamentalists, in contrast to conservatives, insisted on a literalistic version of biblical inerrancy and emphasized Christ's atoning death, his second coming, and the sudden conversion of the believer in accepting Christ as personal savior. Three of the authors of these pamphlets accepted evolution, but two of them attacked it because of its atheistic and materialistic influence.[28] In the next chapter we will look at the Scopes trial in Tennessee in 1925 and the more recent attempts to require that "creation science" be taught in public schools as an alternative to evolutionary biology.

For *Roman Catholicism* evolution was not in principle as disturbing as it was for Protestant conservatism. In Catholicism, revealed truth is to be sought not in scripture alone but in scripture and tradition as interpreted by the living church. Moreover, the doctrine that scripture is divinely inspired had not excluded considerable flexibility and diversity in biblical interpretation, and the concept of different literary genres and "levels of truth" had allowed allegorical rendition of problematic passages, even after the trial of Galileo. Nevertheless, the first reaction of Rome was a strenuous repudiation of evolution, and books by Edward Leroy, John Zahn, and others were withdrawn. The Vatican Council of 1870 and subsequent encyclicals attacked the new trends in biblical scholarship, and the incipient modernist movement among Catholic intellectuals was specifically condemned in 1907.

Gradually, however, the new *biblical scholarship* was more favorably received in Rome, both during the pontificate of Leo XIII (1878–1903) and more recently under Pius XII (1939–1958). Whereas the Pontifical Biblical Commission in 1902 instructed that the "substantial authenticity" of the first five books of the Bible must be taught, by 1948 it not only encouraged reexamination of scriptural problems but also stated that the laws in those books were the product of a long development in response to changing conditions. An encyclical in 1943 said that the Bible uses "the modes of expression of ancient peoples"; the modern interpreter must "go back wholly in spirit to those remote centuries and with the aid of history, archeology, ethnology, and other sciences accurately determine what modes of writing . . . the authors did in fact use."[29] Under this more permissive policy Catholic scholars have made substantial contributions to biblical research.

There has also been cautious but increasing *Catholic acceptance of evolution.* Since long before Darwin, some commentators had interpreted the six days of the creation story in metaphorical terms or had taken them to represent geological epochs. Others held that theological ideas, which were said to constitute the official teaching of Genesis, should be distinguished from the "unofficial," "incidental" and possibly erroneous scientific opinions of its authors; divine inspiration was claimed only for the religious meaning the writer intended to convey. Catholic thought has held, however, that the special creation of Adam's soul was an actual historical event. The doctrine of the fall and the inheritance of original sin were understood to require a single individual from whom all humankind descended. The official teaching has been that the human body evolved organically from earlier animal forms but that the human soul was introduced by God at one distinct point in time, though some recent Catholic authors have questioned this teaching.[30] In a statement in 1996, John Paul II stated that evolution is "more than a hypothesis" since it has been supported by many independent lines of research, and he reaffirmed that each human soul is "immediately created by God."[31]

## 2. THE MODERNIST MOVEMENT

Whereas traditionalists preserved classical doctrines with little modification, modernists departed from them extensively in accommodating to evolution. These were not external critics but reflective people within the church trying to reformulate in the light of modern knowledge what they held to be the essence of Christianity. If parts of the older tradition had to be abandoned, other parts could be liberated to support a more vital religious life. Modernists saw *scripture as a human record,* not of God's revelation, but of a people's search for God—a story of developing ideals and growing religious insights. Biblical history is the progressive evolution of religious awareness from primitive beginnings to its culmination in ethical monotheism. The Bible, for these authors, is not an inspired book, though it is an inspiring one. The first chapters of Genesis are to be read as a poetic expression of religious convictions concerning our dependence on God and the orderliness and the goodness of the world.

*The modernist view of God* was strongly influenced by the concept of evolution. After Darwin, it was urged, divine creative activity must be depicted not as external and once-for-all, but as within the process and continuous in time. God's principal attribute is immanence in nature rather than transcendence. For some of these authors God became an impersonal Cosmic Force, but for most the traditional concept of a personal God was retained, though God's relationship to the world was reconceived. Any dualism of natural and supernatural spheres was attacked, and the unity of God, humanity, and nature was extolled. One divine spirit permeates the universe. This monistic emphasis echoes themes familiar in romanticism and philosophical idealism, modified by the evolutionary view of nature.

The modernist view of *human nature* also differed markedly from the classical doctrine. Not sinfulness and opposition to God but moral progress and unity with God were characteristic themes. Human nature is itself essentially divine, for in humanity is the spark of God. God is immanent in us as well as in nature, and human ideals are the supreme product of God's spirit at work. Religion is rooted in human experience, and theological interpretations are secondary. Human effort, not some special divine action, will bring in the Kingdom. Jesus was not the divine savior but the great teacher of high ideals. Human salvation comes through increased knowledge and noble goals, not through supernatural aid or any basic reorientation of the self. Here, then, was a view of human nature that was in harmony with the optimistic faith so common in the late nineteenth century. The modernists were influenced more by the confidence in inevitable progress expressed by Spencer in his popularization of Darwin than by careful reading of Darwin himself, who was more cautious in his expectations.[32]

Henry Ward Beecher, American preacher and editor, was one of the first *exponents of modernism* to gain a wide hearing, and Spencer was his hero. Spencer was an agnostic, but his law of cosmic evolution could be given a theistic interpretation. Beecher said that geological research has deciphered "the long-hidden record of God's revelation in the material world." The upward march of matter and mind shows us God's way of bringing about progress. "Of one thing I am certain, that whatever may have been the origin, it does not change either the destiny or the moral grandeur of man as he stands in the full light of civilization today."[33] Waste and struggle are preconditions of progress; imperfections are a necessary part of an overall design.

A systematic volume in the same vein is Lyman Abbott's *Theology of an Evolutionist*. The Bible, as he saw it, represents the dawning of religious insight in authors who were children of their times and apprehended truth only slowly and imperfectly. Abbott disagreed with the traditional notion of sin, holding that, since Darwin, an "immoral" act should be understood as simply a lapse into animality. The greatest modification of earlier tradition was his exposition of God's relation to nature. Classical theology, he wrote, pictures God apart from the universe, ruling over it like an emperor and intervening at various times—in creation, in revelation to a chosen people, and in miracles. But in evolution we can see that God works from within by continuous growth. All life is divine, for there is only one cosmic force, an "Infinite and Eternal Energy from which all things proceed."[34]

Abbott seems to make God's action *an immanent force within nature*. As the human spirit dwells in the body, pervading and controlling it, so the Holy Spirit dwells within the universe and shapes it from within. The scientist can describe historical growth but does not deal with its ultimate cause. Does this amount to pantheism? No, said Abbott, because while God's immanence is stressed, transcendence is not omitted. As the human spirit transcends its body, so God is not limited to nature, though God works through its vital processes as a "resident force."

Modernist views found a variety of other formulations. In Henry Drummond, the Scottish layman and scientist, modernism combined with deep personal

piety and devotion to Christ. No special intervention was needed for the creation of mankind, he said, since spirit was always present throughout the
process. Continuing human spiritual evolution was the theme of his book,
*The Ascent of Man*. In John Fiske, who popularized evolution in America,
modernism received more philosophical expression—closer to Spencer's
position, but in a broadly theistic context; Fiske called it *Cosmic Philosophy*, a
ringing affirmation of a progressing universe. The modernist movement in
Roman Catholicism did not depart as radically from orthodox theology. Such
persons as Edward Leroy in France and George Tyrell in England defended
evolution and critical scholarship on the Bible, and they dwelt on the idea of
divine immanence in nature; however, the movement was not widespread
because it encountered official condemnation.

## 3. THE RISE OF LIBERAL THEOLOGY

In the initial controversy over evolution, many theologians adopted traditionalist or modernist views. But by the end of the century a *theological liberalism*,
intermediate between traditionalism and modernism, had gained adherents.
It agreed with modernism in welcoming scientific knowledge of evolution,
but it held that modernism had departed too far from classical views of God
and human nature.

Lux Mundi, a liberal Anglican manifesto published in 1889, included
three essays strongly defending Darwinian evolution. Aubrey Moore emphasized divine immanence: "Either God is everywhere present in nature or He
is present nowhere." People who think God interferes occasionally, said
Moore, must believe that God is usually absent. He defended traducianism,
the thesis that the soul is not a special divine creation but is inherited with
the body in each new human life (as Augustine and several other classical
authors had asserted). Moore said that in evolutionary history, too, no special
creation of the soul was required, since spiritual dimensions have been present all along, and the separation of body and soul is problematic. In another
essay Frederick Temple, who later became Archbishop of Canterbury, wrote,
"God did not make things . . . but made things make themselves." Temple
held that God does not interfere, though he suggested that possibly the soul
is an exception, the product of a direct creative act.[35] Not all Anglicans
agreed with such liberal ideas; the Anglican church included a wide range of
views on both ritual and theology: "high church" Anglo-Catholics, "low
church" evangelicals, and exponents of both liberal and traditional theolo-
gies.

Three significant developments in Germany earlier in the century contributed to the formation of liberal theology. First, *the growth of biblical scholarship* engendered new attitudes toward revelation. In Germany and then in
England and America, in universities and then in seminaries, objective methods of historical and literary research, similar to those applied to other
ancient documents, were being used to analyze the biblical text. In this light,
the first five books of the Hebrew Scriptures (Old Testament), traditionally

ascribed to Moses, showed indications of multiple authorship. Careful examination of duplicated stories and of differences in style, vocabulary, and
thought gave evidence that these books in their present form are a compila-
tion of several accounts of varying antiquity. Some sections, such as the
details of priestly ritual in the Temple, were shown to have been codified in
the exilic period, eight hundred years after Moses. Similar analysis of the
Gospel of John and its differences from the other Gospels in both form and
content led scholars to view it as a theological essay about Christ's life written
more than half a century after the crucifixion.[36]

In *the new view of scripture,* attention was directed to the individual viewpoints and interests of the ancient authors, their purposes in writing, and the
historical and cultural contexts in which they lived. They emerged as very
human figures who shared the assumptions of their day and incorporated
considerable legendary material in their writings. Archaeological evidence
about other early cultures revealed not only many similarities but also characteristic differences, when compared to Hebrew thought. Greater familiarity
with living religions around the world encouraged a "comparative" approach
to their scriptures. The liberals granted the human character of the biblical
record but read it as a treasury of profound religious insights and teachings.
Some of them, instead of rejecting the idea of revelation, reformulated it:
God is revealed, not in the dictation of an infallible book, but in the lives of
the people of Israel, the prophets, and Christ. Scripture, then, was not itself
revelation but rather a human witness to the human experience of revelation.

A second influence was *the appeal to religious experience* as the basis for justifying religious beliefs. This new point of departure was proposed early in the
century by Friedrich Schleiermacher, often called "the father of liberal theology." He held that the basis of religion is not revealed doctrine, as in traditionalism, or cognitive reason, as in natural theology, or even ethical will, as
in Kant's system, but a distinctive religious awareness. Religion is a matter of
living experience, not of formal beliefs; it is not reducible to practical ethics
or speculative philosophy but must be understood in its own terms. Along
with the authors of the romantic movement, Schleiermacher held that God
is known by immediate apprehension rather than indirect inference. The
element common to all religions he described as "a feeling of absolute
dependence," a sense of finitude before the infinite, an awareness of unity
with the whole.[37]

Schleiermacher held that theology should be derived from the *reflective
interpretation of religious experience.* We should start not from "sin" as a theological concept but from our consciousness of guilt and sense of alienation from
God; not from a doctrine of salvation but from the experienced transformation of human life. If we are to dispense with all doctrines not derivable from
our present experience, the traditional belief in miracles and the divinity of
Christ will have to go. The Bible is valuable as the record of the religious
experience of Israel, Christ, and the early church. Schleiermacher himself
found the life of Christ an important source of religious understanding and

believed that the Christian tradition has mediated the awareness of God that is the essence of religion, yet there was little place for historical revelation in the view of theological method that he espoused.

A third theme typical of liberal theology was *the primacy of the ethical* in religion. The legacy of Kant, evident in much of nineteenth-century Protestantism, especially in Germany, was perpetuated in Albrecht Ritschl's "theology of moral values." Ritschl agreed with Kant that religion is a matter of "practical reason," inseparable from conscience and judgments of value. Ritschl, like Schleiermacher, looked to the experiential basis of religion, but for him this was to be found in ethical decision. The central Christian experience is the transformation of an individual's life in response to the personality of Christ. But personal religion, he wrote, goes beyond knowledge of the past, for it involves the experience of forgiveness and reconciliation in the present. Moreover, it has a social dimension, the task of creating on earth the Kingdom of God in which love and service are expressed in human relationships.[38]

Ritschl pictured a sharp contrast between *the human sphere* and *the sphere of nature.* This perpetuated the Kantian distinction between the objective realm, which science investigates, and the realm of history and culture, in which freedom and value are found. It was also a reaction to the image of evolution as a process of conflict and struggle. Ritschl and other liberals defended human dignity not by denying evolution but by affirming the victory of spirit over nature. They defended human personality from mechanical or materialistic interpretations and asserted its value in contrast to the impersonal natural order.[39] Here was another version of the compartmentalization of science and religion that I call the *Independence* model.

In the light of these three trends we can understand *liberal viewpoints concerning evolution.* The liberal conception of the Bible allowed unreserved assent to the scientific evidence for evolution. In contrast to both traditionalists and modernists, the basis of theology was sought in religious and moral experience rather than in either revealed or natural theology. Liberals, in general, were able to take a more open and relaxed attitude toward evolution than did either traditionalists or modernists, since less was at stake theologically. For the knowledge of God, as they saw it, comes primarily from religious and ethical consciousness, not from the Bible or the evolutionary process. This new methodological approach was to be extensively used in the twentieth century.

## 4. NATURALISTIC PHILOSOPHIES OF EVOLUTION

The groups considered so far—traditionalists, modernists, and liberals—all defended some form of theism. But other thinkers used evolutionary ideas to support agnosticism, atheism, or materialism. Herbert Spencer combined *evolution* and *agnosticism* into a comprehensive system. He said that God was "the Unknowable," an incomprehensible Absolute about which we can say nothing beyond the mere affirmation of its existence. As an interpretive principle, evolution was for Spencer far more than a biological theory; it was the unifying key to all areas of knowledge.[40] He asserted a single principle applicable to the growth of stars, organisms, and societies: the law of the integration of matter "from a relatively indefinite, incoherent homogeneity to a relatively definite coherent heterogeneity." The organs of animals—and the "organs" of societies—become more differentiated and specialized but also more integrated and coordinated. Spencer's attempts to derive ethics from evolution, his justification of competitive individualism in social Darwinism, and his faith in automatic progress have already been mentioned.

An interesting *reply to Spencer* was given by the Harvard philosopher Chauncey Wright. He pointed out that Spencer's general principle, "the movement of matter toward a relatively concentrated, multiform and determinate arrangement," was so vague that it could never be verified experimentally. He discussed Spencer's failure to distinguish science from philosophy and his lack of awareness of the methodological limitations of science. Belief in automatic progress, he suggested, cannot be derived from the biological evidence but arises from "the human need for some kind of moral faith." Wright insisted that no wider consequences can be drawn from evolution for cosmology, metaphysics, or religion. Evolution is a biological concept and not a universal explanatory principle.[41]

A materialistic form of naturalism, sometimes called *evolutionary monism,* was defended by the German zoologist Ernst Haeckel. Natural selection and mechanical causality provide the solution to *The Riddle of the Universe,* as his best-known book was entitled; matter and force are the only ultimate reality. His confidence in the all-embracing explanatory power of the new biology is expressed in many passages:

The cell consists of matter called protoplasm, composed chiefly of carbon with an admixture of hydrogen, nitrogen, and sulphur. These component parts properly united produce the soul and body of the animated world, and suitably nursed became man. With this single argument the mystery of the universe is explained, the Deity annulled, and a new era of infinite knowledge ushered in.[42]

*Materialism* asserts that no really new kinds of entity can ever arise, for "every new phenomenon is the equivalent of a rearrangement of existing entities." Materialism as a metaphysical doctrine about the nature of reality was sometimes combined with the additional postulate of determinism. But determinism could be abandoned (because of the element of chance in random variations) without abandoning materialism, if the outcome of evolution was interpreted as the product of purely material factors.[43] Life was said to be the chance product of matter and force, a "mere eddy in the primeval slime." Here was a more pessimistic outlook, contrasting with the confidence in nature that prevailed in the Victorian era. For this minority, nature was not a benevolent parent or hospitable home but an alien realm ruled by blind law and chance, operating on purposeless matter and indifferent to human interests. In such a world a person might lapse into despair or Stoic resignation or might fight back in a Promethean defiance of the sort Bertrand Russell described in the next century:

Man is the product of causes which had no prevision of the end they were achieving; his origin, his growth, his hopes and fears, his loves and his beliefs, are but the outcome of accidental collocations of atoms. . . . Blind to good and evil, reckless of destruction, omnipotent matter rolls on its relentless way. . . . It is for Man, proudly defiant of the irresistible forces that tolerate for a moment his knowledge and his condemnation to sustain alone, a weary but unyielding Atlas, the world that his own ideals have fashioned despite the trampling march of unconscious power.[44]

We may conclude by mentioning briefly the role of evolution in Friedrich Nietzsche's thought. He maintained that if evolution is taken seriously as a norm, our traditional values will have to be turned completely upside down. In the fierce struggle for survival the useful qualities are not the Christian virtues but self-assertion and the will to power. If good is that which survives, strength is the ultimate virtue. "What is good? All that heightens in man the feeling of power, the desire for power, power itself. What is bad? All that comes from weakness." Humility, love, and pity are a morality fit for slaves. A hero's morality consists in courage, vitality, and ruthless egoism, if need be, in the struggle for supremacy. Heroic individuals must emancipate themselves from every moral scruple; they are above every law and through their autonomous wills must realize their own unique and creative individuality. Nietzsche looked forward to the coming Superman, discontinuous with the past, who would be master of the future. He proposed a program of eugenics in which "inferior" strains will be eliminated so that there can come into being the race of heroes who will embody the Will to Power. Here evolution was used to justify ethical norms diametrically opposed to those of the Christian tradition.[45]

## IV. SUMMARY

By the close of the nineteenth century virtually all scientists and most theologians accepted a long history of biological descent from simpler life forms. But the causes of these historical changes were still debated, and the broader interpretations of the evolutionary process varied widely. The *spectrum of theological views* included (from "right" to "left"): biblical literalism, traditionalism, liberalism, modernism, and naturalism. The majority of both theologians and church members were adherents of traditionalism or liberalism (each of which includes a range of views). Let us try to summarize the influence of evolutionary thought on four problems that concern us in this volume.

### 1. Methods in Science

Darwin's scientific work was a brilliant exemplification of empirical observation and theoretical hypothesis in fruitful interplay. But could the methods of science also deal with the wider implications of evolution for beliefs about God, historical progress, and human ethics? The very fact that support from science was claimed for such divergent world views should give us pause. A biological concept was variously converted into an argument for theism, cosmic evolutionism, or atheistic naturalism—each of which, I would submit, must be defended as a philosophical interpretation rather than as a scientific conclusion. Greene writes, "Every great scientific synthesis stimulates efforts to view the whole of reality in its terms, and Darwin's theory of natural selection was no exception. But the views of reality that originate in this way are not in themselves scientific, nor are they subject to scientific verification."[46]

Similarly, considerable ambiguity attended the attempts to derive ethical norms and to justify doctrines of historical progress on the basis of evolutionary evidence alone. Today the relation of evolution to ethics continues to be of great interest, but there is greater awareness of the difference between a scientific theory and its extension into a universal explanatory scheme or an all-embracing worldview. The nineteenth century has taught us the dangers present when theologians too readily interfere in scientific questions or when scientists too readily adjudicate theological questions.

## 2. Methods in Theology

(a) *Revelation.* Among reactions to both evolution and biblical scholarship, the extreme positions were at first most prominent: insistence on biblical literalism by some conservatives and rejection of all forms of revelation by some modernists. In the emerging liberal view, the Bible was valued as the fallible human record of religious experience—and also as witness to revelation, understood not as the dictation of a guaranteed text but as God's presence and activity in the life of Israel, the prophets, and Christ.

(b) *Natural Theology.* The argument from design in the form Paley had popularized was permanently undermined by the theory of evolution. In a reformulated version, purposeful design was seen in the laws and structures through which life and mind emerged and in the directionality of the total process.

(c) *Religious and Moral Experience.* The distinctive new element in nineteenth-century theological method was the appeal to human experience as the basis for theology. Schleiermacher looked to religious awareness and consciousness of God, while Ritschl and his successors emphasized moral experience. We will see that all three of these basic approaches appear in new forms in the twentieth century.

## 3. God and Nature

The "God of the gaps" was as unnecessary in biology after Darwin as it had been in physics after Laplace. Adaptive changes could be accounted for by random variation and natural selection without invoking divine intervention. We have Darwin to thank for finally making it clear that God is neither a secondary cause operating on the same level as natural forces nor a means for filling gaps in the scientific account. J. H. Randall writes:

The nineteenth century definitely abandoned the belief in God as a scientific principle. The watchmaker Creator of the Enlightenment has vanished with the advance of
rational scientific accounts of how the world came into being; and if religious men
still believe in a Creator behind those long processes, they do it on religious rather
than scientific grounds. To them, evolution is merely a more exact description of the
way in which God's creative acts took place.[47]

Liberal theologians and many traditionalists preserved the classical understanding of God but now said that God works continuously through the whole
evolutionary process by means of secondary causes. Modernists, on the other
hand, emphasized God's immanence, often to the virtual exclusion of transcendence, and in some cases God was viewed as a force within a cosmic
process that was itself divine. Two key issues, discussion of which has continued into the contemporary period, are the significance of the directionality of
evolution and the meaning of assertions that God works in or through natural
causes.

### 4. Human Nature

To support his case for the continuity between human and nonhuman life,
Darwin stressed the similarities between humans and animals. As Loren Eiseley
puts it, "Man, theologically, had for so long been accorded a special and
supernatural place in creation that the evolutionists, in striving to carry their
point that he was intimately related to the rest of life, sought to emphasize
those characteristics which particularly revealed our humble origins."[48] We
will see that biologists today fully accept the evolutionary continuity between
human and prehuman forms, while giving attention to the emergence of distinctive human capacities for intelligence, symbolic communication, and the
formation of culture. Among theologians today a more sober estimate of
human limitations prevails than among many of their nineteenth-century
counterparts. The implications of evolution for our understanding of human
nature remain a subject of lively debate today.

# Part Two

## RELIGION AND
## THE METHODS OF SCIENCE

## CHAPTER 4

# Ways of Relating
# Science and Religion

The first major challenge to religion in an age of science is the success of the methods of science. Science seems to provide the only reliable path to knowledge. Many people view science as objective, universal, rational, and based on solid observational evidence. Religion, by contrast, seems to be subjective, parochial, emotional, and based on traditions or authorities that disagree with each other. The methods of inquiry used in science, apart from any particular scientific discoveries or theories, are the topic of part 2. Chapter 4 gives a broad description of contemporary views of the relationship between the methods of science and those of religion. Chapters 5 and 6 explore similarities and differences between the two fields and develop my own conclusions concerning the status of religious beliefs in an age of science.

In order to give a systematic overview of the main options today, I have grouped them in this chapter under four headings: *Conflict, Independence, Dialogue,* and *Integration.* Particular authors may not fall neatly under any one heading; a person may agree with adherents of a given position on some issues but not on others. However, a broad sketch of alternatives will help us in making comparisons in later chapters. After surveying these four broad patterns, I will suggest reasons for supporting *Dialogue* and, with some qualifications, certain versions of *Integration.*[1]

## I. CONFLICT

A historical example of conflict was the Galileo case, which was partly the product of conditions that no longer prevail: the authority of Aristotle and the defensive reactions and political rivalries in a Roman hierarchy that felt threatened by the Protestant Reformation. The Darwin case involved conflicting views, though the responses of both theologians and scientists were far more diverse than the popular image of "the warfare between science and religion." The image of warfare is common today, partly because conflict between extreme views lends itself to dramatic media coverage, while more subtle and complex intermediate positions tend to be neglected.

*Scientific materialism* is at the opposite end of the theological spectrum from *biblical literalism*. But they share several characteristics that lead me to discuss them together. Both believe that there are serious conflicts between contemporary science and classical religious beliefs. Both seek knowledge with a sure foundation—that of logic and sense data, in the one case, that of infallible scripture, in the other. They both claim that science and theology make rival literal statements about the same domain, the history of nature, so that one must choose between them. I will suggest that scientific materialism and biblical literalism both represent a misuse of science. The scientific materialist starts from science but ends by making broad philosophical claims. The biblical literalist moves from theology to make claims about scientific matters. In both schools of thought, the differences between the two disciplines are not adequately respected.

## 1. SCIENTIFIC MATERIALISM

Scientific materialists are the intellectual heirs of the materialism of the French Enlightenment, the empiricism of David Hume, and the evolutionary naturalism of the nineteenth century. Most of them subscribe to two beliefs: (1) the scientific method is the only reliable path to knowledge; (2) matter (or matter and energy) is the fundamental reality in the universe.

The first is an *epistemological* assertion about the characteristics of inquiry and knowledge. The second is a *metaphysical* assertion about the characteristics of reality. The two assertions are linked by the assumption that only the entities and causes with which science deals are real; only science can progressively disclose the nature of the real.

In addition, many forms of materialism express *reductionism*. Epistemological reductionism claims that the laws and theories of all the sciences are in principle reducible to the laws of physics and chemistry. Metaphysical reductionism claims that the component parts of any system constitute its most fundamental reality. The materialist believes that all phenomena will eventually be explained in terms of the actions of material components, which are the only effective causes in the world. Analysis of the parts of any system has, of course, been immensely useful in science, but I will suggest that the study of higher organizational levels in larger wholes is also valuable.

Let us consider the assertion that the scientific method is the only reliable form of understanding. Science starts from reproducible public data. Theories are formulated and their implications are tested against experimental observations. Additional criteria of coherence, comprehensiveness, and fruitfulness influence choice among theories. Religious beliefs are not acceptable, in this view, because religion lacks such public data, such experimental testing, and such criteria of evaluation. Science alone is objective, open-minded, universal, cumulative, and progressive. Religious traditions, by contrast, are said to be subjective, closed-minded, parochial, uncritical, and resistant to change. We will see that historians and philosophers of science have questioned this idealized portrayal of science, but many scientists accept it and think it undermines the credibility of religious beliefs.

Among philosophers, *logical positivism* from the 1920s to the 1940s asserted that scientific discourse provides the norm for all meaningful language. It was said that the only meaningful statements (apart from abstract logical relations) are empirical propositions verifiable by sense data. Statements in ethics, metaphysics, and religion were said to be neither true nor false, but meaningless pseudo-statements, expressions of emotion or preference devoid of cognitive significance. Whole areas of human language and experience were thus eliminated from serious discussion because they were not subject to the verification that science was said to provide. But critics replied that sense data do not provide an indubitable starting point in science, for they are already conceptually organized and theory-laden. The interaction of observation and theory is more complex than the positivists had assumed. Moreover, the positivists had dismissed metaphysical questions but had often assumed a materialist metaphysics. The linguistic analysts argued that science cannot be the norm for all meaningful discourse because language has many differing uses and functions.

Most of the late Carl Sagan's TV series and book, *Cosmos,* is devoted to a fascinating presentation of the discoveries of modern astronomy, but at intervals he interjects his own philosophical commentary, for example, "The Cosmos is all that is or ever was or ever will be."[2] He says that the universe is eternal or else its source is simply unknowable. Sagan attacks Christian ideas of God at a number of points, arguing that mystical and authoritarian claims threaten the ultimacy of the scientific method, which he says is "universally applicable." Nature (which he capitalizes) replaces God as the object of reverence. He expresses great awe at the beauty, vastness, and interrelatedness of the cosmos. Sitting at the instrument panel from which he shows us the wonders of the universe, he is a new kind of high priest, not only revealing the mysteries to us but telling us how we should live. We can indeed admire Sagan's great ethical sensitivity and his deep concern for world peace and environmental preservation. But perhaps we should question his unlimited confidence in the scientific method, on which he says we should rely to bring in the age of peace and justice.

The success of molecular biology in accounting for many of the basic mechanisms of genetics and biological activity has often been taken as a vindication of the reductionist approach. Thus Francis Crick, codiscoverer of the structure of DNA, wrote, "The ultimate aim of the modern movement in biology is in fact to explain *all* biology in terms of physics and chemistry."[3] I will argue in chapter 9 that there is in the biological world a hierarchy of levels of organization. This would lead us to accept the importance of DNA and the role of molecular structures in all living phenomena, but it would also allow us to recognize the distinctiveness of higher-level activities and their influence on molecular components.

Jacques Monod's *Chance and Necessity* gives a lucid account of molecular biology, interspersed with a defense of scientific materialism. He claims that biology has proved that there is no purpose in nature. "Man knows at last that he is alone in the universe's unfeeling immensity, out of which he emerged only by chance."[4] "Chance alone is the source of all novelty, all creation, in the biosphere." Monod espouses a thoroughgoing reductionism: "Anything can be reduced to simple, obvious mechanical interactions. The cell is a machine. The animal is a machine. Man is a machine."[5] Consciousness is an illusion that will eventually be explained biochemically. Monod asserts that human behavior is genetically determined; he says little about the role of language, thought, or culture in human life. Value judgments are completely subjective and arbitrary. But Monod urges us to make the free axiomatic choice that knowledge itself will be our supreme value. He advocates "an ethics of knowledge," but he does not show what this might entail apart from the support of science.

I submit that Monod's reductionism is inadequate as an account of purposive behavior and consciousness in animals and human beings. There are alternative interpretations in which the interaction of chance and law is seen to be more complex than Monod's portrayal and not incompatible with some forms of theism. The biochemist and theologian Arthur Peacocke gives chance a positive role in the exploration of potentialities inherent in the created order, which would be consistent with the idea of divine purpose (though not with the idea of a precise predetermined plan).[6] Monod says that science proves that there is no purpose in the cosmos. Surely it would be more accurate to say that science does not deal with divine purpose; it is not a fruitful concept in the development of scientific theories.

As another example, consider the explicit defense of scientific materialism by the sociobiologist Edward O. Wilson. His writings trace the genetic and evolutionary origins of social behavior in insects, animals, and humans. He asks how self-sacrificial behavior could arise and persist among social insects, such as ants, if their reproductive ability is thereby sacrificed. Wilson shows that such "altruistic" behavior enhances the survival of close relatives with similar genes (in an ant colony, for example); selective pressures would encourage such self-sacrifice. He believes that all human behavior can be reduced to and explained by its biological origins and present genetic structure. "It may not be too much to say that sociology and the other social sciences, as well as the humanities, are the last branches of biology to be included in the Modern Synthesis."[7] The mind will be explained as "an epiphenomenon of the neural machinery of the brain."

Wilson holds that religious practices were a useful survival mechanism in humanity's earlier history because they contributed to group cohesion. But he says that the power of religion will be gone forever when religion is explained as a product of evolution; it will be replaced by a philosophy of "scientific materialism."[8] (If he were consistent, would not Wilson have to say that the power of science will also be undermined when it is explained as a product of evolution? Do evolutionary origins really have anything to do with the legitimacy of either field?) He maintains that morality is the result of deep impulses encoded in the genes and that "the only demonstrable function of morality is to keep the genes intact."

Wilson's writing has received criticism from several quarters. For example, anthropologists have replied that most systems of human kinship are not organized in accord with coefficients of genetic similarity and that Wilson does not even consider cultural explanations for human behavior.[9] In the present context, I would prefer to say that he has described an important area of biology suggesting some of the constraints within which human behavior occurs, but he has overgeneralized and extended it as an all-encompassing explanation, leaving no room for the causal efficacy of other facets of human life and experience. We will consider his views further in chapter 10.

The philosopher Daniel Dennett has defended a strong neo-Darwinist position, drawing from probability theory, cognitive science, and computer simulations. Evolution, he asserts, is the product of *a mindless, purposeless process*. He vehemently rejects all forms of design, including the idea that Darwin set forth in some of his writings that the whole evolutionary process and its laws are the product of design. Dennett claims that he is not a "greedy reductionist" (a person who tries to explain higher-level phenomena by direct appeal to the laws of the lowest level) but rather a "good reductionist" who acknowledges many levels and "new principles of explanation appearing at each level" and seeks to relate the various levels to one another. But he holds that the idea of a unified consciousness is an illusion, and he seeks physical explanations of all mental events. "According to materialists, we can (in principle!) account for every mental phenomenon using the same physical laws and raw materials that suffice to explain radioactivity, photosynthesis, reproduction, nutrition and growth."[10] Other scientific materialists whom I will discuss in later chapters include the biologist Richard Dawkins and the physicist Steven Weinberg.

I suggest that these authors have failed to distinguish between *scientific* and *philosophical* questions. Scientists in their popular writings tend to invoke the authority of science for ideas that are not part of science itself. Articles in journals of physics, chemistry, and biology do not discuss materialism, theism, or other world views that provide philosophical interpretations of science. These are alternative belief systems, each claiming to encompass all reality.

In their epistemology, these authors assume that the scientific method is the only reliable source of knowledge—an assumption sometimes referred to by its critics as "*scientism*." If science is the only acceptable form of understanding, explanation in terms of astronomical origins, evolutionary history, biochemical mechanisms, and other scientific theories will exclude all other forms of explanation. I would reply that science relies on impersonal concepts and leaves out of its inquiry the most distinctive features of personal life. Moreover, the concept of God is not meant to be a hypothesis formulated to explain phenomena in the world in competition with scientific hypotheses. Belief in God is primarily a commitment to a way of life in response to distinctive kinds of religious experience in communities formed by historic traditions; it is not a substitute for scientific research. Religious beliefs offer a wider framework of meaning in which particular events can be contextualized. As a rough approximation, we may say that religion asks *why* and science asks *how,* though we will see that this distinction needs considerable qualification.

In their metaphysics, these authors have extended scientific concepts beyond their scientific use to support comprehensive *materialistic philosophies.* We have seen that Galileo and Descartes distinguished primary qualities (such as mass and motion, which were said to be independent of the observer) from secondary qualities (such as color and sound, which were held to be purely subjective). The identification of the real with measurable properties that can be correlated by exact mathematical relationships started in the physical sciences but influenced scientists in other fields and continues today. But I would argue that these properties of matter have been abstracted from the real world by ignoring the particularity of events and the nonquantifiable aspects of human experience. We do not have to conclude that matter alone is real or that mind, purpose, and human love are only by-products of matter in motion.[11] Theism, in short, is not inherently in conflict with science, but it does conflict with a metaphysics of materialism.

## 2. BIBLICAL LITERALISM

In previous chapters we have seen a variety of *views of scripture* and its relation to science. Medieval writers acknowledged diverse literary forms and levels of truth in scripture, and they gave figurative or allegorical interpretations to many passages. Luther, Calvin, and the Anglicans continued this tradition, though some later Lutherans and Calvinists were more literalistic. We saw that a strict interpretation of scripture by Catholic leaders was one factor in the condemnation of Galileo, though other factors such as the legacy of Aristotle and the authority of the church were equally significant. In Darwin's day, evolution was taken as a challenge to design in nature and as a challenge to the status of humanity, but it was also taken by some groups as a challenge to scripture. Some defended biblical inerrancy and totally rejected evolution. Yet most traditionalist theologians reluctantly accepted the idea of evolution—though sometimes only after making an exception for humanity, arguing that the soul is inaccessible to scientific investigation. Liberal theologians had already accepted the historical analysis of biblical texts ("higher criticism"), which traced the influence of historical contexts and cultural assumptions on biblical writings. They saw evolution as consistent with their optimistic view of historical progress, and they spoke of evolution as God's way of creating.

In the twentieth century, the Roman Catholic church and most of the mainline Protestant denominations have held that scripture is the human witness to the primary revelation, which occurred in the lives of the prophets and the life and person of Christ. Many traditionalists and evangelicals insist on the centrality of Christ without insisting on the infallibility of a literal interpretation of the Bible. But smaller fundamentalist groups and a large portion of some historic denominations in the United States (a majority in the case of the Southern Baptists) have maintained that scripture is inerrant throughout. The 1970s and 1980s saw a growth of fundamentalist membership and political power. For many members of "the New Right" and "the Moral Majority," the Bible provides not only certainty in a time of rapid change, but a basis for the defense of traditional values in a time of moral disintegration (sexual permissiveness, drug use, increasing crime rates, and so forth).

In the Scopes trial in 1925, it had been argued that the teaching of evolution in the schools should be forbidden because it is contrary to scripture. More recently, a new argument called "scientific creationism" or "creation science" asserted that there is scientific evidence for the creation of the world within the last few thousand years. The law that was passed by the Arkansas legislature in 1981 required that "creationist theory" be given equal time with evolutionary theory in high school biology texts and classes. The law specified that creationism should be presented purely as scientific theory, with no reference to God or the Bible.

In 1982 the U.S. District Court overturned the Arkansas law, primarily because it favored a particular religious view, violating the constitutional separation of church and state. Although the bill itself made no explicit reference to the Bible, it used many phrases and ideas taken from Genesis. The writings of the leaders of the creationist movement had made clear their religious purposes.[12] Many of the witnesses against the bill were theologians or church leaders who objected to its theological assumptions.[13]

The court also ruled that "creation science" is not legitimate science. It concluded that the scientific community, not the legislature or the courts, should decide the status of scientific theories. It was shown that proponents of "creation science" had not even submitted papers to scientific journals, much less had them published. At the trial, scientific witnesses showed that a long evolutionary history is central in almost all fields of science, including astronomy, geology, paleontology, and biochemistry, as well as most branches of biology. They also replied to the purported scientific evidence cited by creationists. Claims of geological evidence for a universal flood and for the absence of fossils of transitional forms between species were shown to be dubious.[14] In 1987, the U.S. Supreme Court struck down a Louisiana creationism law; it said the law would have restricted academic freedom and supported a particular religious viewpoint.

"Creation science" is a threat to both religious and scientific freedom. It is understandable that the search for certainty in a time of moral confusion and rapid cultural change has encouraged the growth of biblical literalism. But when absolutist positions lead to intolerance and attempts to impose particular religious views on others in a pluralistic society, we must object in the name of religious freedom. Some of the same forces of rapid cultural change have contributed to the revival of Islamic fundamentalism and the enforcement of orthodoxy in Iran and elsewhere.

We can also see the danger to science when proponents of ideological positions try to use the power of the state to reshape science, whether it be in Nazi Germany, Stalinist Russia, Khomeini's Iran, or creationists in the United States. To be sure, scientists are inescapably influenced by cultural assumptions and metaphysical presuppositions—as well as by economic forces, which in large measure determine the direction of scientific development. The scientific community is never completely autonomous or isolated from its social context, yet it must be protected from political pressures that would dictate scientific conclusions. Science teachers must be free to draw from this larger scientific community in their teaching.

Critics of evolutionary theory such as Phillip Johnson have raised valid objections when scientific materialists have promoted atheistic philosophies as if they were part of science.[15] But both sides err in assuming that evolutionary theory is inherently atheistic, and they thereby perpetuate the false dilemma of having to choose between science and religion. The whole controversy reflects the shortcomings of fragmented and specialized higher education. The training of scientists seldom includes any exposure to the history and philosophy of science or any reflection on the relation of science to society, to ethics, or to religious thought. On the other hand, the clergy has little familiarity with science and is hesitant to discuss controversial subjects in the pulpit. The remainder of this chapter explores alternatives to these two extremes of scientific materialism and biblical literalism.

## II. INDEPENDENCE

One way to avoid conflicts between science and religion is to view the two enterprises as totally independent and autonomous. Each has its own distinctive domain and its characteristic methods that can be justified on its own terms. Proponents of this view say there are two jurisdictions and each party must keep off the other's turf. Each must tend to its own business and not meddle in the affairs of the other. Each mode of inquiry is selective and has its limitations. This separation into watertight compartments is motivated, not simply by the desire to avoid unnecessary conflicts, but also by the desire to be faithful to the distinctive character of each area of life and thought. Some authors assert that science and religion have differing perspectives on a common domain rather than differing domains of inquiry. We will consider first some claims that their methods of inquiry differ radically and then the claim that the languages of science and religion serve very different functions in human life.

### 1. CONTRASTING METHODS

Many *evangelicals* and *conservative Christians* have continued the heritage of the traditionalists of the nineteenth century. They give scripture a central role without insisting on biblical literalism or defending "creation science."

They emphasize Christ's atoning death and the sudden conversion of the believer in accepting Christ as personal savior. They look to the transforming power of the gospel, which is neither threatened nor supported by modern science. For many evangelicals who are not literalists, science and religion are essentially independent spheres of human life, though some have defended natural theology with arguments for design starting from the Big Bang in astronomy or by pointing to the problems faced by scientific theories in accounting for the origin of life or consciousness.[16]

Two theological movements have made a more explicit separation of science and religion. They do so by contrasting the methods of the two fields, continuing the legacy of Kant. Protestant *neo-orthodoxy* sought to recover the Reformation emphasis on the centrality of Christ and the primacy of revelation, while fully accepting the results of modern biblical scholarship and scientific research. According to Karl Barth and his followers, God can be known only as revealed in Christ and acknowledged in faith. God is the transcendent, the wholly other, unknowable except as self-disclosed. Natural theology is suspect because it relies on human reason. Religious faith depends entirely on divine initiative, not on human discovery of the kind occurring in science. The sphere of God's action is history, not nature. Scientists are free to carry out their work without interference from theology, and vice versa, since their methods and their subject matter are totally dissimilar. Science is based on human observation and reason, while theology is based on divine revelation.[17]

In this view, the Bible must be taken seriously but not literally. Scripture is not itself revelation; it is a fallible human record witnessing to revelatory events. The locus of divine activity was not the dictation of a text, but the lives of persons and communities: Israel, the prophets, the person of Christ, and those in the early church who responded to him. The biblical writings reflect diverse interpretations of these events; we must acknowledge the human limitations of their authors and the cultural influences on their thought. Their opinions concerning scientific questions reflect the prescientific speculations of ancient times. We should read the opening chapters of Genesis as a symbolic portrayal of the basic relation of humanity and the world to God, a message about human creatureliness and the goodness of the natural order. These religious meanings can be separated from the ancient cosmology in which they were expressed.

Another movement advocating a sharp separation of the spheres of science and religion is *existentialism.* Here the contrast is between the realm of personal selfhood and the realm of impersonal objects. The former is known only through subjective involvement; the latter is known in the objective detachment typical of the scientist. Common to all existentialists—whether atheistic or theistic—is the conviction that we can know authentic human existence only by being personally involved as unique individuals making free decisions. The meaning of life is found only in commitment and action, never in the spectatorial, rationalistic attitude of the scientist searching for abstract general concepts and universal laws.

Religious existentialists say that God is encountered in the immediacy and personal participation of an I-Thou relationship, not in the detached analysis and manipulative control characterizing the I-It relationships of science. The theologian Rudolf Bultmann acknowledges that the Bible often uses objective language in speaking of God's acts, but he proposes that we can retain the original experiential meaning of such passages by translating them into the language of human self-understanding, the language of hopes and fears, choices and decisions, and new possibilities for our lives. Theological formulations must be statements about the transformation of human life by a new understanding of personal existence. Such affirmations have no connection with scientific theories about external events in the impersonal order of a law-abiding world.[18]

Langdon Gilkey, in his earlier writing and in his testimony at the Arkansas trial, expresses many of these themes. He makes the following distinctions: (1) Science seeks to explain objective, public, repeatable data. Religion asks about the existence of order and beauty in the world and the experiences of our inner life (such as guilt, anxiety, and meaninglessness, on the one hand, and forgiveness, trust, and wholeness, on the other). (2) Science asks objective how questions. Religion asks personal why questions about meaning and purpose and about our ultimate origin and destiny. (3) The basis of authority in science is logical coherence and experimental adequacy. The final authority in religion is God and revelation, understood through persons to whom enlightenment and insight were given, and validated in our own experience. (4) Science makes quantitative predictions that can be tested experimentally. Religion must use symbolic and analogical language because God is transcendent.[19]

In the context of the trial, it was an effective strategy to insist that science and religion ask quite different questions and use quite different methods. It provided methodological grounds for criticizing the attempts of biblical literalists to derive scientific conclusions from scripture. More specifically, Gilkey argued that the doctrine of creation is not a literal statement about the history of nature but a symbolic assertion that the world is good and orderly and dependent on God in every moment of time—a religious assertion essentially independent of both prescientific biblical cosmology and modern scientific cosmology.

In some of his other writings, Gilkey has developed themes that we will consider under the heading of Dialogue. He says there is a "dimension of ultimacy" in the scientist's passion to know, commitment to the search for truth, and faith in the rationality and uniformity of nature. For the scientist, these constitute what Tillich called an "ultimate concern." But Gilkey states there are dangers when science is extended to a total naturalistic philosophy or when science and technology are ascribed a redemptive and saving power, as occurs in the liberal myth of progress through science. Both science and religion can be demonic when they are used in the service of particular ideologies and when the ambiguity of human nature is ignored.[20]

Thomas Torrance has developed further some of the distinctions in neo-orthodoxy. Theology is unique, he says, because its subject matter is God.

Theology is "a dogmatic or positive and independent science operating in accordance with the inner law of its own being, developing its distinctive modes of inquiry and its essential forms of thought under the determination of its given subject-matter."[21] God infinitely transcends all creaturely reality and "can be known only as he has revealed himself," especially in the person of Christ. We can only respond in fidelity to what has been given to us, allowing our thinking to be determined by the given.

## 2. DIFFERING LANGUAGES

An even more effective way of separating science and religion is to interpret them as languages that are unrelated because their functions are totally different. The logical positivists had taken scientific statements as the norm for all discourse and had dismissed as meaningless any statement not subject to empirical verification. The later *linguistic analysts*, in response, insisted that differing types of language serve differing functions not reducible to each other. Each "language game" (as Wittgenstein and his successors called it) is distinguished by the way it is used in a social context. Science and religion do totally different jobs, and neither should be judged by the standards of the other. *Scientific language* is used primarily for prediction and control. A theory is a useful tool for summarizing data, correlating regularities in observable phenomena, and producing technological applications. Science asks carefully delimited questions about natural phenomena. We must not expect it to do jobs for which it was not intended, such as providing an overall world view, a philosophy of life, or a set of ethical norms. Scientists are no wiser than anyone else when they step out of their laboratories and speculate beyond strictly scientific work.[22]

The distinctive function of *religious language*, according to the linguistic analysts, is to recommend a way of life, to elicit a set of attitudes, and to encourage allegiance to particular moral principles. Much of religious language is connected with ritual and practice in the worshiping community. It may also express and lead to personal religious experience. One of the great strengths of the linguistic movement is that it does not concentrate on religious beliefs as abstract systems of thought but looks at the way religious language is actually used in the lives of individuals and communities. Linguistic analysts draw on empirical studies of religion by sociologists, anthropologists, and psychologists, as well as the literature produced within religious traditions.

Some scholars have studied diverse cultures and concluded that religious traditions are *ways of life* that are primarily practical and normative. Stories, rituals, and religious practices bind individuals in communities of shared memories, assumptions, and strategies for living. Other scholars claim that religion's primary aim is the transformation of the person. Religious literature speaks extensively of experiences of liberation from guilt through forgiveness, trust overcoming anxiety, or the transition from brokenness to wholeness. Eastern traditions talk about liberation from bondage to suffering and self-centeredness in the experiences of peace, unity, and enlightenment.[23] These are obviously activities and experiences having little to do with science.

George Lindbeck compares the linguistic view with two other views of religious doctrines:

1. In the *propositional* view, doctrines are truth claims about objective realities. "Christianity, as traditionally interpreted, claims to be true, universally valid, and supernaturally revealed."[24] If doctrines are true or false, and rival doctrines are mutually exclusive, there can be only one true faith. The propositional view is a form of realism, for it believes that we can make statements about reality as it exists in itself.

2. In the *expressive* view, doctrines are symbols of inner experiences. Liberal theology has held that the experience of the holy is found in all religions. Since there can be diverse symbolizations of the same core experience, adherents of different traditions can learn from each other. This view tends to stress the private and individual side of religion, with less emphasis on communal aspects. If doctrines are interpretations of religious experience, they are not likely to conflict with scientific theories about nature.

3. In the *linguistic* view, which Lindbeck himself advocates, doctrines are rules of discourse correlated with individual and communal forms of life. Religions are guides to living; they are "ways of life which are learned by practicing them." Lindbeck argues that individual experience cannot be our starting point because it is already shaped by prevailing conceptual and linguistic frameworks. His approach allows us to accept the particularity of each religious tradition without making exclusive claims for it. This is a nonrealist or instrumentalist position. It does not assume a universal truth or an underlying universal experience; it sees each cultural system as self-contained. By minimizing the role of beliefs and truth claims, the linguistic view avoids conflicts between science and theology that can occur in the propositional view, yet it escapes the individualism and subjectivity of the expressive view.

The three movements we have been considering—neo-orthodoxy, existentialism, and linguistic analysis—all understand religion and science to be independent and autonomous forms of life and thought. Each discipline is selective and has its limitations. Every discipline abstracts from the totality of experience those features in which it is interested. The astronomer Arthur Eddington once told a delightful parable about a man studying deep-sea life using a net on a three-inch mesh. After bringing up repeated samples, the man concluded that there are no deep-sea fish less than three inches in length. Our methods of fishing, Eddington suggests, determine what we can catch. If science is selective, it cannot claim that its picture of reality is complete.[25]

I believe that the *Independence* thesis is a good starting point or first approximation. It preserves the distinctive character of each enterprise, and it is a useful strategy for responding to both types of conflict mentioned earlier. Religion does indeed have its characteristic methods, questions, attitudes, functions, and experiences, which are distinct from those of science. But there are serious difficulties in each of these proposals.

As I see it, *neo-orthodoxy* rightly stresses the centrality of Christ and the prominence of scripture in the Christian tradition. It is more modest in its

claims than biblical literalism, since it acknowledges the role of human interpretation in scripture and doctrine. But in most versions it, too, holds that
revelation and salvation occur only through Christ, which seems to me problematic in a pluralistic world. Most neo-orthodox authors emphasize divine
transcendence and give short shrift to immanence. The gulf between God
and the world is decisively bridged only in the incarnation. While Barth and
his followers do indeed elaborate a doctrine of creation, their main concern
is with the doctrine of redemption. Nature tends to be treated as the unredeemed setting for human redemption, though it may participate in the
eschatological fulfillment at the end of time.

*Existentialism* rightly puts personal commitment at the center of religious
faith, but it ends by privatizing and interiorizing religion to the neglect of its
communal aspects. If God acts exclusively in the realm of selfhood, not in
the realm of nature, the natural order is devoid of religious significance,
except as the impersonal stage for the drama of personal existence. This
anthropocentric framework, concentrating on humanity alone, offers little
protection against the modern exploitation of nature as a collection of
impersonal objects. If religion deals with God and the self, and science deals
with nature, who can say anything about the relationship between God and
nature or between the self and nature? To be sure, religion is concerned with
the meaning of personal life, but this cannot be divorced from belief in a
meaningful cosmos. I will also suggest that existentialism exaggerates the
contrast between an impersonal, objective stance in science and the personal
involvement essential to religion. Personal judgment does enter the work of
the scientist, and rational reflection is an important part of religious inquiry.

Finally, *linguistic analysis* has helped us to see the diversity of functions of
religious language. Religion is indeed a way of life and not simply a set of
ideas and beliefs. But the religious practice of a community, including worship and ethics, presupposes distinctive beliefs. Against instrumentalism,
which sees both scientific theories and religious beliefs as human constructs
useful for specific human purposes, I advocate a critical realism holding that
both communities make cognitive claims about realities beyond the human
world. We cannot remain content with a plurality of unrelated languages if
they are languages about the same world. If we seek a coherent interpretation of all experience, we cannot avoid the search for a unified world view.

If science and religion were totally independent, the possibility of conflict
would be avoided, but the possibility of constructive dialogue and mutual
enrichment would also be ruled out. We do not experience life as neatly
divided into separate compartments; we experience it in wholeness and
interconnectedness before we develop particular disciplines to study different aspects of it. There are also biblical grounds for the conviction that God
is Lord of our total lives and of nature, rather than of a separate "religious"
sphere. The articulation of a theology of nature that will encourage a strong
environmental concern is also a critical task today. I will argue that none of
the options considered above is adequate to that task.

## III. DIALOGUE

*Dialogue* is a diverse group of views that go beyond the *Independence* model but portray relationships between science and religion that are not as close or as direct as those in the *Integration* model. *Dialogue* starts from general characteristics of science or of nature rather than from particular scientific theories such as those invoked by proponents of *Integration*. We will look successively at (1) Presuppositions and Limit Questions, (2) Methodological Parallels, and (3) Nature-centered Spirituality.

### 1. PRESUPPOSITIONS AND LIMIT QUESTIONS

Limit questions are ontological questions raised by the scientific enterprise as a whole but not answered by the methods of science. (They can also be called "boundary questions," but the term may be misinterpreted as referring only to spatial or temporal boundaries or the "boundary conditions" that are required in making predictions from scientific laws.)

In chapter 1 we noted that historians have asked why modern science arose in the Christian West among all world cultures. We explored the claim that the doctrine of creation helped to set the stage for scientific activity. Both Greek and biblical thought asserted that the world is orderly and intelligible. But the Greeks held that this order is necessary and that therefore one can deduce its structure from first principles. Only biblical thought held that the world's order is contingent rather than necessary. If God created both form and matter, the world did not have to be as it is, and one has to observe it to discover the details of its order. Moreover, while nature is real and good, it is not itself divine, as many ancient cultures held. Humans are therefore permitted to experiment on nature.[26] The "desacralization" of nature encouraged scientific study, though it also—along with other economic and cultural forces—contributed to subsequent environmental destruction and the exploitation of nature.

I believe the case for the historical contribution of Christianity to the rise of science is convincing. Some theologians have claimed that theism remains an implicit presupposition or logical requirement of science today, even when scientists do not acknowledge it.[27] But I would argue that once science was well established, its own success was sufficient justification for many scientists, without the need for religious legitimation. Theistic beliefs are clearly not explicit presuppositions of science, since many atheistic or agnostic scientists do first-rate work without them. One can simply accept the contingency and intelligibility of nature as givens and devote one's efforts to investigating the detailed structure of its order. Yet if one does raise these wider questions, one is perhaps more open to religious answers. For many scientists, exposure to the order of the universe, as well as its beauty and complexity, is at least an occasion of wonder and reverence.

We have seen that Torrance maintains the characteristic neo-orthodox distinction between human discovery and divine revelation. But he also says that science raises fundamental questions that it cannot answer. Science shows us an order that is both rational and contingent (that is, its laws and initial conditions were not necessary). It is the combination of contingency and intelligibility that prompts us to search for new and unexpected forms of rational order. The theologian holds that God is the creative ground and reason for the contingent but rational order of the universe. "Correlation with that rationality in God goes far to account for the mysterious and baffling nature of the intelligibility inherent in the universe, and explains the profound sense of religious awe it calls forth from us and which, as Einstein insisted, is the mainspring of science."[28]

The theologian Wolfhart Pannenberg has explored methodological issues in some detail. He accepts Karl Popper's contention that the scientist proposes testable hypotheses and then attempts to refute them experimentally. Pannenberg claims that the theologian can also use universal rational criteria in critically examining religious beliefs. However, the parallels eventually break down, he says, because theology is the study of reality as a whole; reality is an unfinished process whose future we can only anticipate, since it does not yet exist. Moreover, theology is interested in unique and unpredictable historical events. Here the theologian tries to answer another kind of limit question with which the scientific method cannot deal, a limit not of initial conditions or ontological foundations but of openness toward the future.[29]

Three Roman Catholic authors, Ernan McMullin, Karl Rahner, and David Tracy, seem to me to be advocates of *Dialogue*, though with varying emphases. McMullin starts with a sharp distinction between religious and scientific statements that resembles the *Independence* position. God as primary cause acts through the secondary causes studied by science, but these are on radically different levels within different orders of explanation. On its own level, the scientific account is complete and without gaps. McMullin is critical of all attempts to derive arguments for God from phenomena unexplained by science; he is dubious about arguments from design or from the directionality of evolution. God sustains the whole natural sequence and "is responsible equally and uniformly for all events." The theologian has no stake in particular scientific theories, including astrophysical theories about the early cosmos.[30]

McMullin maintains that the doctrine of creation is not an explanation of cosmological beginnings, but an assertion of the world's absolute dependence on God in every moment. The intent of Genesis was not to specify that there was a first moment in time. Moreover, the Big Bang theory does not prove that there was a beginning in time, since the current expansion could be one phase of an oscillating or cyclic universe. He concludes, "What one cannot say is, first, that the Christian doctrine of creation 'supports' the Big Bang model, or, second, that the Big Bang model 'supports' the Christian doctrine of creation."[31] But he says that for God to choose the initial conditions and laws of the universe would not involve any gaps or violations of the sequence of natural causes. McMullin denies that there is any strong logical connection between scientific and religious assertions, but he does endorse the search for a looser kind of compatibility. The aim should be "consonance but not direct implication," which implies that in the end the two sets of assertions are not, after all, totally independent.

For Karl Rahner, the methods and the content of science and theology are independent, but there are important points of contact and correlations to be explored. God is known primarily through scripture and tradition, but he is dimly and implicitly known by all persons as the infinite horizon within which every finite object is apprehended. Kant had asked about the conditions that make knowledge possible, and Rahner asks the same question in a neo-Thomist framework. We know by abstracting form from matter; in the mind's pure desire to know there is a drive beyond every limited object toward the Absolute. Authentic human experience of love and honesty are experiences of grace.[32]

Rahner does also take up particular scientific theories. He holds that the classical doctrines of human nature and of Christology fit well with an evolutionary viewpoint. The human being is a unity of matter and spirit, which are distinct but can only be understood in relation to each other. Science studies matter and provides only part of the whole picture, for we know ourselves to be free, self-conscious agents. Evolution—from matter to life, mind, and spirit—is God's creative action through natural causes, which reach their goal in humanity and the incarnation. Matter develops out of its inner being in the direction of spirit, empowered to achieve an active self-transcendence in higher levels of being. The incarnation is at the same time the climax of the world's development and the climax of God's self-expression. Rahner insists that creation and incarnation are parts of a single process of God's self-communication. Christ as true humanity is a moment in biological evolution that has been oriented toward its fulfillment in him.[33]

David Tracy sees a religious dimension in science. He holds that religious questions arise at the horizons or limit-situations of human experience. In everyday life, these limits are encountered in experiences of anxiety and confrontation with death, as well as in joy and basic trust. He describes two kinds of limit-situations in science: ethical issues in the uses of science, and presuppositions or conditions for the possibility of scientific inquiry. Tracy maintains that the intelligibility of the world requires an ultimate rational ground. For the Christian, the sources for understanding that ground are the classic religious texts and the structures of human experience. All our theological formulations, however, are limited and historically conditioned. Tracy is open to the reformulation of traditional doctrines in contemporary philosophical categories; he is sympathetic to many aspects of process philosophy and recent work in language and hermeneutics.[34]

How much room is there for the reformulation of classical theological doctrines in the light of science? If the points of contact between science and theology refer only to basic presuppositions and limit questions, reformulation will seldom be called for. But if there are some points of contact between particular doctrines and particular scientific theories (such as the doctrine of creation in relation to evolution or astronomy), and if it is acknowledged that all doctrines are historically conditioned, there is in principle the possibility of significant doctrinal development and reformulation, as suggested by advocates of *Integration*.

## 2. METHODOLOGICAL PARALLELS

The positivists had portrayed science as *objective*, meaning that its theories are validated by clear-cut criteria and are tested by agreement with indisputable, theory-free data. Both the criteria and the data of science were held to be independent of the individual subject and unaffected by cultural influences. By contrast, religion seemed *subjective*. We have seen that existentialists made much of the contrast between objective detachment in science and personal involvement in religion.

Since the 1950s, these sharp contrasts have been increasingly called into question. Science, it appeared, is not as objective, nor religion as subjective, as had been claimed. There may be differences of emphasis between the fields, but the distinctions are not as absolute as had been asserted. Scientific data are theory-laden, not theory-free. Theoretical assumptions enter the selection, reporting, and interpretation of what are taken to be data. Moreover, theories do not arise from logical analysis of data but from acts of creative imagination in which analogies and models often play a role. Conceptual models help us to imagine what is not directly observable.

Many of these same characteristics are present in religion. If the data of religion include religious experience, rituals, and scriptural texts, such data are even more heavily laden with conceptual interpretations. In religious language, too, metaphors and models are prominent, as discussed in my writing and in that of Sallie McFague, Janet Soskice, and Mary Gerhart and Allan Russell.[35] Clearly, religious beliefs are not amenable to strict empirical testing, but they can be approached with some of the same spirit of inquiry found in science. The scientific criteria of coherence, comprehensiveness, and fruitfulness have their parallels in religious thought.

Thomas Kuhn's influential book, *The Structure of Scientific Revolutions*, maintained that both theories and data in science are dependent on the prevailing paradigms of the scientific community. He defined a paradigm as a cluster of conceptual, metaphysical, and methodological presuppositions embodied in a tradition of scientific work. With a new paradigm, the old data are reinterpreted and seen in new ways, and new kinds of data are sought. In the choice between paradigms, there are no rules for applying scientific criteria. Their evaluation is an act of judgment by the scientific community. An established paradigm is resistant to falsification, since discrepancies between theory and data can be set aside as anomalies or reconciled by introducing *ad hoc* hypotheses.[36]

Religious traditions can also be looked on as communities that share a common paradigm. The interpretation of the data (such as religious experience and historical events) is even more paradigm-dependent than in the case of science. There is a greater use of *ad hoc* assumptions to reconcile apparent anomalies, so religious paradigms are even more resistant to falsification. We will compare the role of paradigms in science and religion in the next chapter.

The status of the observer in science has also been reconsidered. The earlier accounts had identified objectivity with the separability of the observer from the object of observation. But in quantum physics the influence of the process of observation on the system observed is crucial. In relativity, the most basic measurements, such as the mass, velocity, and length of an object depend on the frame of reference of the observer. Stephen Toulmin traces the change from the assumption of a detached spectator to the recognition of the participation of the observer; he cites examples from quantum physics, ecology, and the social sciences. Every experiment is an action in which we are agents, not just observers. The observer as subject is a participant inseparable from the object of observation.[37]

Michael Polanyi envisions a harmony of method over the whole range of knowledge and says that this approach overcomes the bifurcation of reason and faith. Polanyi's unifying theme is the personal participation of the knower in all knowledge. In science, the heart of discovery is creative imagination, which is a very personal act. Science requires skills that, like riding a bicycle, cannot be formally specified but only learned by example and practice. In all knowledge we have to see patterns in wholes. In recognizing a friend's face or in making a medical diagnosis, we use many clues but cannot identify all the particulars on which our judgment of a total pattern relies. Polanyi holds that the assessment of evidence is always an act of discretionary personal judgment. No rules specify whether an unexplained discrepancy between theory and experiment should be set aside as an anomaly or taken to invalidate the theory. Participation in a community of inquiry is a safeguard against subjectivity, though it never removes the burden of individual responsibility.[38] Polanyi holds that all these characteristics are even more important in religion. Here personal involvement is greater, but not to the exclusion of rationality and universal intent. Participation in the historical tradition and present experience of a religious community is essential.[39]

Several authors have recently invoked similar methodological parallels. The physicist and theologian John Polkinghorne gives examples of personal judgment and theory-laden data in both fields. The data for a religious community are its scriptural records and its history of religious experience. Similarities exist between the fields in that "each is corrigible, having to relate theory to experience, and each is essentially concerned with entities whose unpicturable reality is more subtle than that of naive objectivity."[40] The philosopher Holmes Rolston holds that religious beliefs interpret and correlate experience, much as scientific theories interpret and correlate experimental data. Beliefs can be tested by criteria of consistency and congruence with experience. But Rolston acknowledges that personal involvement is more total in the case of religion, since the primary goal is the reformation of the person. Moreover, there are other significant differences: science is interested in causes, while religion is interested in personal meanings.[41]

Such methodological comparisons seem to me illuminating for both fields, and I discuss them further in the next two chapters. Here I will only note several problems in the use of this approach:

1. In the attempt to legitimate religion in an age of science, it is tempting to dwell on similarities and pass over differences. Although science is indeed a more theory-laden enterprise than the positivists had recognized, it is clearly more objective than religion in each of the senses that have been mentioned. The kinds of data from which religion draws are radically different from those in science, and the possibility of testing religious beliefs is more limited.

2. In reacting to the absolute distinctions presented by adherents of the *Independence* thesis, it would be easy to minimize the distinctive features of religion. In particular, by treating religion as an intellectual system and talking only about religious beliefs, one may distort the diverse characteristics of religion as a way of life, which the linguistic analysts have so well described. Religious belief must always be seen in the context of the life of the religious community and in relation to the goal of personal transformation.

3. Consideration of methodology is an important but preliminary task in the dialogue of science and religion. The issues tend to be somewhat abstract and therefore of more interest to philosophers of science and philosophers of religion than to scientists or theologians and religious believers. Yet methodological issues have rightly come under new scrutiny in both communities. Furthermore, if we acknowledge methodological similarities we are more likely to encourage attention to substantive issues. If theology at its best is a reflective enterprise that can develop and grow, it can be open to new insights, including those derived from the theories of science.

## 3. NATURE-CENTERED SPIRITUALITY

In contrast to the philosophical approach of the authors who discuss limit questions and methodological parallels, another group of authors responds to nature in personal and experiential ways. In writing about *the sacred in nature* they resemble the poets of the romantic movement of the late eighteenth century. Like Thoreau, Emerson, and John Muir in the nineteenth century, they describe the experience of a religious dimension in nature. The earlier poets and nature writers were critical of the attitudes toward nature engendered by science, and they could be classified with advocates of the *Independence* thesis. But some exponents of a nature-centered spirituality today are more interested in science, and they engage in what can be considered a form of *Dialogue*. The term *spirituality* refers to a religious outlook based on individual experience rather than on religious institutions or formal theological doctrines.

Some scientists have described religious responses evoked by their work as scientists but going beyond science itself. Rachel Carson's *Silent Spring* and other writings drew from her scientific knowledge, but she also showed a reverence for the community of living things. Loren Eiseley recorded his awe at the web of life and the ties that connect us to millions of years of evolutionary history. "For many of us the Biblical bush still burns and there is a deep mystery in the heart of a simple seed." He marveled at the amazing powers of life which is "but one mask worn by the Great Face behind."[42] Aldo Leopold wrote with the knowledge of a naturalist but also with the imagination of a poet in portraying his holistic vision of the unity of life.[43]

The American nature writer Annie Dillard finds a living presence in nature. In *Pilgrim at Tinker Creek* she describes moments of illumination in the seemingly insignificant details of natural life, concerning which she is well informed by reading from scientific sources. For her, a backyard tree ablaze with flame is a glimpse of eternity. There is a sublime beauty in nature, but it is not a peaceful and harmonious order. The profusion of creatures seems extravagant, wasteful, and often unruly and untamed. There is a dark side to creation, a violence, cruelty, and death that can be terrifying. But this does not negate her gratitude for creation as a gift. "Beauty itself is the fruit of the creator's exuberance that grew such a tangle, and the grotesques and horrors bloom from that same free growth, that intricate scramble and twine up and down the conditions of time."[44]

The theologian Matthew Fox expresses awe and wonder at the new scientific story of the universe, which can inspire our gratitude. He urges us to celebrate the sacredness of nature in song, dance, ritual, and art as well as in theological reflection. He is critical of the Christian tradition for emphasizing original sin and redemption and for neglecting the idea of creation as "original blessing." But he approves of certain medieval mystics who were life affirming and creation centered, such as Meister Eckhart, Hildegarde of Bingen, and Julian of Norwich. He suggests that in meditation we can realize the divinity within us and within nature. A creation-centered spirituality can put us in touch with ourselves, with one another, and with nature.[45]

Brian Swimme, physicist, and Thomas Berry, theologian, collaborated in writing *The Universe Story.* They recommend setting the Bible aside and taking nature as our primary scripture. They advocate a new spirituality of the earth inspired by the story of the cosmos revealed by science, from the primeval fireball to human culture. The scientific narrative is presented not primarily to provide an intellectual argument for the existence of God but to awaken our reverence and sense of community with all living things. They hold that a biocentric and ecological outlook in science can be reinforced by the respect for the earth found among religious mystics and indigenous cultures. They call for a universal science-based myth or cosmic story in place of the conflicting stories of particular traditions, so that the global community can unite to preserve a planet facing environmental destruction.[46]

Many feminist authors are responsive to the sacred in nature, and some call themselves *ecofeminists.* In chapter 6 I will explore the close connections between the devaluation of women and the devaluation of nature in Western history. I will distinguish two groups: *reformist feminists,* such as Sallie

McFague and Rosemary Ruether, who believe that the patriarchal assumptions of the historic Christian tradition can be rejected without rejecting the whole tradition; and *radical feminists,* such as Starhawk and Charlene Spretnak, who turn to Goddess and Earth Mother figures from early or tribal cultures as inspiration for feminine symbols of the divine and alternative rituals for today. These rituals often express the immance of the divine in nature and the participation of humanity in the natural world.[47] It will be clear at several points in this volume that I am greatly indebted to feminists insights, though I am more interested in reforming the Christian tradition than in pursuing more radical alternatives.

A strong feature of all these versions of nature-centered spirituality is the support they give to *environmental ethics.* But I will suggest below that despite its past inadequacies, the Christian community can reclaim from biblical sources some significant environmental themes that have been neglected in much of its history. I will maintain also that our theology should incorporate both divine immanence in nature and transcendence of nature. Many of the authors mentioned above express a deep commitment to social justice—in the treatment of women, the poor and oppressed, and indigenous populations, for example. Here the record of Christianity is very mixed. The prophetic concern for justice toward the poor and oppressed has always been present in the Christian community, but the institutional church has often collaborated with unjust structures of political and economic power.

Personal responses to the sacred in nature are indeed *more universal and less divisive* than particular theological doctrines in an age of religious pluralism. They encourage humility and openness, avoiding the dogmatism that has often been present in historical religious traditions. But I will suggest in chapter 6 that we should reject both *absolutism,* which claims exclusive truth for one religious tradition, and *relativism,* which holds that no judgments can be made about the truth of any tradition. I will defend the path of *dialogue* between traditions. If we accept a genuine religious pluralism, we can respect the distinctive character of the historic traditions and learn from one another as well as from nature.

Another group of authors has described parallels between the holism of quantum physics and the unity of reality portrayed in Eastern religious traditions. David Bohm was a creative physicist who developed a distinctive mathematical formalism from which the equations of quantum physics can be derived. He went on to postulate an "implicate order" underlying the observable world. He acknowledged that his holistic assumptions were influenced by his commitment to the meditative practices and monistic world view of the Indian mystic Krishnamurti.[48] Fritjof Capra's *The Tao of Physics* is a popular account of parallels between the experience of unity in Eastern religious traditions and the unity of the world as described by quantum physics.[49] The parallels between physics and Eastern mysticism are discussed in chapter 7.

There is also a wide range of what are sometimes called *New Age movements* that combine interest in meditation, harmony with nature, and various purportedly scientific claims that are more esoteric. One common theme, despite their great diversity, is interest in "higher consciousness," "cosmic consciousness," or the power of mind over matter. Another is advocacy of a "holistic approach" designed to overcome all prevalent dualisms, such as those of matter and spirit, masculine and feminine, and humanity and nature. The scientific claims of some of these groups are dismissed by most scientists as "pseudoscience," for example astrology, communication with the dead through mediums, reports of visitors from space (UFOs), and the concentration of spiritual energies by crystals.[50] Other claims have been the subject of serious scientific research but have been difficult to verify, such as paranormal experiences of mental telepathy and precognition. From a scientific viewpoint, there are two problems with these claims: (1) the *data* cited can seldom be reliably reproduced, and (2) few *theories* have been proposed that can be tested against data.

In this volume I will be looking mainly at mainstream science and its relation to mainstream religion. However, I am critical of the reductionist assumptions of many scientists, and I welcome the careful testing of more holistic hypotheses. I am sympathetic with the hunger for spirituality in a materialistic culture and the widespread dissatisfaction with traditional institutions, whether scientific or religious. I, too, wish to encourage personal religious experience that is significant in people's lives. I am therefore open to an extension of what are taken to be the boundaries of acceptable science and religion and to the possibility of new paradigms that are more inclusive. In both science and religion I believe that alternatives outside the mainstream should be carefully evaluated and neither dismissed out of hand nor uncritically accepted.

## IV. INTEGRATION

The final group of authors holds that some sort of integration is possible between the content of theology and the content of science. Here the relationships between theological doctrines and particular scientific theories are more direct than in any of the forms of *Dialogue* above. There are three distinct versions of *Integration*. In natural theology, it is claimed that the existence of God can be inferred from the evidences of design in nature, of which science has made us more aware. In a theology of nature, the main sources of theology lie outside science, but scientific theories may affect the reformulation of certain doctrines, particularly the doctrines of creation and human nature. In a systematic synthesis, both science and religion contribute to the development of an inclusive metaphysics, such as that of process philosophy.

### 1. NATURAL THEOLOGY

Previous chapters have traced the changing fortunes of natural theology in earlier centuries. Thomas Aquinas offered several versions of the *cosmological argument* for a First Cause (or a necessary being on whom all contingent beings are dependent). He also presented the *teleological argument* for the orderliness and intelligibility of nature in general and the evidence of design in particular natural phenomena. Newton, Boyle, and other key figures in the rise of modern science frequently extolled the evidences of benevolent design in nature. Hume criticized these arguments in the eighteenth century, but they were still popular in the early nineteenth century. Paley argued that the coordination of many complex parts for a single function (such as vision in the case of the eye) testifies to an intelligent Designer. Darwin in turn showed that adaptation can be explained by random variation and natural selection, though he continued to hold (at least until late in his life) that the evolutionary laws were themselves the product of intelligent design. In the *reformulation of the argument* after Darwin, design was said to be present not in the particular structures of individual organisms but in the properties of matter and the laws of nature through which the evolutionary process could produce such organisms. It is in the design of the total process that God's wisdom is evident. In the 1930s, F. R. Tennant argued that nature is a unified system of mutually supporting structures that have led to living organisms and have provided the conditions for human moral, aesthetic, and intellectual life.[51] Reformulations of the teleological argument are common in Roman Catholic thought, where natural theology has traditionally held a respected place as a preparation for the truths of revealed theology.[52]

The British philosopher Richard Swinburne has given an extended defense of natural theology. He starts by discussing *confirmation theory* in the philosophy of science. In the development of science, new evidence does not make a theory certain. Instead, a theory has an initial plausibility, and the probability that it is true increases or decreases with the additional evidence (Bayes's Theorem). Swinburne suggests that the existence of God has an initial plausibility because of its simplicity and because it gives a personal explanation of the world in terms of the intentions of an agent. He then argues that the evidence of order in the world increases the probability of the theistic hypothesis. He also maintains that science cannot account for the presence of conscious beings in the world. "Something outside the web of physical laws" is needed to explain the rise of consciousness. Finally, religious experience provides "additional crucial evidence." Swinburne concludes, "On our total evidence, theism is more probable than not."[53]

The most recent rendition of the design argument is *the Anthropic Principle* in cosmology. Astrophysicists have found that life in the universe would have been impossible if some of the physical constants and other conditions in the early universe had differed even slightly from the values they had. The universe seems to be "fine-tuned" for the possibility of life. For example, Stephen Hawking writes, "If the rate of expansion one second after the big bang had been smaller by even one part in a hundred thousand million million, the universe would have recollapsed before it even reached its present size."[54] Freeman Dyson draws the following conclusion from such findings:

I conclude from the existence of these accidents of physics and astronomy that the universe is an unexpectedly hospitable place for living creatures to make their home in. Being a scientist, trained in the habits of thought and language of the twentieth century rather than the eighteenth, I do not claim that the architecture of the universe proves the existence of God. I claim only that the architecture of the universe is consistent with the hypothesis that mind plays an essential role in its functioning.[55]

John Barrow and Frank Tipler present many other cases in which there were extremely critical values of various forces in the early universe.[56] The philosopher John Leslie defends the Anthropic Principle as a design argument. But he points out that an alternative explanation would be the assumption of many worlds (either in successive cycles of an oscillating universe or in separate domains existing simultaneously). These worlds might differ from each other, and we just happen to be in one that has the right variables for the emergence of life.[57] Moreover, some of these apparently arbitrary conditions may be necessitated by a more basic unified theory, on which physicists are currently working. We will examine these alternatives in chapter 8.

The former bishop of Birmingham, Hugh Montefiore, claims that there are many instances of design in the universe, including the Anthropic Principle and the directionality of evolution. Some of his other examples, such as James Lovelock's "Gaia Hypothesis" and Rupert Sheldrake's "morphogenetic fields," are much more controversial and have little support in the scientific community. Montefiore does not claim that these arguments prove the existence of God, but only that the latter is more probable than other explanations.[58]

Debates continue about the validity of each of these arguments, to which we will return in later chapters. Natural theology has a great appeal in a world of religious pluralism, since it starts from scientific data on which we might expect agreement despite cultural and religious differences. Moreover, such arguments may overcome some obstacles to belief by showing that the idea of a Designer is as reasonable as alternative interpretive proposals. But even if the arguments are accepted, they would not lead to the personal, active God of the Bible, as Hume pointed out, but only to an intelligent designer remote from the world. Moreover, few persons have actually acquired their religious beliefs by such arguments. Natural theology can show that the existence of God is a plausible hypothesis, but this kind of reasoning seems far removed from the actual life of a religious community.

## 2. THEOLOGY OF NATURE

A theology of nature does not start from science, as some versions of natural theology do. Instead, it starts from a religious tradition based on religious experience and historical revelation. But it holds that some traditional doctrines need to be reformulated in the light of current science. Here science and religion are considered to be relatively independent sources of ideas, but with some areas of overlap in their concerns. In particular, the doctrines of creation, providence, and human nature are affected by the findings of science. If religious beliefs are to be in harmony with scientific knowledge, some adjustments or modifications are called for. The theologian will want to draw mainly from broad features of science that are widely accepted, rather than risk adapting to limited or speculative theories that are more likely to be abandoned in the future. Theological doctrines must be consistent with the scientific evidence even if they are not required by it.

Our understanding of the general characteristics of nature will affect our models of God's relation to nature. Nature is today understood to be a dynamic evolutionary process with a long history of emergent novelty, characterized throughout by chance and law. The natural order is ecological, interdependent, and multileveled. These characteristics will modify our representation of the relation of both God and humanity to nonhuman nature. This will, in turn, affect our attitudes toward nature and will have practical implications for environmental ethics. The problem of evil will also be viewed differently in an evolutionary rather than a static world.

For biochemist and theologian Arthur Peacocke, the starting point of theological reflection is past and present religious experience in an ongoing religious community. Religious beliefs are tested by community consensus and by criteria of coherence, comprehensiveness, and fruitfulness. But Peacocke is willing to reformulate traditional beliefs in response to current science. He discusses at length how chance and law work together in cosmology, quantum physics, nonequilibrium thermodynamics, and biological evolution. He describes the emergence of distinctive forms of activity at higher levels of complexity in the multilayered hierarchy of organic life and mind. He gives chance a positive role in the exploration and expression of potentialities at all levels. God creates through the whole process of law and chance, not by intervening in gaps in the process. God creates "in and through" the processes of the natural world that science unveils. Peacocke speaks of chance as God's radar sweeping through the range of possibilities and evoking the diverse potentialities of natural systems. In other images, artistic creativity is used as an analogy in which purposefulness and open-endedness are continuously present.[59] I am sympathetic with Peacocke's position at most points. He gives us vivid images for talking about God's relation to a natural order whose characteristics science has disclosed. But I believe that in addition to images that provide a suggestive link between scientific and religious reflection, we need philosophical categories to help us unify scientific and theological assertions in a more systematic way.

The writings of the Jesuit paleontologist Teilhard de Chardin are another example of a theology of nature. Some reviewers take *The Phenomenon of Man* to be a form of natural theology, an argument from evolution to the existence of God. I have suggested that it can more appropriately be viewed as a synthesis of scientific ideas with religious ideas derived from Christian tradition and experience. Teilhard's other writings make clear how deeply he was molded by his religious heritage and his own spirituality. But his concept of God was modified by evolutionary ideas, even if it was not derived from an analysis of evolution. Teilhard speaks of continuing creation and a God immanent in an incomplete world. His vision of the final convergence to an "Omega Point" is both a speculative extrapolation of evolutionary directionality and a distinctive interpretation of Christian eschatology.[60]

In any theology of nature there are theological issues that require clarification. Is some reformulation of the classical idea of God's omnipotence called for? Theologians have wrestled for centuries with the problem of reconciling omnipotence and omniscience with human freedom and the existence of evil and suffering. But a new problem is raised by the role of chance in diverse fields of science. Do we defend the traditional idea of divine sovereignty and hold that what appears to the scientist to be chance is really providentially controlled by God? Or do both human freedom and chance in nature represent a self-limitation on God's foreknowledge and power, required by the creation of this sort of world?

How do we represent God's action in the world? The traditional distinction of primary and secondary causes preserves the integrity of the secondary causal chains that science studies. God does not interfere but acts through secondary causes, which at their own level provide a complete explanation of all events. This tends toward deism if God has planned all things from the beginning so they would unfold by their own structures (deterministic and probabilistic) to achieve the goals intended. Is the biblical picture of the particularity of divine action then replaced by the uniformity of divine concurrence with natural causes? Should we then speak only of God's one action, the whole of cosmic history? These are some of the questions that a theology of nature must answer. We will return to them in part 4.

A theology of nature today must also provide motivation for action to *preserve the environment* of our endangered planet. Environmentalists have rightly criticized classical Christianity for emphasizing divine transcendence at the expense of immanence and for drawing too sharp a line between human and nonhuman nature. The idea of dominion over nature in Genesis 1:28 has sometimes been used to justify unlimited domination in which other creatures are treated simply as means to human ends. But many recent authors have urged the recovery of biblical themes that give strong support to environmentalism.[61]

1. *Stewardship of Nature.* The land belongs ultimately to the God who created it; we are only trustees or stewards, responsible for its welfare and accountable for our treatment of it. The Sabbath is a day of rest for the earth and other living things as well as for people. Every seventh year the fields are to lie fallow; the land deserves respect, and it will cry out if mistreated. However, stewardship has often been interpreted as assigning only utilitarian value to nature, and it can easily be distorted into domination over nature unless other themes are combined with it.

2. *Celebration of Nature.* Celebration goes beyond stewardship because it implies that nature is valuable in itself. The first chapter of Genesis ends with an affirmation of the goodness of the created order; the idea of creation is a

great unifying framework encompassing all forms of life. The covenant after the flood includes all creatures. Many of the psalms refer to the value of nature apart from its usefulness to us, and they celebrate the rich diversity in the natural world. At the end of his dialogue with God, Job is overwhelmed by the majesty of natural phenomena, including strange creatures that are of no use to humanity. Christ spoke of God's care for the lilies of the field and the sparrows of the air, and several of his parables use images from the natural world.

3. *A Sacramental View of Nature.* Even greater value is attributed to nature when it is believed that the sacred is present in and under it. Eastern Orthodoxy and Celtic Christianity celebrate the goodness of creation and find God's presence in it. Some Anglican authors hold that all of nature and not just the bread, wine, and water of the sacraments can be vehicles of God's grace. These traditions envision the redemption of the whole creation rather than the rescue of human souls from the world. They have much in common with the nature-centered spirituality discussed earlier, but place more emphasis on transcendence and the person of Christ.

4. *The Holy Spirit in Nature.* In the opening verses of Genesis, "the Spirit of God was moving over the face of the water." Several of the psalms speak of the presence of the Spirit in nature. After praising God for diverse plants and animals around us today, Psalm 104 affirms: "When thou sendest forth thy Spirit, they are created." But the Spirit also inspires the prophets and the worshiping community. Christ received the Spirit at his baptism, and the activity of the Spirit marked the birth of the church at Pentecost. Reference to the Spirit thus ties together God's work as Creator and Redeemer. The same God whom we encounter in nature can be encountered in the life of Christ and the church.

I have discussed *environmental ethics* at greater length elsewhere,[62] but the topic is taken up at many point in this volume (see Index of Selected Topics). I seek a theology that can bring together concern for the environment and for social justice. I will maintain in chapter 11 that process theology offers a promising conceptuality for articulating environmental and human values.

## 3. SYSTEMATIC SYNTHESIS

A more systematic integration can occur if both science and religion contribute to a coherent world view elaborated in a comprehensive metaphysics. Metaphysics is the search for a set of general categories in terms of which diverse types of experience can be interpreted. An inclusive conceptual scheme is sought that can represent the fundamental characteristics of all events. Metaphysics as such is the province of the philosopher rather than of either the scientist or the theologian, but it can serve as an arena of common reflection. The Thomistic framework provided such a metaphysics, but one in which, I would argue, the dualisms of spirit/matter, mind/body, humanity/nature, and eternity/time were only partially overcome.

*Process philosophy* is a promising candidate for a mediating role today because it was itself formulated under the influence of both scientific and religious thought, even as it responded to persistent problems in the history of Western philosophy (for example, the mind/body problem). Alfred North Whitehead has been the most influential exponent of process categories, though theological implications have been more fully investigated by Charles Hartshorne, John Cobb, and others. The influence of biology and physics is evident in the process view of reality as a dynamic web of interconnected events. Nature is characterized by change, chance, and novelty as well as order. It is incomplete and still coming into being. Process thinkers are critical of reductionism; they defend organismic categories applicable to activities at higher levels of organization. They see continuity as well as distinctiveness among levels of reality; the characteristics of each level have rudimentary forerunners at earlier and lower levels. Against a dualism of matter and mind, or a materialism that has no place for mind, process thought envisages two aspects of all events as seen from within and from without. Because humanity is continuous with the rest of nature (despite the uniqueness of reflective self-consciousness), human experience can be taken as a clue to interpreting the experience of other beings. Genuinely new phenomena emerge in evolutionary history, but the basic metaphysical categories apply to all events.

Process thinkers understand God to be the source of novelty and order. Creation is a long and incomplete process. God elicits the self-creation of individual entities, thereby allowing for freedom and novelty as well as order and structure. God is not the unrelated Absolute, the Unmoved Mover, but instead interacts reciprocally with the world, an influence on all events though never the sole cause of any event. Process metaphysics understands every new event to be jointly the product of the entity's past, its own action, and the action of God. Here God transcends the world but is immanent in the world in a specific way in the structure of each event. We do not have a succession of purely natural events, interrupted by gaps in which God alone operates. Process thinkers reject the idea of divine omnipotence; they believe in a God of persuasion rather than compulsion, and they have provided distinctive analyses of the place of chance, human freedom, evil, and suffering in the world. Christian process theologians point out that the power of love, as exemplified in the cross, is precisely its ability to evoke a response while respecting the integrity of other beings. They also hold that divine immutability is not a characteristic of the biblical God who is intimately involved with history. Hartshorne elaborates a "dipolar" concept of God: unchanging in purpose and character, but changing in experience and relationship.[63]

In *The Liberation of Life*, Charles Birch and John Cobb have brought together ideas from biology, process philosophy, and Christian thought. Early chapters develop an ecological or organismic model in which (1) every being is constituted by its interaction with a wider environment, and (2) all beings are subjects of experience, which runs the gamut from rudimentary responsiveness to reflective consciousness. Evolutionary history shows continuity but also the emergence of novelty. Humanity is continuous with and part of the natural order. Birch and Cobb develop an ethics that avoids anthropocentrism. The goal of enhancing the richness of experience in any form encourages concern for nonhuman life, without treating all forms of life as equally valuable. These authors present a powerful vision of a just and sustainable society in an interdependent community of life.[64] In other books they indicate their commitment to the Christian tradition and their attempt to reformulate it in the categories of process thought. Writing with David Griffin, for example, Cobb seeks "a truly contemporary vision that is at the same time truly Christian."[65] God is understood both as "a source of novelty and order" and as "creative-responsive love." Christ's vision of the love of God opens us to creative transformation. These authors also show that Christian process theology can provide a sound basis for an environmental ethics.

I am in basic agreement with the "Theology of Nature" position, coupled with a cautious use of process philosophy. Too much reliance on science in natural theology can lead to the neglect of the areas of experience that I consider most important religiously. As I see it, the center of the Christian life is an experience of reorientation, the healing of our brokenness in new wholeness, and the expression of a new relationship to God and to the neighbor. Existentialists and linguistic analysts rightly point to the primacy of personal and social life in religion, and neo-orthodoxy rightly says that for the Christian community it is in response to the person of Christ that our lives can be changed. But the centrality of redemption need not lead us to belittle creation, for our personal and social lives are intimately bound to the rest of the created order. We are redeemed in and with the world, not from the world. Part of our task, then, is to articulate a theology of nature, for which we will have to draw from both religious and scientific sources.

In articulating a theology of nature, a systematic metaphysics can help us toward a coherent vision. But Christianity should never be equated with any metaphysical system. There are dangers if either scientific or religious ideas are distorted to fit a preconceived synthesis that claims to encompass all reality. We must always keep in mind the rich diversity of our experience. We distort it if we cut it up into separate realms or watertight compartments, but we also distort it if we force it into a neat intellectual system. A coherent vision of reality can still allow for the distinctiveness of differing types of experience. In the chapters that follow I will try to do justice to what is valid in the *Independence* position, though I will be mainly developing the *Dialogue* position concerning methodology and the *Integration* thesis with respect to the doctrines of creation and human nature.

## CHAPTER 5

# Models and Paradigms

This chapter examines some parallels between the methods of science and those of religion. It develops the "Methodological Parallels" version of *Dialogue* in the previous chapter. Whereas advocates of *Independence* see only the differences between science and religion, advocates of *Dialogue* usually point to similarities. The differences will not be ignored here, though they will be more specifically explored in chapter 6.

We begin with a comparison of the general structures of scientific and religious thought. Then the role of conceptual models in both fields is analyzed. A summary of the debate over the role of paradigms in science follows, and some possible parallels in religion are presented. In the final section, we consider the balance between tentativeness and commitment in each field.

## I. THE STRUCTURES OF SCIENCE AND RELIGION

We look first at the relation between the two basic components of science: data and theory. It is then suggested that in religion the data are religious experience, story, and ritual and that religious beliefs have some functions similar to those of scientific theories. The distinctive features of religious story and ritual are also discussed.[1]

### 1. THEORY AND DATA IN SCIENCE

In describing the work of Galileo, Newton, and Darwin I suggested that the fundamental components of modern science are (1) particular observations and experimental data, and (2) general concepts and theories. How are theories related to data? Since Bacon and Mill, the *inductive view* has held that the scientist starts with observations and formulates theories by generalizing the patterns in the data (this would be represented by an arrow *upward* from data to theories in figure 1). But this view is inadequate because theories involve novel concepts and hypotheses not found in the data, and they often refer to entities and relationships that are not directly observable.

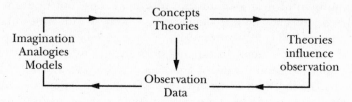

Fig. 1 The Structure of Science

There is, then, no direct upward line of logical reasoning from data to theories in the diagram, but only the indirect line at the left, representing acts of *creative imagination* for which no rules can be given. Often a new concept or relationship is first thought of by analogy with a more familiar concept or relationship, but with a novel modification or adaptation. Frequently the analogy is systematically developed as a *conceptual model* of a postulated entity that cannot be directly observed. The model leads to the formulation of a generalized and abstract theory. For example, the billiard ball model of a gas postulated invisible gas particles that were imagined to collide and bounce off each other like billiard balls. From the model, the kinetic theory of gases was developed.

To be scientifically useful, a theory must be tested experimentally. A theory leads us to expect some observations and not others. This is the *hypothetico-deductive* view of science, represented by the *downward arrow* from theory to observation. The context of discovery (left-hand loop) differs from the context of justification (downward arrow). If a theory or hypothesis is valid, then particular observational patterns are expected, though the reasoning process always involves a variety of background assumptions, auxiliary hypotheses, and rules of correspondence linking theoretical and observational terms. In the case of the kinetic theory of gases, we can calculate the change in the momentum of the hypothetical particles when they strike the walls of the containing vessel. If we assume perfectly elastic collisions and particles of negligible size, we can derive Boyle's Law relating the observed pressure and volume of a gas sample. The corroboration of such deductions leads us at least tentatively to accept a theory.[2]

This hypothetico-deductive view dominated philosophy of science in the 1950s and early 1960s. It assumed that data are describable in a theory-free observation language and that alternative theories are tested against these fixed, objective data. Even though *agreement* with data does not *verify* a theory (since there may be other theories that would also agree), it was claimed by Karl Popper and others that *disagreement* with data will conclusively *falsify* a theory. But studies in the history of science cast doubt on this claim.

In some cases, discordant data were brought into harmony with a theoretical prediction by the introduction of *ad hoc auxiliary hypotheses*. Early opponents of Copernican astronomy said the hypothesis that the earth moves around the sun must be false because there is no visible annual change in the apparent position of near stars relative to distant stars. But Copernicus dismissed this discrepancy by introducing the hypothesis (for which there was then no independent evidence) that all the stars are very distant compared to the size of the solar system. In other historical cases a theory was retained without modification and the discordant data were simply set to one side as an *unexplained anomaly*. Newton in his *Principia* admitted that the observed motion of the apogee (the most distant point) of the moon's elliptical orbit in successive revolutions was twice that predicted by his theory. For sixty years the disagreement, which far exceeded the limits of experimental error, could not be accounted for, yet it was never taken to disprove the theory.

We can never test a theory alone, but only as part of *a network of theories*. If a theory fits poorly with the data at one point, other parts of the network can usually be adjusted to improve the fit. Theories with terms far from the observational boundaries are not uniquely determined by the data.[3] Normally, a group of background theories is simply assumed and treated as unproblematic while attention is directed to a new or controversial theory. In many scientific disputes, the contending parties agree on most of these background assumptions, and so they can agree on the kinds of experimental data that both sides will accept as a crucial test for adjudicating between rival theories. But in some cases two theories of broad scope involve differing ways of interpreting the data, or they are correlated with differing bodies of data or differing types of explanation, and no simple experimental adjudication is possible.

Moreover, *all data are theory-laden*. There simply is no theory-free observational language. Theories influence observations in many ways (as shown in the right-hand loop in the diagram). The selection of phenomena to study and the choice of variables considered significant to measure are theory-dependent. The form of the questions we ask determines the kind of answers we receive. Theories are reflected in our assumptions about the operation of our equipment and in the language in which observations are reported.[4] This account differs sharply from the empiricist account, in which the edifice of knowledge is built on the secure foundation of unchanging facts.

In addition, the object observed may be altered by *the process of observation* itself. We will see that this is particularly problematic in the microworld of quantum physics and in the complex networks of ecosystems. We are not detached observers separate from observed objects; we are participant observers who are part of an interactive system.

Thomas Kuhn has argued that scientific data are strongly dependent on dominant *paradigms*. A paradigm, as we have seen, is a cluster of conceptual and methodological presuppositions embodied in an exemplary body of scientific work, such as Newtonian mechanics in the eighteenth century or relativity and quantum physics in the twentieth century. A paradigm implicitly defines for a given scientific community the kinds of questions that may fruitfully be asked and the types of explanations to be sought. Through standard examples, students learn what kinds of entities exist in the world and what methods are suitable for studying them. A paradigm shift is "a scientific revolution," "a radical transformation of the scientific imagination," which is not unequivocally deter-mined by experimental data or by the normal criteria of research. Accepted paradigms are thus more resistant to change and more difficult to overthrow than are particular theories. Paradigms are the products of particular historical communities.[5] Here we see a contextualism, a historicism, and a relativism con-trasting with the formalism and the empiricism of Popper's account.

There are four criteria for assessing theories in normal scientific research:

*1. Agreement with Data.* This is the most important criterion, though it never provides proof that a theory is true. For other theories not yet devel-oped may fit the data as well or better. Theories are always underdetermined by data. Nor does disagreement with data prove a theory false, since *ad hoc* modifications or unexplained anomalies can be tolerated for an indefinite period. However, agreement with data and predictive success—especially the prediction of novel phenomena not previously anticipated—constitute impressive support for a theory.

*2. Coherence.* A theory should be consistent with other accepted theories and, if possible, conceptually interconnected with them. Scientists also value the internal coherence and simplicity of a theory (simplicity of formal struc-ture, smallest number of independent or *ad hoc* assumptions, aesthetic ele-gance, transformational symmetry, and so forth).

*3. Scope.* Theories can be judged by their comprehensiveness or generality. A theory is valued if it unifies previously disparate domains, if it is supported by a variety of kinds of evidence, or if it is applicable to wide ranges of the relevant variables.

*4. Fertility.* A theory is evaluated not just by its past accomplishments but by its current ability and future promise in providing the framework for an ongoing research program. Is the theory fruitful in encouraging further the-oretical elaboration, in generating new hypotheses, and in suggesting new experiments? Attention is directed here to the continuing research activity of a scientific community rather than to the finished product of their work.

Western thought has included three main *views of truth,* and each empha-sizes particular criteria from the list above. The *correspondence* view says that a proposition is true if it corresponds to reality. This is the common-sense understanding of truth. The statement "it is raining" is true if in fact it is raining. This is the position adopted by classical realism, and it seems to fit the empirical side of science as specified by the first criterion: theories must agree with data. But we have said that there are no theory-free data with which a theory can be compared. Many theories postulate unobservable enti-ties only indirectly related to observable data. We have no direct access to reality to compare it with our theories.

The *coherence* view says that a set of propositions is true if it is comprehen-sive and internally coherent. This view has been adopted by rationalists and philosophical idealists, and it seems to fit the theoretical side of science. We have said that a single theory can never be evaluated in isolation, but only as part of a network of theories, so scope should be considered along with coherence. But this position is also problematic, since there may be more than one internally coherent set of theories in a given domain. Moreover, judgments of agreement with data differ in character from judgments of internal coherence and cannot be assimilated to the latter. In addition, reality seems to be more paradoxical and less logical than the rationalists assume.

The *pragmatic* view says that a proposition is true if it works in practice. We should judge by the consequences. Is an idea fruitful and suggestive? Is it useful in satisfying individual and social needs and interests? Ideas and theories are guides to action in particular contexts. Instrumentalists and linguistic analysts usually dismiss questions of truth, and they talk only about the diverse functions of language. But they often adopt a pragmatic view of scientific language. There is a pragmatic element in Kuhn's thesis that scientific inquiry is problem-solving in a particular historical context and within a particular paradigm community. This side of science is reflected in our last criterion: fertility. But taken alone this criterion is inadequate; whether an idea "works" or is "useful" remains vague unless these concepts are further specified by other criteria.

My own conclusion is that the *meaning* of truth is correspondence with reality. But because reality is inaccessible to us, the *criteria* of truth must include all four of the criteria mentioned above. The criteria taken together include the valid insights in all these views of truth. One or another of the criteria may be more important than the others at a particular stage of scientific inquiry. Because correspondence is taken as the definition of truth, this is a form of realism, but it is a *critical realism* because a combination of criteria is used. I will be advocating such a critical realism throughout this volume.

In sum, science does not lead to certainty. Its conclusions are always incomplete, tentative, and subject to revision. Theories change in time, and we should expect current theories to be modified or overthrown, as previous ones have been. But science does offer reliable procedures for testing and evaluating theories by a complex set of criteria. We will later examine the role of individual judgment and the traditions of particular scientific communities in the application of these criteria.

## 2. BELIEF AND EXPERIENCE IN RELIGION

The basic structure of religion is similar to that of science in some respects, though it differs at several crucial points. The data for a religious community consist of the distinctive experiences of individuals and the stories and rituals of a religious tradition. Let us start by considering *religious experience,* which is always interpreted by a set of concepts and beliefs. These concepts and beliefs are not the product of logical reasoning from the data; they result from acts of creative imagination in which, as in the scientific case, analogies and models are prominent (figure 2). Models are also drawn from the stories of a tradition and express the structural elements that recur in dynamic form in narratives. Models, in turn, lead to abstract concepts and articulated beliefs that are systematically formalized as theological doctrines.

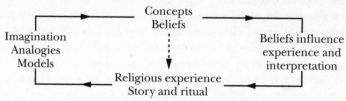

Fig. 2 The Structure of Religion

The experiential testing of *religious beliefs* is problematic (so the downward arrow is shown as a dashed line), though we will find that there are criteria for judging the adequacy of beliefs. Moreover, there are no uninterpreted experiences, as there are no theory-free data in science. Religious beliefs influence experience and the interpretation of traditional stories and rituals (the loop on the right of the diagram)—an even stronger influence than that of scientific theories on data. Here, too, paradigms are extraordinarily resistant to change, and when paradigm shifts do occur a whole network of conceptual and methodological assumptions is altered. We will examine in turn each of these features of religious life and thought.

Six distinctive types of religious experience recur in a variety of traditions around the world.[6]

*1. Numinous Experience of the Holy.* Persons in many cultures have described a sense of awe and reverence, mystery and wonder, holiness and sacredness. Participants may experience a sense of otherness, confrontation, and encounter, or of being grasped and laid hold of. Here individuals typically express awareness of their dependence, finitude, limitation, and contingency. The experience is often interpreted in terms of a personal model of the divine. This pattern is more common in the monotheistic religions (Judaism, Christianity, and Islam) but is found also in Mahayana Buddhism and the *bhakti* tradition of Hinduism. It emphasizes a strong contrast between the finitude of the human and the transcendence of the divine.

*2. Mystical Experience of Unity.* Mystics in many traditions have spoken of the experience of the unity of all things, found in the depth of the individual soul and in the world of nature. Unity is achieved in the discipline of meditation and is characterized by joy, harmony, serenity, and peace. In its extreme form the unity may be described as selflessness and loss of individuality and the joy as bliss or rapture. The experience is often correlated with impersonal models of the divine, especially in Eastern traditions, though it occurs in the West with both personal and impersonal models. Here the unity rather than the separation of the human and divine is emphasized. The numinous and the mystical seem to be the most common types of religious experience around the world.

*3. Transformative Experience of Reorientation.* In the lives of some individuals, acknowledgment of guilt has been followed by the experience of forgiveness. Others have described a transition from brokenness and estrangement to wholeness and reconciliation. Some experience a healing of internal divisions or a restoration of relationship with other persons. Such reorientation and renewal, whether sudden or gradual, may lead to self-acceptance, liberation from self-centeredness, openness to new possibilities in one's life, a greater sensitivity to other persons, or perhaps dedication to a style of life based on radical trust and love. Such transformative experiences are prominent in the Christian tradition, but parallels are found in many traditions.

4. *Courage in Facing Suffering and Death.* Suffering, death, and transiency are universal human experiences, and responses to them are found in virtually every religious tradition. Meaninglessness is overcome when people view human existence in a wider context of meaning, beyond the life of the individual. Attitudes toward suffering and death are affected when trust replaces anxiety (in the West), or when detachment replaces the attachment that gives suffering and death their power over us (in the East). Such experiences can, of course, be described in psychological terms, but in religious traditions they are understood in relation to a view of ultimate reality beyond the individual.

5. *Moral Experience of Obligation.* Many people have felt moral demands overriding their own inclinations. Though the voice of conscience is in part the product of social conditioning, it may also lead persons to express judgment on their culture or moral outrage in the face of evil, even at the risk of death. Judgments of good and evil, right and wrong, are made in the light of one's view of the nature of ultimate reality. Moral demands may be understood as the will of a God of justice and love or as a requirement for harmony with the cosmic process. In the West, prophetic protest against social injustice has been viewed as a response to God's purposes.

6. *Awe in Response to Order and Creativity in the World.* At the intellectual level, the presence of order and creativity in nature has served as the basis for inferring a divine source of order, beauty, and novelty (as in the classical argument from design). At the experiential level, people have responded to the world with reverence and appreciation, with gratitude for the gift of life, and with wonder that nature has a rational order intelligible to our minds. In the numinous tradition this is expressed as a dependence on a Creator who is the ground of order and creativity. In the mystical tradition it is more often articulated as dependence on a creative force immanent within nature.

Such experiences sometimes appear private and individual, but they occur *in the context of a community.* Experience is always affected by prior expectations and beliefs. The founders of new traditions started with inherited cultural assumptions, even if they challenged some of those assumptions. After their distinctive experiences, they evoked powerful responses among their followers. In subsequent generations, the experiences of individuals were subjected to a process of sorting and selecting within the ongoing community. The group affirmed some forms of experience and not others, and it set limits on acceptable beliefs—though these limits have changed historically and may allow for considerable reformulation. Most traditions have included prophetic figures who criticized accepted ideas and practices, while those in priestly roles were more often dedicated to continuity and the preservation of the past. There have been periods of codification and institutionalization, and periods of reformation and change.

If the task of the theologian is systematic reflection on the life and thought of the religious community, this will include critical assessment according to particular criteria. I suggest that assessment of beliefs *within a paradigm community* can be undertaken with the same criteria listed above for scientific theories, though the criteria will have to be applied somewhat differently. (The questions of assessing the paradigms themselves and judging among religious traditions are taken up in the next chapter.)

*1. Agreement with Data.* Religious beliefs must provide a faithful rendition of the areas of experience that are taken by the community to be especially significant. I have argued that the primary data are individual religious experience and communal story and ritual. Here the data are much more theory-laden than in the case of science. We will have to examine the influence of beliefs on experience and on the interpretation of story and ritual.

*2. Coherence.* Consistency with other accepted beliefs ensures the continuity of a paradigm tradition. The intersubjective judgment of the community provides protection against individualism and arbitrariness. But there is room for reformulation and reinterpretation, and the ideas of religious communities have indeed undergone considerable change throughout history. There are also close internal relationships among a set of religious beliefs.

*3. Scope.* Religious beliefs can be extended to interpret other kinds of human experience beyond the primary data, particularly other aspects of our personal and social lives. In a scientific age, they must also at least be consistent with the findings of science. Religious beliefs can contribute to a coherent world view and a comprehensive metaphysics.

*4. Fertility.* In the case of science, theories are judged partly by their promise for encouraging an ongoing research program, which is the central activity of science. Because religion involves a greater diversity of activities and serves some functions quite different from those of science, fertility here has many dimensions. At the personal level, religious beliefs can be judged by their power to effect personal transformation and the integration of personality. What are their effects on human character? Do they have the capacity to inspire and sustain compassion and create love? Are they relevant to urgent issues of our age, for example, environmental destruction and nuclear war? Judgments on such questions will of course be paradigm-dependent, but they are an important part of the evaluation of religion as a way of life. These questions are explored later in this chapter.

## 3. STORY AND RITUAL IN CHRISTIANITY

In addition to religious experience, religious tradition includes a second form of data, namely a set of stories and rituals. Traditions are transmitted primarily through stories and their reenactment in rituals, rather than through abstract concepts and doctrinal beliefs. Religious stories were initially the products of experiences and events, interpreted imaginatively (an activity belonging on the left side of the diagram in figure 2). But the stories were later recorded in *scriptures* and became part of the data to which people responded in subsequent generations. Many scholars of religion use the term *myths* to refer to the central narratives of a religious tradition, insisting that the term does not imply any judgment either for or against the narratives' historicity or validity. However, in popular usage, a myth refers to a fictional and untrue tale, so I have come to prefer the term *story*, since the status of a story is clearly left open.

The central *religious stories* are taken to manifest the character of the cosmic order and our relationship to it. They are significant in personal and communal life because they endorse particular ways of ordering experience, and they provide exemplary patterns for human actions. Such stories inform us about ourselves; our self-identity as individuals and as communities is in part constituted by these narratives. They are recalled in liturgy and acted out in ritual. Past events become present (re-presented) in symbolic reenactment. Creation stories found in most cultures portray the essential structures of reality and the cosmic context for human existence. Other stories exhibit a saving power in human life that can overcome some of its flaws or distortions (variously seen as sin, ignorance, or attachment). The power to transform life and restore relationships may be expressed in a personal redeemer or in a law or discipline to be followed.[7]

It is important to look at particular religions rather than at religion in general; I will primarily consider the Christian tradition, though I will give some examples from other traditions. Christianity re-presents three central stories.

1. *The Creation of the World.* The opening chapters of Genesis set human life in a framework of significance and meaning. They portray a world that is good, orderly, and coherent. They picture a God who is free, transcendent, and purposeful. These theological affirmations are conveyed through a dramatic narrative, which assumes a prescientific cosmology. In chapter 8 we will consider the interpretation of this story in a scientific age. We will note the connections of the creation story with human experience, theological doctrine, ritual practice, and ethical action. For example, the liturgies of ancient psalms and modern hymns and prayers give recurrent voice to gratitude for the created order. We will see also how a view of creation affects attitudes toward nature and the ways in which we treat the environment.

2. *The Covenant with Israel.* The Exodus stories of liberation from captivity in Egypt and the giving of the covenant at Sinai are central in Judaism but are also significant in Christian identity. Here the community's existence is understood as response to a God who is liberator and redeemer as well as creator. It is not surprising that liberation theology among oppressed groups today (blacks, women, Third World nations) has given prominence to the exodus theme. Rituals such as Passover and the liturgies expressing gratitude for the Torah lie at the heart of Judaism and have influenced Christian worship and ethics. Most biblical scholars today hold that many of the details of

the Law come from later centuries, but they trace the distinctive features of ethical monotheism and the concept of covenant to the time of Moses. The stories, that is, originated in historical events, but as they appear in scripture they involve centuries of elaboration and interpretation.

3. *The Life of Christ.* The most important stories for the Christian community recount the life, teachings, death, and resurrection of Christ. These narratives, historically based but inescapably involving interpretation, are central to individual and communal religious identity. The most prominent ritual (Eucharist or Lord's Supper) and festivals (Christmas and Easter) celebrate and re-present crucial portions of this story. The early Christians wrote of their experience of liberation from anxiety and the fear of death and their empowerment to new patterns of life, which for them was connected with the person of Christ and the continuing activity of God as Holy Spirit. The story continues in the community's response to the life of Christ (recorded in the book of Acts, Paul's letters, and subsequent Christian literature).

Each of the major world religions has its own central stories. Hinduism, for instance, tells creation stories portraying the cosmic order as a context for human life. The most popular Hindu scripture, the Bhagavad Gita, recounts the story of Arjuna's dialogue with Krishna (in the form of a charioteer) on the eve of battle. In the course of the dialogue, the three classical patterns of Hindu religious life are set forth: the way of works (carrying out one's social duties and home rituals without excessive attachment to them); the way of knowledge (disciplined meditation seeking unity with the all-inclusive Brahman); and, finally, the way of devotion (loving devotion to a personal deity, such as the compassionate Krishna). The Gita includes examples of numinous experience (Arjuna's awe-inspiring vision of the power of the god Vishnu) and examples of mystical experience (liberation from the illusion of selfhood through the peace of participation in the Infinite, which pervades all things). These two strands come together when the personal deity, Krishna, is recognized as one of the manifestations or faces of Brahman, the impersonal Absolute.[8]

The data of religion, then, are the characteristic experiences, stories, and rituals of particular religious communities. Often the early memories of formative experiences and events are recorded in scriptures, to which members of the community respond in later generations, adding new layers of experience and ritual. Systematic concepts, beliefs, and doctrines are elaborated and reformulated to interpret these primary religious phenomena.

## II. THE ROLE OF MODELS

Within these general structures of experience and interpretation, the role of models is particularly interesting both in science and in religion.

### 1. MODELS IN SCIENCE

We have seen that in science there is no direct route by logical reasoning from data to theory. Theories arise in acts of creative imagination in which models often play a role. Here we are talking about conceptual or theoretical models, not experimental or scale models constructed in the laboratory, nor logical or mathematical models, which are abstract and purely formal relationships. Theoretical models usually take the form of imagined mechanisms or processes postulated in a new domain by analogy with familiar mechanisms or processes.

Three general characteristics may be noted in theoretical models:[9]

*1. Models are analogical.* A scientist working in a new domain may posit entities having some of the properties of a familiar entity (the positive analogy) and some properties unlike those of the familiar entity (the negative analogy). The Bohr model of the atom, in which "planetary" electrons revolve in orbits around a central nucleus, resembled the familiar solar system in some of its dynamic properties, but the key assumption that only certain orbits are allowed (quantization) had no classical analogue at all. The model aided the formulation of the mathematical equations for the theory (for example, the equations for the energy levels of the electrons). It also suggested how theoretical terms characterizing entities not directly observable might be related to observable variables (for example, how the transition of an electron between two orbits might be related to the frequency of the light emitted).

*2. Models contribute to the extension of theories.* Some claim that a model is a temporarily useful psychological aid that can be discarded once the equations of the theory are formulated. But this ignores the fact that it is often the model rather than the theory that suggests its application to new phenomena or new domains. It was the billiard ball model that suggested how the kinetic theory of gases might be applied to gas diffusion, viscosity, and heat conduction. Moreover, the model was crucial to the modification of the theory. Gases under high pressure depart significantly from Boyle's Law. This could be accounted for with a revised model (elastic spheres with finite volume and attractive forces), which departs from the simple billiard ball model, but which would not have occurred to anyone without the earlier model. The suggestiveness and open-endedness of models provide a continuing source of possible applications, extensions, and modifications of theories.

*3. Models are intelligible as units.* Models provide a mental picture whose unity can be more readily understood than that of a set of abstract equations. A model can be grasped as a whole, giving a vivid summary of complex relationships, which is useful in extending and applying the theory as well as in teaching it. Images are creative expressions of imagination in the sciences as well as in the humanities. The intuitive intelligibility of a model is, of course, no guarantee of its validity. Deductions from the theory to which the model leads must be tested carefully against the data, and more often than not the proposed model must be amended or discarded. Models are used to generate promising theories to test by the diverse criteria outlined earlier.

In the quantum theory that has replaced the Bohr model, mechanical models are given up and there are severe limitations on the use of visualizable models. Nevertheless, two basic models, the *wave model* and the *particle model,* underlie the formalisms of quantum theory and suggest ways of correlating theory and experiment. These two basic models cannot be satisfactorily unified (the wave/particle paradox), even though a unified set of equations can be provided in the abstract theory. From the theory we can predict only the probability that a measurement in the atomic or subatomic world will have a particular value; we cannot predict exact values for a measurement. The models are more than a temporary expedient, for they continue to contribute to the interpretation of the mathematical formalism and to the modification of the theory and its extension to new domains.

Some of the novel characteristics of quantum physics will be discussed in a later chapter. Here we note only that *complementary models* are used despite their problematic status. Bohr formulated the Complementarity Principle, recognizing that "a complete elucidation of one and the same object may require diverse points of view which defy a unique description."[10] He acknowledged the interaction between subject and object and the importance of the particular experimental arrangement. But he also stressed the conceptual limitations of human understanding. We must choose between causal or spatiotemporal descriptions, between wave and particle models, between accurate knowledge of momentum or of position. We have successive and incomplete perspectives that cannot be neatly unified.

Such models and theories clearly cannot be taken as literal descriptions of entities in the world, as *classical realism* assumed. At the opposite extreme, *instrumentalism* holds that models and theories are calculating devices whose only function is to allow the correlation and prediction of observations. Instrumentalism sees them as useful intellectual instruments for organizing research and for controlling the world. According to instrumentalists, models and theories do not describe or refer to real entities in the world.

I have elsewhere defended the intermediate position of *critical realism*.[11] On this view, models and theories are abstract symbol systems, which inadequately and selectively represent particular aspects of the world for specific purposes. This view preserves the scientist's realistic intent while recognizing that models and theories are imaginative human constructs. Models, on this reading, are to be taken seriously but not literally; they are neither literal pictures nor useful fictions but limited and inadequate ways of imagining what is not observable. They make tentative ontological claims that there are entities in the world something like those postulated in the models.

*Opponents of realism* argue that successive scientific theories are not convergent, cumulative, or progressive. New theories often exhibit radical changes in conceptual framework rather than refinements that preserve and add to earlier concepts. The history of science is said to be littered with theories that were successful and fruitful in their day, but that were later totally rejected rather than being modified—including Ptolemaic astronomy, phlogiston chemistry, catastrophic geology, Lamarckian evolution, caloric heat theory, and ether theories in physics.[12]

But recent years have seen a revival of interest in *realism*. Many books and articles on the subject have appeared in the last few years.[13] For example, some have pointed out that new theories exhibit *continuity* as well as discontinuity in relation to the theories they replace. Usually some of the concepts in the old theory and much of the data accumulated under its guidance are carried over into the new context. Sometimes the laws of the old theory are actually included in the new theory as limiting cases. Thus the laws of classical mechanics are limiting cases of relativistic laws at low velocities, though the fundamental concepts have been radically redefined. Later theories typically provide a better empirical fit and extend to wider domains, so that one can indeed speak of progress according to the criteria listed earlier.

We have greater confidence in *the existence of a theoretical entity,* such as the electron, if it is linked to many different kinds of phenomena explored in diverse types of experiment. With a new theory, scientists believe they have a better understanding of the structure of the world, not just a more accurate formula for correlating observations. Theoretical concepts are tentative and revisable, but they are taken to characterize and refer to the world. Unless a theory is at least partially true, how can we account for its success in predicting entirely new phenomena with types of observation radically different from those that led to the theory? Science, in short, is at the same time a process of discovery and a venture in human imagination.

The basic assumption of realism is that *existence* is prior to *theorizing.* Constraints on our theorizing arise from structures and relationships already existing in nature. Scientific discoveries are often quite unexpected. Humility before the given is appropriate; we learn from nature in order to set limits on our imagination. While the history of science exhibits no simple convergence or "successive approximation," it does include a body of well-attested theory and data, most of which can be considered trustworthy, even though any part of it is revisable. Can anyone doubt, for example, that we know more about the human body than we did five hundred years ago, even though there is still much to be known, and some of our current ideas may be rejected?

Ernan McMullin defends *a critical realist view of models,* especially those postulating hidden structures. He holds that "a good model gives us insight into real structures, and that the long term success of a theory, in most cases, gives reason to believe that something like the theoretical entities of that theory actually exist."[14] A good model, he says, is not a dispensable temporary expedient but a fruitful and open-ended source of continuing ideas for possible extensions and modifications. Like a poetic metaphor, it offers tentative suggestions for exploring a new domain. A structural model may change as research progresses, McMullin observes, but it also exhibits substantial continuity as the original model is extended. One of his examples is the model of continental drift, which proved inconsistent with geological data but which itself suggested the tectonic plate model—a model supported by more recent evidence concerning midocean rifts and earthquake zones.

Most scientists are incurably realist, but their confidence in *the status of models and theoretical entities* varies among fields and in different historical periods. Models of larger scale and more familiar types of structure tend to be viewed more realistically. A geologist is not likely to doubt the existence of tectonic plates or prehistoric dinosaurs, though neither can be directly observed. In 1866, Mendel postulated hypothetical "units of hereditary transmission," which were later identified as genes in chromosomes and more recently as long segments of DNA. As we move further from familiar objects, instruments greatly extend our powers of direct or indirect observation.

When we get to the strange *subatomic world,* common sense fails us and we cannot visualize what is going on. Quarks behave like nothing familiar to us, and their quantum numbers (arbitrarily named strangeness, charm, top, bottom, and color) specify abstract rules for the ways they combine and interact. Even here, I will propose later, our theories are an attempt to represent reality, though microreality is not like the everyday world and ordinary language is inadequate to describe it.

## 2. MODELS IN RELIGION

Religious models, we have said, lead to beliefs that correlate patterns in human experience. In particular, models of the divine are crucial in the interpretation of religious experience. They represent in images the characteristics and relationships portrayed in narrative form in stories. But models are less conceptually articulated and less systematically developed than beliefs and doctrines, which take the form of propositional statements rather than narratives or images.

Like scientific models, religious models are *analogical.* Religious language often uses imaginative metaphors, symbols, and parables, all of which express analogies. The most frequently used and systematically developed analogies are incorporated in models, such as the model of God as Father. Religious models, too, are *extensible.* A model originating in religious experience and key historical events is extended to interpret other areas of individual and communal experience, and it may be modified in the process. Religious models are also *unitary;* they are grasped as a whole with vividness and immediacy.[15]

As in the scientific case, I defend a *critical realism* that takes religious models seriously but not literally. They are neither literal descriptions of reality nor useful fictions, but human constructs that help us interpret experience by imagining what cannot be observed. The biblical prohibition of graven images or "any likeness" (Exodus 20:4) is both a rejection of idolatry and an acknowledgment that God cannot be adequately represented in visual imagery. The sense of awe and mystery associated with numinous experience is an additional safeguard against literalism. But we do not have to go to the opposite extreme and take religious models as psychologically useful fictions whose only function is to express and evoke distinctive ethical attitudes, as some instrumentalists hold.[16]

Janet Soskice has advocated a form of *critical realism* concerning models in both science and religion. In both cases, she suggests, there were originating experiences and events in which a model was first introduced, and there was a subsequent linguistic community and interpretive tradition which perpetuated it. "The sacred literature thus records the experience of the past and provides the descriptive language by which new experience may be interpreted."[17] Particular models are emphasized if they illuminate similar experiences in the later history of the community. The models supported by the experience of many generations find continued literary expression and are used in liturgy and devotional practices.

Soskice also claims that the continuity of the linguistic community guarantees *a continuity of reference* for models in both science and religion (for example, reference to "electrons" or "God"), even though the descriptive terms used are revisable and change over time. I find her portrayal of the interaction of experiences and interpretive linguistic traditions very illuminating. But I suggest that our acceptance of the referential character of religious language must rest on contemporary evaluation by the criteria outlined above, rather than on linguistic continuity. There has been a continuous interpretive tradition in astrology for several thousand years, but I do not believe that the connections it makes between the planets and human life patterns are referential. Theologians have the tasks of analysis and reformulation as well as passing on a tradition.

Frank Brown has raised some questions about the relation between *metaphoric* and *conceptual* thought in theological reflection that are relevant to the discussion of models.[18] He starts from the prominence of metaphor in scripture. Should theologians translate such metaphors into concepts and doctrines that can be systematized and analyzed? No, says Brown, because metaphors cannot be fully expressed in concepts; their implications are open-ended and contextual. Moreover, metaphors will always be valuable in enabling us to redescribe our own experience and in their power to transform our personal lives. Concepts are abstract, but metaphoric symbols are experientially rich and are thus central in ritual and worship. Brown concludes that we have to move back and forth between metaphoric and conceptual modes of thought. I suggest that models can facilitate this dialectic, since they are more fully developed than metaphors and yet they are less abstract than concepts.

Religious models have additional functions without parallel in science, especially in expressing and evoking *distinctive attitudes*. We have said that religion is a way of life with practical as well as theoretical goals. The life-orienting and emotional power of religious models and their ability to affect value commitments should not be ignored. Models are crucial in the *personal transformation and reorientation* sought in most religious traditions. Some linguistic analysts and instrumentalists hold that religious language has only these noncognitive functions. I argue, in reply, that such noncognitive functions cannot stand alone because they presuppose *cognitive beliefs*. Religious traditions do endorse particular attitudes and ways of life, but they also make claims about reality.[19]

In science, models are always ancillary to theories. In religion, however, the models themselves are as important as conceptual beliefs, partly because of their close association with the *stories* prominent in religious life. Christian worship is based on those stories of creation, the covenant, and especially the life of Christ. The individual participates in communal ritual and liturgy that reenact and refer to portions of these stories. Narratives in dramatic form are more personally involving and evocative than models, which are relatively static, though models are less abstract than concepts. Moreover, biblical stories can often be correlated with our own life stories, which are also narrative in form. Nevertheless, the movement from stories to models to concepts and beliefs is a necessary part of the theological task of critical reflection.

## 3. PERSONAL AND IMPERSONAL MODELS

The atomic and subatomic world cannot be directly observed, and its behavior suggests that it is very unlike the world of everyday objects. We have seen that it cannot be represented by any single model, but it can be partially understood through theories formulated with *complementary models*, such as wave and particle. In religion, too, we are dealing with a reality that cannot be directly observed and that is beyond our capacity to visualize. Here, too, we can admit our conceptual limitations and accept the role of complementary models.

Ninian Smart has traced among world religions the two basic types of religious experience described in the previous section: *numinous encounter* and *mystical union*. The first received its classic description in Rudolf Otto's *Idea of the Holy*. Its characteristics are a sense of awe and reverence, mystery and wonder, holiness and sacredness. Typical examples are Isaiah's vision in the temple, the call of Paul or Muhammad, or the theophany of Krishna to Arjuna in the Bhagavad Gita. Human responses to experiencing the numinous include worship, humility, and obedience.[20]

Smart shows that numinous experience is usually interpreted in *personal models*. Worshipers think of God as distinct and separate from themselves. The overwhelming character of the experience suggests an exalted view of the divine and an emphasis on transcendence, with a corresponding human self-abasement and recognition of finitude or sinfulness. The sense of being grasped and laid hold of unexpectedly seems to point to a divine initiative independent of human control. The gulf between God and humanity may seem to be so great that it can be bridged only by revelation from God's side or by a divine savior. Winston King speaks of "the gap between worshiping man and the worshiped Ultimate," and he describes its symbolization in the rituals of personalistic theism, such as sacrifice, prayer, and devotional liturgy and practice.[21]

The second type of experience is *mystical union*, which does seem to have common features in different cultures, despite their diversity. Among these, we have seen, are intensity, immediacy, unitary consciousness, unexpectedness, joy, and serenity. The realization of unity can lead to liberation from self-centeredness. All dichotomies (human/divine, subject/object, time/eternity) seem to be overcome in identity with the One beyond time and space. Mysticism

is expressed in meditation, contemplation, and an inner quest for enlightenment, rather than in communal worship or ritual.

The mystic is cautious in the use of models and may say that the object of
the experience cannot be described. The *via negativa* asserts only what the
divine is not. But the writings of mystics do make extensive use of analogies
and models. Sometimes union with the divine is said to be like the most
intense union of two lovers. In other cases, ultimate reality is thought of as a
Self identical in essence with the individual self, or a world Soul with which
one's own soul is merged. More often mystical experience is interpreted with
*impersonal models*. The self is absorbed in the pantheistic All, the impersonal
Absolute, or the divine Ground. The distinction between subject and object
is overcome in an all-embracing unity beyond all personal forms. The self
loses its individuality "as a raindrop loses its separate identity in the ocean."

Smart demonstrates that although Western traditions have been predominantly numinous and Eastern traditions predominantly mystical, all the major
world religions have included *both types of experience* and *both types of models*.[22]
Judaism, Christianity, and Islam all have influential mystical writings, along
with more common patterns of worship of the holy as personal; in these writings, the gap between God and humanity is narrowed, but it is never obliterated in total identity. Early Buddhism followed more mystical meditative
disciplines, but Mahayana Buddhism includes the numinous strand in the
worship of the Eternal Buddha and the Bodhisattvas (especially in Amida
Buddhism). In Hinduism, the *bhakti* path of devotion to personal deities has
accompanied the *jnana* path of meditation, unitive awareness, and an impersonal Absolute. Ramanuja developed the more personal side of Hinduism,
whereas Shankara developed the more impersonal side. Modern followers of
the *jnana* path say that their view should be called nondualism rather than
monism, since ultimate reality cannot be described in positive terms.

It seems to me appropriate, then, to speak of personal and impersonal
religious models as *complementary*. People who use personal models are often
the first to insist that they are inadequate and that God is not literally a person. Sometimes it is said that God is *more* than a person, and the more is usually spelled out in predominantly impersonal terms (divine Ground, creative
power, and so forth). And those who rely mainly on impersonal models may
speak of love and grace, or they may hold that the impersonal Absolute is
approached through devotion to its personal manifestations. All models are
partial and inadequate representations of what is beyond our ordinary categories of thought. Religious models often are analogies of relationships rather
than attributes of the divine in isolation. Moreover, differing human tem-
peraments may be more congenial to some patterns of experience and some
kinds of models than to others.

The *relative priority* of personal and impersonal models is not, of course, a
minor matter. Only with a personal God can there be decisive divine initiative. The ontological and epistemological distance between the divine and
the human is a correlate of ideas of historical revelation, grace, and redemp-

tion. Western traditions have found more room for human individuality (which in extreme forms becomes individualism) and social activism, whereas the oriental quest for inner peace has more often led to quietism, though often accompanied by exemplary compassion and respect for all forms of life.

Because a model functions within a total network of ideas and attitudes, I do *not* suggest that the Hindu Brahman and the Christian God, or other models from *different* religious traditions, be considered complementary. But we could consider the use of personal and impersonal models *within* one paradigm community as *complementary,* paralleling the use of wave and particle models within quantum physics. Nevertheless, recognizing the diversity of models in our own tradition might help us appreciate the models of other traditions, which would be an important contribution in a religiously pluralistic world. Complementarity encourages us to view models neither as literal pictures nor as useful fictions, but as partial symbolic representations of what cannot be directly observed.

## 4. CHRISTIAN MODELS

The writings of the theologian Sallie McFague provide a good example of the exploration of models in Christian thought. In *Metaphorical Theology* she starts from Paul Ricoeur's insights on the importance of *metaphor* in religious language. A metaphor asserts similarity but it denies identity. In a metaphor, one term "both is and is not" like its analogue. Recognition of the limitations of religious language prevents idolatry of any one formulation, which is the temptation of literalism.[23]

McFague then discusses *models* in science and religion, drawing extensively on my earlier writing on this topic. She considers a model to be a systematic and relatively permanent metaphor. A model is more emotionally rich and less abstract than a concept, but it is more precise than a metaphor. Religious models arise from human experience, especially the experience of healing, renewal, and reorientation of patterns of life. Models order our experience, and their implications are systematically developed in doctrines. Whereas Ricoeur says that the purpose of theological interpretation is to return us to experience, McFague gives more emphasis to conceptual clarity and comprehensive ordering. Against naive realism on the one hand and instrumentalism on the other, she defends critical realism in both science and religion. Models are tentative, partial, open-ended, and paradigm-dependent. The dominant paradigm of a tradition sets limits on acceptable models.

McFague defends the use of *a multiplicity of models* within a paradigm community—a greater multiplicity than is typical of science. Such multiplicity guards against the temptations of idolatry, absolutism, and literalism, which appear when one model is dominant. Multiplicity is also appropriate because in both science and religion we are modeling relationships, patterns, and processes rather than separate entities or things-in-themselves. Religious models are analogies for our experience of relating to God, which takes a variety of forms that are not mutually exclusive. God can be related to us in both a fatherly and a motherly way—and a rich diversity of other ways.

In her more recent book, *Models of God*, McFague discusses *criteria* for evaluating Christian models. She mentions general criteria such as comprehensiveness, internal consistency, and potential for dealing with anomalies. Another criterion is continuity with earlier expressions of the Christian paradigm. Scripture is important as the earliest witness to the experience of the transforming power of God and the earliest interpretations of the life and death of Christ as the transformative event. Moral fruitfulness serves as an additional criterion, and she gives special attention to relevance for the crises of "an ecological and nuclear age."[24] As she turns to specific models, McFague criticizes the *monarchical model*, which has been dominant historically. God as King or Ruler is related to the world externally, not intrinsically. Here God controls by domination, acting on the world rather than through it, which undermines human responsibility. McFague's first proposed alternative is to consider *the world as God's body*. This goes to the opposite extreme in stressing immanence rather than transcendence. It suggests that the language of scientific laws and the language of divine intentions may be alternative ways of describing cosmic history.

The second half of her book examines in detail three personal models: God as *Mother, Lover,* and *Friend*. Each represents not the power of domination but the power of love in a particular form, described classically as *agape, eros,* and *philia,* respectively. The three models express in turn God's activity as Creator, Savior, and Sustainer, and together they illuminate many of the themes of traditional theology. Thus God as *Mother* can draw on the experiences of the mystery of human birth and the nurturing of life. The model suggests an ethic of care and of justice. A mother's concern for present and future life can be broadened to "universal parenthood," which includes care not only for the needs of present and future human generations but for the life of other species.

Similarly, the model of God as *Friend* points to a reciprocal mutual bond and also to a common vision that demands our action as coworkers. God suffers with us and works with us to extend the inclusive, holistic, and nonhierarchical vision of the fulfillment of all beings. I find these models very helpful in thinking about God's relation to humanity and humanity's relation to nature, but they seem less helpful in thinking about God's relation to nature. McFague indicates at several points that she is sympathetic to process theology, but she does not explore the ways in which a process metaphysics might facilitate the conceptual articulation of the relationships suggested by the models. We will consider these and other specific Christian models in chapter 12.

## III. THE ROLE OF PARADIGMS

In addition to parallels in the structures of scientific and religious inquiry, and in the role of imaginative models, there are some interesting similarities in the role of paradigms in the two fields. There are also, of course, some important differences that must be explored. We will look successively at paradigms in science, in religion in general, and then in Christian thought.

## 1. PARADIGMS IN SCIENCE

Thomas Kuhn defined *paradigms* as "standard examples of scientific work that embody a set of conceptual and methodological assumptions." In the postscript to the second edition of his book he distinguished several features that he had previously treated together: a research tradition, the key historical examples through which the tradition is transmitted, and the metaphysical assumptions implicit in the fundamental concepts of the tradition. The key examples, such as Newton's work in mechanics, implicitly define for subsequent scientists the type of explanations that should be sought. They mold assumptions as to what kinds of entity there are in the world, what methods of inquiry are suitable for studying them, and what counts as data. A paradigm provides an ongoing research community with a framework for "normal science." Science education is an initiation into the habits of thought presented in standards texts and into the practices of established scientists.

Kuhn describes a major paradigm shift as a *scientific revolution*. A growing list of anomalies and *ad hoc* modifications within an existing paradigm produces a sense of crisis. Instead of simply acquiring further data or modifying theories within the existing framework, some scientists look for a new framework, which may involve a questioning of fundamental assumptions. Within the new paradigm, new kinds of data are relevant and the old data are reinterpreted and seen in a new way. The choice between the new and the old is not made by the normal criteria of research, Kuhn maintains. Adherents of rival paradigms will try to persuade each other. "Though each may hope to convert the other to his way of seeing his science and its problems, neither may hope to prove his case."[25] Kuhn analyzes several historical "revolutions" in some detail. For example, he describes the radical change in concepts and assumptions that occurred when quantum physics and relativity replaced classical physics. Three features of Kuhn's account are of particular interest.[26]

*1. All data are paradigm-dependent.* We noted earlier that there is no observation-language independent of theoretical assumptions. All data are theory-laden, and theories are paradigm-laden. The features of the world considered most important within one paradigm may be incidental in another. Kuhn claimed initially that paradigms are "incommensurable" (that is, they cannot be directly compared with each other). However, his later writings acknowledged that usually a core of observation statements exists on which the protagonists of rival paradigms can agree, a level of description that they can share. These common data are not free of theoretical assumptions, but some assumptions can be shared even by adherents of rival paradigms. If data were totally paradigm-dependent, they would be irrelevant to the choice of paradigms, which has not been the case historically.

2. *Paradigms are resistant to falsification.* Comprehensive theories, and the even broader paradigms in which they are embedded, are very difficult to overthrow. Discordant data, as we have seen, can usually be reconciled by modifying auxiliary assumptions or introducing special *ad hoc* hypotheses, or they can be set aside as unexplained anomalies. Paradigms are not rejected because there is contradictory evidence; they are replaced when there is a more promising alternative. Research can proceed when the theories of a paradigm do not fit all the data, but systematic research cannot proceed in the absence of a paradigm. Commitment to a research tradition and tenacity in developing its potentialities and extending its scope are scientifically fruitful. But observations do exert some control over a paradigm, and an accumulation of *ad hoc* hypotheses and unexplained anomalies can undermine confidence in it. Without persistent concern for fidelity to the data, science would be an arbitrary and subjective human construction.

3. *There are no rules for paradigm choice.* A paradigm change is a revolution, achieved more by "persuasion" and "conversion" than by logical argument. Kuhn initially maintained that criteria for choice are themselves paradigm-dependent. In response to his critics, he said that the decision to choose a certain paradigm is not arbitrary or irrational, since reasons can be given for the choice. He acknowledged that there are values common to all scientists and shared criteria of simplicity, coherence, and supporting evidence; but the way the criteria are applied and their relative weight are matters of personal judgment, not rules to be followed. The decision is like that of a judge weighing evidence in a difficult case, not like a computer performing a calculation. There is no court of appeal higher than the judgment of the scientific community itself. The presence of shared values and criteria allows communication and facilitates the eventual emergence of scientific consensus.[27] Kuhn thus qualified his more extreme claims.

In recent decades there has emerged what Harold Brown calls "the new philosophy of science." Brown describes the move from empiricism to a more historical view of science as itself a paradigm shift in the philosophy of science. He describes the contributions of Toulmin, Polanyi, and others, along with Kuhn, in the emergence of this new view that draws heavily on the history of science. Brown gives this summary:

Our central theme has been that it is ongoing research, rather than established results, that constitutes the life blood of science. Science consists of a sequence of research projects, structured by accepted presuppositions which determine what observations are to be made, how they are to be intepreted, what phenomena are problematic, and how these problems are to be dealt with.[28]

Brown gives examples of "normal science," in which work was conducted within an accepted framework, and he describes several scientific revolutions that involved alternative presuppositions and "fundamental changes in the way we think about reality." But he maintains that a revolution shows continuity as well as discontinuity:

For the most part, old concepts are retained in altered form, and old observations are retained with new meanings. The continuity provides the basis for rational debate between alternative fundamental theories. . . . Thus the thesis that a scientific revolution requires a restructuring experience akin to a gestalt shift is compatible with the continuity of science and the rationality of scientific debate.[29]

Brown takes up the charge that the new view makes science appear subjective, irrational, and historically relative. To be sure, science does not fulfill the empiricists' definition of objectivity as reliance on strict empirical verification or falsification, nor its definition of rationality as the application of impersonal rules. But science does conform to more appropriate definitions of objectivity and rationality. Objectivity should be identified with intersubjective testability and informed judgment in the community of qualified scientists. It is rational to accept a paradigm if it solves important problems and provides a guide to further research. Brown holds that "crucial decisions as to how a conflict between theory and observation is to be resolved, or how a proposed new theory is to be evaluated, are not made by the application of mechanical rules, but by reasoned judgments on the part of scientists and through debate within the scientific community."[30]

We can summarize our conclusions about scientific paradigms in three sentences. The first half of each sentence represents a *subjective and historically relative* feature of science that was neglected in the earlier empiricist accounts. The second half of each sentence represents a reformulation of the *objective, empirical, and rational* features of science that prevent it from being arbitrary or purely subjective:

1. All data are paradigm-dependent, but there are data on which adherents of rival paradigms can agree.
2. Paradigms are resistant to falsification by data, but data does cumulatively affect the acceptability of a paradigm.
3. There are no rules for paradigm choice, but there are shared criteria for judgment in evaluating paradigms.

Compared to empiricist accounts, then, Kuhn gives a much larger role to historical and cultural factors. He insists that a theory is judged within a network of theories and against a background of assumptions, in terms of its success in solving problems in a particular historical context. Kuhn is a contextualist, in contrast to the earlier formalists, but I do not think that this makes him a subjectivist or an unqualified relativist, for in his view the data do provide empirical constraints, and the presence of shared criteria does represent a defensible form of rationality.

## 2. PARADIGMS IN RELIGION

As in the scientific case, a religious tradition transmits a broad set of metaphysical and methodological assumptions that we can call a paradigm. As in science, traditions in religion are passed on by particular communities, partly through respected historical texts and key examples. Here, too, new members enter a tradition by being initiated into the assumptions and practices of the community, and they normally work within its accepted framework of thought, which we can call "normal religion," corresponding to "normal science."

As in science, normal criteria are difficult to apply to major historical "revolutions" or to the choice between competing paradigms. Let us focus first on the relation of paradigm choice to religious experience, returning later to the role of story and ritual and their transmission through scriptures. Each of the three subjective and historically relative features of scientific paradigms listed above is even more evident in the case of religion. Each of the corresponding objective, empirical, and rational features of religion is more problematic.

1. *Religious experience is paradigm-dependent.* But are some experiences common to the adherents of rival paradigms? Religious experience seems to be so strongly molded by the believer's interpretive framework that a skeptic might claim that the experience is entirely the product of prior expectations. Religious experiences are not as publicly accessible as scientific data are, even though both are theory-laden. Yet there are common features of experience within a religious community that exert some control on the subjectivity of individual beliefs. And there do seem to be some characteristics of religious experience in diverse traditions that point beyond cultural relativism, and that make communication between traditions possible.

2. *Religious paradigms are highly resistant to falsification.* But does cumulative experience influence paradigm choice at all? Discordant data, we have said, does not lead directly to the overthrow of a paradigm. Instead, *ad hoc* modifications are introduced, or the data are set aside as an anomaly. Yet people may eventually modify or abandon their most fundamental religious beliefs in the light of their experience, especially if they see a promising alternative interpretive framework.

3. *There are no rules for paradigm choice in religion.* But are there shared criteria for evaluating religious paradigms? Some criteria were proposed above for evaluating beliefs *within* a dominant paradigm. Can these be applied to the choice *between* paradigms? Are the criteria themselves totally paradigm-dependent? I will suggest that there are indeed criteria transcending paradigm communities, though their application is a matter of individual judgment in more problematic ways than in the case of science.

Frederick Streng maintains that the idea of paradigms is applicable to Christianity but not to Buddhism. He says that the center of any religious tradition is the experience of *personal transformation and reorientation.* Religion is above all a "strategy for living." Religious conversion is a change in awareness and in mode of living. Streng holds that discussion of paradigms makes us look at systems of belief and doctrine, which are indeed important in Christianity. But Buddhism is more concerned about the transformation of consciousness to a less ego-centered awareness, and it urges nonattachment to doctrinal expressions and changing intellectual forms. It offers spiritual practices to achieve enlightened consciousness and to release us from the attachments that cause our suffering.[31] In reply I would point out that Buddhism includes a network of characteristic *concepts and beliefs*, including the doctrine of "no-self," which imply ontological claims as well as existential commitments. Moreover, major historic changes have taken place in Buddhist thought as well as practice, such as the emergence of Mahayana from Theravada Buddhism. Buddhism may urge nonattachment to doctrinal forms, but it does not seem to have dismissed them entirely.

## 3. PARADIGMS IN CHRISTIANITY

Hans Küng has applied the concept of *paradigm change* to the history of Christian thought. He cites five major historical paradigms: Greek Alexandrian, Latin Augustinian, Medieval Thomistic, Reformation, and Modern-Critical. Each paradigm provided a framework for normal work and cumulative growth (comparable to "normal science"), in which the scope of the paradigm was extended and major changes were resisted. As in the scientific case, Küng shows, each new paradigm arose in a period of crisis and uncertainty—for example, the challenge of gnosticism in the Hellenistic world, or the rise of science and biblical criticism in the modern period. In each case, conversion to the new paradigm involved subjective factors and personal decisions as well as rational argument. These paradigm shifts involved both continuity and discontinuity.[32]

Küng brings out some *distinctive features* of paradigm shifts in Christian thought as compared to those in science. The centrality of the scriptural witness to Christ is without parallel in science. "The biblical message," not scripture itself, is the enduring norm. Each new paradigm arose from a fresh experience of the original message, as well as from institutional crises and external challenges. The gospel thus contributed to both continuity and change. Moreover, there is always a personal dimension to the decision of faith, along with the more intellectual task of showing that a new paradigm is both responsive to the Christian message and relevant to the present world of experience and contemporary knowledge. Küng says that we can acknowledge the distinctive features of religion and yet find the comparison with scientific paradigms helpful in understanding processes of change in the history of a religious tradition. In a similar vein, Stephan Pfürtner shows that it is illuminating to consider Luther's idea of *justification by faith* as a new paradigm. It led to the reconstruction of prior beliefs and the reinterpretation of previous data in a new framework of thought.[33]

This leads me to ask: How large a group is a *paradigm community*, and how does one determine its boundaries? When should one consider a historical change to be an evolutionary modification within a paradigm, and when should one consider it a revolutionary paradigm shift? Thomas Kuhn's earlier writing reserved the term *scientific revolution* for the rare instances when a sweeping change took place in a whole network of assumptions and concepts. Critics felt that he had drawn too sharp a line between normal science and revolutionary science, leaving out changes of intermediate scale. Kuhn's later writing referred to more modest "micro-revolutions" and said that a paradigm community could be as small as twenty-five persons in a subdiscipline.

In religion, too, there are communities and subcommunities, and there are large and small historical changes. I suggest that the concept of paradigm shift is most helpful in understanding historical change if we use the term for relatively rare *comprehensive conceptual changes*. Clearly, the emergence of early Christianity from Judaism represents such a paradigm shift, for despite the continuities, people experienced far-reaching discontinuities in belief and practice. By the time of Paul's letters, it was evident that Christianity could not be a sect within Judaism or a movement to reform Judaism, and individuals had to choose one paradigm community or the other, focusing on either Christ or the Torah. The discontinuities in the Protestant Reformation were perhaps not as radical, but major changes took place in doctrine and practice as well as in institutional organization.

Would it be illuminating to consider all of Christianity as one paradigm and refer to "the Christian paradigm"? One could then speak of a "paradigm shift" when an individual converted to another religious tradition (or atheism) and joined another paradigm community. The parallels with science would be stretched, for there seem to be few shared data or criteria common to diverse traditions, to which appeal could be made in giving reasons for choice among them. Should we seek such shared data and criteria in a global age, or can the assessment of beliefs be carried out only within a well-defined religious tradition? We will return to the problem of religious pluralism in the next chapter.

## IV. TENTATIVENESS AND COMMITMENT

In the popular stereotype, the scientist's theories are tentative hypotheses that are continually criticized and revised, while religious beliefs are unchanging dogmas that the faithful accept without question. The scientist is seen as open-minded, the theologian as closed-minded. Is not faith a matter of unconditional commitment? Are not Christian beliefs attributed to divine revelation rather than human discovery? Have we perhaps lost sight of the distinctive features of religious faith by tracing some limited parallels with science?

### 1. TRADITION AND CRITICISM

Let us ask first how the scientific and religious communities each balance the importance of an ongoing tradition against the value of criticism and change. When major historical changes take place, does continuity or discontinuity predominate?

Whereas Popper identifies rationality and objectivity in science with adherence to explicit rules, Kuhn maintains that the locus of authority is the scientific community itself. Decisions rest on *the informed judgment of the community*. Shared values and criteria underlie such judgment, but the application and weighting of the criteria are not governed by logic or rules. Kuhn claims that authoritative tradition transmitted by the dominant paradigm provides the framework for thought and action in "normal science." This is a historical and social view of the process of inquiry in which the ongoing community is emphasized.[34]

As there is no private science, so also there is no private religion. In both cases, the initiate joins *a particular community* and adopts its modes of thought and action. Even the comtemplative mystic is influenced by the tradition in which he or she has lived. Paradigms in religion, as in science, are acquired by example and practice, not by following formal rules. Individual insights are tested against the experience of others, as well as in one's own life. Here, too, the historical and social context affects all modes of thought and action.

Kuhn pictures *normal science* as conservative and controlled by *tradition*. Working within the prevailing paradigm is an efficient way of solving the distinctive problems it raises. Exploring its potentialities and extending its range provide a focus for research. Within that tradition, a person benefits from the work of others, and there is cumulative progress. According to Kuhn, paradigm shifts are relatively rare and occur only when an accumulation of anomalies has produced a real crisis. One cannot speak of progress across the transitions; Kuhn describes paradigm changes in the political metaphor of revolution, which emphasizes discontinuity and the overthrow of the established order.

Kuhn's critics reply that even in *scientific revolutions* the old data are preserved (though reinterpreted) and the new concepts and theories can be related to the old (though displacing them). Moreover, shared values and criteria of judgment persist across the change. Most scientists are familiar with other scientific disciplines and subfields, which provide continuity when their own area of specialization is in transition. A scientist has a higher loyalty to the wider scientific community and its values, which goes beyond loyalty to a particular paradigm. The critics urge us to view science as evolutionary and subject to *continual reformation*, rather than as bound by tradition except during revolutions. Nevertheless, historical studies have tended to support the view that theories are not evaluated separately but as part of networks of assumptions which sometimes change together rather radically.[35]

*Normal theology* does indeed show the dominance of *tradition*. The theologian is concerned to develop the potentialities of a particular paradigm. This provides focus and encourages communication and cumulation. But the process can include considerable reinterpretation, reformulation, and innovation. Scripture is unchanging, but ways of understanding and appropriating it have changed greatly, especially since the rise of historical-critical methods. Theology, we have said, is critical reflection on the life and thought of the religious community, and this implies the revisability of ideas. The Protestant Reformation was not a once-for-all revolution, but rather a vision of a church that is *semper reformanda,* always reforming. Cardinal Newman defended the development of ideas and the evolution of doctrine within the basic continuity of the Catholic tradition.[36]

*Theological revolutions,* such as the Protestant Reformation, or the emergence of Mahayana from Theravada Buddhism, do involve extensive and fundamental changes. Yet here, too, there are impressive continuities amid the discontinuities. There is a common loyalty to the founding leader, common scriptures, and a shared early history. In an ecumenical age, Catholic and Protestant thinkers read each others' writings and affect each other, as do Buddhists of diverse schools. Feminist theologians criticize the gender biases of Christian thought and propose major reconstruction of traditional doctrines, yet in most cases they affirm a large portion of a common heritage. The theologian, however, does not seem to have a loyalty to an overarching and universal religious community, with shared criteria and values comparable to those shared by all scientists. In a global age, could such wider loyalties be encouraged, without undermining the distinctiveness of each religious tradition?

## 2. CENTRAL AND PERIPHERAL BELIEFS

Popper maintains that scientific theories are held with great tentativeness and that basic assumptions should be continually questioned and criticized. Kuhn, by contrast, says that there is normally great tenacity in commitment to a prevailing paradigm, which is questioned only in rare times of crisis. Imre Lakatos proposes an intermediate position in which there is commitment to a *"hard core"* of central ideas that are preserved by making adjustments in a "protective belt" of more tentative *auxiliary hypotheses.* In place of competing individual theories (Popper) or successive paradigms (Kuhn), Lakatos pictures research programs, which sometimes compete over a protracted period of time. He does not accept the formal criteria for the acceptability of theories proposed by Popper, but he offers more definite and rational criteria than Kuhn acknowledges.

Lakatos maintains that a *research program* is constituted by a hard core of ideas that is deliberately exempted from falsification so that its positive potentialities can be systematically developed and explored. Anomalies are accommodated by changes in the auxiliary hypotheses, which can be sacrificed if necessary. This strategy calls for commitment in sticking with central ideas, without being distracted from them, as long as the program is "progressive" in predicting "novel facts" (which may refer to new phenomena or to already known facts not previously related to the program). A program should be abandoned when it is stalled and not growing for a considerable period and when there is a promising alternative. The old program is not falsified but rather is displaced as a research strategy. Lakatos believes his scheme *describes* the best scientific practice and *prescribes* how scientific programs should be evaluated, namely by comparing their progress as strategies for research over a period of time.[37]

We can apply Lakatos's analysis to religious communities, which also make a *central core* of ideas immune to falsification and protect them by adjusting *peripheral beliefs.* Commitment to a core program allows it to be systematically explored without continual distraction. Rival programs may compete over long periods. The component beliefs are not verified or falsified separately in isolation; they are parts of an ongoing program that can be compared to other programs. Here progress is presumably not judged by the power to predict totally new phenomena, but by the ability to account for known data not previously considered. When anomalies arise—from historical events, from new experience, or perhaps from new discoveries in science—adjustment would be made in auxiliary hypotheses before core beliefs were abandoned.[38]

Ancient Israel held a central belief in the existence of a God of power and justice. An important but less central assumption was that God punishes wrongdoers. I suggest that we could see efforts to deal with the anomaly of *undeserved suffering* as attempts to preserve the central core by modifying auxiliary hypotheses. In the book of Job, the protagonist is told by his friends that he must have sinned in secret to deserve such suffering. But Job maintains both his innocence and the existence of God, at the cost of the hypothesis that all suffering is deserved. Israel faced the same anomaly on a national scale in its long exile in Babylon. Some people saw the exile as God's punishment for Israel's failure to observe the Torah rigorously, and they counseled stricter observance. Others developed new ways of understanding God's action in history, which allowed for undeserved suffering (including the vicarious suffering or suffering servant motif in Isaiah 53 and elsewhere). But even the latter "auxiliary hypothesis" is put in question by the magnitude of evil and suffering in the Nazi Holocaust. For some people this historical event required reformulation of concepts of God's power. For a few it led to abandoning theism itself. The Holocaust is an anomaly that is only partly resolved within the traditional beliefs of both the Jewish and Christian communities.

Nancey Murphy proposes using Lakatos's methodology in Christian theology. The primary data would be the practices of the Christian community, including its devotional experience and its use of scripture. The idea of a plurality of competing *theological research programs* can both illuminate past history and offer a possible pattern for current theological inquiry. As one example, Murphy traces three forms of the doctrine of atonement, in which Christ's death is understood as a victory over the forces of evil or as a satisfaction of God's justice or as a demonstration of God's love. The first program was largely replaced by the other two historically, but it could be revived today with a new auxiliary hypothesis in which the forces of evil are reinterpreted in social and political terms.[39]

How broad a set of ideas should be thought of as *a theological program*? An interpretation of a single doctrine, such as one view of the atonement, is perhaps too limited to consider as a "core belief" to which enduring commitment is given. Perhaps a school of Christian thought, such as neo-orthodoxy, Thomism, or process theology, can fruitfully be portrayed as a program. Alternatively, in the context of religious pluralism, one might think of

Christianity as a program whose core is belief in a personal God and the centrality of Jesus Christ—with all other beliefs as auxiliary hypotheses that can be modified to maintain that core. Gary Gutting goes even further in proposing that belief in the existence of a personal God constitutes the Lakatos core to which decisive assent should be given, but this seems to me too broad to define an identifiable religious community.[40] I will suggest in chapter 12 that *process theology* can be viewed as a theological program in which the "hard core" of the Christian tradition is taken to be belief in God as creative love, revealed in Christ, while divine omnipotence is treated as an "auxiliary hypothesis" that can be modified to allow for the data of human freedom, evil and suffering, and evolutionary history.

Lakatos's *programs*, then, are very similar to Kuhn's *paradigms*, but they offer two advantages as ways of analyzing both science and religion. First, they allow one to distinguish between the central core to which a group is committed and the peripheral beliefs that are more readily modified or abandoned—though Lakatos recognizes that the distinction is not absolute and can change historically. Second, rival programs can coexist during protracted periods, allowing for greater pluralism. We are to look at the fruitfulness of a program in a community over a period of time, rather than evaluating a fixed set of ideas at any moment in abstraction from the ongoing life of the community.

## 3. REVELATION, FAITH, AND REASON

Even if peripheral beliefs are tentative and revisable, are not the core beliefs of a religious community held with absolute and unconditional commitment? Job may have given up the idea that suffering is always deserved, but his basic faith in God was unshaken. No evidence could count against it: "Though he slay me, yet will I trust in him" (Job 13:15 KJV). St. Paul was confident that "neither death nor life. . . . nor anything else in all creation will be able to separate us from the love of God which is in Christ Jesus our Lord" (Rom. 8:39). In chapter 4 we noted the existentialist thesis that faith is a matter of passionate personal commitment and decision, far removed from the dispassionate weighing of hypotheses. We also referred to the neo-orthodox theme that faith's confidence rests on revelation, which was the result of divine initiative rather than of human discovery. Can our account do justice to the importance of faith and revelation in the Christian tradition?

Basil Mitchell contrasts the *tentative hypotheses* of science with *unconditional commitment* in religion. But he goes on to qualify the contrast from both sides. He describes the tenacity of a scientist's commitment to a Kuhnian paradigm. He also insists that ultimate religious commitment is to God and not to Christianity or any other system of belief. And here the cumulative weight of evidence should be decisive. All religious ideas are open to revision, according to Mitchell. There must be grounds for accepting a claim of divine revelation in history, even if revelation shows us possibilities that we could not have anticipated. Mitchell says that knowledge of God in religious experience is also not self-authenticating, for there is no uninterpreted experience, and any particular interpretation involves claims that must be judged more plausible than the alternatives. There is thus a continuing dialectic between commitment and reflection, or between faith and reason.[41]

In the biblical view, *faith* is personal trust, confidence, and loyalty. Like faith in a friend or faith in a doctor, it is not "blind faith," for it is closely tied to experience. But it does entail risk and vulnerability in the absence of logical proof. If faith were the acceptance of revealed propositions it would be incompatible with doubt. But if faith means trust and loyalty, it is compatible with considerable doubt about particular beliefs. Doubt frees us from illusions of having captured God in a creed. It calls into question every religious symbol. Self-criticism is called for if we acknowledge that no church, book, or creed is infallible and no formulation is irrevocable. The claim to finality by any historical institution or theological system must be questioned if we are to avoid absolutizing the relative.

Religious faith does demand a more total *personal involvement* than occurs in science, as the existentialists maintain. Religious questions are of ultimate concern, since the meaning of one's existence is at stake. Religion asks about the final objects of a person's devotion and loyalty. Too detached an attitude may cut a person off from the very kinds of experience that are religiously most significant. But such religious commitment can be combined with critical reflection. Commitment without inquiry tends toward fanaticism or narrow dogmatism. Reflection alone without commitment tends to become trivial speculation unrelated to real life. Perhaps personal involvement must alternate with reflection, since worship and critical inquiry do not occur simultaneously.

*Divine revelation* and *human response* are always inextricably interwoven. Revelation is incomplete until it has been received by individuals, and individuals always live within interpretive communities. The God-given encounter was experienced, interpreted, and reported by fallible human beings. In the history of Israel, crucial events were revelatory only when interpreted in the light of the prophet's experience of God. God acts in the lives of individuals and communities, especially in the life of Christ, we have said, but the records of these events reflect particular personal and cultural perspectives. There is no uninterpreted revelation.

Moreover, revelation is recognized by its ability to illuminate *present experience*. Revelation helps us to understand our lives as individuals and as a community today.[42] Special events in the past enable us to see what is present at other times but may have been ignored. The cross reveals God's universal love, everywhere expressed but not everywhere acknowledged. The power of reconciliation in Christ's life is the power of reconciliation in all life.[43] Revelation leads to a new relation to God in the present; thus it is inseparable from reorientation and reconciliation. It is not a system of divine propositions completed in the past but an invitation to new experience of God today. So revelation and experience, like faith and reason, are not mutually exclusive.

To sum up, there are many *parallels* between science and religion: the interaction of data and theory (or experience and interpretation); the historical character of the interpretive community; the use of models; and the influence of paradigms. In both fields there are no proofs, but there can be good reasons for the judgments rendered by the paradigm community. There are also important *differences* between science and religion, but some of them turn out to be differences in emphasis or degree rather than the absolute contrasts sometimes imagined. We have traced a number of polarities in which the first term was more prominent in science and the second in religion: objectivity and subjectivity; rationality and personal judgment; universality and historical conditioning; criticism and tradition; and tentativeness and commitment. But some features of religion seem to be *without parallel* in science: the role of story and ritual; the noncognitive functions of religious models in evoking attitudes and encouraging personal transformation; the type of personal involvement characteristic of religious faith; and the idea of revelation in historical events. Some additional comparisons are explored in the next chapter before we draw overall conclusions.

## CHAPTER 6

# Similarities and Differences

The general structure of science has been described in terms of data, theory, models, and paradigms. A number of parallels in religion were proposed. We can now pursue some additional comparisons. There are indeed striking similarities, but also significant differences, and both need discussion if we are to represent these two areas of human life fairly. We first examine the character of historical inquiry, since nature has a history, and so do religious communities. The second section asks whether objectivity is possible if it is recognized that all knowledge is historically and culturally conditioned; the contribution of feminist thinkers is especially significant here. The third section responds to the challenge of religious pluralism by exploring a path between absolutism and relativism. These three sections address differing though related issues; they may be read selectively in accordance with the reader's interests. The chapter closes with a summary and discussion of the conclusions of part 2.

## I. HISTORY IN SCIENCE AND RELIGION

A brief examination of the nature of historical inquiry can contribute to the comparison of the methods of science and religion. History is usually grouped in the curriculum with the humanities rather than with the social sciences because it deals with the unrepeatable ideas and actions of human agents. But there is today a new recognition of the importance of history in science. Nature is understood in historical and evolutionary terms, and science itself is acknowledged to be a historical and culturally conditioned enterprise. In addition, religious stories are related to particular events in history, and so we need to look at the relationships between story and history in religious thought.

### 1. HISTORICAL EXPLANATION

How might one compare historical explanation with scientific explanation? Five distinctive features of historical explanation have been proposed.

#### 1. The Interpretive Viewpoint

The interests and commitments of historians influence the way they select from among the myriad details those that might be relevant to a historical account.

Changing cultural presuppositions also affect perceptions of what is significant in the social world. The historian Carl Becker writes, "The history of any event is never precisely the same to two different persons, and it is well known that every generation writes the same history in a new way, and puts upon it a new construction."[1] A historical narrative has a coherence of meaningful patterns and unifying themes that are partly a product of the narrator's vision. Meaning always depends on contexts; historical writing exhibits a dialectic between individual events and larger wholes. The American Civil War, for example, can be seen variously as part of the history of slavery or of federal union, states' rights, regional economies, ethical concerns, or democratic ideals.

But despite the presence of interpretation, the historian cannot ignore the demands of *objectivity* understood as intersubjective testability. Scholarly integrity requires open-mindedness, self-criticism, and fidelity to evidence. The interaction among historians provides some correction for personal limitations and individual biases. There are common standards, which go beyond private judgment. Historians are held responsible by their colleagues to justify their inferences and conclusions by the citation of historical evidence. We can acknowledge such constraints while recognizing that the standards and methodological assumptions of historians, like those of every community of inquiry, reflect intellectual assumptions that vary among cultures and historical periods.

In historical inquiry, *subjectivity* and *cultural relativism* are more evident than in scientific inquiry, but I submit that this is a difference of degree rather than an absolute distinction. The data of science are theory-laden, while the events of history are interpretation-laden. Objective controls are less prominent and variations in individual and cultural interpretation are more evident as we move across the disciplinary spectrum from the natural sciences, through the social sciences and history, to religion. Such a continuum reveals significant differences, but no sharp lines can be drawn.

## 2. The Intentions of Agents

It has sometimes been said that to explain a human action means to account for it in terms of the ideas and choices of the actors. To answer the question "Why did Brutus kill Caesar?" one must study Brutus's experiences, dispositions, loyalties, and motives. The philosopher William Dray writes, "There is a sense of 'explain' in which an action is only explained when it is seen in a context of rational deliberation, when it is seen from the point of view of an agent."[2] R. G. Collingwood maintains that only by imaginative identification with persons in the past can the historian enter into the meanings and intentions that governed their actions. Such empathy is possible because we are human beings ourselves; introspection and self-knowledge provides the basis of our understanding of other persons.[3] The linguistic analysts, however, remind us that thought and language always occur in a social context. Individual actions must be understood in relation to the rules and expectations of the society in which they occurred, not in relation to our rules and expectations.[4]

If historical explanation were limited to accounts of the intentions of agents, it would exclude any *history of nature*. Some historians have in fact portrayed a strong contrast between history and science based on precisely this distinction. But the writings of historians include many pages with little or no reference to human intentions. They may portray social and economic forces of which the participants were unaware. Even in the lives of individuals, decisions may have been swayed by unconscious motives more than by rational ideas. If we recognize that diverse factors are at work in human history, we can speak also of the history of nature. We can see similarities as well as differences in comparing human history and natural history.

## 3. Particularity and Lawfulness

Typical explanations in science consist in showing that a given state of a system can be deduced from knowledge of a previous state, plus a set of *general laws*. Hempel insists that an event in history is explained only when it is similarly subsumed under a covering law: "General laws have quite analogous functions in history and in the natural sciences. In view of the structural equality of explanation and prediction, it may be said that an explanation is not complete unless it might as well have functioned as a prediction."[5] Scientific and historical explanation, he says, do not differ in principle, because only one kind of procedure is explanatory.

Dray and others have replied that historical inquiry inescapably involves *singular statements about particulars*. Every historical event is unique. Historians do not explain the Reformation by showing it to be a case of reformations-in-general. Generalizations about revolutions throw little light on the American, French, or Russian revolutions; it is precisely the peculiarities of the Russian Revolution—the role of Lenin, let us say—that are of interest. If historians are challenged, they do not invoke laws but fill in additional details in their narrative accounts. Historical explanation is a configurational understanding of the relation of parts in larger wholes. The historian tries to establish an intelligible context for an event rather than trying to deduce it from laws.[6]

It seems to me that both sides of this debate have overstated their cases. Every event is *unique* in some respects. No occurrence, even in the physics laboratory, is ever exactly duplicated in all its inexhaustible detail. But this does not exclude the presence of regular and repeatable features. On the other hand, no event is absolutely unique, even in history. The use of language presupposes common characteristics, such as those reflected in the words *revolution, nation,* and the like. The individuality of the exact pattern of weeds in the botanist's garden is trivial, but the individuality of a great historical figure is interesting and important to us. Uniqueness, then, is relative to the purposes of inquiry, not a property of some events but not of other events.

Moreover, historians do use *lawlike generalizations* of limited temporal and geographical scope, even if they do not use universal laws. They explain particular actions in terms of the conventions and principles by which people at the time would have understood and justified their actions, and this requires generalizations about the culture and period in question. In tracing connections between events, historians also draw on implicit generalizations about human motives for action. They are guided by parallels with patterns in other historical situations and by common-sense observations about human behavior. They may even use theories from sociology, psychology, or economics. While they are indeed interested in understanding particular events, they can do so only by pointing to relationships with which they are familiar in other similar situations.[7]

## 4. The Unpredictability of History

The limitations of the covering-law model are further underscored by the unpredictability of history. One source of unpredictability in practice is the occurrence of factors entering from outside a previously assumed framework of analysis: the microbe that brought Alexander the Great to an untimely death; the birth of a girl instead of a boy to Henry VIII; the storm that contributed to Cornwallis's defeat at Yorktown; the stray bullet that killed Stonewall Jackson. Another source of unpredictability is human freedom and creativity. The Gettysburg address, Beethoven's Ninth Symphony, and Newton's *Principia* were products of the creativity of particular individuals at particular times and could not conceivably have been predicted in advance.

Narratives of unpredictable events do indeed appear characteristic of human history, but they also appear in *the history of nature*. We will see in part 3 that there are irreducible unpredictabilities in quantum physics, thermodynamics, and genetic mutation and recombination. Unrepeatable events, which happened only once, are studied in cosmology, geology, and evolutionary biology. Why does the Indian rhinoceros have one horn and the African rhinoceros two? No one claims that such details of evolutionary history could possibly have been predicted. The laws of mechanics permit the prediction of the state of a system at one time from knowledge of its state at an earlier time, without any investigation of its intervening history. But DNA has a kind of historical memory representing the accumulation of information from many unpredictable events over a long span of time. Even a simple cell has the accumulated experience of a billion years of history encoded in its genes. We have biological theories to help explain regular patterns in these events, but the history of nature can be told only in narrative form.[8]

## 5. Diverse Types of Explanation

The previous points can be drawn together by suggesting that there is a variety of types of explanation within each of the disciplines. Historical inquiry and scientific inquiry are not mutually exclusive processes. Gordon Graham shows that there is both *theoretical* and *historical* explanation within science. In the former one appeals to general theories and laws, while in the latter one gives narratives of particulars.[9] In dealing with human history, on the other hand, we can recognize many different kinds of connections between events.

Sometimes historians refer to the intentions of agents, but at other times they invoke lawlike generalizations of limited scope or refer to economic and social forces or to theories derived from the social sciences. In the chapters that follow, then, we will give considerable attention to the history of nature, without denying the distinctive features of human history.

Stephen Toulmin says that a phenomenon is explained by *placing it within a context* that makes sense of the phenomenon. In the natural sciences, events are typically placed within the context of a law; a law is explained by situating it within a theory; and a theory is viewed within an "ideal of natural order." A historical event, he says, is explained by placing it within a series of events. A passage in a text is explained by considering its relation to the text as a whole. The various kinds of explanation and understanding thus each have a characteristic form of rationality.[10] Phillip Clayton holds that an explanation makes some area of experience comprehensible, either in terms of its components and details or by placing it in a broader context within which its meaning and significance become clear. He says that *different types of rationality* operate in the natural sciences, the social sciences, and theology, but they are all rational because each discipline has criteria of judgment accepted by everyone in the discipline. Clayton contends that in theology the criterion of internal coherence is more relevant than the criterion of empirical fit. He accepts Lakatos's argument that it is not isolated hypotheses that are evaluated but ongoing programs within historical contexts.[11]

We should note, finally, that these views allow us to do justice to *the historical character of science.* Instead of understanding science as a strictly logical enterprise, we have maintained that it is historically and culturally conditioned. The philosophy of science should be based on the history of science, not on idealized rational reconstructions. We have seen that Kuhn's paradigm shifts must be considered historically and Lakatos's programs can be evaluated only by their fruitfulness over a period of time. Toulmin applies evolutionary concepts to science itself. Scientific theories evolve; new ideas are like mutations that survive if they are selected by the scientific community. While there are limitations to this analogy, which I will point out later, it is a vivid representation of the historicity of science.

## 2. STORY AND HISTORY IN CHRISTIANITY

In the previous chapter we saw that stories are central in the life of religious communities. Recent exponents of *narrative theology* claim that biblical stories should be distinguished from both historical accounts and theological propositions. They insist that Christian convictions are communicated only by the biblical narrative itself. Let us consider the relation of story to history here.

One source of narrative theology is the writing of the *literary critics,* who insist that the meaning of a poem or story is carried by the text and cannot be extracted from it. Stories involve the interaction of characters and events. Often a plot moves over time through conflict toward resolution. Paul Ricoeur holds that it is the plot that makes a story an intelligible whole rather than a series of scattered events. Configurational patterns emerge among the events, even if surprises and contingencies rule out the possibility of predicting the outcome. Here again we see a dialectic between the meaning of the part and the meaning of the whole; every event in a story must be viewed contextually.[12]

Beyond these general characteristics of stories, theologians have outlined three features of biblical stories.[13]

*1. Canonical Story.* The Bible contains many shorter narratives within an overarching story. Crucial turning points occur, especially in the Exodus and Easter events. David Tracy says that the story form is indispensable and carries a distinctive disclosive and transformative power.[14] Hans Frei asserts that biblical narratives introduce God as a character in a set of stories. The character's identity cannot be extracted from the story or expressed exhaustively in theological concepts. The gospel message, he says, cannot be separated from the biblical story, which is central in preaching and ritual.[15] Other authors have pointed to Christ's use of parables—short stories that often present an unexpected reversal of values and a challenge to the hearer's response and decision.[16]

*2. Community Story.* Stories create communities, and communities create stories, in an ongoing interaction. Religious communities transmit stories and traditions of interpretation and add new stories about their own struggles and experiences. The internal stories of a community carry the interpretive categories it uses to understand its present life.[17] Stories are vehicles of self-understanding, but they also provide an impetus for action, for they affect emotions and motives more powerfully than conceptual propositions. Stories are vindicated by patterns of living, not by philosophical arguments. As the linguistic analysts have pointed out, the functions of stories in religious communities are very different from the functions of historical accounts among academic historians.

*3. Personal Story.* The story of our lives is always related to the larger stories within which we see ourselves. Moreover, the stories of other persons' lives disclose new possibilities for our own lives. In most of the stories of our culture, men have had the dominant roles, and women are now asserting that women must tell their own stories. James McClendon shows how our lives are challenged by the story of other lives, which were in turn inspired by scriptural stories. Martin Luther King, Jr., for example, understood himself in the light of the Exodus and the crucifixion, and these motifs of liberation and self-sacrifice come to us in turn through the story of King's life, not through theological propositions.[18] Stanley Hauerwas insists that stories change our attitudes and actions. Christian ethics do not consist of applying principles in discrete moments of decision but in our ongoing patterns of response shaped by stories. Character and vision are embodied in stories rather than in concepts or principles.[19]

I agree with these authors concerning the importance of biblical stories, but I believe that we also have to face the question of *the veracity of historical claims.* If no Exodus took place, and if Christ did not go willingly to his death, the power of the stories would be undermined. Moreover, the interpretation of particular biblical texts is not always obvious; there has been a continual process of interpretation and reinterpretation. Since the eighteenth century it has been widely recognized that the work of the theologian must take historical criticism into account. The existentialists have minimized the importance of historicity and have said that faith is individual decision and obedience in the present moment. But this neglects both the role of the community and the conviction that faith is a response to what God has done in the past.

The biblical stories of creation, covenant, and Christ differ greatly in their historicity. In chapter 8, I will argue that the stories of *creation and fall* should not be viewed as narratives of historical events. The Genesis story, I suggest, is a symbolic assertion of God's relation to the world and of the ambivalence of human existence. Moses, however, was a historical figure, and *the covenant* at Sinai was based on historical events. But the story as we have it in Exodus was recorded many centuries later and reflects the experience of Israel during that interval. Most scholars hold, for example, that the Ten Commandments may go back to Moses' day, but the long lists of detailed instructions for the rituals of the Jerusalem temple were of later origin.

*Jesus of Nazareth* was a historical person, and we have more historical information about him than we do about Moses. But in calling him Christ and in testifying to his redemptive role we are making statements of faith that are not historically provable, though they are related to historical evidence. The Gospels were written at least a generation after his death, and they reflect the experience and theological interpretations of the early Christian community. The theologian's task goes beyond that of the historian, but the theologian cannot ignore historical research concerning the Bible and the events it narrates.

In addition to asking about the veracity of historical claims, the theologian must examine *the validity of ontological claims* implicit in the biblical story. The God of the Bible is also understood to be the God of nature and history and the Lord of our lives. If the Bible is the story of what God has done, we must ask how today in an age of science we may conceive of God's action. This task requires the articulation of systematic theological concepts. The stories are the starting point of philosophical and theological reflection. The theologian must consider the coherence and validity of beliefs as well as the pragmatic effects and transformative power of the stories. Moreover, if we take stories alone, we end with total relativism. If each person or community lives in a particular story and there is no common story, there can be no communication. The use of stories alone hinders the search for common elements in the religious experience of diverse cultures.

Van Harvey suggests that we can never escape from the historically conditioned categories of *a community of interpretation* but we can partially transcend this limitation by imaginatively sharing in the outlook of other communities.[20] Michael Goldberg holds that there can be rational discourse across story lines, exposing us to "the various ways the world might reasonably be envisaged, sensitizing us to the richness and complexity of the diverse possibilities for our lives."[21] Starting from story and moving to history, philosophy, and theology, we do not escape the problems of cultural relativism, but we can enter forms of dialogue that are not possible if we stay within a story.

## II. OBJECTIVITY AND RELATIVISM

We have seen that paradigms and theories influence scientific data. Paradigms and beliefs even more decisively shape the interpretation of religious experience and religious stories. Similar assertions have been made in more extreme form in recent writings on the social construction of science. Third World critics have maintained that economic and political interests affect the results of both scientific research and theological reflection. Feminist authors have shown that gender biases are prevalent in both fields. These diverse movements all criticize claims of objectivity and assert the cultural relativity of theories and beliefs. Are these more radical criticisms valid?

### 1. THE SOCIAL CONSTRUCTION OF SCIENCE

Popper upholds the traditional view of science as an *autonomous* rational enterprise following its own internal logic in testing hypotheses against reliable observations. Many scientists accept this view, both as an ideal to be sought and as a description of typical scientific practice. Kuhn does try to trace some external influences (including the metaphysical assumptions of the wider culture), but he deals for the most part with ideas within the scientific community. In the 1970s and 1980s, more radical challenges have arisen from several quarters. Not only are data theory-laden and theories paradigm-laden, but it now appears that paradigms are culture-laden and value-laden. Here Kuhn's contextualism, relativism, and historicism are carried much further.

One source of the new *"externalist"* accounts has been the social history of science, including studies of science as an institution in a cultural context. Another has been writings in the sociology of knowledge, especially those by Habermas and others in the Frankfurt school, who argue that ideological biases, intellectual assumptions, and political forces are at work in all inquiry. A related source is the Marxist thesis that economic and class interests lie at the root of all human social activity, including science. Science as a social reality is a source of power; power over nature becomes power over people. You might think that if you want to know how science works, you should ask scientists. Not at all, say the critics, for scientists will give you an idealized and selective reconstruction, a rationalization that justifies their interests in the guise of objectivity and autonomy. The myth of the neutrality of science allows it to be used to achieve the goals of those who hold power in society.[22]

Most scientists will grant that *technology* and applied science are controlled by government and industry, but they will argue that *basic research* ("pure science") maintains its independence. But the critics point out that this distinction is increasingly dubious. The time between a scientific discovery and an industrial application is often very short, as in the case of solid state physics or molecular biology, and so industry has a stake in basic research. Many fields of "big science" are capital-intensive, requiring expensive equipment and teams of scientists. The "industrialization of science" erodes its autonomy. Subsidy of basic science by government and by the military-industrial complex also extends far into the academic world.[23]

Many scientists will go a step further and grant that the *selection of research problems* and the direction and rate of advance in different areas of science are determined by political and economic forces. The setting of priorities and the allocation of limited funds are carried out by government and industry in accordance with social and institutional goals. Some kinds of problems are ignored, and others are given high priority. But even if the direction of scientific advance is socially managed, are not the actual discoveries of sciences objectively determined by nature?

Not so, say the authors in the *social construction of science* movement, especially the more extreme versions of the "strong program." The design of research is not given to us by nature. The kinds of question we ask, the type of explanation we seek, and even the criteria of rationality we use are all socially formed. Models often originate outside of science, as in Darwin's chance reading of Malthus. Theories are underdetermined by data, and diverse theories may be consistent with the data. The cognitive and intellectual interests of scientists will affect their thought patterns. Personal motives, such as professional recognition and the securing of research grants, will tend to favor working within the prevailing paradigm. Institutions and individuals may have a greater stake in one theory than another. Rapid acceptance of a particular theory and resistance to a rival one may have complex social, political, and economic causes. Here is a cultural relativism that goes well beyond that suggested by Kuhn.[24]

Proponents of these views have presented a variety of case studies, often based on careful historical research. Newtonian physics was more readily accepted because a mechanistic view of nature excluded the pantheistic and occult philosophies associated with alchemy and astrology. Maxwell's electromagnetic theory of the ether was welcomed because it seemed to provide an antidote to the philosophy of materialism.[25] One author argues that the indeterminism of quantum theory in the Weimar Republic was influenced by the romanticism and anarchism of postwar Germany.[26] Studies of scientific disputes reveal complex reasons for favoring one theory over another when the evidence is ambiguous, as in quark theory in physics from 1974 to 1976, following the discovery of the J-psi particle.[27]

These various delineations of inputs from outside science are a valuable corrective to the "internalist" view of an autonomous, rational, scientific community. But in the history of ideas the causal or explanatory role of interests is often speculative and difficult to document. I believe these authors lean too far toward relativism and underestimate the constraints placed on theories by the data arising from our interaction with nature. Their interpretation of science fails to account for its success in making predictions and generating applications. Ideologies and interests are often present, but their distorting influence can be reduced by using the criteria mentioned earlier, especially the testing of theories against data. Extrascientific input is indeed evident in the imaginative origination of theories, but it is less evident in their subsequent justification. Finally, the extreme relativists are inconsistent, for they assert that their own analysis is valid for all cultures. Their own claims somehow escape the charges of cultural relativism of which everyone else is accused.

## 2. THIRD WORLD CRITIQUES

A critique of Western science similar to that of the "strong program" was given by several delegates from the Third World at a conference sponsored by the World Council of Churches at MIT. They claimed that science today predominantly serves the interests of the rich nations, not those that are poor and oppressed. Scientific resources are distributed in radically unequal ways, with only 3 or 4 percent of the world's research and development funds aimed at problems typical of developing nations. Medical research is mostly directed at the diseases of the affluent, with little going to tropical diseases that affect a far larger population. The technologies transferred to developing countries have frequently not been appropriate for their situation. Most of these critics referred to problem selection or technological application, but some discussed Western biases in scientific concepts and theories.[28]

Might there be a distinctively different science in an Asian or African culture? Most scientists would quickly dismiss the idea. They would assert that the laws of nature are universal and that scientific meetings and publications are international. Historical evidence provides no clear answer, since modern science arose in the West and was then transplanted to other cultures; indigenous forms of inquiry were not developed. Most non-Western scientists or their teachers were trained in the West and write for journals published in the West. In another culture, mathematical physics would perhaps not have been the first science to be established, despite the fact that the phenomena it studies are in some ways simpler than those of other sciences. Would another culture have escaped reductionism and maintained a more holistic approach in both experiment and theory—or might it still do so in the future? Some adherents of Eastern religions think so, as we will see in the next chapter. Science does contribute to the most general categories of interpretation, which are systematically explored in metaphysics, but the metaphysical assumptions of a culture also influence the character of scientific paradigms, as Kuhn recognized. In short, I believe that culture does influence paradigms in all the sciences, but I do not think that this implies incommensurability or unrestrained cultural relativism.

Third World authors, especially advocates of *liberation theology*, have similarly criticized the biases they see in Western religious thought. They maintain that all theology is written from a social location, which influences perception and interpretation. What we see depends on where we stand. In the past, theology has usually legitimated existing power structures, and its purported political neutrality has perpetuated the status quo. Gustavo Gutiérrez proposes that theology should be based on an interplay of theory and action; it should be critical reflection on the church's engagement in the world. We have to start from the gospel and also from our own historical situation. In Latin America, that situation is one of abject poverty, the product of a long history of colonialism, repressive local governments allied with the rich, and continued dependence on an international economy from which affluent nations have been the main beneficiaries.[29]

The liberation theologians hold that we all read scripture selectively. From the Third World perspective, God is primarily *Liberator.* The Exodus motif is central. God liberated the Israelites from slavery in Egypt and continues to side with the poor and oppressed, not the privileged. For the prophets, "to know God is to do justice." In his first sermon, Jesus quoted Isaiah: "The Spirit of the Lord is upon me, because he has anointed me to preach good news to the poor. . . . to set at liberty those who are oppressed" (Luke 4:18). According to liberation theology, the Christian is called to solidarity with the poor and to the struggle to change unjust and dehumanizing economic and political structures. The gospel is a message of liberation, not only from individual sin, but from the social sins of exploitative institutions. Individuals feel helpless, but they can be empowered by God and can work through small grass-roots religious groups ("base communities") and political movements. Most liberation theologians advocate some form of socialism as the only possible path to social justice in their historical situation.

Liberation theology has been criticized for its indebtedness to Marxism and its tendency to condone violence and revolution. But most theologians who accept the Marxist analysis of economic exploitation do not accept other tenets of Marxism. They also point to the protracted covert violence of the status quo, and they give diverse assessments of the circumstances in which revolution might be justified; many of them acknowledge that a revolutionary government might impose new forms of oppression.[30] But our concern here is with the liberation theologians' insistence that all theology is culture-laden and reflects *economic and political interests.* Black theologians in the United States have asserted that Christian theology has reflected racial as well as economic biases.[31] Here, too, is a thesis on the social construction of theology resembling the thesis that science is a social construction.

## 3. FEMINIST CRITIQUES

In a similar way, feminists have analyzed the presence of gender biases in both science and religion. Their critique of science occurs on several levels. They state concerns about *equal access* for women in science education and employment, studying overt and covert forms of discrimination in schools and on the job. Next are criticisms of gender biases in *the selection of problems* for research, especially in biology and the health sciences. A more fundamental criticism is that male biases have affected *scientific theories* and *interpretation of data*. One example is the assumption by Darwin and his successors that competition and struggle are the main forces in natural selection ("the survival of the fittest"). This assumption seems to have reflected the bias of a male-dominated culture, which valued competition. Only much later was it recognized that cooperation and symbiosis are often crucial in evolutionary survival. More blatant examples of gender bias are evident in studies on the biological basis of sex differences, such as claims that there is a neurological difference between the sexes in brain lateralization and that this accounts for the purportedly innate superiority of males in mathematics and spatial visualization.[32]

Helen Longino, a philosopher of science, holds that a feminist perspective can contribute to objectivity in science by facilitating *the critique of auxiliary hypotheses* and by suggesting alternative ones. For example, it has often been said that "man the hunter" was the key to the evolution of the earliest humans from primates and hominids. Male hunting would have encouraged tool use, upright posture, and mental capacities. But did not women use similar capacities as gatherers and nurturers? Longino holds that in our culture science reflects gender-related preferences in the choice of problems, models, and concepts, which affect the content as well as the practice of science.[33]

Evelyn Fox Keller has described Barbara McClintock's work on genetic transposition, which waited thirty years for recognition and eventually received a Nobel Prize. McClintock was unable to find a university job, and after she found a research post, her ideas were considered unorthodox. The "central dogma" of molecular biology had posited a one-way transfer of information: always from DNA, never to it (except by natural selection). While most research was being done on genetic structure, McClintock was interested in function and organization and the relation of genes to cells, organisms, and developmental patterns. Her work on transposition was finally vindicated, and the idea that the wider environment could indirectly affect genetic changes (though not directly, as Lamarck had thought) was finally accepted. Keller portrays McClintock's painstaking attention to small variations and anomalies (such as a few corn kernels with colors different from the others) and her "feeling for the organism"—not implying a mystic intuition but rather a sense of humility and a "listening to the material." Keller says we should not see this as "feminist science," but she thinks McClintock's "outsider" role and her distinctive attitudes may have given her a greater freedom to consider diverse kinds of interrelationship.[34]

All of these authors seek a *gender-free science* within the prevailing norms of scientific objectivity. Male biases are to be rejected not simply because they are patriarchal but because they are "bad science," and they can be corrected by a greater commitment to objectivity and openness to evidence. But some feminists go much further in advocating a new *"feminist science"* and in rejecting objectivity itself as a male ideology. If there can be no value neutrality in science, then one can only seek a differently gendered science, accepting the inevitability of relativism. Sandra Harding calls this "feminist postmodernism," describing it as skeptical about the possibility of value neutrality, rationality, and objectivity. She concludes, "It has been and should be moral and political beliefs that direct the development of both the intellectual and social structures of science. The problematics, concepts, theories, methodologies, interpretations of experiments, and uses have been and should be selected with moral and political goals in mind, not merely cognitive ones."[35]

These more radical critiques arise partly from considering the *dualisms* that have been so pervasive in Western thought: mind/body, reason/emotion, objectivity/subjectivity, domination/submission, impersonal/personal, power/love. In each case, the first term has been identified in our culture as male, the second as female. But precisely these first terms are taken to characterize science: mind, reason, objectivity, domination, impersonality, power. Science is stereotypically male, and nature is referred to in female images. Bacon spoke of nature as the mind's bride: "Make her your slave, conquer and subdue her." In a patriarchal society, the exploitation of women and nature have a common ideological root. In this interpretation, scientists share these alienating and manipulative attitudes when they make control and prediction, rather than understanding, their goal.[36] Another source of radical critiques is the psychoanalytic theory claiming that a growing girl achieves selfhood by identifying with her mother, while a growing boy does so by separating from his mother—leading men to value separation, independence, objectivity, and power, the attitudes typical of contemporary science.[37]

I cannot agree with those postmodernist feminists who recommend that we should reject objectivity and accept relativism. Western thought has indeed been dualistic, and men have perhaps been particularly prone to dichotomize experience. But the answer surely is to try to avoid dichotomies, not merely to relativize them. Nor do we want to perpetuate them in inverted form by rejecting the first term and affirming the second in each polarity. Such a move would be shortsighted, even as a temporary corrective strategy, if we seek to acknowledge the wholeness of life. We can grant that our inquiry is not free of values and interests without having to adopt an anarchic relativism. As Keller says, "Science is neither a mirror of nature nor simply a reflection of culture." If we insist that objectivity is a product of male consciousness, we deny the possibility of a feminist voice within current science. Moreover, no clear proposal for an alternative feminist science has been spelled out.

We also need to ask what people mean by *objectivity* and decide which of these ideas we can affirm as valid ideals for science, whether or not they are adhered to in current practice. Two of these meanings of objectivity I would defend: (1) *data* should be intersubjectively reproducible, even though they are theory-laden, and (2) *criteria* should be impartial and shared by a broad community of inquiry, even though they are difficult to apply. But two other ideas seem to me dubious. First, objectivity cannot mean that theories are determined *only by the object*, for we have said repeatedly that data are theory-laden and that we cannot separate the subject and the object in an experiment. Inquiry involves participation and interaction, not detachment. Second, objectivity does not imply *reductionism*, as if the physicochemical laws of the component parts were more valid as explanations than attempts to describe the higher-level activities of integrated wholes. *Holistic thinking* is not limited to women, but it appears that in our culture women may be more sensitive than men to connections, contexts, and interdependencies and more attuned to development, cooperation, and symbiosis. There may be a biological basis for some of these gender differences, but they are mainly attributable to cultural patterns of socialization.

In *religion*, too, feminist critiques have occurred at a variety of levels. Some authors express concern about equal access to education and employment, including the ordination of women. But the more fundamental critique is of gender biases in concepts and beliefs. Reformers seek an equal-gendered Christianity or Judaism, while radicals believe the inherited traditions are so inherently patriarchal that they should be rejected.

The *reformist feminists* agree that Christianity and Judaism have been strongly patriarchal in both practice and thought. Religious leadership and images of God have been overwhelmingly male and have supported male domination in society. But the reformers argue that the essential biblical message is not patriarchal. Female images of God appear in the Bible, though rarely. Isaiah asserts that God will not forget Israel: "Can a woman forget her suckling child?" (Isa. 49:15). Individual women figure significantly in the Bible: Deborah, Esther, Ruth, and of course Mary, as well as such later saints as St. Teresa of Avila and Julian of Norwich. Jesus was not sexist, and he exhibited the virtues stereotyped as "feminine," such as love and emotion, as much as the "masculine" virtues of courage and leadership.[38] Contemporary feminists seek inclusive language, not only for brothers and sisters in the church, but for a God who is like a mother as well as like a father, as we have seen in Sallie McFague's writing.

The theologian Rosemary Ruether sharply criticizes patriarchal assumptions in the Catholic tradition, but she believes the church's essential message can be *reformulated* in nonsexist terms. The mind/body dualism, in particular, came into Christian thought less from biblical than from Neoplatonic sources, and it can be replaced with a more biblical vision of the whole person in community. Ruether brings together the central concerns of feminist theology, liberation theology, and the ecology movement. She holds that all three are opposed to dualism, hierarchy, and domination. She seeks a more participatory epistemology and an inclusive and equitable social order, combining social justice with concern for nature and nonhuman life. She has given a powerful critique of traditional Christianity without completely rejecting it.[39]

The *radical feminists*, on the other hand, hold that the biblical tradition is incurably patriarchal and that new religious forms must be sought outside the church. The starting point must be such distinctive experiences of women as sisterhood, pregnancy, and motherhood, as well as the experiences considered inferior in a patriarchal culture: intuition, emotion, the body, and harmony with nature. In addition, the new approach must be based on the liberation and empowerment made possible by women's self-definition, self-expression, support groups, and solidarity with other oppressed groups (though progress in moving beyond a white, middle-class movement has been slow). Some radical feminists have developed new religious rituals for women. Others have drawn from goddess and Earth Mother myths in early cultures to provide female symbols of the divine. Another alternative is to symbolize the ultimate as impersonal—as the Ground of Being, for instance—which avoids attribution of gender.[40]

As in the case of proposals for a feminist science, I disagree with those radical feminists who perpetuate dualistic thinking by inverting the prevailing cultural dualisms. In both cases, the effort to eliminate what is invalid in the tradition can result in eliminating whatever is valid in it also. Absolutizing the feminine seems as dubious as absolutizing the masculine. Surely the goal should be for each of us as men and women to express all our diverse capacities, whether stereotyped in our culture as male or female—and to symbolize the same diversity of creative characteristics in our models of God.

## III. RELIGIOUS PLURALISM

Despite the influence of cultural assumptions on scientific paradigms, there is substantial agreement among scientists around the world concerning theories and data. Religious pluralism is a more serious problem in a global age. Agreement is more elusive, and the consequences of disagreement are sometimes more disastrous. What are we to make of the diversity of interpretations of religious experience? Can we find a middle ground between absolutism in religious claims and total relativism? Are there any criteria that can be applied cross-culturally in evaluating religious traditions?

### 1. THE INTERPRETATION OF RELIGIOUS EXPERIENCE

How should we view cultural relativism in the interpretation of religious experience? Some people have argued that it is not really a serious problem. Richard Swinburne says that we ordinarily *accept people's reports* of what they claim to have experienced, unless there are grounds for thinking that their testimony is unreliable or their claims implausible. Similarly, says Swinburne, when persons say they have an awareness of God, both they and other people should accept this at face value unless there are strong grounds to doubt it. "From all this, of course, it follows that if it seems to me that I have a glimpse of Nirvana or a vision of God, that is good grounds for me to suppose that I do. And, more generally, the occurrence of religious experiences is prima facie reason for all to believe in that of which the experience was purportedly an experience."[41] He grants that some experiences are deceptive and that we use cultural concepts to describe all experience; religious testimony, in particular, produces conflicting claims. But the basic religious experiences are rather similar, and the burden of proof should rest on the skeptic. Swinburne concludes that "religious perceptual claims deserve to be taken as seriously as perceptual claims of any other kind."

William Alston maintains that we accept sense experience as evidence of an independently existing object if (1) the experience occurs *under favorable circumstances,* and (2) the interpretation is *consistent with other beliefs.* The acceptance can be overridden if it is not consistent with other beliefs (for example, we question our perception that the moon is larger near the horizon). Alston says that similar conditions apply to the interpretation of religious experience. We should acknowledge the favorable circumstances provided by the spiritual disciplines undertaken by the masters of the religious life. And we can test their conclusions against a larger framework of beliefs. But Alston grants that there are greater cultural variations in religious experience than the cultural variations in sense experience that anthropologists have reported.[42]

Steven Katz, at the opposite extreme, says that a report of religious experience is determinatively *shaped by the concepts* a person brings to it. He examines mystical writings in various traditions and is impressed by their diversity. For example, Jewish mysticism does not involve loss of identity in the experience of unity but preserves a sense of God's otherness. Belief in a personal God and in the importance of ritual and ethical action is simply assumed. "The mystic brings to his experience a world of concepts, images, symbols and values which shape as well as color the experience he eventually and actually has."[43] Prior expectations impose both form and content on experience; we cannot say there is a universal experience that is then interpreted by diverse cultural concepts. The symbols of religious communities are at work before, during, and after the experience. Buddhists hold that suffering and impermanence are the basic human problem, and therefore they seek liberation from suffering. Christians believe that sin is our basic problem, and they seek forgiveness and unity with God.

Peter Donovan takes an intermediate position. He argues that in religion, as in science, there is *no neutral description without interpretation.* "All that theoretical background is not found in the experience itself, but is brought to it by way of interpretation, making it the experience it is."[44] Experience can indeed support an overall theoretical scheme, but "one's estimate of the value of any particular experience will depend on how one evaluates the total belief system in terms of which the experience is thought to be significant."[45] Donovan holds that particular experiences, even those that are life transforming, must be systematically related to a coherent conceptual framework, which is judged as a whole.

In a similar vein Ninian Smart points to common elements in the reports of mystics but acknowledges that they diverge in *doctrinal interpretation:*

The fact that mysticism is substantially the same in different cultures and religions does not, however, entail that there is a "perennial philosophy" common to mystics. Their doctrines are determined partly by facts other than mystical experience itself. . . . The distinction between experience and interpretation is not clear-cut. The reason for this is that the concepts used in describing and explaining an experience vary in their degree of ramification. That is to say, where a concept occurs as part of a doctrinal scheme it gains its meaning in part from a range of doctrinal statements taken to be true.[46]

Smart recommends that we use low-level descriptive terms, with minimal doctrinal ramification, to try to formulate a more phenomenological account on which both the mystic and other persons can concur. This would be consistent with my own view that the distinction between experience and interpretation, like that between data and theory in science, is never absolute; in both cases the distinction is relative and is drawn at differing points at various times for particular purposes.

If there is no uninterpreted experience, there can be *no immediate religious knowledge,* no "self-authenticating" awareness of God, no incorrigible intuition for which finality may be claimed. For when interpretation is present there is always the possibility of misinterpretation, especially through wishful thinking, which reads into experience more than is warranted. Nor can there be any certain inference from experience to a Being who is its independent cause. Even the sense of confrontation and encounter is no guarantee of the existence of a source beyond us.[47]

The key question is whether religious experience exercises any control on interpretation. A set of basic beliefs has the tendency to produce experiences that can be cited in support of those beliefs, which are then self-confirming. A suggestible person may experience what he or she has been taught to expect. Yet people also have unexpected and surprising experiences that challenge their previous assumptions and lead them to reformulate their beliefs.

We can deny that God is an immediate and uninterpreted datum without going to the opposite extreme of saying that God is *only inferred,* without being experienced. To make God a hypothesis to be tested or a conclusion of an argument (as in the argument from design) is to lose the experiential basis of religion. In my view, God is known through *interpreted experience.*[48] Our knowledge of God is like knowledge of another self in being neither an immediate datum nor an inference. Another self is not immediately experienced; it must express itself through various media of language and action, which we interpret. Yet we do not merely infer that another self is present; as a precondition for taking words and gestures as expressions of purpose and intention we must already understand ourselves to be dealing with another self.[49] Members of religious communities similarly understand themselves to be dealing with God; such an understanding is so basic that it may seem almost as much a part of interpreted experience as encounter with another human self.

I conclude that beliefs are both brought to religious experience and derived from it. In religion, more than in science, paradigms influence interpretive beliefs, which affect experience. But religious experience does influence beliefs and paradigms. Although there is no neutral descriptive language, there are degrees of interpretation. Thus members of various religious traditions can communicate even though they are dependent on culturally formed languages.

## 2. BETWEEN ABSOLUTISM AND RELATIVISM

Religious communities have varied widely in their attitudes toward other religions. We can distinguish five types of attitudes.[50]

### 1. Absolutism

Here the claim is that there is only one true religion and all others are simply false. There is one exclusive path to salvation. Judaism always balanced the particularism of the covenant with Israel and the idea of the chosen people against the universalism of the covenant with Noah, and salvation was never restricted to Jews. In Christianity, the uniqueness of the incarnation was the basis for the traditional assertion that salvation is possible only through Christ. Roman Catholicism expressed it classically as, "Outside the church, no salvation." In Protestant fundamentalism, exclusivism is based on the idea of a uniquely revealed book. Critics of this position hold that it absolutizes finite expressions of the infinite, whether in an institution, a book, or a set of doctrines. They also point out that such views have led to intolerance, crusades, inquisitions, religious wars, and the rationalization of colonialism. The grim history of Christian persecution of Jews is one consequence of such absolutism. Religious imperialism is particularly dangerous in a nuclear age.

### 2. Approximations of Truth

In this view other religions are believed to hold elements of the truth that is more fully presented in one's own tradition. Christianity is said to be the fulfillment of what is implicit or only partially understood in other religions. God is at work in these other traditions, which are genuine responses to God and real ways of salvation for their adherents, despite their limitations. There are prefigurations of Christ, not just in the Old Testament (Hebrew Scriptures), but in all the major world religions. This is a common view in Protestant liberalism. Catholic authors since Vatican II have said that in other traditions there is "the hidden Christ" (Raymond Panikkar), "the anonymous Christian" (Karl Rahner), or (in an older terminology) "the latent church," whereby the salvation won by Christ is available to all humankind. As Rahner puts it, "There are many ways, but one norm." This view goes far toward mitigating the intolerance of the first position. However, it tends to be somewhat condescending toward other traditions. Presumably it would see no value in dialogue except to persuade the other party. We have nothing to learn if our tradition already possesses the full truth, which is only partially available elsewhere.

## 3. Identity of Essence

Perhaps all religions are basically the same, though expressed in differing cultural forms. To some writers, the central religious experience is mysticism, in which there is awareness of the unity of all things (as in Aldous Huxley's "perennial philosophy"). To others, the feeling of absolute dependence (Schleiermacher) or the numinous power of the holy (Otto) is the essence of religion. Doctrines are looked on as symbolic statements of inner experiences, which are what is important religiously. In this view, we should all agree on the common core, without claiming that one set of doctrines is superior to another. This would encourage us to work for the emergence of a global religion, in which no one group would impose its views on others. The problem with this position is that there is disagreement as to what the common essence is. Moreover, a rich diversity exists within every tradition as well as among traditions. A watered-down global religion would have to rely on private experiences and abstract ideas, stripped of all the historical memories, communal stories and rituals, and particular patterns of behavior found in actual religious communities.

## 4. Cultural Relativism

Anthropologists study cultures in their totality, and they view religion as an expression of a culture. Each religion functions in its own cultural setting. Linguistic analysts hold that religious symbols and concepts shape our experience; since cultural and linguistic forms vary widely, it is not surprising that there is great diversity in religious experience. Forms of life and their associated "language games" are self-contained, culturally relative, and incommensurable. The primary religious language is "prayer, praise and preaching," while both doctrine and experience are secondary (Lindbeck). Here the central place of particular stories and rituals in worship and practice can be appreciated.

The great strength of linguistic analysis is its recognition of the multiple functions of religion as a way of life. Moreover, a relativistic approach clearly avoids the problems presented by claims of superiority and claims of identity. It affirms the particularity of each tradition as well as its internal diversity. But it also makes the study of another religion of limited relevance, since it must be understood as part of its cultural system. Little can be learned that might illuminate our lives in our own cultural setting. Any beliefs claiming to be true would have to be discounted, and there is no motive to try to transcend the limitations and blind spots of our own culture. There is no basis for criticism of one's own culture. Acceptance of tradition would predominate over critical reflection and reformulation.

## 5. Pluralistic Dialogue

The starting point here is affirmation of the presence of God in the faith and life of persons in other traditions. We can be open to the diverse ways of being human and recognize that there are diverse possibilities for our own lives. We can be sensitive to persons in other cultures and try to see the world from their point of view, even though we can never totally leave behind our cultural assumptions. We can take a confessional approach and testify to what has happened in our own lives, without passing judgment on others. Loyalty to our own tradition can be combined with respect for other traditions. This view offers a stronger basis for genuine dialogue and mutual learning than any of the alternatives above.

As an example of this position, consider the writings of John Hick, who holds that "God has many names." The divine reality is encountered, conceptualized, and responded to in multiple ways. "These different human awarenesses of the Eternal One represent different culturally conditioned perceptions of the same infinite divine reality."[51] Hick says that religious traditions are like reports from explorers of a Himalayan mountain whose higher altitudes are always hidden in the clouds. The explorers have taken different routes and have different impressions of the mountain from varying perspectives, and none has reached the top. But Hick goes beyond this analogy in proposing that divine initiative has been revealed within many traditions, in the framework of the cultural assumptions of each. The variety of traditions exhibit multiple forms of revelation as well as differences in human perception.

Moreover, says Hick, salvation occurs within many traditions. Here he is referring not to eternal life but to the transformation of personal existence in this life, "the transformation from self-centeredness to Reality-centeredness," variously referred to as salvation, fulfillment, liberation, or enlightenment. The spiritual and moral fruits of such changes are not confined to any one religion. Each tradition can be effective in the lives of persons who have been spiritually formed by it. We should each be loyal to our own heritage:

We can revere Christ as the one through whom we have found salvation, without having to deny other points of reported contact between God and man. We can commend the way of Christian faith without having to discommend other ways of faith. We can say that there is salvation in Christ, without having to say there is no salvation other than in Christ.[52]

In common with the Identity of Essence position, Hick holds that there is a common object of devotion in all religions. However, he differs in emphasizing the influence of cultural traditions on experience as well as on doctrinal interpretation. He also welcomes diversity and commitment to particular traditions, rather than the search for a single global religion. He agrees with Cultural Relativism in acknowledging the formative influence of culture and language. Moreover, his insistence that the heart of religion is personal transformation rather than doctrine is consistent with relativism. He sees no necessary conflict between differing means of transformation in diverse cultures, whereas doctrines make mutually exclusive claims. But Hick avoids a total relativism by affirming a transcendent reality beyond the variations of culture and by advocating an epistemology in which religious language can make cognitive claims, even though they are always partial, symbolic, and tradition-laden.

In his treatment of Christ, Hick starts on common ground with the Approximations of Truth school, but in the end he departs from it. How might we compare Christ with the Hebrew prophets, Christian saints, or founders and leading figures in other world religions? Hick cites several authors who defend the uniqueness of Christ but who understand that uniqueness as a difference in degree and in relationship to God, rather than as an absolute difference in kind or in metaphysical substance and nature. He accepts the preeminence of Christ as the definitive expression of God's presence for himself as a Christian. But he affirms the possibility that people in other traditions may find definitive expressions elsewhere.[53]

This fifth position, then, goes beyond tolerance of other positions to advocate dialogue that may be mutually enriching. If we are open to new insights, we can learn from other religions and perhaps come to appreciate aspects of the divine and potentialities for human life that we have ignored. Thus Hick thinks that Christianity has had a positive influence on Hinduism in encouraging a greater concern for social justice, while the current interest in meditation among Christians is in part indebted to Hinduism. Again, Buddhism has less frequently been associated with imperialism and warfare than Christianity and has shown a greater respect for nature; but Christianity seems to have provided greater impetus for material progress and social change. Exposure to another religion can also lead us to rediscover neglected themes in our own heritage.[54]

A similar view is developed by Paul Knitter, who holds that one can accept the possibility of *other saviors* without undermining *commitment to Christ*. Christ is God's revelation, but not the only one. The Christian vision can be decisive for us, he says, but we do not need to pass judgment on other visions. Ultimate reality is perceived in differing ways and interpreted in varying symbols among the diverse religious traditions. Knitter suggests that people should be encouraged toward a deeper experience within their own tradition and at the same time be open to dialogue with other traditions. Instead of being a source of conflict and fragmentation, religion could then be a powerful force for global unity.[55]

## 3. CONCLUSIONS

Religion is indeed *a way of life*. Religious language serves diverse functions, many of which have no parallel in science. It encourages ethical attitudes and behavior. It evokes feelings and emotions. Its typical forms are worship and meditation. Above all, its goal is to effect personal transformation and reorientation (salvation, fulfillment, liberation, or enlightenment). All of these aspects of religion require more total personal involvement than does scientific activity, affecting more diverse aspects of personality. Religion also fills psychological needs, including integration of personality and the envisioning of a larger framework of meaning and purpose. Many of these goals are fulfilled primarily through religious experience, story, and ritual.

In all these functions, the use of language is *noncognitive* and no explicit propositional assertions about reality are made. Yet each function presupposes *cognitive beliefs* and assertions. The appropriateness of a way of life, an ethical norm, a pattern of worship, a particular understanding of salvation, or a framework of meaning depends in each case on beliefs about the character of ultimate reality.

Let us look again at the four criteria presented in the previous chapter, considering first their use *within a religious tradition* or paradigm community.

*1. Agreement with Data.* It is sometimes said that the distinctive feature of science is that from theories one can make *predictions*, which can be tested in *controlled experiments*. But not all sciences are predictive and experimental. Geology and astronomy are based on observations rather than experiments; in geology there are no predictions (though aspects of present or past states could have been predicted from earlier states). We have said that evolutionary history could not have been predicted in detail, and only certain portions of evolutionary theory can be tested experimentally. In science, then, we should talk about the *intersubjective testing* of theories against various kinds of data, with all the qualifications suggested earlier about theory-laden data, paradigm-laden theories, and culture-laden paradigms. Moreover, we have seen that because auxiliary hypotheses can usually be adjusted, we must reject any simple notion of verification and falsification.

In religion, the *intersubjective testing* of beliefs does occur within religious communities, and it provides some protection against arbitrariness and individual subjectivity. The interpretation of initiating events, formative experiences, and subsequent individual and communal experiences goes through a long process of testing, filtering, and public validation in the history of the community. Some experiences recur and are accepted as normative, others are reinterpreted, ignored, or discounted. But clearly the testing process is far less rigorous than in science, and religious communities are not as intercultural as scientific communities.

*2. Coherence.* Consistency with accepted theories and internal coherence are sought in science. We have learned from Lakatos that the continuity of a research program is maintained by commitment to its central core, which is protected by making modifications in auxiliary hypotheses. Religious beliefs, too, are judged by their consistency with the central core of a tradition, but here the core is correlated with story and ritual. The interpretation of story and ritual involves auxiliary hypotheses that are subject to modification. Anomalies can be tolerated for considerable periods, but the capacity to respond to them creatively without undermining the central core is a sign of the vitality of a program. Theological formulations are corrigible and have changed substantially in the course of history. New principles of scriptural interpretation and new concepts of God are characteristic of the modern period. More recently, feminist and Third World writers have helped us see some of the biases in the classical tradition. Theology as critical reflection is also concerned about the coherence and systematic interconnection of beliefs.

*3. Scope.* A scientific theory is more secure if it is broad in scope and extensible, correlating diverse types of phenomena in domains different from those in which the theory was first developed. Religious beliefs, too, can be judged by their comprehensiveness in offering a coherent account of diverse kinds of experience, beyond the primary experiences from which they arose. Religious beliefs must be consistent with the well-supported findings of science, and this may sometimes require the reformulation of theological auxiliary hypotheses, as we will see in subsequent chapters. Religious beliefs can also contribute to a comprehensive metaphysics, though they are not the only source of such wider integrative frameworks that are broader than either science or religion. Metaphysical assumptions in turn feed back to affect paradigms in religion, as they do in science.

*4. Fertility.* Theories in science are judged by their achievement and promise in contributing to the vitality of an ongoing program over a period of time. In line with the goals of science, scientific fertility refers to the ability to stimulate theoretical development and experimental research. Religion has more diverse goals, so fertility here has many facets. It includes the capacity to stimulate creative theological reflection. But it also includes evidence of power to nourish religious experience and to effect personal transformation. Beyond this, fertility includes evidence of desirable influence on human character and the motivation to sustain ethical action. The apostle Paul said that "the fruit of the Spirit is love, joy, peace, patience, kindness, goodness, faithfulness, gentleness, self-control" (Gal. 5:22). The philosopher William James discusses saintliness as one criterion. We can also ask about practical implications for the most urgent problems of our time, such as the ecological crisis and world peace. Criteria for evaluating such individual and social consequences are of course strongly paradigm-dependent.

In short, religion cannot claim to be scientific or to be able to conform to the standards of science. But it can exemplify some of the same spirit of inquiry found in science. If theology is critical reflection on the life and thought of the religious community, it is always revisable and corrigible. There are no controlled experiments, but there is a process of testing in the life of the community, and there should be a continual demand that our concepts and beliefs be closely related to what we have experienced. There is no proof, but there is a cumulative case from converging lines of argument. Rational argument in theology is not a single sequence of ideas, like a chain that is as weak as its weakest link. Instead, it is woven of many strands, like a cable many times stronger than its strongest strand.[56] Or, to use an analogy introduced earlier, religious beliefs are like an interlocking network that is not floating freely but is connected at many points to the experience of the community.

Can these same criteria be applied to *comparative judgments* between religious traditions? Ninian Smart refers to world religions as "experiments in living."[57] Could one ask about their comparative success as experiments in living? By the first criterion above, it appears that each set of religious beliefs is in agreement with experience, but each focuses selectively on particular types of experience. Next, each has elaborated beliefs that are coherent, consistent with its heritage, and expressive of its stories and rituals. Moreover, thinkers in each tradition have worked out comprehensive conceptual systems of wide scope. The transformation of personal life has occurred in varying degrees within all the major religious traditions.

When it comes to ethical consequences, there seem to be saints and hypocrites around the world. The ideal of love may be extolled in each tradition, but it has been realized only by rare individuals or in monastic orders and relatively small, dedicated communities—though the ideal may have affected the lives of millions. The actual history of each tradition has seen violence, cruelty, and greed as well as compassion, reconciliation, and dedication to justice. Each heritage seems to have its characteristic strengths and weaknesses, its particular virtues and temptations. One can indeed make some comparative judgments between them in terms of their ideals, if not in terms of their practice. But these judgments are inescapably ambiguous and reflect the norms of one's own traditions.[58]

I believe that the Christian tradition has the potential to meet these criteria better than other traditions, but I have to acknowledge that it has seldom lived up to this potential. I can learn from other traditions, coming to appreciate some of their ethical sensitivities, meditation practices, and models of God, which can be part of my life. Even after trying to learn from them, I am still an outsider whose understanding is fragmentary, and I am not in a position to pass judgment on them. If I take a confessional stance, I can only witness to what has happened in my life and in that of the Christian community; my main task is to respond to the deepest insights of my own heritage.[59]

The differences among religions are too great for us to adopt the Identity of Essence thesis, despite the appeal of its universalism in a global age. The Approximations of Truth position seems difficult to maintain if beliefs and criteria are strongly paradigm-dependent. It may be defended, however, by reliance on revelation, which has no parallel in science. The dangers of Absolutism can be avoided if revelation is not identified with infallible scriptures, revealed doctrines, or authoritative institutions. If revelation occurs through the lives of persons, the human character of theology and the human failings of the church can be acknowledged.

Pluralistic Dialogue allows us to give preeminence to revelation and salvation in Christ without denying the possibility of revelation or salvation in other traditions. It differs from Approximations of Truth in its greater openness to the possibility of distinctive divine initiative in other traditions. It also goes further in accepting the historical conditioning of our interpretive categories. Yet it differs from Cultural Relativism in insisting that there are criteria of judgment, so we do not have to end in skepticism.

The first three criteria, in particular, do exhibit some similarities with science, even if their application is more ambiguous and paradigm-dependent. If we looked only at the noncognitive functions of religious language, such as personal transformation and liturgical celebration, we might accept a total relativism because no truth claims about reality would be asserted. But if religious language does make implicit and explicit claims about reality—even tentative and partial claims—we cannot abandon the use of criteria to evaluate concepts and beliefs. Critical reflection guided by such criteria is primarily motivated by our own search for truth rather than by the desire to prove our superiority over others. But it does imply that there are limits to tolerance. We cannot avoid passing judgment on cannibalism, Satanism, or Nazism or raising questions about what we see as the inadequacies of other religious traditions.

Perhaps Pluralistic Dialogue ends closer to relativism than to absolutism, but it can be distinguished from both. It brings liberation from the quest for *certainty,* which is one of the motivations of absolutism. We have said that certainty is not possible, even in science, and that all understanding is historically conditioned. Yet we do not need to accept the *skepticism* to which extreme relativism leads in the interpretation of both science and religion. Such skepticism would in the long run undermine the commitment that is balanced against tentativeness in both the scientific and the religious community. Of all the alternatives, this path offers the greatest prospect for religious cooperation in a global age.

Pluralistic Dialogue between religions is compatible with *Dialogue* between science and religion concerning questions and methodological parallels (chapter 4). But it is also compatible with a closer *Integration* between science and religion (through natural theology, a theology of nature, or systematic synthesis). Critical realism encourages such integration, for it holds that some statements in the two disciplines refer to a common world. Instrumentalists maintain that ideas of various kinds have dissimilar functions in life; linguistic analysts hold that there are independent language games having little in common. But critical realists affirm that the theories of science and the beliefs of theology both make claims about reality—and that at least some points these claims are related to each other. Some of these relationships are explored in part 3.

# Part Three

## RELIGION AND
## THE THEORIES OF SCIENCE

## CHAPTER 7

# Physics and Metaphysics

In part 3 we turn from the methods of science to the content of particular scientific theories. In successive chapters we look at three scientific disciplines: physics, astronomy, and evolutionary biology. In each case, current scientific theories are outlined and their philosophical and theological implications are explored.

Physics is the study of the basic structures and processes of change in matter and energy. Dealing with the lowest organizational levels, and using the most exact mathematical equations, it seems of all sciences furthest removed from the concerns of religion for life, mind, and human existence. But physics is of great historical and contemporary importance because it was the first science that was systematic and exact, and many of its assumptions were taken over by other sciences. Its methods were seen as ideals for other sciences to emulate. It exerted a major influence on philosophy and theology.

Moreover, though physicists study only the inanimate, they look today at entities from a variety of domains, from quarks and atoms to solid state crystals, planets, and galaxies—including the physical basis of living organisms. Already in the field of physics we confront issues of the observer and the observed, chance and law, and parts and wholes. But the issues here are inevitably complex, and readers who find the details difficult to follow can find a summary of the conclusions at the end of the chapter.

Three assumptions of *Newtonian physics* have been called into question in the twentieth century:

1. Newtonian epistemology was *realistic*. Theories were believed to describe the world as it is in itself, apart from the observer. Space and time were held to be absolute frameworks in which every event is located, independently of the frame of reference of the observer. The "primary" qualities, such as mass and velocity, which can be expressed mathematically, were considered objective characteristics of the real world.

2. Newtonian physics was *deterministic*. In principle, it was held, the future of any system of matter in motion could be predicted from accurate knowledge of its present state. The universe, from the smallest particle to the most distant planet, seemed to be governed by the same inexorable laws.

3. The Newtonian outlook was *reductionistic* in holding that the behavior of the smallest parts, the constituent particles, determines the behavior of the

whole. Change consists in the rearrangement of the parts, which themselves remain unchanged. Here was a powerful image of nature as a law-abiding machine, an image that strongly influenced the development of science and Western thought. This view of the world as a clockwork mechanism led to the deistic view of God as the clockmaker who designed the mechanism and left it to run itself.

The eighteenth century saw the further elaboration of Newtonian mechanics. In the nineteenth century, new types of conceptual schemes were introduced in physics, including electromagnetic theory and the kinetic theory of gases. But the basic assumptions remained unchanged. All laws seemed to be derivable, if not from the mechanics of particles, at least from the laws governing a few kinds of particles and fields. In kinetic theory and thermodynamics, the behavior of gases was described in terms of probability, but this procedure was considered to be only a convenience in calculation. It was assumed that the motion of all gas molecules is precisely determined by mechanical laws, but because these motions are too complex to calculate, we can use statistical laws to predict the average behavior of large groups of molecules.

All three of these assumptions—realism, determinism, and reductionism—have been challenged by twentieth-century physics. The changes in concepts and assumptions were so great that it is not surprising that Kuhn uses it as a prime example of a scientific revolution, a paradigm shift. We will examine quantum theory and relativity as well as recent work in thermodynamics, chaos theory, and complexity, and then explore their implications for religious thought.

## I. QUANTUM THEORY

We have seen that *particle* models, such as the billiard ball model, dominated the classical physics of matter. By the nineteenth century, theorists used another basic type of model, that of *waves* in continuous media, to account for a different group of phenomena involving light and electromagnetism. But early in the present century a number of puzzling experiments seemed to call for the use of both *wave* and *particle* models for both types of phenomena. On the one hand, Einstein's equations for the photoelectric effect and Compton's work on photon scattering showed that light travels in discrete packets, with definite energy and momentum, behaving very much like a stream of particles. Conversely, electrons, which had always been viewed as particles, showed the spread-out interference effects characteristic of waves. Waves are continuous and extended, and they interact in terms of phase; particles are discontinuous, localized, and they interact in terms of momentum. There seems to be no way to combine them into one unified model.[1]

Suppose, for example, that *a stream of electrons* is sent through two parallel slits in a metal screen and strikes a photographic film placed a few centimeters behind the screen. Each electron registers as a single tiny dot on the film; it seems to arrive as a particle, and it must presumably have gone through either one slit or the other if the charge and mass of the electron are indivisible. Yet the dots on the film fall in an interference pattern of parallel bands, which can be explained only if one assumes a wave passing through both slits. This same *wave-particle duality* is found throughout atomic physics. But a unified mathematical formalism can be developed that allows the observed events to be predicted statistically. It yields wave functions for a mixture of possibilities, a "superposition of states." One can calculate the *probability* that an electron will strike the film at any given point. Within the calculated probability distribution, however, the exact point at which a particular electron will strike cannot be predicted.

Similarly, *no unified model* of the atom has been developed in quantum theory. The earlier "Bohr model" of the atom could be easily visualized; particle-like electrons followed orbits around the nucleus, resembling a miniature solar system. But the atom of quantum theory cannot be pictured at all. One might try to imagine patterns of *probability waves* filling the space around the nucleus like the vibrations of a three-dimensional symphony of musical tones of incredible complexity, but the analogy would not help us much. The atom is inaccessible to direct observation and unimaginable in terms of sensory qualities; it cannot even be described coherently in terms of classical concepts such as space, time, and causality. The behavior of the very small is radically different from that of everyday objects. We can describe by statistical equations what happens in experiments, but we cannot ascribe familiar classical attributes consistently to the inhabitants of the atomic world.

The extensions of quantum theory in recent years into the nuclear and subnuclear domains have maintained the probabilistic character of the earlier theory. *Quantum field theory* is a generalization of quantum theory that is consistent with special relativity. It has been applied with great success to electromagnetic interactions and subnuclear interactions (quantum chromodynamics or quark theory) and electroweak theory.[2] Let us trace, then, the challenge that quantum theory presents in turn to realism, determinism, and reductionism.

## 1. COMPLEMENTARITY

Niels Bohr defended the use of wave and particle models and other pairs of sharply contrasting sets of concepts. His discussion of what he called the Complementarity Principle included several themes. Bohr emphasized that we must always talk about an atomic system in relation to an experimental arrangement; we can never talk about it in isolation, in itself. We must consider *the interaction between subject and object* in every experiment. No sharp line can be drawn between the process of observation and what is observed. We are actors and not merely spectators, and we choose the experimental tools we will employ. Bohr held that it is the interactive process of observation, not the mind or consciousness of the observer, that must be taken into account.

Another theme in Bohr's writing is the *conceptual limitation* of human understanding. The human as knower, rather than as experimenter, is the center of attention here. Bohr shares Kant's skepticism about the possibility of knowing the world in itself. If we try, as it were, to force nature into certain conceptual molds, we preclude the full use of other molds. Thus we must choose between complete causal *or* spatiotemporal descriptions, between wave *or* particle models, between accurate knowledge of position *or* momentum. The more one set of concepts is used, the less the complementary set can be applied simultaneously. This reciprocal limitation occurs because the atomic world cannot be described in terms of the concepts of classical physics and observable phenomena.[3]

How, then, are the concepts of quantum physics related to the real world? Three differing views of the status of theoretical entities in science yield differing interpretations of quantum theory.

*1. Classical Realism.* Newton and almost all physicists through the nineteenth century said that theories are descriptions of nature as it is in itself apart from the observer. Space, time, mass, and other "primary qualities" are properties of all real objects. Conceptual models are replicas of the world that enable us to visualize the unobservable structure of the world in familiar classical terms. Einstein continued this tradition, insisting that a full description of an atomic system requires specifying the classical spatiotemporal variables that define its state objectively and unambiguously. He held that since quantum theory does not do this, it is incomplete and will eventually be superseded by a theory that fulfills classical expectations.

*2. Instrumentalism.* Here theories are said to be convenient human constructs, calculating devices for correlating observations and making predictions. They are also practical tools for achieving technical control. They are to be judged by their usefulness in fulfilling these goals, not by their correspondence to reality (which is inaccessible to us). Models are imaginative fictions used temporarily to construct theories, after which they can be discarded; they are not literal representations of the world. We cannot say anything about the atom between our observations, though we can use the quantum equations to make predictions about observable phenomena.

It is often assumed that Bohr must have been an instrumentalist because he rejected classical realism in his protracted debate with Einstein. He did indeed say that classical concepts cannot be used unambiguously to describe independently existing atomic systems. Classical concepts can be used only to describe observable phenomena in particular experimental situations. We cannot visualize the world as it is in itself apart from our interaction with it. Bohr did agree with much of the instrumentalist critique of classical realism, but he did not endorse instrumentalism specifically, and more careful analysis suggests that he adopted a third alternative.

*3. Critical Realism.* Critical realists view theories as partial representations of limited aspects of the world as it interacts with us. Theories allow us to correlate diverse aspects of the world manifest in differing experimental situations. To the critical realist, models are abstract and selective but indispensable attempts to imagine the structures of the world that give rise to these interactions. The goal of science, in this view, is understanding, not control. The corroboration of predictions is one test for valid understanding, but prediction is not in itself a goal of science.

A good case can be made that Bohr adopted a form of critical realism, though his writings were not always clear. In the debate with Einstein, he was not denying the reality of electrons or atoms, but claiming instead that they are not the sort of things that admit of precise classical space-time descriptions. He did not accept Mach's phenomenalism, which questioned the reality of atoms. Summarizing the dispute, Henry Folse says, "He discarded the classical framework and kept a realistic understanding of the scientific description of nature. What he rejects is not realism, but the classical version of it."[4] Bohr presupposed the reality of the atomic system that is interacting with the observing system. In contrast to subjectivist interpretations of quantum theory, which take observation to be a mental-physical interaction, Bohr talks about *physical interactions* between instrumental and atomic systems in a total experimental situation. Moreover, wave and particle or momentum and position or other complementary descriptions apply to *the same object,* even though the concepts are not unambiguously applicable to it. They represent different manifestations of the same atomic system. Folse writes:

Bohr argues that such representations are "abstractions" which serve an indispensable role in allowing a phenomenon to be described as an interaction between observing systems and atomic systems, but which cannot picture the properties of an independent reality. . . . We can describe such a reality in terms of its power to produce the various different interactions described by the theory as providing complementary evidence about the same object.[5]

Bohr did not accept the classical realist view of the world as consisting of entities with determinate classical properties, but he still held that there is a real world, which in interacting has the power to produce observable phenomena. Folse concludes his book on Bohr with this summary:

The ontology implied by this interpretation of Bohr's message characterizes physical objects through their powers to appear in different phenomenal manifestations rather than through determinate properties corresponding to those of phenomenal objects as was held in the classical framework. The case is then made that, within the framework of complementarity, it is possible to preserve a realistic understanding of science and accept the completeness of quantum theory only by revising our understanding of the nature of an independent physical reality and how we can have knowledge of it.[6]

In short, we do have to abandon the sharp separation of the observer and the observed that was assumed in classical physics. In quantum theory, the observer is always a participant. In complementarity, the use of one model limits the use of other models. Models are symbolic representations of aspects of interactive reality that cannot be uniquely visualized in terms of analogies with everyday experience; they are only very indirectly related to either the atomic world or the observable phenomena. But we do not have to accept an instrumentalism that makes theories and models useful intellectual and practical tools that tell us nothing about the world.

Bohr himself proposed that the idea of complementarity could be *extended to other phenomena* susceptible to analysis by two kinds of models: mechanistic and organic models in biology, behavioristic and introspective models in psychology, models of free will and determinism in philosophy, or of divine justice and divine love in theology. Some authors go further and speak of *the complementarity of science and religion*. Thus C. A. Coulson, after explaining the wave-particle duality and Bohr's generalization of it, calls science and religion "complementary accounts of one reality."[7]

I am dubious about such extended usage of the term. I would set down several conditions for applying the concept of complementarity.[8]

1. Models should be called complementary only if they refer to *the same entity* and are of *the same logical type*. Wave and particle are models of a single entity (for example, an electron) in a single situation (for example, a two-slit experiment); they are on the same logical level and had previously been employed in the same discipline. These conditions do not apply to "science and religion." They arise typically in differing situations and serve differing functions in human life.[9] For these reasons I speak of science and religion as alternative languages and restrict the term *complementary* to models of the same logical type within a given language, such as personal and impersonal models of God (chap. 5).

2. One should make clear that the use of the term outside physics is *analogical and not inferential*. There must be independent evidence of the value of two alternative models or sets of constructs in the other field. It cannot be assumed that methods found useful in physics will be fruitful in other disciplines.

3. Complementarity provides *no justification for an uncritical acceptance of dichotomies*. It cannot be used to avoid dealing with inconsistencies or to veto the search for unity. The paradoxical element in the wave-particle duality should not be overemphasized. We do not say that an electron is both a wave and a particle, but only that it exhibits wavelike and particlelike behavior; moreover we do have a unified mathematical formalism, which provides for at least probabilistic predictions. We cannot rule out the search for new unifying models, even though previous attempts have not yielded any theories in better agreement with the data than quantum theory. Coherence remains an important ideal in all reflective inquiry, even if it is qualified by acknowledgment of the limitations of human language and thought.

## 2. INDETERMINACY

We have seen that for individual events quantum theory typically makes only predictions of probability. For example, we can predict when half of a large group of radioactive atoms will have disintegrated, but we cannot predict when a particular atom will disintegrate; we can predict only the probability that it will disintegrate in a given time interval. The Heisenberg Uncertainty

Principle states that the more accurately we determine the position of an electron, the less accurately we can determine its momentum, and vice versa. A similar uncertainty relation connects other pairs of conjugate variables, such as energy and time.

Do these uncertainties represent the limitations of our knowledge or real indeterminacy and chance in the world? Three possible answers were given in the early years of quantum theory, and the debate among them continues today:

1. Uncertainty may be attributed to *temporary human ignorance*. Exact laws will eventually be discovered.

2. Uncertainty may be attributed to *inherent experimental or conceptual limitations*. The atom in itself is forever inaccessible to us.

3. Uncertainty may be attributed to *indeterminacy in nature*. There are alternative potentialities in the atomic world.

The three positions parallel the three epistemological positions of the preceding section. The first is classically realist (in epistemology) and *deterministic* (in metaphysics). The second is instrumentalist and *agnostic about determinism;* we can never know how the atom itself behaves between observations. The third, which I defend, is critically realist and *indeterministic*. Let us look at each of these interpretations.[10]

## 1. Uncertainty as Human Ignorance

Some of our uncertainties reflect our lack of knowledge about systems that conform to precise laws. Kinetic theory assumed that the motion of gas molecules is precisely determined but is too complicated to calculate. The uncertainty was thought to be entirely *subjective,* representing incompleteness of information. A minority of physicists, including Einstein and Planck, have maintained that the uncertainties of quantum mechanics are similarly attributable to our present ignorance. They believed that detailed subatomic mechanisms are rigidly causal and deterministic; someday the laws of these mechanisms will be found and exact prediction will be possible.

Einstein wrote, "The great initial success of quantum theory cannot convert me to believe in that fundamental game of dice. . . . I am absolutely convinced that one will eventually arrive at a theory in which the objects connected by laws are not probabilities but conceived facts."[11] Einstein expressed his own faith in the order and predictability of the universe, which he thought would be marred by any element of chance. "God does not play dice," he said. As we saw, Einstein was a classical realist, holding that the concepts of classical physics must "refer to things which claim real existence independent of perceiving subjects."

David Bohm has tried to preserve determinism and realism by constructing a new formalism with hidden variables at a lower level. The apparent randomness at the atomic level would arise from variations in the concurrence of exact forces at the postulated subatomic level.[12] So far his calculations yield no empirical conclusions differing from those of quantum mechanics, though Bohm hoped that in the future hidden variables may play a detectable role. Most scientists are dubious about such proposals. Unless someone can actually develop an alternative theory that can be tested, they say, we had better accept the probabilistic theories we have and give up our nostalgia for the certainties of the past.

## 2. Uncertainty as Experimental or Conceptual Limitations

Many physicists assert that uncertainty is not a product of temporary ignorance but a fundamental limitation permanently preventing exact knowledge of the atomic domain. The first version of this position, found in the early writings of Bohr and Heisenberg, claims that the difficulty is an experimental one; the uncertainty is introduced by *the process of observation*. Suppose that we want to observe an electron. To do so we must bombard it with a quantum of light, which disturbs the situation we were attempting to study. The disturbance of the system is unavoidable, since there must be at least a minimal interaction of the observer and the observed. Although this interpretation fits many experiments, it appears unable to account for uncertainties when nothing is done to disturb the system—for example, the unpredictability of the time at which a radioactive atom spontaneously disintegrates or the time at which an isolated atom makes a transition from an excited state.

The second version of the argument attributes uncertainty to our *inescapable conceptual limitations*. By our choice of experimental situations we decide in which of our conceptual schemes (wave or particle, exact position or exact velocity) an electron will manifest itself to us. The structure of the atomic world is such that we must choose either causal descriptions (using probability functions that evolve deterministically) or spatiotemporal descriptions (using localized variables that are only statistically connected)—but we cannot have both at once. This interpretation is *agnostic* as to whether the atom itself, which we can never know, is determinate or indeterminate (though a particular author expounding it may on other grounds favor one assumption or the other). As indicated above, many physicists since Bohr have been instrumentalists, though I have claimed that he himself was closer to critical realism.

## 3. Uncertainty as Indeterminacy in Nature

In his later writings, Heisenberg held that indeterminacy is *an objective feature of nature* and not a limitation of human knowledge.[13] Such a viewpoint would accord with the critical realism I have advocated in which scientific theories are held to be representations of nature, albeit limited and imperfect ones. These limitations help to remind us that the denizens of the atomic realm are of a very different sort from the objects of everyday experience—but this does not mean that they are less real. Instead of assuming that an electron has a precise position and velocity that are unknown to us, we should conclude that it is not the sort of entity that always has such properties. Observing consists in extracting from the existing probability distribution one of the many *possibilities* it contains. The influence of the observer, in this view, does not consist in disturbing a previously precise though unknown value, but in forcing one of the many existing potentialities to be actualized. The observer's activity becomes part of the history of the atomic event, but it is an objective history, and even the spontaneously disintegrating atom, left to itself, has its history.

If this interpretation is correct, indeterminacy characterizes the world. Heisenberg calls this "the restoration of the concept of *potentiality*." In the Middle Ages the idea of potentiality referred to the tendency of an entity to develop in a particular way. Heisenberg does not accept the Aristotelian manner of describing a potentiality as a striving to attain a future purpose, but he does suggest that the probabilities of modern physics refer to tendencies in nature that include a *range of possibilities*. The future is not simply unknown. It is "not decided." More than one alternative is open and there is some opportunity for unpredictable novelty. Time involves a unique historicity and unrepeatability; the world would not repeat its course if it were restored to a former state, for at each point a different event from among the potentialities might be actualized. Potentiality and chance are objective and not merely subjective phenomena.

A more exotic version of objective indeterminacy is Hugh Everett's *many-universes interpretation*. Everett proposed that every time a quantum system can yield more than one possible outcome, the universe splits into many separate universes, in each of which one of these possible outcomes occurs.[14] We happen to be in the universe in which there occurs the outcome that we observe, and we have no access to the other universes in which duplicates of us observe other possibilities. Since there are many atoms and many quantum events each second, the universe would have to divide into a mind-boggling proliferation of universes. Moreover, the theory seems to be in principle untestable, since we have no access to other universes containing the potentialities unrealized in ours. It seems much simpler to assume that potentialities not actualized in our universe are not actualized anywhere. Then we would have one universe which is objectively indeterminate.

In any case, adherents of the second and third of these basic positions—which between them include by far the majority of contemporary physicists—agree in rejecting the determinism of Newtonian physics, even if they do not agree on their reasons for doing so.

## 3. PARTS AND WHOLES

Beyond the challenges to realism and determinism, quantum theory calls into question the *reductionism* of classical physics. We have already discussed the inseparability of observer and observed and the need to consider both the experimental apparatus and the atomic system. But the necessity of talking about wholes is also evident in many other ways.

It was once thought that protons, neutrons, and electrons were indivisible, the basic building blocks of matter. During the 1950s and 1960s, experiments with high-energy accelerators produced a variety of other types of particles, each with distinctive mass, charge, and spin, some existing for only a billionth of a second or less. Systematic order within this "zoo" of strange particles appeared when it was proposed in 1963 that they are all composed of even smaller particles dubbed *quarks*. There seem to be only a few types of quarks (arbitrarily identified by "flavors" and "colors") and a few simple rules for the ways they can combine. But quarks are a strange type of "component": free quarks have never been observed, and it appears that a quark cannot exist alone, according to the theory of quark confinement. A proton is made up of three quarks, for example, but if you try to separate them you need a great deal of energy and you end by creating more quarks, which combine with the ones you already had to make new protons and other particles. Quarks are parts that apparently cannot exist except in a larger whole.[15]

The various "elementary particles" composed of quarks seem to be temporary manifestations of shifting patterns of waves that combine at one point, dissolve again, and recombine elsewhere. A particle begins to look more like a local outcropping of a continuous substratum of vibratory energy. A force between two particles (protons, for example) can be thought of as arising from a field or from a rapid exchange of other kinds of particles (mesons, in this case). A bound electron in an atom has to be considered as a state of *the whole atom* rather than as a separate entity. As more complex systems are built up, *new properties* appear that were not foreshadowed in the parts alone. New wholes have distinctive principles of organization as systems and therefore exhibit properties and activities not found in their components.

Consider the helium atom, composed of two protons and two neutrons (in its nucleus) and two orbital electrons. In the planetary model it was pictured as a nucleus around which circled two separate identifiable electrons; the atom's parts were clearly distinguishable, and the laws of its total behavior were derivable from analysis of the behavior of these components. But in quantum theory the helium atom is a total pattern with *no distinguishable parts*. Its wave function is not at all the sum of two separate single-electron wave functions. The electrons have lost their individuality; we do not have electron A and electron B but simply a two-electron pattern in which all separate identity is lost. (In the statistics of classical physics, an atom with A in an excited energy state and B in a normal state counts as a different configuration from the atom with A and B interchanged, but in quantum theory it does not.)

In the case of helium and more complex atoms with additional electrons, we find that their configurations are governed by the *Pauli Exclusion Principle*, a law concerning the total atom that cannot conceivably be derived from laws concerning individual electrons. The principle states that in a given atom no two electrons can be in identical states (with the same quantum numbers specifying energy, angular momentum, and spin). To this remarkable and far-reaching principle can be attributed the periodic table and the chemical properties of the elements. When another electron is added to a given atom, it must assume a state different from all electrons already present. If one used classical reasoning, one would have to assume that the new electron is somehow influenced by all the other electrons; but this "exclusion" does not resemble any imaginable set of forces or fields. In quantum reasoning any attempt to describe the behavior of the constituent electrons is simply abandoned; the properties of the atom as a whole are analyzed by *new laws* unrelated to those governing its separate "parts," which have now lost their identity. A bound electron is a state of the system, not an independent entity.[16]

The energy levels of an array of atoms in the solid state (such as a crystal lattice) are a property of the whole system rather than of its components. Again, some of the disorder-order transitions and the so-called *cooperative phenomena* have proved impossible to analyze atomistically—for example, the cooperation of elementary magnetic units when a metal is cooled or the cooperative behavior of electrons in a superconductor. Such situations, writes one physicist, "involve a new organizing principle as we proceed from the individual to the system," which results in "qualitatively new phenomena." There seem to be *system laws* that cannot be derived from the laws of the components; distinctive explanatory concepts characterize higher organizational levels.[17] Interpenetrating fields and integrated totalities replace self-contained, externally related particles as fundamental images of nature. The being of any entity is constituted by its relationships and its participation in more inclusive patterns. Without such holistic quantum phenomena we would not have chemical properties, transistors, superconductors, nuclear power, or indeed life itself. Such holism contrasts with the reductionism of Newtonian physics.

## 4. BELL'S THEOREM

Some fascinating but complex experiments have thrown further light on the relation between the three classical assumptions—realism, determinism, and reductionism. (Readers who find the argument difficult to follow can skip to the next section.) In 1935, Einstein proposed a type of experiment that has become possible to carry out only in the last few years.[18] In one version, a source emits two particles, A and B, which fly off in opposite directions, say left and right. If the system initially had total spin zero, conservation laws require that the spin of B is equal and opposite to that of A. If a directionally sensitive detector is placed perpendicular to the flight path at some distance to the left, one can measure a particular component of the spin of A. One can then predict the precise value of the corresponding component of the spin of B (namely, equal and opposite), which can be measured with a second detector at the right. Quantum theory describes each particle in flight as a mixture of waves, representing with equal probability various possible spin orientations. Each set of waves collapses to a single value only when a measurement is made. Thus B will behave differently according to what one chooses to measure on A. How can B know which component of A's spin one will choose to measure?

Einstein argued that while in flight B's spin must already have had a definite value, not a probability distribution. He made two assumptions: (1) *classical realism* (individual particles possess definite classical properties at all times, even when we are not observing them), and (2) *locality* (no causal influence can be transmitted between two isolated systems faster than the speed of light, which we will see shortly is a limit set by relativity theory). Einstein concluded from his "thought experiment" that the probability descriptions of quantum theory must be incomplete, and that there must be hidden variables in each of the traveling particles, determining a particular outcome. Bohr replied that Einstein's form of realism was misguided because we cannot talk about the property of a particle except in relation to a measuring process. In particular, we must think of the two particles and the two detectors as a single indivisible experimental situation. The wave function encompasses both particles, even though they are distant from each other.

In 1965 John Bell calculated the statistical correlation one would expect between the data at the two detectors if Einstein's assumptions are correct. Recent experiments by Alain Aspect and others have not been consistent with these expectations, indicating that one of Einstein's assumptions is incorrect. In a "delayed choice" version of the experiment in 1983, Aspect was able to switch the orientation of the left detector at the last minute while the particles were in flight—too late for any signal to reach the right particle before it arrived at its detector.[19] The particles behaved as if there were some communication between them, but they were too far apart to communicate in the time available. *Classically realistic local theories* seem to be ruled out by these experiments.

Most physicists conclude that we should follow Bohr here, *giving up classical realism* and *keeping locality* (the finite limit on the speed with which any influence can be transmitted). They insist that particles A and B originated in one event and must be regarded as a single system even when they are far apart. The quantum wave function must include both particles. Only after an observation can they be regarded as having separate identities and independent existence. But it is possible to maintain a critical realism concerning the probabilistic whole while abandoning classical realism concerning the separate parts. Thus the physicist Paul Davies concludes, "The system of interest cannot be regarded as a collection of things, but as an indivisible, unified whole."[20] Polkinghorne writes, "Quantum states exhibit an unexpected degree of togetherness. . . . The experiment points to a surprisingly integrationist view of the relationship of systems which have once interacted with each other, however widely they may subsequently separate."[21]

Another option is to keep classical realism and give up locality. Among defenders of *realistic nonlocal* theories is David Bohm. He has developed the equations for a quantum potential that acts as a kind of instantaneous pilot wave guiding particles; the wave incorporates encoded information about both local and distant events and does not fall off with distance. Bohm holds that there is a holistic underlying *implicate order* whose information unfolds into the explicate order of particular fields and particles. One analogy he uses is a TV signal with information enfolded in an electromagnetic wave, which the TV receiver unfolds as a visual image. Another analogy is a holographic photograph, of which every part has three-dimensional information about the whole object photographed.[22] Bohm's scheme shows a dramatic wholeness by allowing for *nonlocal, noncausal,* instantaneous connections. Events separated in space and time are correlated because they are unfolded from the same implicate order, but there is no direct causal connection between them since one event does not itself influence another event. (It would be like two TV screens showing images of a moving object taken from different angles; the two images are correlated, but one image does not influence the other.) The theory does not violate the relativistic prohibition of signals faster than the speed of light, for there is no way to use it to send a signal from one detector to the other.[23] Most physicists acknowledge that Bohm's view is consistent with the experiments, but they are reluctant to abandon Bohr's view until there is experimental evidence against it. The development of quantum potential theory by Bohm and his coworkers may lead to distinctive testable predictions, but it has not done so to date.

In sum, Einstein's classically realist, determinist, and local interpretation seems to be ruled out by the Aspect experiments. Bohm's theory, with its classical realism, determinism, and extreme nonlocal holism, cannot yet be experimentally distinguished from standard quantum theory. The instrumentalists claim that we cannot say anything about the world between observations and therefore questions about determinism and holism should be dismissed as meaningless. I have advocated a combination of critical realism, indeterminacy, and a more limited form of holism, and I have suggested that Bohr himself was actually closer to this view than to instrumentalism.

## II. RELATIVITY

Let us consider next the other major revolution in twentieth-century physics, Einstein's theory of relativity, and examine the new understanding of space and time to which it leads.

### 1. SPACE, TIME, AND MATTER

For Newton and throughout classical physics, space and time are separable and absolute. Space is like an empty container in which every object has a definite location. Time passes uniformly and universally, the same for all observers. The cosmos consists of the total of all such objects in space at the present moment, which is a simultaneous and shared "now." The length and mass of an object are unchanging, intrinsic, objective properties, independent of the observer. All of this is close to our everyday experience and common-sense assumptions, but it is challenged by relativity.

In 1905, at the age of twenty-six, Einstein wrote his first paper proposing *special relativity.* His search for symmetry in the equations for moving electromagnetic fields, along with the Michaelson-Morley experiments with light, led him to postulate *the constancy of the velocity of light* for all observers. This hypothesis had unexpected and far-reaching implications. Imagine that an observer at the middle of a moving railway train sends light signals, that reach the equidistant front and rear of the train at the same instant. For an observer on the ground, the signals travel *different distances* to the two ends (since the train moves while the signals are traveling); therefore if the signals travel at constant velocity in his framework they must arrive at *different times*. The two events are simultaneous in one frame of reference but not in the other. The effect would be very small with a train but would be large with a space rocket or a high-energy particle approaching the velocity of light.[24]

There is also a *time dilation,* which has been confirmed in many experiments. For example, a mu-meson has a lifetime of 2 microseconds. But if it is traveling at very high velocity in a circular orbit in an accelerator, its lifetime as measured on the ground will be much longer, and it will go around many more times than one would expect. Measurements of *mass* and *length* as well as time vary according to the frame of reference. The mass of a particle, such as the circulating meson, becomes much larger as its velocity relative to the measuring apparatus approaches the velocity of light. Lengths contract, so a moving object appears much shorter in the direction of motion (though from the moving object, it is the other objects that appear compressed). The theory also predicts the equivalence of *mass* and *energy* ($E = mc^2$, confirmed in the atomic bomb explosion), and also the creation and annihilation of matter and antimatter (confirmed in the creation and mutual annihilation of electron-positron pairs).

Because there is no universal simultaneity and no common present separating past and future, the division between *past* and *future* will vary among observers. Some events, which are past for one observer, may still be future for other observers. However, for any two events that could be causally connected (a light signal could pass between them), the order of before and after is the same for all possible observers. No one could conclude that an effect preceded its cause. There is no way to influence the past or to change history. People could leave the earth on a spaceship in the year 2000, travel at high velocity for five years, and return to earth five years older to find themselves in the year 3000. But there is no way they can go back to the year 1000. ("Time travel" works only in one direction, so no one will face the science fiction question of what would happen if you went back and killed one of your ancestors.)

Space and time, then, are not independent but are united in a *spacetime continuum.* The spatial separation of two events varies according to the observer, and the temporal separation also varies, but the two variations are correlated in a definite way. Different observers "project" spatial and temporal dimensions of the four-dimensional spatiotemporal interval in different ways, but each can calculate what the other will be observing. There are rules for translating into equivalent relationships in another frame of reference.

In 1915, Einstein went on to develop the *general theory of relativity*, extending his earlier ideas to include gravity. He reasoned that an observer in a windowless elevator or spaceship cannot tell the effects of a gravitational field from the effects of accelerated motion. From this he concluded that the geometry of space is itself affected by matter. Gravity bends space, giving it a four-dimensional curvature (here the fourth dimension is spatial rather than temporal, and it is reflected in the altered geometry of three-dimensional space). As John Wheeler puts it, "Space tells matter how to move, and matter tells space how to curve."[25] Dramatic confirmation was obtained in 1919, when it was observed during an eclipse that light rays from distant stars were slightly bent by the sun's gravitational field. Time is also shrunk by gravity, and clocks slow down as they do from relative motion. In 1959, very accurate experiments at Harvard showed that a photon traveling from the basement of a building to the top floor changes its frequency slightly because of the difference in gravitational field.

One of the most striking conclusions from general relativity is that the universe may be *finite, curved, and unbounded* (that is, closed) rather than infinite (that is, open). If so, a person setting out from the earth into space in one direction would return eventually from the opposite direction. As we will see in the next chapter, it is not clear from present evidence whether there is sufficient matter in the universe for space to be closed rather than open. But what has been clear since Hubble's red-shift measurements is that space itself is everywhere expanding. The present motion indicates the expansion of all parts of the universe from a common explosion 15 billion years ago. This was not the explosion of matter into a preexisting void, but the expansion of space itself.

## 2. THE STATUS OF TIME

Let me first discuss three claims supposedly based on relativity that seem to me dubious.

*1. "Time is illusory and events are determined."* We can draw graphs showing time as if it were another spatial dimension. It is sometimes said that we can represent the cosmos as a static spatiotemporal block that different observers "project" as spatial and temporal dimensions in differing ways. Taken as a whole, the block does not "happen"; it just "is." In reply, I would insist that temporal change *does* occur in every frame of reference. We should speak of "the temporalization of space" rather than "the spatialization of time."[26] Dynamic events, not unchanging substances, are now taken to constitute reality. It may appear deterministic to say that what is future for one observer is already past (and therefore "determined") for another observer. But this is not true for causally related events, among which futurity is shared. Special relativity and quantum theory have been combined in relativistic quantum theory, in which indeterminacies become determinate only with the passage of time.

*2. "Reality is mental."* Length, mass, velocity, and time, once thought to be objective, primary properties of objects in themselves, are now known to be relative to the observer. This has sometimes been taken as evidence that the human mind forms the reality of the world. But the "frame of reference of the observer" does not require a human mind. It might consist of clocks and meter sticks and measuring devices that could be recorded by an automatic camera. The mesons circulating in an accelerator are "observed" by Geiger counters connected to computer printouts. The lesson here is interconnectedness, not the pervasiveness of consciousness or mentality.

3. *"Relativity supports relativism."* Science is said to have shown that everything is relative and there are no absolutes, and this has been cited in support of moral and religious relativism. But the claim is dubious even in physics. Many absolutes have been given up (space, time, mass, and so forth), but there are new ones. The velocity of light is absolute, and the spacetime interval between two events is the same for all observers. Everyone carries their own clock and their own time zone, but the order of causally related events does not change. Moreover, Einstein took pains to show that while phenomena do vary among frames of reference, the laws of physics are invariant among them. There is a core of relationships that is not observer-dependent, though it is described from multiple points of view.[27]

In relativity there is greater diversity among observations than in classical physics, but there is an underlying unity. In the previous chapter, I asked whether there is any such underlying unity among diverse religious traditions, any invariants in religious experience, any equivalencies in translating from one tradition to another. In that context I sought a middle path between an unequivocal absolutism and a total relativism—a path not unlike that in relativistic physics, though obviously not expressed in mathematical equations.

If we reject these three dubious claims, does relativity have other metaphysical implications that can be defended? Yes, it shows us a *dynamic* and *interconnected* universe. Space and time are inseparable, mass is a form of energy, and gravity and acceleration are indistinguishable. There is an interplay between the dynamics of matter and the form of space, a dialectic between temporal process and spatial geometry. Matter is, if you will, a wrinkle in the elastic matrix of spacetime. Instead of separate enduring things, externally related to each other, we have a unified flux of interacting events. Gravity and quantum theory have not yet been united, but physicists are currently working on such a supertheory in which electromagnetic, nuclear, and gravitational forces will be shown to be forms of one basic force. Along with this wholeness and interdependence, however, relativity introduces a new form of separateness and isolation. It takes time for connections to be effective, so we are momentarily alone in each present. There are some regions of space so distant that it takes billions of years for a signal to reach us from them. We are isolated from most of the universe for incredibly long stretches of time.

Does relativity provide any analogies for talking about God? Perhaps it can help us to imagine God as *omnipresent* yet *superspatial*. Karl Heim speaks of

God and selfhood as other "spaces" and "in another dimension." The same set of events can be differently ordered in different spaces. Spaces are concurrent frameworks with incommensurable dimensions; they permeate each other without boundaries.[28] Heim is extending terms from relativity as analogies for religious thought, not making direct inferences from science.

A further question is raised by the fact that apparently there can be no physical communication faster than the velocity of light. Do we say that God has an array of local projects in isolated parts of the universe? Or is God timeless and eternal, transcending time as well as space? I suggest that God is omnipresent and knows all events instantaneously. The limitation on the speed of transmission of physical signals between distant points would not apply, since God is immanent at all points and in all events. God is neither at rest nor in motion relative to other systems. We would have to assume that God influences an event in terms of the pattern of events relevant to its situation and its causal past, which, of course, is uniquely defined for all frames of reference.[29]

## III. ORDER AND COMPLEXITY

Let us turn next to recent work in thermodynamics and chaos theory and the implications for our understanding of order and complexity.

### 1. THERMODYNAMICS AND ORDER

In classical and relativistic physics, all interactions are exactly *reversible* in time. If you are watching a film of colliding billiard balls, and the film is alternately run forward and backward, you cannot tell which direction was the original, since both sets of motions obey the laws of mechanics. But in phenomena among large numbers of particles there is an *irreversible* change from order to disorder, which indicates the directionality of time. A bottle of perfume is opened and the scent fills the room; the molecules do not spontaneously return from the room to the bottle. A bomb explodes and scatters its fragments, dissipating heat to the surroundings; the reverse does not occur. Past and future are here clearly distinguishable.

The Second Law of Thermodynamics expresses this change: in every closed system there is an increase of *entropy*, which is a measure of *disorder*. A high-entropy disordered system has high probability (because there are many arrangements of the constituents by which it can be achieved) and low information content (since it appears random). An ordered system, by contrast, has lower entropy, lower probability, and higher information content. In closed systems, *order* and *information* are dissipated over time. On a cosmic scale this is referred to as the "running down" of the universe. Energy becomes less available as temperature differences come to an equilibrium.

*Living systems* have a high degree of order and information. They have a very low probability of occurring from the random assembly of their constituent atoms or molecules. How, then, could they have come into existence in evolutionary history? And how can a living system grow and maintain itself today? Living organisms do not violate the Second Law because they are open rather than closed systems. They receive a constant inflow of materials and energy from the environment, deriving primarily from the sun's energy. An organism is a relatively stable self-maintaining system, an island of high local order drawing on the order of its wider environment. A local change in entropy is paid for by a change in entropy elsewhere.[30]

In chapter 9 we will ask about the evolutionary origin of life. But already within physics we find some interesting examples of the emergence of *higher levels of order* in self-organizing systems. Most physical systems will return to the most probable, disordered, equilibrium state if disturbed from it. But sometimes, if they are unstable and far from equilibrium, a new level of collective order will appear and achieve a stable form. Ilya Prigogine won a Nobel Prize for his work on nonequilibrium thermodynamics. One of his examples is the appearance of a vortex in the turbulence of a flowing river. Again, complex patterns of convection cells are formed in the circulation of a fluid heated from below. In such cases a small fluctuation is amplified and leads to a new and more complex order, which resists further fluctuations and maintains itself with a throughput of energy from the environment. Sometimes there is a "bifurcation of paths" (for example, the convection cells can go clockwise or counterclockwise). The choice of paths seems to be the result of very small chance fluctuations.[31]

Prigogine has analyzed many inanimate self-organizing systems in which *disorder* at one level leads to *order* at a higher level, with new laws governing the behavior of structures showing new types of complexity. Randomness at one level leads to dynamic patterns at another level. In some cases the new order can be predicted by considering the average or statistical behavior of the myriad components. But in other cases, Prigogine shows, there are many possible outcomes, and no unique prediction can be made. Multiple divergent solutions arise from these nonlinear instabilities. The formation of such self-organizing, self-perpetuating systems at the molecular level was perhaps the first step in the emergence of life. As in quantum theory, there seems to be a complex interplay of law and chance; here, too, we must look at larger wholes and higher levels of organization and not just at the component parts. Once again, determinism and reduction are called into question.

## 2. CHAOS THEORY AND COMPLEXITY

Another field in which determinism and reduction have been challenged is *chaos theory*. Like the thermodynamic systems studied by Prigogine, chaotic systems are non-linear, and a very small initial change can result in a very large change at a later time. Deterministic equations describe dynamic physical systems (such as a set of billiard balls or a pair of coupled pendulums) or certain interactive social systems (in economics or population demographics, for instance). If one assumes an exact set of initial conditions, the equations can be run on a computer to give a determinate result. But the outcome is highly sensitive to very small initial variations, and the solutions sometimes diverge exponentially.[32]

In chaotic systems, *an infinitesimally small uncertainty* concerning initial conditions can lead to enormous uncertainties in predicting subsequent behavior. This has been called "the butterfly effect" because a butterfly in Brazil might alter the weather a month later in New York. The effect of moving an electron on a distant galaxy might be amplified over a long period of time to alter events on the earth. Deterministic laws are strictly applicable only to closed systems; they are an approximation to reality because actual systems that are extremely sensitive to initial conditions can never be totally isolated from outside influences. If God acted by making infinitesimal changes in chaotic systems it would be undetectable scientifically; divine action could not be proved, but it could not be disproved either, as we will see in chapter 12.[33]

According to Stephen Kellert, the *unpredictability* of chaotic systems is not merely a reflection of temporary human ignorance. Prediction over a long time period would require more information than could be stored on all the electrons of our galaxy, and the calculations would take longer than the phenomena we were trying to predict. Moreover chaotic systems would amplify the quantum indeterminacies that set limits to the accurate specification of initial conditions in both theory and practice. Kellert also notes that in classical physics the behavior of a larger whole is deduced from predictive causal laws governing interactions of its constituent parts. Chaos theory, by contrast, studies the qualitative form of *large-scale patterns* that may be similar even when the constituents are very different. Chaos theory examines holistic geometrical relationships and systemic properties rather than seeking reduction to detailed causal mechanisms. One example is the repetition of geometrical "patterns within patterns" on smaller and smaller scales (known as fractals). There can also be a deeper order within apparent randomness in a series of numbers or a sequence of events. Order is a broader concept than law because it includes formal, holistic, historical, and probabilistic patterns.[34]

The *holistic* and *anti-reductionist* character of chaos theory has been described by one of its best-known exponents, James Gliek:

Chaos is anti-reductionist. This new science makes a strong claim about the world: namely, that when it comes to the most interesting questions, questions about order and disorder, decay and creativity, pattern formation and life itself, the whole cannot be explained in terms of the parts. There are fundamental laws about complex systems, but they are new kinds of law. They are laws of structure and organization and scale, and they simply vanish when you focus on the individual constituents of a complex system—just as the psychology of a lynch mob vanishes when you interview individual participants.[35]

Similar conclusions are suggested by studies of *self-organization* in complex systems. Stuart Kauffman finds common patterns in the integrated behavior of systems that appear very different, such as molecules, cells, neural networks, ecosystems, and technological and economic systems. In each case feedback mechanisms and nonlinear interactions make cooperative activity possible in larger wholes. The systems show similar emergent *systemic properties* not present in their components. Kauffman gives particular attention to the behavior of networks. For example, an array of 100,000 light bulbs, each of which goes on or off as an adjustable function of input from its four neighbors, will cycle through only 357 states from among the astronomical number of possible states. Genes are also connected in networks; in the simplest case, gene A represses gene B and vice versa, so only one of them is turned on. Kauffman notes that there are only 256 cell types in mammals, and suggests that this may be the result of system principles and not merely an historical accident.[36]

Many of Kauffman's ideas are speculative and exploratory, but they lead to a new way of looking at prebiotic molecular evolution and the origins of life. He finds that order emerges spontaneously in *complex systems,* especially on the border between order and chaos. Too much order makes change impossible; too much chaos makes continuity impossible. Complexity at one level leads to simplicity at another level. Disorder is often the precondition for the appearance of a new form of order. Kauffman concludes that we should see ourselves not as a highly improbable historical accident but as an expected fulfillment of the natural order. In his book *At Home in the Universe,* he calls for awe and respect for a process in which such self-organization occurs. These issues of order, holism, complexity, and self-organization will of course recur when we look at evolution in a later chapter.

## IV. METAPHYSICAL IMPLICATIONS

In the last two decades a proliferation of claims has arisen alleging that physics has far-reaching metaphysical implications. Some authors claim that quantum physics has demonstrated the mental character of reality. Quantum indeterminacy is also said to be compatible with life, human freedom, and God's action, as Newtonian determinism was not. Other authors have delineated parallels between contemporary physics and Eastern mysticism.

### 1. THE ROLE OF MIND

Associated with physics has been a long tradition of *philosophical idealism,* the belief that reality is essentially mental in character. The Pythagoreans held that mathematical relationships are the underlying reality of nature. The Platonists took nature to be an imperfect reflection of another realm of perfect eternal forms. Both these themes were expressed in the writings of Kepler and Copernicus at the dawn of modern science. In the eighteenth century, Kant and his successors held that the structures of time, space, and causality are categories of human thought, which we impose on nature; we can never know things as they are in themselves.

New versions of idealism have claimed support from modern physics. Writing in the 1930s, James Jeans said, "The universe begins to look more like a great thought than like a great machine. Mind no longer appears as an accidental intruder in the realm of matter."[37] Arthur Eddington assigned the determinative influence in all knowledge to the human mind. He pictures us following footsteps in the sand, only to discover that the tracks are our own. We impose our own patterns of law so that "the mind may be regarded as regaining from Nature that which the mind has put into Nature."[38] In relativity, all the basic properties of objects, such as length, time, and mass, are relative to the observer. This have sometimes been cited as evidence of the priority of mind over matter, though as indicated earlier I am critical of this claim.

In quantum physics, the connection between theory and experiment is very indirect. Instrumentalists stressed the experimental side, arguing that theories are only useful fictions for correlating observations. But other scientists, focusing on the theoretical concepts, which are abstract and mathematical, found encouragement for idealistic interpretations. One major problem is *the act of measurement,* in which the multiple potentialities of an atomic system become one actuality. Physicists have been puzzled by the sharp discontinuity that occurs when the wave function (the "superposition of states" representing alternative outcomes) collapses to the one value that is observed. Along the route between the microsystem and the human observer, where does the initially indeterminate result get fixed?

The physicist Eugene Wigner holds that quantum results are fixed only when they enter somebody's *consciousness.* "It is not possible to formulate the laws in a fully consistent way without reference to consciousness."[39] He maintains that the distinctive feature of human consciousness, which causes the wave function to collapse, is introspection or self-reference; consciousness can give an account of its own state, cutting the chain of statistical coordinations. But why then do two different observers agree on the result of a quantum experiment?

Another physicist, John Wheeler, asserts that this is *an observer-created universe.* The collapse of the wave function is the product of intersubjective agreement in which the key feature is not consciousness but communication. He argues that the past has no existence until it is recorded in the present. He tells the story of a conversation among three baseball umpires. One says, "I calls 'em as I see 'em." The second claims, "I calls 'em as they really are." The third replies, "They ain't nothin' until I calls 'em." As observers of the Big Bang and the early universe, says Wheeler, we have helped to create those events. Before there were observers, atoms were only partially individuated; they had enough reality to enter chemical reactions but were not fully real until they were later observed. He grants that it seems an anomaly that the present could influence the past, but he says that, in the quantum world of indeterminacy and acausality, ideas of before and after are meaningless. The past has no meaning unless it exists as a record in the present. So human beings are central in a participatory and observer-dependent universe.[40]

I do not find these interpretations of quantum physics convincing. Surely it is not mind as such that affects observations, but the process of *interaction* between the detection apparatus and the microsystem. The experimental results might be automatically recorded on film or on a computer printout, which no one looks at for a year. How could looking at the film or printout alter an experiment that has been recorded for a year? The Wheeler view seems very strange, for observers of the Big Bang are themselves products of the evolution of the cosmos, which included billions of years when there was no human consciousness and no observers. Atoms that affect subsequent evolutionary events must surely be considered fully real.

The Bell's Theorem experiments, in which there is a correlation of distant events, have sometimes been cited as evidence of instant communication and hence as supporting the plausibility of mental telepathy. But I have indicated that the experiment does not imply that a signal or other communication can be transmitted instantaneously or faster than the speed of light. In all these cases the lesson to be learned is that phenomena in the world are interdependent and interconnected, not that they are mental in character or intrinsically dependent on the human mind.

## 2. LIFE, FREEDOM, AND GOD

Is there any connection between atomic-level indeterminacy and biological life, human freedom, or God's action in the world? These questions will all be discussed in later chapters but may be briefly considered here.

### 1. Biological Life

Quantum theory is the basis of the periodic table and the properties of the chemical elements and molecular bonds, without which there could be no life. But indeterminacy at first appears irrelevant to phenomena at the level of a living cell containing millions of atoms, among which statistical fluctuations will tend to average out. Quantum equations give exact predictions for large ensembles, though not for individual events. Moreover, atoms and molecules have an inherent stability against small perturbations, since at least a quantum of energy is required to change their states. However in many biological systems individual microevents can have macroconsequences. Even in nonequilibrium thermodynamics, small random changes can have large-scale effects. One mutation in a single component of a genetic sequence can change evolutionary history. In the nervous system and the brain, a microevent can trigger the firing of a neuron whose affects are amplified by the neural network.

Holmes Rolston portrays the interaction patterns between cells and atoms: "The macromolecular system of the living cell, like the physicist's apparatus, is influencing by its interaction patterns the behavior of the atomic systems. . . . There is a kind of downward causation that complements an upward causation, and both feed on the openness, if also the order, in the atomic substructures."[41] Rolston says that "biological events are superintending physical ones." Physics leaves out this "upstairs control" but it does allow for a looseness among the lower-level parts. He broadens this analysis to include the action of the mind and human freedom:

If we turn from the *random* element of indeterminacy to the *interaction* concept also present, we gain a complementary picture. We are given a nature that is not just indeterminate in random ways, but is plastic enough for an organism to work its program on, for a mind to work its will on. Indeterminacy does not in any straightforward way yield either function, purpose, or freedom, as critics of too swiftly drawn conclusions here are right to observe. Yet physics is, as it were, leaving room in nature for what biology, psychology, social science, and religion may want to insert, those emergent levels of structure and experience that operate despite the quantum indeterminacies and even because of them. We gain space for the higher phenomena that physics has elected to leave out.[42]

## 2. Human Freedom

Clearly we cannot identify freedom with randomness. Within physics, the only alternatives are determinate cause and indeterminate chance, and neither can be equated with freedom. But several physicists have asserted that whereas Newtonian determinism excluded human freedom, quantum indeterminacy at least allows for it. They have usually assumed a mind/body dualism; they suggest that a free immaterial mind can determine the behavior of brain atoms which would otherwise be indeterminate.

In place of such a dualism I shall defend the idea of levels of organization and activity. Human experience as an integrated event shows a new type of unpredictability derived not from atomic indeterminacy but from its unitary activity at a higher level. Atomic indeterminacy and human freedom are not, on this view, directly related to each other, and they occur on quite different levels. Coordinated individual events at various levels have multiple potentialities, but only at the level of human selfhood is there freedom in which choices are made in terms of present motives, future goals, and moral ideals. We can talk about freedom only in relation to a model of selfhood that includes past conditioning, continuity of character, personal decision, and individual responsibility.

## 3. God's Action in the World

Some authors have suggested that atomic indeterminacies are the domain in which God providentially controls the world. William Pollard, a physicist and priest, has proposed that such divine action would violate no natural laws and would not be scientifically detectable. God, he says, determines which actual value is realized within the range of probability distribution. The scientist can find no natural cause for the selection among quantum alternatives; chance, after all, is not a cause. The believer may view the selection as God's doing. God would influence events without acting as a physical force. Since an electron in a superposition of states does not have a definite position, no force is required for God to actualize one among the set of alternative potentialities. By a coordinated guidance of many atoms, God providentially governs all events. God, not the human mind, collapses the wave function to a single value.[43]

Pollard's proposal is consistent with current theories in physics. God would be the ultimate nonlocal "hidden variable." But I have three objections to his ideas: (1) Pollard asserts divine sovereignty as *total control* over all events, and he defends predestination. This seems to me incompatible with human freedom and the reality of evil. It also denies the reality of chance, which becomes only a reflection of human ignorance of the true divine cause. (2) For Pollard, God's will is achieved through the *unlawful* rather than the lawful aspects of nature. This may be a needed corrective to deism's opposite emphasis, but it seems equally one-sided. (3) There is an *implicit reductionism* in assuming that God acts at the lowest level, that of the atomic components. Do we not want to allow also for God's influence on higher levels, "from the top down" rather than "from the bottom up"? Isn't God related to the integrated human self, for example, and not just to the atomic events in the brain?

Arthur Peacocke takes quantum effects to be only one example of chance, which occurs at many points in nature. Moreover, he portrays God as acting through the whole process of *chance and law,* not primarily through chance events. God does not predetermine and control all events; chance is real for God as it is for us. The creative process is itself God's action in the world. We will examine these views in detail in chapter 12.

## 3. PHYSICS AND EASTERN MYSTICISM

Several volumes appeared in the 1970s and 1980s claiming close parallels between contemporary physics and Eastern mysticism.[44] The most influential and widely read of these is Fritjof Capra's *The Tao of Physics,* which starts by setting forth epistemological parallels. According to Capra, both physics and Asian religions recognize *the limitations of human thought and language.* Paradoxes in physics, such as the wave/particle duality, are reminiscent of the yin/yang polarity in Chinese Taoism, which portrays the unity of apparent opposites; Bohr himself put the yin/yang symbol at the center of his coat of arms. Zen Buddhism asks us to meditate on *koans,* the famous paradoxical sayings to which there is no rational solution. Capra also says that mind plays an essential role in the construction of reality: "Ultimately, the structures and phenomena we observe in nature are nothing but the creations of our measuring and categorizing minds."[45] He also cites Wigner's assertion that quantum variables have no definite values until the intervention of human consciousness.

*The wholeness of reality* is another theme Capra finds in both cases. Quantum physics points to the unity and interconnectedness of all events. Particles are local disturbances in interpenetrating fields. In relativity, space and time form a unified whole, and matter-energy is identified with the curvature of space. Eastern thought likewise presents the unity of all things and speaks of the experience of undifferentiated oneness encountered in the depth of meditation. There is one ultimate reality, referred to as Brahman in India and the Tao in China, with which the individual is merged. The new physics says that the observer and the observed are inseparable, much as the mystic tradition envisages the union of subject and object.

Next, both physics and Eastern thought are said to see the world as *dynamic and ever-changing*. Particles are patterns of vibration that are continually being created and destroyed. Matter appears as energy and vice versa. Hinduism and Buddhism hold that life is transitory, all existence is impermanent and in ceaseless motion. The dance of Shiva is an image of the cosmic dance of form and energy. But in both fields there is also an underlying *timeless realm*. Capra maintains that in relativity spacetime is timeless; the eternal now of mystical experience is also timeless.

In general, I think Capra has overstressed the similarities and virtually ignored the *differences* between the two disciplines. Often he finds a parallel by comparing particular terms or concepts, abstracted from the wider contexts that are radically different.[46] For example, Asian traditions speak of undifferentiated unity. But the wholeness and unity that physics expresses is highly differentiated and structured, subject to strict constraints, symmetry principles, and conservation laws. Space, time, matter, and energy are all unified in relativity, but there are exact transformation rules. The mystic's structureless unity, in which all distinctions are obliterated, also seems very different from the organized interaction and cooperative behavior of higher-level wholes, seen already in physics but much more evident in biology. If mechanists see only the parts, Capra gives one-sided attention to wholes. Process thought seems to me to strike a more tenable balance between unity and diversity, with a basic pluralism rather than a monism.

I believe the relation between *time* and *timelessness* is also significantly different in physics and in mysticism. Physics deals with the realm of temporal change. I agree with Capra that in the atomic world there is impermanence and an ever-changing flux of events. But I do not agree that spacetime is a static and timeless block. I have argued that relativity points to the temporalization of space rather than the spatialization of time. On the other hand, for much of Eastern mysticism, especially the Advaita tradition in Hinduism, the temporal world is illusory and ultimate reality is timeless. Beneath the surface flux of *maya* (illusion) is the unchanging center, which alone is truly real, even though the world exhibits regular patterns to which a qualified reality can be ascribed. In Buddhism, timelessness also refers to the realization of our unity with all things, which releases us from bondage to time and the threat of impermanence and suffering. Meditative disciplines do bring the experience of a sense of timelessness (though this may be partly the product of absorptive attention that stops the flow of thought and shifting consciousness).

Capra ignores the diversity among and within Eastern religions and says nothing about Western mysticism. Moreover, he says little about the *difference in the goals* of physics and mysticism, or the distinctive functions of their languages. The goal of meditation is not primarily a new conceptual system but the transformation of personal existence, a new state of consciousness and being, an experience of enlightenment. We have seen that the mystical strand in both East and West emphasizes experience. There are implicit or explicit beliefs, to be sure, but they must always be considered as components of mysticism as a total way of life.

David Bohm is more cautious in delineating parallels between physics and mysticism. We discussed earlier his idea of instantaneous, nonlocal, noncausal correlations, which would provide an explanation of the Bell's Theorem experiments. He has extended these ideas as a more general metaphysical system. He proposes that mind and matter are two different projections of the underlying implicate order; they are two related expressions of a single deeper reality. Bohm also finds in Eastern religions a recognition of the basic unity of all things; in meditation there is a direct experience of undivided wholeness. Fragmentation and egocentricity can be overcome in the absorption of the self in the undifferentiated and timeless whole.[47] Here is an ultimate monism that contrasts with the greater pluralism of Western religions and of process theology. For Bohm, the answer to the fragmentation of personal life is the dissolution of the separate self, rather than the healing of brokenness by the restoration of relationships to God and the neighbor that Christian thought advocates.

In a recent volume, *Science and Mysticism,* Richard Jones gives a detailed comparison of themes in the new physics, Advaita Hinduism, and Theravada Buddhism; he emphasizes the differences among them.[48] He subscribes basically to what I have called the *Independence* thesis: science and mysticism are independent and separate, but both have cognitive value. Science has authority concerning objective structures and regularities in the realm of becoming and change, while mysticism is an experience of the unstructured, nonobjectifiable reality beneath the surface multiplicity. For the most part, their claims are incommensurable, and no integration is possible, for they refer to different realms. Science deals objectively with differentiated lawful structures, while the mystic encounters the undifferentiated wholeness of the underlying reality in the experience of meditation. Jones is critical of the vague parallels that Capra draws and his use of phrases abstracted from their contexts.

Jones grants that the classical forms of these Eastern traditions devalued the world of phenomena in a way that offers no encouragement to science. He himself defends *the cognitive value* of both science and mysticism, each on its own level. He acknowledges that mysticism does not start from uninterpreted experience but inescapably uses theoretical interpretive concepts. Some beliefs might conflict with or be supported by science, and we do not end with total independence. For example, one belief shared by many Eastern traditions is the idea of *karma,* the infinite cycle of rebirths, which requires an infinite span of time—and this belief might conflict with some astronomical theories but not others.

Jones accepts the *timelessness* of ultimate reality in these Eastern traditions. I have greater reservations about this concept. Medieval Christian thought also asserted the timelessness of God, though God was there understood in predominantly personal terms, and the doctrine of creation gave a stronger affirmation of the reality and goodness of the temporal world than is found in most of the East. The God of medieval thought was eternal, unchanging, impassible, omniscient, and omnipotent, influencing the world but not influenced by it. But both biblical thought and process theology have had a dynamic understanding of a God who is intimately involved in the temporality of the world. In Hartshorne's dipolar theism, God is unchanging in purpose but changes in experience of the world.[49] We will return in a later chapter to this question of divine temporality and timelessness. At the moment I am suggesting that while timelessness is an important idea in religious thought of both East and West, we can find little support for it in current physics.

## 4. CONCLUSIONS

I have suggested that twentieth-century physics has some important epistemological implications and some modest metaphysical ones. Among the former, *the downfall of classical realism* has been described. In its place, some interpreters have defended instrumentalism, but I have advocated a critical realism. Theories and models can no longer be taken as literal descriptions of atomic reality, but they can be taken as selective and symbolic attempts to represent the structures of nature that are responsible for particular observable phenomena. The limitations of our theoretical concepts and models are dramatized by the Complementarity Principle, which is a valuable reminder of the partial character of human knowledge. I proposed earlier that there are parallels in the use of complementary models within theology.

Another epistemological lesson can be learned from contemporary physics: *the participation of the observer.* I have argued that in quantum physics this is required because of the holistic character of wave functions and the interactive character of observation processes. In relativity, it reflects the fact that temporal and spatial properties are now understood to be *relationships* rather than intrinsic features of separate objects in themselves. In religion, too, knowledge is possible only by participation, though of course the forms of participation differ from those in science. We can ask how God is related to us, but we can say little about the intrinsic nature of God.

Advocates of *Independence* and *Dialogue* between science and religion (chap. 4) would want to stop here. They welcome the greater epistemological caution and humility that physics encourages, but they are wary of any direct metaphysical implications, and also theological ones. The deists were too dependent on the Newtonian world view. They ended with the clockmaker God who designed the world machine. Their error was not just that they used ideas derived from a physics that is now known to be scientifically inadequate. Their mistake, according to these interpreters, was in using *any* ideas from physics in the formulation of theology. The deists tried to build a metaphysics by an unwarranted extrapolation of the physics of their day. The new epistemology can help liberate theology from bondage to mechanistic physics, but it can equally warn us of the danger of bondage to twentieth-century physics. The chief lesson of the new physics, on this reading, is a negative one—a warning against repeating the mistakes of the past—not a positive contribution to the theologian's task.

Moreover, we have seen that many of the alleged implications of recent physics appear to be questionable. The involvement of the observer in both quantum physics and relativity has often been cited as evidence of the central role of mind. I have argued that it points to the interaction of the observational system with the system observed, not to the presence of mind as such. It is evidence of interconnectedness and holism, not of the pervasiveness of mentality or consciousness. Probability waves may seem less substantial than billiard ball atoms, and matter that converts to radiant energy may appear immaterial. But the new atom is no more spiritual or mental than the old, and it is still detected through physical interactions. If science is indeed selective and its concepts are limited, it would be as questionable to build a metaphysics of idealism on modern physics as it was to build a metaphysics of materialism on classical physics. I have criticized the attempt of Capra and others to portray direct metaphysical parallels between physics and Eastern mysticism, especially with respect to timelessness and holistic unity.

We would also be guilty of a new form of *reductionism* if we tried to base an inclusive metaphysics on current physics, which deals only with the lowest levels of organization among inanimate structures. But I believe reductionism can be avoided in four ways. (1) We have seen that already within physics we have to look at wholes as well as parts; reductionism is inadequate even within this discipline. (2) We will find that some of the characteristics of nature seen in physics (such as temporality, chance, and wholeness) are also prominent in other sciences. (3) We will go on in subsequent chapters to trace the emergence of higher levels of organization, including life and mind, which cannot be reduced to physics. (4) We will seek metaphysical categories that are adequate for the coherent interpretation, not simply of scientific data, but of all areas of human experience.

This will lead us toward the last of the views in chapter 4, a concern for the *Integration* of science and religion. I see three *metaphysical implications* of current physics, which form a coherent pattern with the implications of other sciences and other areas of human experience.

## 1. Temporality and Historicity

Time enters into the structure of reality in a more fundamental way in the new physics than in classical physics. The quantum world consists of vibrations that, like musical notes, are nothing at an instant and require time in order to exist. It is a world of dynamic flux in which particles come and go. It is a world of probability states; only the passage of time will disclose which of the alternative potentialities will be actualized. Time is not the unwinding of a predetermined scroll of events but the novel coming-to-be of unpredictable events in history. In relativity, time is inseparable from space. There are no purely spatial relationships, only spatiotemporal ones. All of this is radically different from the Newtonian world of absolute space and time, in which change consisted of the rearrangement of particles that are themselves unchanging. We will find a similar emphasis on change and the emergence of genuine novelty in astronomy and evolutionary biology. The historicity of nature is evident in all the sciences.

## 2. Chance and Law

There are alternative potentialities for individual events. In accordance with critical realism and the later views of Bohr and Heisenberg, I have interpreted the Uncertainty Principle as an indication of objective indeterminacy in nature rather than the result of subjective uncertainty and human ignorance. The choice between bifurcation paths in nonequilibrium thermodynamics also seems to be a chance phenomenon. In chaos theory, prediction is impossible because the outcome is sensitive to infinitesimally small differences in initial conditions or influences from outside the system. We will find the same combination of chance and law in other fields, including quantum effects in the early instants of the cosmos and random mutations in evolutionary history. Human freedom occurs at a totally different level from quantum indeterminacy, but it also exhibits the presence of unpredictable novelty. T. S. Eliot points to the importance of an open future:

Time present and time past
Are both perhaps present in our future
And time future contained in time past.
If all time is eternally present
All time is unredeemable.[50]

## 3. Wholeness and Emergence

Against reductionism, which seeks to explain the activity of complex entities in terms of the laws of their components, I have maintained that higher organizational levels involve distinctive patterns of behavior. The Pauli Exclusion Principle, which links physics to chemistry—but which cannot be derived from the laws governing separate particles—was offered as one illustration. The inseparability of the observer and the observed was presented as further evidence of interdependence. The correlations between distant events shown in the Bell's Theorem experiments is a dramatic example of such interconnectedness. In relativity, the unification of space, time, matter, and energy represents wholeness of a fundamental kind. Nonequilibrium thermodynamics describes the emergence of higher levels of systemic order from lower-level disorder. In chaos theory and complexity theory, behavior is described by principles applied to whole systems rather than by detailed causal mechanisms among the parts.

Later chapters will consider the new wholes that arise with the emergence of life, mind, and society. Looking back, it will not seem unreasonable to claim that even in physics we can see the beginning of a *historical, ecological,* and *many-leveled* view of reality. I will suggest that these three characteristics— temporality and historicity, chance and law, wholeness and emergence—are prominent in the metaphysics of process philosophy. These reflections will take us far beyond physics, but they will form a pattern coherent with our understanding of the characteristics of physical reality.

# Astronomy and Creation

On Christmas Eve 1968, the first astronauts in orbit around the moon appeared live on TV in millions of American homes. Frank Borman read the opening verses of Genesis:

In the beginning God created the heavens and the earth. The earth was without form and void, and darkness was upon the face of the deep; and the Spirit of God was moving over the face of the water. And God said, "Let there be light"; and there was light.

Borman's message concluded: "Greetings from the crew of Apollo 8. God bless all of you on the good earth." Those astronauts were the first people to see the beauty of the earth as a blue and white gem spinning in the vastness of space, and the reading from Genesis seemed an appropriate response. But how can the Genesis story be reconciled with the findings of twentieth-century astronomy? What are the theological implications of recent cosmological theories?

## I. THE BIG BANG

Let us look first at the scientific evidence concerning the early history of the universe and some initial theological responses to it. In subsequent sections, recent cosmological theories and interpretations of the doctrine of creation are examined in greater detail.

### 1. THEORIES IN ASTROPHYSICS

Physical cosmology is the study of the physical structure of the cosmos as a whole.[1] In 1917, Willem de Sitter, working with Einstein's general relativity equations, found a solution that predicted *an expanding universe*. In 1929, Edwin Hubble, examining the "red shift" of light from distant nebulae, formulated Hubble's Law: the velocity of recession of a nebula is proportional to its distance from us. Space itself, not just objects in space, is everywhere expanding. Extrapolating backward in time, the universe seems to be expanding from a common origin about fifteen billion years ago. In 1965, Arno Penzias and Robert Wilson discovered a faint background of microwaves coming from all directions in space. The spectrum of those waves corresponded very closely to the 3°K residual radiation, which had been predicted from relativity theory. The radiation is the cosmic fireball's afterglow, cooled by its subsequent expansion. In 1992, data obtained by NASA's Cosmic Background Explorer (COBE) satellite showed small variations in this microwave background among different regions in space. The existence of such variations early in cosmic history would account for the clumping of matter in galaxies.

Indirect evidence concerning the very early moments of the Big Bang have come from both theoretical and experimental work in high-energy physics. Einstein himself spent his later years in an unsuccessful search for a unified theory that would integrate gravity with other physical forces. More recent research has moved closer to this goal. There are *four basic physical forces:* (1) the electromagnetic force responsible for light and the behavior of charged particles; (2) the weak nuclear force responsible for radioactive decay; (3) the strong nuclear force that binds protons and neutrons into nuclei; and (4) the gravitational force evident in the long-distance attraction between masses. Recent attempts to develop a theory that would integrate these forces have moved through several stages.

In 1967, Steven Weinberg and Abdus Salam showed that the electromagnetic and weak forces could be unified within an *Electro-weak Theory.* The theory predicted the existence of two massive particles, the W and Z bosons, which mediate between the two kinds of force. In 1983, Carlo Rubbia and coworkers found particles with the predicted properties of W bosons among the products of high-energy collisions in the CERN accelerator in Geneva.

There has been some progress in attempts to unite the electro-weak and strong forces in a *Grand Unified Theory* (GUT). The unification would be mediated by very massive X-particles, which could only exist at energies higher than those in any existing accelerator. However, the GUT theory implies that protons decay spontaneously, very slowly, rather than being stable, as previously supposed. Physicists are trying to detect this extremely low level of proton decay with experiments in deep mines, where other stray particles are screened out. A GUT theory would help us understand the structure of matter today, and it would also contribute to our understanding of the very early moments of the Big Bang.

The unification of gravity with the other three forces within one *Supersymmetry Theory* has appeared more difficult because we have no successful quantum theory of gravity. But there has been recent excitement concerning Superstring Theory, which escapes the anomalies of previous attempts. The basic constituents would be incredibly massive, tiny, one-dimensional strings that can split or loop. With differing patterns of vibration and rotation, they can represent all known particles from quarks to electrons. There is no experimental evidence for strings; the energy required for their existence would be far beyond those in the laboratory, but it would have been present at the very earliest instants of the Big Bang.[2] Physicists have a strong commitment to simplicity, unity, and symmetry, which motivates the search for a unified theory even when direct experimentation is impossible.

Putting together the evidence from astronomy and high-energy physics, a plausible reconstruction of cosmic history can be made. Imagine a trip backward in time. Twelve billion years after the Big Bang, microscopic forms of life were beginning to appear on our planet. Ten billion years after the bang, the planet itself was formed. One billion years from the beginning, the galaxies and stars were coming into being. At t = 500,000 years, the constituent atoms appeared. A mere 3 minutes from the beginning, the nuclei were starting to form out of protons and neutrons. Plausible theories concerning these events can account for the relative abundance of hydrogen and helium and for the formation of heavier chemical elements in the interior of stars (see fig. 3).[3]

Fig. 3 Major Cosmological Transitions

| TIME | TEMP. | TRANSITION |
|---|---|---|
| 15 billion yrs. | | (today) |
| 12 " | | Microscopic life |
| 10 " | | Planets formed |
| 1 " | | Galaxies formed (heavy elements) |
| 500,000 yrs. | 2000° | Atoms formed (light elements) |
| 3 mins. | $10^9$ | Nuclei formed (hydrogen, helium) |
| $10^{-4}$ sec. | $10^{12}$ | Quarks to protons and neutrons |
| $10^{-10}$ " | $10^{15}$ | Weak and electromagnetic forces separate |
| $10^{-35}$ " | $10^{28}$ | Strong nuclear force separates |
| $10^{-43}$ " | $10^{32}$ | Gravitational force separates |
| (0 | Infinite | Singularity) |

The farther back we go before 3 minutes, the more tentative are the theories, because they deal with states of matter and energy further from anything we can duplicate in the laboratory. Protons and neutrons were probably forming from their constituent quarks at $10^{-4}$ seconds (a ten-thousandth of a second from the beginning), when the temperature had cooled to $10^{12}$ (a thousand billion) degrees. This fantastically dense sea of hot quarks had been formed at about $10^{-10}$ seconds from an even smaller and hotter fireball—which had expanded and cooled enough for the electro-weak forces to be distinguishable from the strong and gravitational forces.[4]

Before $10^{-35}$ seconds, the temperature was so high that all the forces except gravity were of comparable strength. This is the period to which a Grand Unified Theory would apply. We have almost no idea of events before $10^{-43}$ seconds, when the temperature was $10^{32}$ degrees. The whole universe was the size of an atom today, and the density was an incredible $10^{96}$ times that of water. At these very small dimensions, the Heisenberg uncertainties of quantum theory were significant, and all four forces were united. This would have been the era of Supersymmetry. I will return later to examine some remarkable features of these very early stages.

But what happened before that? At the time t = 0, was there a dimensionless point of pure radiation of infinite density? In standard Big Bang theory, t = 0 appears as a singularity to which the laws of physics do not apply. I will examine later some recent speculative theories that try to account for that singularity.

## 2. THEOLOGICAL RESPONSES

Some theologians have welcomed Big Bang cosmology. After the conflicts between theologians and astronomers in previous centuries, they saw common ground in the idea that the universe had a beginning—a beginning that standard Big Bang theory cannot explain. They identified the point of radiation of infinite density with the words in Genesis, "Let there be light," since light is pure radiation. Pope Pius XII said that the Big Bang theory supports the biblical idea of creation.[5] The astrophysicist Robert Jastrow has argued that "the astronomical evidence leads to a biblical view of the origin of the world." He ends his book *God and the Astronomers* with this striking passage:

At this moment it seems as though science will never be able to raise the curtain on the mystery of creation. For the scientist who has lived by his faith in the power of reason, the story ends like a bad dream. He has scaled the mountains of ignorance; he is about to conquer the highest peak; as he pulls himself over the final rock, he is greeted by a band of theologians who have been sitting there for centuries.[6]

At a press conference in 1992 announcing the findings from *the COBE satellite program*, the team leader, George Smoot, said, "If you're religious, it's like seeing God." Smoot later said, "Science can never answer the religious questions. You still have 'what came before?' and you can ask 'who designed it all?' " The NASA team leader, John Mather, told *The Washington Post* that he saw a parallel between the biblical version of creation and the scientific version. The media picked up these comments, and one paper ran a headline: "The Grand Unification of Religion and Science."[7]

I want to start with a word of caution about identifying the religious idea of creation too closely with scientific ideas of cosmology. Later I will indicate some points at which I think contemporary cosmology is relevant to theology. One reason for caution is that in the past God has often been invoked to explain gaps in the prevailing scientific account. This has been a losing enterprise as one gap after another has been filled by the advance of science—first in seventeenth-century astronomy and physics, then in nineteenth-century geology and biology. The present case appears different because events at the time t = 0 seem to be in principle inaccessible to science. Yet this situation might conceivably change, for much of contemporary cosmology is tentative and speculative.

Thirty years ago, some astronomers thought they had avoided the problem of a beginning by postulating an infinite span of time. The *Steady State Theory* proposed that hydrogen atoms come into being, slowly and continuously, throughout an infinite time and space. Fred Hoyle, in particular, defended the theory long after most of his colleagues had abandoned it. Hoyle's writings make clear that he favored the Steady State Theory, not just on scientific grounds, but partly because he thought infinite time was more compatible with his own atheistic beliefs.[8] But today Big Bang theories have clearly won the day.

However, it is possible to combine the Big Bang and infinite time if one assumes *an oscillating cosmos*. Before the present era of expansion there could have been an era of contraction—a Big Crunch before the Big Bang. Any evidence for past cycles would have to be indirect, since their structure would have been totally wiped out in the fireball. Concerning the future of the cosmos, observations suggest that the velocity of expansion is very close to the critical threshold between expanding forever (an *open* universe) and expanding a very long time before contracting again (a *closed* universe). Evidence announced recently suggests that black holes may provide sufficient mass at least to slow the expansion, and additional mass may be present in neutrinos and interstellar dark matter.

Some atheistic or agnostic astronomers feel more comfortable with the idea of an infinite series of oscillations, just as some theists welcome a beginning of time. But I would say it is equally difficult to imagine a beginning of time or an infinite span of time. Both are unlike anything we have experienced. Both start with an unexplained universe. I do not think that major theological issues are at stake, as has often been assumed. If a single, unique Big Bang continues to be the most convincing scientific theory, the theist can indeed see it as an instant of divine origination. But I will suggest that this is not the main concern expressed in the religious notion of creation.

## II. CREATION IN JUDAISM AND CHRISTIANITY

What is the theological content of the doctrine of creation? To answer this question we must start with the biblical creation story and briefly trace the historical development of the idea of creation. We must also look at the function of creation stories in the life of religious communities. Only then will we be able to ask about the compatibility of the doctrine of creation with contemporary cosmology.

### 1. HISTORICAL IDEAS OF CREATION

Look again at the opening verses of Genesis: "In the beginning, God created the heavens and the earth. The earth was without form and void, and darkness was upon the face of the deep, and the Spirit of God was moving over the face of the waters." The relation between those first two sentences is not clear in the Hebrew, and the RSV Bible gives the alternative translation: "When God began to create the heavens and the earth, the earth was without form and void. . . ." Instead of creation from nothing, *ex nihilo,* there is the creation of *order from chaos.* Scholars see here an echo of the Babylonian creation story, which also starts with a primeval watery chaos. Several biblical passages refer to taming the waters and conquering the sea monster Rahab, which are also features of the Babylonian story.[9] Many texts in the Hebrew Scriptures (the Christian Old Testament) assume a continuing struggle between order and chaos and acknowledge the persistence of evil and the fragility of creation.[10]

But clearly the biblical story differs from other ancient creation stories in its assertion of the sovereignty and transcendence of God and the dignity of humanity. Creation is orderly and deliberate, following a comprehensive plan and resulting in a harmonious and interdependent whole. God is portrayed as purposive and powerful, creating by word alone. In the Babylonian story, humanity was created to provide slaves for the gods; in Genesis, humanity was given a special status in God's plan, superior to the rest of creation.[11] The biblical narrative asserts the essential goodness and harmony of the created order. After each day, God saw that it was good; after the sixth day, "God saw everything that he had made, and behold, it was very good." It is a cosmos, a structured, harmonious whole.

Most historical scholars hold that within the Hebrew scriptures the first chapter of Genesis (through 2:3) is a relatively late writing, probably from the fifth century B.C.E. (We will consider the story of Adam and Eve in a later chapter.) It appears that God was worshiped as the redeemer of Israel before being worshiped as the creator of the world. The exodus and the covenant at Sinai were the formative events for Israel as a people. Early Israelite religion centered on God's act of liberation and revelation in history—that is, the creation of Israel. Von Rad argues that the Genesis story was of secondary importance, a kind of cosmic prologue to Israel's history, written to give the covenant faith a more universal context.[12]

But Westermann, Anderson, and most scholars today hold that creation was of considerable importance throughout the Hebrew scriptures.[13] Challenged by the nature gods of surrounding cultures, the people of Israel asserted that Yahweh was both Redeemer and Creator. Several early psalms celebrate Yahweh's enthronement as Creator and King (Pss. 47, 93, and 99). Again, Psalm 19 expresses gratitude for *both* creation and revelation: "The heavens are telling the glory of God," but also "The law of the Lord is perfect." "Our help comes from the Lord, who made heaven and earth" (Ps. 121:2). In Job, the voice from the whirlwind asks, "Where were you when I laid the foundations of the earth?" and goes on to portray with poetic power the wonders of the created order (Job 38–41). In the book of Proverbs, Wisdom is personified as God's agent in creation. Isaiah gives the most powerful synthesis of creation and redemption, tying past, present, and future together. God is indeed the creator of Israel, but also of all humanity and all nature. Moreover, says Isaiah, God will in the future recreate a people out of the chaos of bondage and exile (Isa. 40, 45, and 49). Here is the theme of a new creation, including a new harmony in nature, which is picked up in the later apocalyptic literature. The idea of creation thus pervades the Hebrew scriptures; we do not have to rely on Genesis alone.

In the New Testament, too, creation is closely linked to redemption. The opening verse of John's Gospel recalls Genesis: "In the beginning was the Word, and the Word was with God. . . . All things were made through him." Here the term *Word* merges the *logos,* the Greek principle of rationality, with the Hebrew image of God's Word active in the world. But John then links creation to revelation: "And the Word became flesh." In Christ's life and death, according to the early church, God had made known the purpose of creation. Paul, in his devotion to Christ, gives him a kind of cosmic role in several passages: "In him all things were created in heaven and on earth. . . . he is before all things and in him all things hold together" (Col. 11:16–17; cf. 1 Cor. 8:6). The Spirit was understood as God's continuing presence in nature, in individual life, and in the gathered community.

The Nicene Creed (381 C.E.) refers to God as "maker of heaven and earth." The creed was important in the liturgical life of the church in affirming its identity and its commitment to God and Christ. The doctrine of creation was formulated more explicitly as part of the self-definition of the Christian community in relation to rival philosophies, especially in response to the challenge of Hellenistic dualism. The idea of *creatio ex nihilo,* creation out of nothing, was elaborated to exclude the gnostic teachings that matter is evil, the work of a lesser being, not the work of the God who redeems. Against claims that preexisting matter limited God's creativity, it asserted that God is the source of matter as well as of form. Against pantheism, it asserted that the world is not divine or part of God but is distinct from God. Against the idea that the world was an emanation of God, made of the divine substance and sharing its characteristics, it asserted that God is transcendent and essentially different from the world. It is such ontological assertions, and not any specific reference to a temporal beginning, that were of theological importance.

By the fourth century, Augustine was willing to accept metaphorical or figurative interpretations of Genesis, and he said that it was not the intent of scripture to instruct us about such things as the form and shape of the heavens. "God did not wish to teach men things not relevant to their salvation." He held that creation is not an event in time; time was created along with the world. Creation is the timeless act through which time comes to be and the continuous act by which God preserves the world. He said that it is meaningless to ask what God was doing before creating the world, for there was no time without the created world.[14]

Thomas Aquinas in the thirteenth century accepted a beginning in time as part of scripture and tradition and said that creation in time helps to make God's power evident. But he argued that a universe that had always existed would equally require God as creator and sustainer. What is essential theologically could be stated without reference to a beginning or a singular event. To be sure, one of the versions of his cosmological argument did assume a beginning in time: every effect has a cause, which in turn is the effect of a previous cause, back to a First Cause, which initiated the causal chain. But in another version, he asks, Why is there anything at all? He replies that the whole causal chain, whether finite or infinite, is dependent on God. God's priority is ontological rather than temporal.

But we must note also that there has been a subordinate theme of *continuing creation* from biblical times to the present. Edmund Jacob has said that while there are many biblical texts referring to a primordial creation in the beginning, "Other texts, generally more ancient, draw much less distinction between the creation and conservation of the world, and make it possible for us to speak of a *creatio continua*."[15] There is a recurring witness to God's continuing sovereignty over both history and nature. God is still creating through natural processes. "Thou dost cause the grass to grow for cattle and the plants for man to cultivate. . . . When thou sendest forth thy Spirit, they are created; and thou renewest the face of the ground" (Ps. 104: 14 and 30).

Jaroslav Pelikan shows that the continuing creation theme was present but subordinate throughout the Middle Ages, the Reformation, and the Enlightenment. He holds that it assumes great importance in considering evolution and contemporary science.[16] I will suggest that astrophysics, along with geology and evolutionary biology, shows us a dynamic world with a long history of change and development and the appearance of novel forms. Coming-to-be is a continuing process throughout time, and it continues today. We can see the emergence of new forms as a sign of God's creativity.

## 2. THE INTERPRETATION OF GENESIS TODAY

How then are we to understand the opening chapter of Genesis? A literal interpretation of the six days would conflict with many fields of science, as we saw in chapter 4. The attempt to find scientific information in Genesis is dubious theology as well as dubious science. By treating it as if it were a book of science ahead of its times, we tend to neglect both the human experiences that lie behind it and the theological affirmations it makes.

I would list the *human experiences* that lie behind the idea of creation as follows: (1) a sense of dependence, finitude and contingency; (2) a response of wonder, trust, gratitude for life, and affirmation of the world; and (3) a recognition of interdependence, order, and beauty in the world. These were all part of the experience of the astronauts as they looked at the earth from the moon, and their reading of Genesis seems an appropriate expression of their response. The religious idea of creation starts from wonder and gratitude for life as a gift.

What are the basic *theological affirmations* in that chapter of Genesis? I would list the following: (1) the world is essentially good, orderly, coherent, and intelligible; (2) the world is dependent on God; and (3) God is sovereign, free, transcendent, and characterized by purpose and will. Note that these are all assertions about characteristics of God and the world in every moment of time, not statements about an event in the past. They express ontological rather than temporal relationships.[17]

The intent of the story was not to exclude any scientific account but to exclude, in the first instance, the nature gods of the ancient world. In later history it stood *against alternative philosophical schemes,* such as pantheism, dualism, and the belief that the world and matter are either illusory or evil or ultimate. Against these alternatives it asserted that the created order is good, an interdependent whole, a community of being, but not the object of our worship. These theological affirmations were expressed in Genesis in terms of a prescientific cosmology that included a three-decker universe and creation in six days. But the affirmations are not dependent on that physical cosmology. Reform and Conservative Judaism, the Catholic church, and most of the mainline Protestant denominations today maintain that we do not have to choose between cosmology and creation. We can look on the Big Bang and subsequent evolution as God's way of creating.[18]

But should we take a *beginning of time* literally, even if we do not interpret the six days in Genesis literally? Here theologians are divided. For one thing, the biblical concept of finite linear time has contributed to the Western view of history. The West has differed from the ancient cultures and Eastern religions that assumed an infinite succession of cycles; these cultures have generally evidenced less interest in historical development. But other theologians suggest that even a beginning of time is not crucial to the theological notion of creation. David Kelsey, for instance, says that the basic experience of gratitude for life as a gift has no essential connection with speculations about unique events at the beginning. Science and religion, he maintains, address different question, which should not be confused.[19]

Without denying the distinctive features of Genesis, we can note that *creation stories* in various cultures fulfill similar functions. They locate human life within a cosmic order. The interest in origins may be partly speculative or explanatory, but the main concern is to understand who we are in a framework of larger significance. Anthropologists and scholars of the world's religions have looked at a variety of creation stories, studying their function in the ordering of human experience in relation to a meaningful world. These stories provide patterns for human behavior, archetypes of authentic human life in accord with a universal order. They portray basic relationships between human life and the world of nature. Often they express structures of integration and creativity over against powers of disintegration and chaos.

A religious community appropriates and participates in its sacred stories in various ways. Often the stories are symbolized or enacted in rituals. Streng speaks of one generation passing on to another stories that "manifest the essential structure of reality." Eliade says that exemplary patterns in primordial time are made present in ritual and liturgy.[20] Consider an example from the traditional Jewish morning prayer, which uses the present tense:

Praised are You, O Lord our God, King of the universe.
You fix the cycles of light and darkness;
You ordain the order of all creation. . . .
In Your goodness the work of creation
Is continually renewed day by day.[21]

At this point one might conclude that the biblical idea of creation and scientific theories of cosmology are distinct and unrelated types of assertion, as represented by the *Independence* model in chapter 4. The methods of inquiry of the astronomer and the theologian are very different, as neo-orthodoxy maintains. Each mode of inquiry is selective and has its limitations. The language of science and the language of religion serve very different functions in human life, as linguistic analysts have pointed out. The goal of science is understanding lawful relations among natural phenomena, while that of religion is a way of life within a larger framework of meaning. The *Independence* model is indeed a good first approximation, and it rules out any possibility of *Conflict* between the two fields if they are separate and independent enterprises.

But we can go beyond *Independence* to examine some areas of possible *Dialogue*. We will later (section IV) consider the possibilities for a closer *Integration* of scientific and theological ideas that would avoid any simple identification of the Big Bang with the doctrine of creation.

## III. DESIGN, CHANCE, AND NECESSITY

Several significant questions are raised by recent cosmological theories that constitute topics of *Dialogue* between scientists and theologians. The general character of the argument can be followed, even if the details are somewhat technical. We will look at design, chance, and necessity and their relation to religious beliefs.

### 1. DESIGN: THE ANTHROPIC PRINCIPLE

In the traditional argument from design, it was claimed that both biological forms and the physical conditions favorable for life must be the product of an intelligent designer because it is inconceivably improbable that they could have occurred by chance. Even before Darwin, Hume and other critics replied that when we have only one case (one universe) from which to judge, we cannot make judgments of probability. But the argument from design has been revived by recent cosmologists who compare our universe with the set of *possible universes* allowed by the laws of physics.

A striking feature of the new cosmological theories is that even a small change in the physical constants would have resulted in an uninhabitable universe. Among the many possible universes consistent with Einstein's equations, ours is one of the few in which the arbitrary parameters are right for the existence of anything resembling organic life. Thus Carr and Rees conclude that the possibility of life as we know it "depends on the value of a few basic constants" and is "remarkably sensitive to them."[22] Among these *fine-tuned phenomena* are the following:

*1. The Expansion Rate.* Stephen Hawking writes, "If the rate of expansion one second after the Big Bang had been smaller by even one part in a hundred thousand million million it would have recollapsed before it reached its present size."[23] On the other hand, if it had been greater by a part in a million, the universe would have expanded too rapidly for stars and planets to form. The expansion rate itself depends on many factors, such as the initial explosive energy, the mass of the universe, and the strength of gravitational forces. The cosmos seems to be balanced on a knife edge.

2. *The Formation of the Elements.* If the strong nuclear force were even slightly weaker we would have only hydrogen in the universe. If the force were even slightly stronger, all the hydrogen would have been converted to helium. In either case, stable stars and compounds such as water could not have been formed. Again, the nuclear force is only barely sufficient for carbon to form; yet if it had been slightly stronger, the carbon would all have been converted into oxygen. Particular elements, such as carbon, have many other special properties that are crucial to the later development of organic life as we know it.[24]

3. *The Particle/Antiparticle Ratio.* For every billion antiprotons in the early universe, there were one billion and one protons. The billion pairs annihilated each other to produce radiation, with just one proton left over. A greater or smaller number of survivors—or no survivors at all if they had been evenly matched—would have made our kind of material world impossible. The laws of physics seem to be symmetrical between particles and antiparticles; why was there a tiny asymmetry?[25]

One could list other unexplained "remarkable coincidences," such as the fact that the universe is homogenous and isotropic. The simultaneous occurrence of many independent improbable features appears wildly improbable. Reflection on the way the universe seems to be fine tuned for intelligent life led the cosmologists Dicke and Carter to formulate the *Anthropic Principle:* "What we can expect to observe must be restricted by the conditions necessary for our presence as observers."[26] The principle does underscore the importance of the observer, to which quantum theory also testifies. But it does not in itself provide any casual explanation of those conditions. However, this fine tuning could be taken as an argument for the existence of a designer, perhaps a God with an interest in conscious life.

Some physicists see *evidence of design* in the early universe. Stephen Hawking, for example, writes, "The odds against a universe like ours emerging out of something like the Big Bang are enormous. I think there are clearly religious implications."[27] And Freeman Dyson, in a chapter entitled "The Argument from Design," gives a number of examples of "numerical accidents that seem to conspire to make the universe habitable." He concludes, "The more I examine the universe and the details of its architecture, the more evidence I find that the universe in some sense must have known we were coming."[28]

I do not think that the Anthropic Principle provides a convincing design argument in the tradition of *natural theology*—partly because chance and necessity remain as options for the atheist, as we shall see. But I find the principle quite consistent with a *theology of nature* (an alternative form of the *Integration* model). The fine tuning of the physical constants is just what one would expect if life and consciousness were among the goals of a rational and purposeful God. Such a theology of nature would have to draw from many fields in addition to astrophysics in articulating a coherent overall interpretation of cosmic history and human life.

## 2. CHANCE: MANY-WORLDS THEORIES

One way of explaining the apparent design in these "remarkable coincidences" is to suggest that many worlds existed either successively or simultaneously. If there were billions of worlds with differing constants, it would not be surprising if *by chance* one of them happened to have constants just right for our forms of life. That which is highly improbable in one world might be probable among a large enough set of worlds. There are several ways in which many worlds could occur.

*1. Successive Cycles of an Oscillating Universe.* Wheeler and others suggest that the universe is reprocessed in each Big Crunch before the next Big Bang. The universe and all its structures completely melt down and make a new start as it expands and cools again. In the quantum uncertainties entailed by those very small dimensions, indeterminate possibilities are present. If the constants vary at random in successive cycles, our particular combination will eventually come up by chance, like the winning combination on a Las Vegas slot machine. As indicated earlier, present evidence does not favor cyclic theories, but they cannot be ruled out.

*2. Multiple Isolated Domains.* Instead of multiple bangs in successive cycles, a single Big Bang might have produced multiple domains existing simultaneously. The domains would be like separately expanding bubbles isolated from each other because their velocity of separation prevents communication even at the speed of light. The universe might have split into many domains with differing constants or even differing laws.[29] Some of the new inflationary models of the universe involve infinite time and regions very unlike ours, beyond our horizon of possible observation. Perhaps this just happens to be one of the few regions in which life could be present.

*3. Many-Worlds Quantum Theory.* In the previous chapter we noted Everett's proposal that every time there are alternative quantum potentialities in an atom, the universe splits into several branches.[30] This interpretation of quantum theory involves a mind-boggling multiplicity of worlds, since each world would have to split again into many branches during each of the myriad atomic and subatomic events throughout time and space. But being mind-boggling is not enough to disqualify an idea, though this proposal violates Occam's Razor with a vengeance. More to the point, it seems to be inherently unverifiable, since no communication could take place between the various branching worlds.

*4. Quantum Vacuum Fluctuations.* A strange feature of quantum theory is that it permits very brief violations of the law of conservation of energy. It is permissible for a system's energy to go into debt if the debt is rapidly paid back—so rapidly that it could never be detected within the limits of the uncertainty principle. In the laboratory, a vacuum is really a sea of activity in which pairs of virtual particles come into being and almost immediately anni-hilate each other again. The energy needed to create a universe could be borrowed for only a fantastically brief instant (the magnitude of the allow-able energy debt is inversely proportional to the repayment time), but con-ceivably this could get things going. Moreover, the energy needed might be small or even zero if the negative gravitational energy is taken into account. Quantum fluctuations are sometimes presented as a secular version of cre-ation *ex nihilo* that dispenses with the idea of God. The theory starts with a vacuum, which seem to be "nothing."[31] But actually the theory has to assume the existence of a quantum field and the laws of quantum physics. How do we account for the situation in which a gigantic quantum fluctuation could occur?

All four of these theories—many cycles, many domains, many quantum worlds, or many quantum fluctuations—would allow us to explain the com-bination of constants favorable to life as *a chance occurrence* among a set of worlds, most of which would be lifeless. John Leslie has argued that the God hypothesis is simpler and more plausible as an explanation of the fine tuning than these many-worlds hypotheses.[32] These theories, he says, are all very *ad hoc*, highly speculative, and unsupported by any independent evidence, whereas one can appeal to other kinds of evidence in support of belief in God. Note that Leslie assumes here that God and chance are mutually exclu-sive hypotheses.

## 3. NECESSITY: A THEORY OF EVERYTHING

We have tried to account for the value of parameters favorable to the emer-gence of life, first on the basis of design and then on the basis of chance. But there is a third possibility: *necessity*. Perhaps the values of the constants, which appear arbitrary, are in fact dictated by a more basic structure of relation-ships. Perhaps there is a more fundamental theory that will show that the constants can have only the values that they have. In the history of science are recorded many apparent coincidences or apparently arbitrary numbers that later received theoretical explanation.

We have seen that a *Grand Unified Theory* (GUT) offers the prospect of bringing the two nuclear forces and the electromagnetic force into a single theory. Such a theory would help us understand that momentary era, prior to the hot quark era, when these three forces were merged. The theory already suggests that the slight imbalance between particles and antiparticles may have arisen from a slight asymmetry in the decay processes of the X and the anti-X bosons (the very heavy particles that mediate the unified force of the GUT theory).

There are also promising new *inflationary theories* that may explain why the present expansion rate is so close to the critical balance between an open and a closed universe (the so-called flatness problem). Inflationary theories could also explain why the microwave radiation is nearly isotropic (arriving equally from all directions). These theories entail a very rapid expansion at about $10^{-35}$ seconds, due to the tremendous energy released in the breaking of symmetry when the strong force separated out. Before inflation, the universe would have been so small that its parts could have been in communication and thus could have achieved thermal equilibrium, which would account for its later homogeneity over vast distances.[33]

Current theories are quite inadequate to deal with the even earlier period before $10^{-43}$ seconds when the temperature would have been so high that the fourth force, gravity, would have been united with the other three. Scientists hope to develop theories of *Supersymmetry* or *Supergravity,* which would provide a quantum theory of gravity. We saw that String Theory, in particular, may bring these diverse phenomena together. Because it would unite all the basic physical forces, it has been referred to as a Theory of Everything (TOE). Perhaps the whole cosmos can be derived from one simple and all-inclusive equation. Such a theory has been called the Holy Grail of the current quest in physics.

Successful GUT and TOE theories would seem to undermine the argument from design in the early universe. Perhaps self-consistency and fundamental laws will show that only one universe is possible, that is, that the universe is *necessary* and not contingent. I would reply that such theories would only push the argument back a stage. For it is all the more remarkable if a highly abstract physical theory, which itself has absolutely nothing to say about life, turns out to describe structures that have the potential for developing into life. The theist could welcome this as part of God's design. Such an orderly universe seems to display a grander design than a universe of chance. A theory that starts with a superlaw and a singularity would leave unanswered the question, Why that superlaw and that singularity? And why the laws of logic that end with such amazing consequences? Can a TOE ever explain itself or how it comes to be instantiated in the real world?

Stephen Hawking has developed a theory of quantum gravity that assumes neither infinite time nor a beginning of time. Instead, time is *finite but unbounded.* There is no initial singularity. The equations are relationships involving imaginary time, which is indistinguishable from the three spatial dimensions. Just as the two-dimensional surface of the earth is finite but unbounded, and three-dimensional relativistic ("curved") space is finite but unbounded, so Hawking's spatial and imaginary time dimensions are all finite but unbounded. In that imaginary time frame, real time gradually emerges. He grants that the interpretation of events in imaginary time is not clear. It also seems to me inconsistent to think of time as emerging, since emergence refers to changes in real time.

Hawking makes some interesting comments on the *theological implications* of a self-contained universe without boundaries or initial conditions. Earlier Big Bang theory assumed a singularity at which the laws of physics break down. At the singularity, God would have had freedom to choose both the initial conditions and the laws of the universe. But in Hawking's universe there are no initial conditions, and the choice of laws is restricted by self-consistency and by the Anthropic Principle: the early universe must provide the conditions for the later existence of humanity. He concludes,

[God] would, of course, still have had the freedom to choose the laws that the universe obeyed. This, however, may not really have been all that much of a choice; there may well be only one, or a small number, of complete unified theories, such as the heterotic string theory, that are self-consistent and allow the existence of structures as complicated as human beings who can investigate the laws of the universe and ask about the nature of God.

Even if there is only one possible unified theory, it is just a set of rules and equations. What is it that breathes fire into the equations and makes a universe for them to describe? The usual approach of science of constructing a mathematical model cannot answer the questions of why there should be a universe for the model to describe.[34]

Hawking says here that the equations of a unified theory could not answer the question of why there is a universe at all. Yet his final paragraph seems to hold out the hope that a complete scientific theory may someday answer just that question:

However, if we do discover a complete theory, it should in time be understandable in broad principle by everyone, not just a few scientists. Then we shall all, philosophers, scientists, and just ordinary people, be able to take part in the discussion of the question of why it is that we and the universe exist. If we find the answer to that, it would be the ultimate triumph of human reason—for then we would know the mind of God.[35]

In sum, these various cosmological theories are at one level simply alternative scientific hypotheses proposed to account for empirical data. But at another level their proponents have often presented *chance* and *necessity* as alternatives to *design*, alternatives that would make the idea of a Creator superfluous. I have tried to show that even if it turns out that the Big Bang is not a unique singularity, none of these theories is inconsistent with theism. No support for the *Conflict* model can be found in a careful analysis of current cosmology.

## IV. THEOLOGICAL IMPLICATIONS

Let us consider the theological implications of recent cosmology under four headings: (1) Intelligibility and Contingency, (2) *Ex nihilo* and Continuing Creation, (3) The Significance of Humanity, and (4) Eschatology and the Future.

### 1. INTELLIGIBILITY AND CONTINGENCY

Science has a number of presuppositions that are not themselves objects of scientific investigation. I also called them limit questions and suggested that they can be topics of *Dialogue* between science and religion. Among these presuppositions are the *orderliness, unity, simplicity,* and *intelligibility* of nature. I take order to be a broader concept than law, since it can include probabilistic, geometrical, and historical patterns as well as causal regularities, as we saw in the case of chaos theory. Unity refers to the presence of common interrelationships underlying apparently diverse phenomena. Let us look particularly at the status of intelligibility.

The search for a unified theory in physics and cosmology is motivated by the conviction that the cosmos is orderly, simple, and *rationally intelligible.* Physicists must, of course, check their theories against experimental evidence, but they are convinced that a valid general theory will be conceptually simple and aesthetically beautiful. To the critical realist, simplicity in our theories reflects a simplicity in the world and not just in our minds. Einstein said that the only thing that is incomprehensible about the world is that it is comprehensible.

Historically, the conviction that the cosmos is unified and intelligible had both Greek and biblical roots. The Greeks, and later the Stoics in the Roman world, saw the universe as a single system. The Greek philosophers had great confidence in the power of reason, and it is not surprising that they made significant progress in mathematics and geometry. We saw in chapter 1 that historians have claimed that the biblical doctrine of creation made a distinctive contribution to the rise of experimental science because it combined the ideas of *rationality* and *contingency.* If God is rational, the world is orderly; but if God is also free, the world did not have to have the particular order that it has. The world can then be understood only by observing it, rather than by deducing its order from necessary first principles, as the Greeks tried to do.[36] The church fathers said that God voluntarily created form as well as matter *ex nihilo,* rather than imposing preexisting eternal forms on matter.

Thomas Torrance has written extensively on the theme of "*contingent order.*" He stresses God's freedom in creating as an act of voluntary choice. God alone is infinitely free, and both the existence and the structure of the world are contingent in the sense that they might not have been. The world might have been differently ordered. We can discover its order only by observation. Moreover, the world can be studied on its own because in being created it has its own independent reality, distinct from the transcendent God. Science can legitimately assume a "methodological secularism" in its work, while the theologian can still assert that the world is ultimately dependent on God.[37]

Einstein, on the other hand, saw any contingency as a threat to belief in the rationality of the world, which he said is central in science. "A conviction, akin to religious feeling, of the rationality or intelligibility of the world lies behind all scientific work of a high order."[38] He spoke of a "cosmic religious sense" and "a deep faith in the rationality of the world." He rejected the idea of a personal God whose acts arbitrarily interfere in the course of events; he subscribed to a form of pantheism, identifying God with the orderly structure itself. When asked if he believed in God, he replied, "I believe in Spinoza's

God, who reveals himself in the orderly harmony of what exists."[39] Einstein equated rationality with orderliness and determinism; he never abandoned his conviction that the uncertainties of quantum theory only reflect temporary human ignorance, which will be left behind when the deterministic underlying mechanisms are discovered. He felt that Bohr's ideas of paradox and complementarity were a departure from rationality. He was mainly concerned about the necessity of events, but he also thought that the laws of physics are logically necessary. In a similar vein, Geoffrey Chew holds that all the laws of physics will be uniquely derivable from the requirement of self-consistency alone.[40]

The physicist James Trefil describes the search for unified laws in cosmology, and in an epilogue he writes,

But who created those laws? . . . Who made the laws of logic? . . . No matter how far the boundaries are pushed back, there will always be room both for religious faith and a religious interpretation of the physical world. For myself, I feel much more comfortable with the concept of a God who is clever enough to devise the laws of physics that make the existence of our marvelous universe inevitable than I do with the old-fashioned God who had to make it all, laboriously, piece by piece.[41]

Here the assumption seems to be that of deism rather than pantheism: the laws of physics are contingent but events governed by those laws are "inevitable."

John Polkinghorne, physicist and theologian, discusses the intelligibility of the world in a theistic framework. The key to understanding the physical world is mathematics, an invention of the human mind. The fit between reason in our minds and in the world would be expected if the world is the creation of mind. God is *the common ground of rationality* in our minds and in the world. Orderliness can also be understood as God's faithfulness, but it does not exclude an important role for chance. Polkinghorne invokes the early Christian concept of *logos*, which, as we have seen, combined the Greek idea of a rational ordering principle and the Hebrew idea of the active Word of God. He maintains that the theist can account for the intelligibility that the scientist assumes.[42]

Robert Russell makes a helpful distinction between global, nomological, and local contingency.[43] In the light of my earlier discussion of cosmology, I suggest a fourfold distinction:

1. *Contingent Existence.* Why is there anything at all? This is the question of greatest interest to theologians. The existence of the cosmos as a whole is not self-explanatory, regardless of whether it is finite or infinite in time. The details of particular scientific cosmologies are irrelevant to the contingency of the existence of the world. Even if a theory shows that there is only one possible universe, the universe would still only remain possible; nothing in the theory provides that a universe actually exists or that the theory is instantiated.[44]

2. *Contingent Boundary Conditions.* If there was a beginning, it was a singularity to which the laws of physics do not apply, and as such it cannot be

scientifically explained. If time is infinite, there would be no beginning, but at any point in time, no matter how far back, one would have to postulate a particular state of affairs, treating it as a "given."

3. *Contingent Laws.* Many of the laws of cosmology appear to be arbitrary. But some of them may turn out to be necessary implications of more fundamental theories. If a unified theory is found, however, it will itself be contingent, and the argument only moves back a stage. Insofar as it is required by laws of logic (for example, two-valued logic), those laws reflect axioms that are not necessary in any absolute sense. Moreover, some laws applicable to higher emergent levels of life and mind are not derivable from the laws of physics. Such higher laws would only be instantiated with the novel occurrence of the phenomena they describe. It is misleading to refer to a unified theory in physics as a "Theory of Everything," for its unity would be achieved only by a very high degree of abstraction that leaves out all of the diversity and particularity of events in the world and the emergence of more complex levels of organization from simpler ones. We could hardly expect a TOE to tell us very much about an amoeba, much less about Shakespeare, Beethoven, or Newton.

4. *Contingent Events.* To the critical realist, uncertainty in quantum physics reflects indeterminacy in the world and not simply the limitations of our knowledge. (Similar contingency is present in the bifurcations of nonequilibrium thermodynamics, random mutations in evolution, and freedom in human life.) We have seen that quantum phenomena played a role in the very early history of the Big Bang. The cosmos is a unique and irreversible sequence of events. Our account of it must take a historical form rather than consist of general laws alone.

Of course, many scientists today are atheists or agnostics and confine themselves to strictly scientific questions. Yet wider reflection on cosmology seems to be an important way of raising what the theologian David Tracy calls "limit questions."[45] At the personal level, cosmologists often express a sense of mystery and awe at the power unleashed in the Big Bang and the occurrence of phenomena at the limits of our experience, language, and thought. If there was an initial singularity, it appears to be inaccessible to science. Cosmology encourages the examination of our presuppositions about time and space, law and chance, necessity and contingency. Above all, the intelligibility of the cosmos suggests questions that arise in science but cannot be answered within science itself.

## 2. *EX NIHILO* AND CONTINUING CREATION

In the Christian community, belief in God rests primarily on the historical witness to redemption in the covenant with Israel and the person of Christ, and on the personal experience of wholeness and renewal. The doctrine of creation represents the extension of these ideas of redemption to the world of nature. We have said that it also expresses the experience of wonder, dependence on God, gratitude for life as a gift, and recognition of interdependence, order, and novelty in the world. I suggested that these theological affirmations can be made apart from any particular cosmology, ancient or modern, as represented by the *Independence* thesis.

Nevertheless, there are theological parallels to each of the four kinds of contingency mentioned above. The first two (on *ex nihilo*) could perhaps be considered limit questions (a form of *Dialogue*), since particular cosmological theories do not answer them. The second two (on continuing creation) suggest a theology of nature (a form of *Integration*) to which particular scientific theories are relevant.

1. *The contingency of existence* corresponds to the central religious meaning of creation *ex nihilo*. In both the scientific and the theological contexts the basic assertions can be detached from the assumption of an absolute beginning. On the scientific side, it now appears likely that the Big Bang was indeed an absolute beginning, a singular event, but if there is new evidence for a cyclic universe or infinite time, the contingency of existence would remain. On the theological side, we have seen that Genesis portrays the creation of order from chaos, and that the *ex nihilo* doctrine was formulated later by the church fathers to defend theism against an ultimate dualism or a monistic pantheism. Its message applies to the whole of the cosmos at every moment, regardless of questions about its beginning or its detailed structure and history. In its theological articulation, *ex nihilo* has served to assert the transcendence, power, freedom, and purposefulness of God, and to express our dependence on God.

2. *The contingency of boundary conditions* also expresses the message of *ex nihilo* without requiring an absolute beginning. If it turns out that past time was finite, there was indeed a singularity at the beginning, inaccessible to science. Such a beginning was assumed by the church fathers in the classical *ex nihilo* doctrine, even though it was not their chief concern. As Aquinas said, such a beginning would provide an impressive example of dependence on God. On the other hand, if time were infinite, we would still have contingent boundary conditions; scientists could not avoid dealing with situations or states that they would have to treat as unexplained givens. In neither case could it be said that our particular universe was necessary.

3. *The contingency of laws* can be identified with the orderly aspect of *continuing creation*. Traditionally, creation has been identified with the provision of *order*. Such order, it was assumed, was introduced at the beginning, though it had to be continually sustained by God. By the eighteenth century, the order of nature seemed to be all-embracing, mechanical, and self-sustaining. But now we know that the history of the cosmos involves both law and chance, both structure and novelty. I will argue in the next chapter that the laws applicable to *emergent higher levels* of reality are not reducible to laws governing lower levels. New and more complex forms of order have emerged in successive eras. Life and consciousness would not be possible without these underlying structures going back to the early cosmos, but they cannot be explained by the laws of physics.

4. *The contingency of events* corresponds to the novel aspect of *continuing creation*. We can no longer assume the static universe of the Middle Ages, in which the basic forms of all beings were thought to be unchanging. Coming-to-be is a continuing process throughout time, and it continues today. Nature in all its forms must be viewed historically. Astrophysics adds its testimony to that of evolutionary biology and other fields of science. Time is irreversible and genuine novelty appears in cosmic history. Continuing creation expresses the theme of God's immanence and participation in the ongoing world. God builds on what is already there; each successive level of reality requires the structures of lower levels. Here we are moving beyond *Dialogue* to *Integration* in a theology of nature in which particular findings of science are relevant to the reformulation of theological ideas, as we will see in the chapter on evolution. I will suggest in chapter 11 that process philosophy is particularly helpful at this point, since it takes seriously the contingency of events (from indeterminacy in physics to the freedom of human beings), but it also represents a role for God in the unfolding of every event.

## 3. THE SIGNIFICANCE OF HUMANITY

We noted earlier that the function of creation stories is not primarily to explain events in the distant past but to locate present human experience in a framework of larger significance. Creation stories manifest the essential structure of reality and our place in it. They provide archetypes of authentic human life in accord with a universal order. They are recalled and celebrated in liturgy and ritual because they tell us who we are and how we can live in a meaningful world.

Much of the resistance to Copernicus and Galileo arose because in their cosmologies the earth was no longer the center but only one of several planets going around the sun. Darwin carried further the demotion of humanity from its central place in the cosmic scheme, and this seemed to challenge the biblical understanding of the significance of human life. What are the implications of modern cosmology for our self-understanding? Can they be reconciled with the message of the biblical creation story?

1. *The Immensity of Space and Time.* Humanity seems insignificant in the midst of such vast stretches of time and space. But today those immensities do not seem inappropriate. We now know that it takes about fifteen billion years for heavy elements to be cooked in the interior of stars and then scattered to form a second generation of stars with planets, followed by the evolution of life and consciousness. A very old expanding universe has to be a huge universe—on the order of fifteen billion light years. Moreover, as Teilhard de Chardin pointed out, we should not measure significance by size and duration, but by such criteria as complexity and consciousness.[46] The greatest complexity has apparently been achieved in the middle range of size, not at atomic dimensions or galactic dimensions. There are a hundred trillion synapses in a human brain; the number of possible ways of connecting them

is greater than the number of atoms in the universe. A higher level of organization and a greater richness of experience occurs in a human being than in a thousand lifeless galaxies. It is human beings, after all, that reach out to understand that cosmic immensity.

2. *Interdependence.* Cosmology joins evolutionary biology, molecular biology, and ecology in showing the interdependence of all things. We are part of an ongoing community of being; we are kin to all creatures, past and present. From astrophysics we know about our indebtedness to a common legacy of physical events. The chemical elements in your hand and in your brain were forged in the furnaces of stars. The cosmos is all of a piece. It is multileveled; each new higher level was built on lower levels from the past. Humanity is the most advanced form of life we know, but it is fully a part of a wider process in space and time. The new view may undercut anthropocentric claims that set humanity completely apart from the rest of nature, but it by no means makes human life insignificant. But along with this interconnectedness, we have to recognize that cosmic distances are so vast that we are cut off from communication with most of the universe.

3. *Life on Other Planets.* Planets are so numerous that if even a small fraction of them are habitable, life could exist in many stellar systems. In 1996 meteorites from Mars were discovered in Antarctica containing tiny carbonate strings that were in some respects similar to carbonates formed by bacteria on earth—though many scientists thought inorganic explanations more plausible. NASA missions to the surface of Mars will be seeking more direct evidence as to whether life forms once existed there. Most scientists are open to the possibility of intelligent life on relatively nearby galaxies, though biologists seem to consider it less likely than do astronomers or science fiction writers. But the possibility of beings superior to us, living in more advanced civilizations, is a further warning against anthropocentrism. It also calls into question exclusive claims concerning God's revelation in Christ. Here we can recall that even on our planet the work of the *logos,* the Eternal Word, was not confined to its self-expression in Christ. If that Word is active in continuing creation throughout the cosmos, we can assume that it will also have revealed itself as the power of redemption at other points in space and time, in ways appropriate to the forms of life existing there.

4. *Chance and Purpose.* Traditionally, we said, God's purpose in creation was identified with order. An emphasis on God's sovereignty led to a determinism in which everything was thought to happen in accordance with a detailed divine plan. Any element of chance was viewed as a threat to God's total control. It is not surprising, then, that some scientists and philosophers who are impressed by the role of chance are led to reject theism. (Bertrand Russell, Jacques Monod, Stephen Jay Gould, and Steven Weinberg, for example, view life as the accidental result of chance and assume that chance and theism are incompatible.) The appropriate response to design would be gratitude and thanksgiving, but the response to pure chance would be a sense of futility and cosmic alienation.

One possible answer is to say that God really controls all the events that appear to us to be chance—whether in quantum uncertainties, evolutionary mutations, or the accidents of human history. This would preserve divine determinism at a subtle level undetectable to science. But I will argue in the next chapter that the presence of genuine chance is not incompatible with theism. We can see design in the whole process by which life came into being, with whatever combination of probabilistic and deterministic features the process had. Natural laws and chance may equally be instruments of God's intentions. There can be purpose without an exact predetermined plan.

The contingency of events in personal life faces each of us at the existential level. We are all vulnerable to unpredictable events: the actions of other people, natural catastrophes, illness, and, above all, death. Our freedom is always limited by events we cannot control. We know the anxiety and insecurity of temporality and finitude. In the face of all such contingency, the gospel does not promise immunity from suffering or loss but rather the courage to affirm life in spite of them and the confidence that God's love is with us in the midst of them.

## 4. ESCHATOLOGY AND THE FUTURE

We ask, finally, how religious and scientific visions of the future might be compared. We focus here on the future of *the cosmos,* though this is inescapably tied to two other dimensions of eschatology: the future of *the individual* and the future of *society.* The basic experience involved in eschatology is our orientation toward the future and our need for hope. In all cultures people search for meaning in the face of suffering and death. Death intensifies the problem of cosmic justice, for the incidence of suffering in this life does not seem to be related to any deserved rewards and punishments. Eschatology can be understood as an extrapolation into the future of convictions about the present cosmic order. Most cultures have had stories about the cosmic future, as they have about the cosmic past.

There are two basic types of eschatological story.[47] First are the *myths of cyclical return* in which the world is repeatedly destroyed and reconstituted. Here time and history are viewed as cycles. Hinduism, for example, portrays a cycle of four ages: creation, deterioration, destruction, and recreation. Vishnu will be reincarnated in a new avatar, setting a new age in motion. There is also an eternal cycle of rebirth, in which every individual dies and is reborn in a higher or lower form, human or nonhuman, according to the merit (*karma*) earned during the previous life. Over an extended series of rebirths, the justice of the cosmic moral order is fulfilled. The cycle can be escaped only by enlightenment and absorption in Brahman, the all-embracing unity. In contrast to the short time span and geocentric outlook of the Bible, Hinduism has always assumed the vastness of time and space, which are features of modern cosmology. This cyclical view makes events in history appear less significant in Hinduism and other Asian religions than in the biblically based religions. If the cosmic cycle repeats itself endlessly, there is no beginning and no ending, no sense of overall historical progress, and no long-term motivation to make the world a better place. Instead, the main goal is to find a transhistorical reality and to achieve through meditation a timeless mode of being.

The second type is the *end-of-time myth*, which expresses a linear and irreversible view of time and history. Both Judaism and Christianity look to a future messianic age, but the ways in which that future has been envisaged have varied greatly in differing historical periods. (There have also been varying conceptions of resurrection, immortality, and heaven, but these are not our main concern here.) How did these ideas about the end of time develop, and how might we interpret them today?

The *early prophets* (for example, Amos, Micah, or Isaiah 9–11) held that Israel and its leaders had departed from the covenant. Believing in a God of justice, they saw God's judgment in the disasters threatening the nation but hoped that a return to the covenant and the presence of a new leader from the Davidic lineage would restore the nation to peace, justice, and prosperity. But after the exile, when Israel was occupied by successive foreign armies, the prospect that human actions could liberate the nation from oppression seemed dim indeed. The only hope seemed to lie in a more dramatic intervention by God. The *apocalyptic literature* (for example, Daniel) looked to a supernatural defeat of the worldly powers. Here the Messiah, who would bring deliverance and establish the Kingdom, was portrayed as a supernatural being rather than a political or military leader. The struggle would involve the whole cosmos and not just the nation. The coming Kingdom was envisaged in increasingly otherworldly terms. This shift also reflected a strong dualistic influence from Persia and Zoroastrianism; the world was said to be the theater of conflict between two coeternal forces, those of light and darkness, or God and Satan. The last days would bring a cosmic battle and the final victory of good over evil.

*The Kingdom of God* was a central theme in Christ's teachings, and he said that it was "at hand" (Mark 1:15). Sometimes he spoke of present aspects of the Kingdom; it is "in your midst" and it grows like a mustard seed. More often, he said it would come suddenly and unexpectedly. After his death, his disciples asserted that he was the promised Messiah and that the fulfillment of the Kingdom would come soon with his return. But with the postponement of these expectations, diverse responses arose in the early church. Some writings, such as the book of Revelation, continued the apocalyptic tradition and identified Christ's return with the final conflict between good and evil. Others, including the Gospel of John, focused on the community's continuing experience of the living Christ, understood as a kind of "realized eschatology" or future made present. By the time of Augustine, the institutional church was equated with the Kingdom already present on earth, though a distant consummation was still expected. In the Middle Ages and Reformation, much attention was given to the end of the world and the last judgment, but this did not preempt concern for justice and righteousness in this world. The three main biblical stories were extended to five stages of history: Creation, Covenant, Christ, Church, and Consummation.[48]

The *diversity of future expectations* continues among Christians today.[49] Some groups take the book of Revelation literally and think that the final conflict is imminent. They seek a detailed timetable among the rich profusion of biblical images, and they look for "signs of the end" today. Global crises and the threat of a nuclear holocaust have encouraged such apocalyptic thinking, but it engenders irresponsibility if it leads people to assume that they can do nothing about the future. Neo-orthodox and existentialist theologians, on the other hand, take Christ's teachings on the imminence of the Kingdom to be a symbolic way of expressing the urgency of decision and the importance of obedience to God's rule in the present. For them, the Kingdom is not a future event but a dimension of current existence. Liberal Protestants and exponents of liberation theology go back to the early prophets, for whom the Kingdom involved obedience to God and commitment to justice in society. In addressing their nation, the prophets combined a sense of God's judgment with hope for a new beginning. The majority of Christians would probably say that we must work to build the Kingdom, but that it is also the work of God, both within history and beyond history. This offers a middle ground between relying on God alone and relying on ourselves alone in facing the future.

What can scientists tell us about *the future of the universe?* We have seen that the expansion of the universe is slowing down, but current evidence is insufficient to decide whether it is open (expanding forever) or closed (expanding to a maximum before collapsing). If it is *closed,* it will eventually contract to a very small size (the Big Crunch), but it could bounce back again and continue in an indefinite series of cycles. This resembles the Hindu view of a cyclic universe with ages of destruction and ages of creation. The current structures of the world would be wiped out in such a "heat death," but new structures would appear in future cycles. The current expanding phase will last at least a hundred billion years, though our sun may not last longer than five or ten billion years. This is an incredibly long future in comparison to the half million years that human beings have been around, but it is not infinite.

Some scientists find this prospect very depressing. The astrophysicist Steven Weinberg holds that humanity is alone in an immense and impersonal universe, headed for oblivion. The earth is "just a tiny part of an overwhelmingly hostile universe." Scientific activity itself is the only source of consolation in a meaningless world:

The more the universe seems comprehensible, the more it also seems pointless. But if there is no solace in the fruits of research, there is at least some consolation in the research itself. . . . The effort to understand the universe is one of the very few things that lifts human life above the level of farce, and gives it some of the grace of tragedy.[50]

In a recent book Weinberg elaborates: "I did not mean that science teaches us that the universe is pointless, but only that the universe itself suggests no point."[51] That qualification would allow one to reply that if purpose is not ruled out by science, it is possible that cosmic history can be coherently interpreted as an expression of God's purposes. The emergence of intelligent persons would be a plausible goal of an intelligent, personal God. Theism and materialism are alternative metaphysical commitments, not scientific conclusions in either case. If we accept that interpretation we can move beyond *Conflict* at least to *Dialogue* on such questions.

If the universe is *open,* it will continue to expand and cool forever, but at a decreasing rate. It has usually been assumed that this would lead to the "freezing death" of all life as temperatures continue to fall. But Freeman Dyson has argued that biological life will be able to adapt to such new conditions in the future. Moreover, we could use genetic engineering to redesign organisms for extreme conditions. The energy requirements of a system are proportional to the square of the temperature; very little energy is required at low temperatures. Dyson also holds that the "software programs" that exist in the human brain could be transferred to computers and other kinds of "hardware," so that new forms of intelligence and consciousness will be able to survive at very low temperatures. "Life and intelligence are potentially immortal."[52]

A similar vision is set forth by Frank Tipler. The human brain, he says, is essentially a computer. As we colonize space, *information processing* in various forms will spread in networks throughout the universe. The information processing rate and the memory storage could both increase without limit, which would produce an essentially infinite intelligence. The cosmic computer network would be an "evolving God" emerging from the process and taking total control of the universe. There would be "an eternal continuation of intelligence," even if human beings are extinct, for computers would be able to replicate themselves. Even if we live in a closed universe, there could be an infinite number of thoughts before the Big Crunch, and this can be considered a form of this-worldly immortality.[53]

These projections are, of course, highly speculative and rest on many unverified assumptions. They seem to me inconsistent with *the biblical message,* not because they disagree with some of the imaginative future scenarios in the Bible, but because they reflect views of humanity, God, and the future that are at odds with basic biblical convictions. The Bible views the person as a unity of body, mind, and spirit (see chapter 10), not as a purely rational intellect defined by information-processing ability. Moreover, Dyson and Tipler propose a technologically based salvation that seeks control of the cosmos, whereas the Bible speaks of the need for personal transformation and social reconstruction in response to God. Though biblical eschatology takes many forms, all agree that future fulfillment will be the work of a personal God as well as of humanity, not the work of humanity apart from God.

Dyson and Tipler think that a future *heat death* or *freezing death* can be avoided. But if they cannot be avoided, would that contradict biblical assumptions? Would such a future imply that the universe is meaningless, as Weinberg suggests? I do not think so. I would argue that biblical stories about both the beginning and the end of time are symbolic expressions of trust in God. Together they represent an ultimate framework for temporal history, not events in that history.[54] The future of the cosmos, like the past, can also be seen as a phase of continuing creation. The long time scale does indeed make us aware that evolution will continue. It would be grossly anthropocentric to assume that we are the goal or the only purpose of creation. There is an immensely long time for this part of the cosmic experiment to continue. In the meantime, there are meaningful challenges to action in our own lifetime—above all, to move toward a just and sustainable planetary society. Our hope is based on the conviction that God is at work in the world and that we can cooperate in that work.

According to *process thought,* every entity has value in three ways. First, as a moment of experience it has intrinsic value. The value of these experiences is inherent in each present moment. Second, every entity is valuable for its contribution to the future of other beings in the world—both in the immediate future and in the distant future. Third, every entity is valuable for its ongoing contribution to the life of God. The values achieved in this world are preserved in God's eternal life, and this is part of their enduring significance and permanence beyond the flux of time. In addition, some entities, such as human beings, will have a fourth kind of future value, if as conscious individuals we survive death.

If we think that life on earth or in this universe will eventually be extinguished, only a portion of the second of these *sources of value and meaning* is threatened, namely the contribution of our present actions to the very distant future. The others are all unaffected. Moreover, there may be forms of life on other planets or in other universes. Who is to say what are the limits of new possibilities for God in this cosmic cycle or in future cycles or in other domains of creation?

In conclusion, then, I think we can join the astronauts in celebrating the beauty of our amazing planet and in expressing gratitude for the gift of life. Standing under the stars at night, we can still experience wonder and awe. Now we know that the cosmos has included stretches of space and time that we can hardly imagine. What sort of world is it in which those strange early states of matter and energy could be the forerunners of intelligent life? Within a theistic framework it is not surprising that there is intelligent life on earth; we can see here the work of a purposeful Creator. Theistic belief makes sense of this datum and a variety of other kinds of human experience, even if it offers no conclusive proof. We still ask: Why is there anything at all? Why are things the way they are? With the psalmist of old we can say, "O Lord, how manifest are thy works! In wisdom thou has made them all. . . . When thou sendest forth thy Spirit, they are created" (Ps. 104:30).

## CHAPTER 9

# Evolution and Continuing Creation

The publication of Charles Darwin's *On the Origin of Species* in 1859 was the initiating event in an intellectual revolution that continues to affect many areas of thought. We noted that evolutionary theory presented a fourfold challenge to traditional Christianity in the nineteenth century: (1) a challenge to biblical literalism, (2) a challenge to design, (3) a challenge to the status of humanity, and (4) the challenge of evolutionary ethics and social Darwinism. We traced a variety of theological responses, ranging from traditionalism through liberalism and modernism to naturalistic philosophies of evolution. All four of these initial challenges continue to be important today. The first two (concerning scripture and design) are taken up in this chapter, the others (concerning human nature and ethics) in the subsequent chapter. But before discussing theological implications, we must examine scientific developments in evolutionary biology in the twentieth century.

## I. EVOLUTIONARY THEORY

Since Darwin's day, scientists have accumulated an immense amount of evidence supporting both the historical occurrence of evolution and the hypothesis that variations and natural selection are the main causes of evolutionary change. But vigorous debates continue concerning some of the details of their operation and the role of other factors. We must look at the role of DNA and current theories about the origin of life. Information theory and systems theory also throw light on the historical evolution of organisms and their present functioning.

### 1. THE MODERN SYNTHESIS

In the twentieth century, work in *population genetics* has greatly advanced our understanding of the inheritance of variations, about which Darwin could only speculate. Mendel's laws of heredity were studied in plant, insect, and animal populations, both in the field and in the laboratory. It was also found that an occasional individual had a characteristic, such as eye color, that differed markedly from the rest of the population. The frequency of such mutations could be increased by exposure to X rays and certain chemicals. Mutations and the recombination of units of heredity (genes) from two parents were seen to be the main sources of variation, and both were evidently random processes unrelated to the needs of the organism. Genetics and evolutionary theory were brought together in a systematic neo-Darwinian framework, to which Julian Huxley in 1942 gave the name "the Modern Synthesis."[1] Among its exponents have been Ernst Mayr, Theodosius Dobzhansky, and Gaylord Simpson.[2]

Population studies also greatly extended our understanding of *natural selection*. A "species" was identified with a reproductive population rather than a characteristic type. There is usually considerable diversity within a population, and evolution occurs when a shift takes place in the relative frequency of genes. In the Modern Synthesis, evolution was thought to occur slowly and gradually by the accumulation of small changes. Often these changes are induced by a changing environment. Mutants not useful in one environment may turn out to be highly adaptive in other surroundings. Among a species of light-colored moths there occurs a rare dark mutation, which is conspicuous against light-colored tree trunks and is picked off more rapidly by birds. But on the soot-darkened trees of industrial areas, the dark moth is less conspicuous; in the past century it has completely supplanted the light-colored form in parts of England.

In Darwin's day, natural selection was understood primarily as the survival of the fittest under conditions of competitive struggle. In this century, selection was equated with differential reproduction and survival, and the importance of *cooperation* as well as *competition* was recognized. Sometimes symbiotic cooperation between two species enables both to survive. At other times a division of labor among diverse members of a social group, such as a termite colony, may be the key to its success. The study of ecosystems has traced complex patterns of interdependence in biotic communities.

Recent techniques for *comparing the molecular structure* of similar proteins in various living species allow us to estimate the time since their lineages diverged. For example, the enzyme cytochrome-C in human beings consists of a sequence of 104 amino acids. In the comparable sequence in rhesus monkeys, only one of these amino acids is different; horses have 12 that differ, and in fish there are 22, indicating increasingly distant kinship. The evolutionary history established by this biochemical method agrees well with evidence derived from two completely different disciplines: the study of fossil records by paleontologists, and the comparison of the anatomy of living species by taxonomists.[3]

Before Darwin, Lamarck had claimed that evolution occurred because an animal's behavior produced physiological modifications that were inherited by its offspring. The giraffe's neck is long, he said, because it has been stretched by generations of reaching for leaves on trees. As we have seen, such a direct *inheritance of acquired characteristics* was subsequently discredited. In reaction to Lamarckianism, Darwinians tended to minimize the role of the organism's own behavior in its evolution. Change was viewed as the product of the external forces of natural selection acting on an essentially passive population.

But early in this century, Baldwin and Lloyd Morgan defended "organic selection"; they granted that the environment selects organisms, but they pointed out that organisms also select their own environments (the Baldwin effect). More recently, C. H. Waddington's idea of genetic assimilation underscores the importance that *behavior* can have, without violating Darwin's basic postulates. He assigns great significance to an indirect effect whose long-term results are similar to Lamarckianism. Suppose that during a time of food scarcity a species of birds adopts a new habit of probing for insects under the bark of trees. Thereafter, those mutations or variations associated with longer beaks will tend to survive more efficiently and will be selected. Novel activities can thus bring about novel forms. Functional changes may precede structural ones. A new behavior pattern can thus produce an evolutionary change, though not in the simple way Lamarck assumed.[4]

Alister Hardy contends that modern biologists have emphasized the mechanical role of external forces acting on random mutations and have neglected the fact that *internal drives* can decisively modify evolution. He discusses the curiosity and initiative of animals, their self-adaptation, instinct and learning, and other findings of ethology. He concludes, "I think we can say, from the many different lines of argument, that internal behavioral selection due to the 'psychic life' of the animal, whatever we think about its nature, is now seen to be a most powerful creative element in evolution."[5] We do not have to imagine that random mutations at the molecular level are the chief agent in the initiation of change; they may serve rather to perpetuate changes first introduced by the initiative of the organism itself. Of course, this does not imply that organisms were trying to evolve, but only that purposive behavior as well as chance mutation was important in setting the direction of evolutionary change.

## 2. CURRENT DEBATES

Several features of the Modern Synthesis have been challenged in recent years. In some cases the critics call for an extension of the synthesis; in others they modify some of its assumptions.

### 1. Punctuated Equilibrium

Starting in the 1930s, Goldschmidt and others challenged the assumption that evolution occurs through the gradual accumulation of small changes. They said that laboratory studies had documented only changes within species, not the formation of new species. Few fossils had been found representing transitions between species, much less between major types (classes or phyla). They proposed that new species and phyla arise suddenly from very rare cases in which a viable creature is produced by "systemic" mutations, such as those that modify an early stage of the embryo's development.[6]

More recently, Stephen Jay Gould and Niles Eldredge have defended "punctuated equilibrium." The fossil record shows long periods of *stasis—*

millions of years with very little change—interspersed with bursts of rapid speciation in relatively short periods. They postulate that whole developmental sequences changed at once, leading to major structural changes. Speciation could occur rapidly if a small population was geographically isolated. They claim that previous evolutionary theory was not false but incomplete, especially in accounting for speciation.[7] Proponents of the Modern Synthesis reply that their theory is more varied and flexible than these critics acknowledge. The absence of transitional forms is a result of the incompleteness of the fossil record. Changes that appear rapid on the scale of geologic time (over a period of fifty thousand years, let us say) can encompass many generations. Thus Stebbins and Ayala think that many of Gould's ideas can be included in an enlarged version of the neo-Darwinian synthesis.[8]

## 2. Nonadaptive Changes

The Modern Synthesis held that natural selection is the primary directive force in evolution and that every new trait is an adaptation contributing to survival. Some critics suggest that this is an unfalsifiable claim, since one can always think up a possible selective advantage or introduce *ad hoc* auxiliary hypotheses for which there is no independent evidence. Gould and Lewontin attack such "panselectionism" and suggest that selection is an important but not exclusive factor. "Selection may be the ultimate source of evolutionary change, but most actual events owe more of their shape to its nonadaptive sequelae."[9]

It has been known for some time that *detrimental changes* do occur. For example, the antlers of the Irish elk evolved to such enormous size that they became very unwieldy. Many such changes can be explained as byproducts of other changes, since a constellation of genes controls a whole package of developmental processes. (In this case, larger antlers may have accompanied larger and stronger bone structures, which would have conferred a selective advantage.) Organisms are integrated wholes, and a particular gene may hitchhike with other genes that are selected. Structures originally arising for one function can later be coopted for other purposes that contribute to survival.

*Genetic drift* from neutral mutations is another form of nonadaptive change. Many variations neither foster nor hinder survival, and their perpetuation seems to have been a matter of chance. If a large population is broken up into small groups, statistical or sampling variations will be present among the groups. In changing environments, a small isolated population might have been a bottleneck of evolutionary history, and the particular genes that it perpetuated may have been a matter of chance rather than selective advantage.[10]

## 3. Multilevel Selection

In the Modern Synthesis, individual organisms are selected and their genes are passed on. But Wyne-Edwards, Hamilton, and others focused attention on groups of related organisms. A bird's warning cry endangers individual survival, but it helps the survival of a *kinship group* with shared genes. Such "altruistic" behavior would contribute to inclusive fitness and kin selection. These phenomena are prominent in the writings of Wilson, Dawkins, and other sociobiologists; in the next chapter we will examine their claims concerning altruism and genetic determinism. Here we note that they see selection as operating on kinship groups to maximize the transmission of their genes. Critics have seen these views as reductionistic, and they propose a hierarchical model in which selection occurs at a variety of levels.

Hull and others have argued that a *species* is an important unit of selection. The history of a species is similar to that of an organism, but on a much longer time scale. An organism produces other organisms by reproduction; a species produces other species by speciation. An organism perishes in death; a species perishes in extinction. As we ask about high reproductive rates in organisms, so we might ask what characteristics of a species produce high speciation rates. There can thus be branching, persistence, and selection of inheritable variations on several levels at once. Changes at one level will constrain those at another level.[11]

## 4. The Active Role of Genes

In neo-Darwinism, random mutations and the recombination of genes provide the raw material of change, but the directionality of evolution is entirely the result of natural selection. The genes are completely passive before the selective forces of the environment. But some biologists suggest that genes play a more active role in their own evolution. For one thing, the mutational repertoire of a gene is a function of its structure, which limits the operation of chance. Some changes are the result of the transposition of genes, and transposability is a function of gene structure. Some enzymes also promote mutation. The ability to evolve faster depends on internal as well as external factors. A species can in effect learn to evolve, using strategies successful in the past.[12]

Most molecular biologists have accepted the assumption (often called the Central Dogma) that information in organisms passes in only one direction, from genes to proteins. But Stuart Kauffman and others have shown that there are ways in which proteins affect genes.[13] Some enzymes manipulate the genetic message in response to signals from the environment. Immune systems act as sensors for environmental and bodily changes, and there are codes for gene repair in response to damage. Moreover, embryonic development takes place according to basic forms, structures, and rules that limit the options. The developmental pathways channel change and constrain the morphological possibilities. Some of this developmental information resides in the cell's cytoplasm.[14] These claims suggest the need for a considerable enlargement of the Modern Synthesis, though not its total rejection.

## 3. DNA AND THE ORIGIN OF LIFE

The discovery of the structure of DNA by Watson and Crick in 1953 opened the door to the analysis of genes at the molecular level. The DNA molecule was shown to be a double strand. At regular intervals along each strand is a projecting nucleotide base (one of four bases, abbreviated A, C, G, and T), which is linked to a base in the opposite strand. The base pairs form cross-links like the rungs of a ladder. An A base will link only with a T base, and C only with G. Here was a mechanism for one of the crucial properties of genes: *replication.* If the two strands separate, every base in each strand will attract a new partner base (from the surrounding fluid) and build up a new partner-strand identical to the old one, with A, C, G, and T units in exactly the same order. Mutations are apparently caused by damage to a portion of the DNA molecule or by defective replication.

The other important property of genes is the control of developmental processes. All living organisms are composed of *protein chains* built out of simpler building blocks, the twenty amino acids. The DNA remains in the cell nucleus, but its distinctive sequences are copied on single strands of messenger-RNA and carried to other parts of the cell, where amino acids are assembled into protein chains. It was found that there is a *genetic code* in which a distinctive group of three bases corresponds to each of the twenty amino acids. The order of the triplets in the DNA determines the order in which the amino acids are assembled into protein chains.

In the DNA, then, an "alphabet" of just four "letters" (A, C, G, and T bases), grouped in three-letter "words" (each specifying one of the amino acids), is arranged in "sentences" (specifying particular proteins). Thousands of sentences of varying length and word order can be made from the twenty basic words, so there are thousands of possible proteins. Long paired strands, made of exactly the same four bases in various sequences, constitute the genes of all organisms, from microbes to human beings. In all known organisms, the same code is used to translate from DNA to protein, which seems to indicate a common origin for all living things.

*The origin of life* remains a mystery, but some possible pieces of the puzzle have been proposed. In 1953, Stanley Miller passed sparks through a flask containing only a mixture of simple gases and heated water (the inorganic compounds that were probably present in the early atmosphere and ocean). He found that he had produced many of the amino acids. Other scientists detected the spectra of simple organic compounds in interstellar gas clouds, and amino acids were found inside meteorites arriving from outer space. Glycine was the most abundant amino acid in both the Miller experiments and in the meteorites, as it is in living organisms. Alanine was second in all three cases. Perhaps the earliest forms of life arose in such a prebiotic soup. More complex proteins can form microspheres, which in some cases grow and split into two smaller spheres, resembling rudimentary cells.[15]

An alternative theory proposes that a primitive form of replication occurred first in *crystals of clay* or other minerals. For a given mineral, one of the alternative crystal structures, and whatever flaws are present in it, is copied onto successive layers. A small piece of mineral dust, dropped in a supersaturated solution, acts as a "seed" around which a new crystal grows, replicating the flaws in the original. If some versions survive better than others, there would be a rudimentary selection system. Certain organic molecules are known to facilitate such crystal replication. Perhaps organic molecules at first assisted inorganic replication and later achieved self-replication on their own.[16]

But how could DNA and *the genetic code* have arisen? The coding molecules in an organism today are themselves the product of coded instructions. We seem to face a chicken-and-egg dilemma, as far back as we go. But Manfred Eigen has shown that if you string nucleotide bases together, some combinations are more stable than others. There could have been an early form of chemical evolution, a prebiological selection of more stable combinations. The most stable and abundant triplet, GGC, corresponds to the simplest and most abundant amino acid, glycine. GCC is second in abundance; it corresponds to alanine, also second. Eigen proposes a hypothetical "hypercycle" of four simple RNA chains, which could replicate and also synthesize proto-proteins.[17] This would still be a long way from DNA, and much remains puzzling, but the gap between nonliving and living forms does not seem as wide as it did a few decades ago.

It has often been assumed that the Second Law of Thermodynamics excludes *the emergence of more highly ordered states,* since entropy or disorder tends to increase in closed systems. But I pointed out in chapter 7 that organisms are open systems, citing Prigogine's work on the appearance of more complex patterns of order in physical systems far from equilibrium. In discussing the origins of life, Jeffrey Wicken has shown that self-organizing dissipative systems can contribute to the production of entropy in irreversible energy flows. The accumulation of organization and structure provides boundary conditions on the operation of physico-chemical processes; there is randomization within constraints. The given chemical affinities and bonding preferences provide internal limitations on structural possibilities. Wicken observes that to explain a state in classical physics, one needs only a set of initial conditions and a set of laws. But to explain a state in the biological world, one needs a historical account of change and cumulative selection. Moreover, an organism is selected as part of a total ecosystem that constitutes a flow of energy and materials. Wicken argues that evolutionary explanations must be holistic in both time and space.[18]

## 4. DNA, INFORMATION, AND SYSTEMS THEORY

The evolutionary role of DNA as an encoded message is illuminated by work in *information theory*. In chapter 7 we saw that order and information in thermodynamics are represented by improbable combinations of components. Entropy and disorder tend to increase in a closed system, leading to a loss of information. In World War II the reliable communication of messages by radio was sought. In that context, noise is disorder that degrades a message. According to information theory, there are two ways of reducing such loss: (1) *redundancy,* in which portions of the message are repeated, and (2) *rules,* which set constraints by restricting the allowable combinations, while still allowing novelty and diversity. With the advent of computers, information could be reliably encoded in a binary or digital representation (0/1 or off/on) and quantified as "bits" of information. The computer responds to instructions in the program, which specify connections in its electrical circuits. It can then manipulate the representation of the information fed into it ("information processing") and activate some form of output.

*Information* is an ordered pattern (of auditory sounds, alphabetical letters, binary digits, DNA bases, or any other distinguishable elements) that is one among many possible states of a system. *Information is communicated* when another system (a listener, reader, computer, or organic process) responds to the pattern selectively—that is, when information is coded, transmitted, and decoded. In the case of proteins formed by DNA there are internal structural rules that limit the possible combinations and restrict the operation of chance. Yet there is ample opportunity for novel messages. For stable forms to evolve, mutations must be neither too rare nor too frequent. Jeremy Campbell writes, "The lesson of information theory is that choice and constraint can coexist as partners, enabling a system, be it a living organism, a language, or a society, to follow the arrow not of entropy but of history."[19]

For evolution to occur information must flow in two directions, both from and to the genes. Consider first *the expression of the DNA* in the growing organism. The linear message of the DNA molecule produces a linear protein chain, but because there are characteristic bonding angles and folds in the chain, the result is a distinctive three-dimensional protein structure, with sites for side groups. Message leads to structure, and structure leads to function. A very complex set of genetic regulatory programs with activators and repressors switches the activity of other genes on and off, so that the right kind of cell is produced at the right place and at the right time in the growing embryo and in the continuing functioning of the organism. In this context, the DNA embodies effective information, that is, a set of instructions.

*Information about the environment* is also transmitted to the gene pool through natural selection. There is information on what has proved viable and how the organism can make its way through the world, including encoded instinctive behavioral patterns. This represents a memory capacity through which the story of life is written in the DNA. We could say that the system shows a kind of learning ability, a trial-and-error testing in a series of information-gathering experiments reaching up to larger units: organisms, populations, and ecosystems. Considerable unused information is stored in the DNA, which can be called on under altered environmental conditions. Here is a cybernetic or feedback system for gaining, storing, retrieving, and using information. The action of DNA is context-dependent and requires a two-way flow of information between levels. Information, along with matter and energy, is thus a basic constituent of reality, and it is relational in character. Words convey a message only when they are read. Information is always context-dependent.

Imagine a person *writing a book* that is organized in chapters, paragraphs, sentences, words, and letters. The choice of letters is determined by the choice of words, and the words are governed by the formulation of sentences, and so forth. The writer also assumes a whole set of encoding conventions: grammatical rules, linguistic practices, and the alphabet and vocabulary of a particular language-using community. The reader, in turn, uses the same rules to decode the message. The book can be translated into another language, or it can be read aloud, expressing the same message in another medium.

In the case of DNA, too, the meaning of the part depends on *larger wholes*. Control sequences (operons) regulate whole blocks of activities. Recognition codes provide responses to particular molecular structures. Developmental pathways aid the differentiation and growth of cells in particular organs. Homeostatic feedback mechanisms, such as those for temperature regulation, represent norms for the functioning of the organism as a whole. In each case the patterns among components at one level set boundary conditions for activities at lower levels. The patterns in the DNA do not violate the laws of physics and chemistry, but they could never be deduced from those laws. Information is recorded and utilized in hierarchically organized patterns. The meaning of the parts is determined relationally by their participation in larger wholes.[20] A similar hierarchical ordering is present in computer programs. In that case, too, the message (software) can be distinguished from the medium (hardware). The meaning of a message, whether in a DNA code or a computer code, depends on its wider context.

DNA constitutes a *developmental* and *functioning* program only in conjunction with molecules in the cytoplasm, which provide a milieu and support structure. The genetic program has been preserved from the past and functions in the present because of the behavior of larger units—including, finally, the whole interdependent ecosystem with its cycles and interactions of energy, materials, and information. Each unit achieves stability by being nested in a larger whole to whose stability and dynamism it contributes. As Wicken puts it, "Nature produces itself hierarchically—one level establishing the ground of its own stability by utilizing mechanisms made available by lower levels, and finding functional contexts at higher levels."[21]

The relation among levels of order has been analyzed in systems theory, especially in *hierarchy theory*. Information theorist Herbert Simon asks us to imagine a watchmaker whose work is disrupted occasionally. If the watchmaker has to start over again each time, he may never finish his task. But if he assembles groups of parts in stable subassemblies, which are then combined, he will finish the task more rapidly. Living organisms have many such *stable subassemblies*, with differing bonding strengths, which are preserved intact and only loosely coupled to each other. The higher level of stability often arises from functions that are relatively independent of variations in the microscopic details. The collective integrated behavior can be described in a simpler way at a higher organizational level.[22]

Here is a clue as to how evolution can exhibit both *chance* and *directionality*. Chance is present at many levels: mutations, genetic recombination, genetic drift, climatic variations, and so forth. Evolution is an unrepeatable series of events that no one could have predicted; it can only be described historically. Yet history has seen an ascent to higher levels of organization, a trend toward greater complexity and sentience. The dice are thrown, but the dice are loaded; there are built-in constraints. In particular, modular structures are *relatively stable,* and so the advances are conserved. Think of a gear that can make small random rotations in either direction. If it has a ratchet that occasionally clicks in place, rotation in one direction will be favored in the long run. Another analogy is a ball on a hill with small terraces, offering "metastable states" in which the ball can rest without returning to the bottom.

There are two kinds of hierarchy. First, considered historically, is *genealogical hierarchy:* gene, organism, and species. The units are identified by their historical role in replication and evolutionary change. Second, considered at any point in time, is an *organizational hierarchy:* atom, molecule, cell, organ, organism, population, and ecosystem. Here units are identified by their relative stability and their action and interaction as integrated units. Entities at any level share many properties with other entities at that level and share relatively few properties with entities at other levels. In both hierarchies information flows between levels. In the second case, Niles Eldredge and Stanley Salthe speak of an "upward influence" when many lower-level subsystems work together as necessary conditions of a larger whole, and a "downward influence" when many subsystems are constrained by the boundary conditions set by higher-level activities.[23] How are these hierarchical levels related to each other?

## II. A HIERARCHY OF LEVELS

Francis Crick, the codiscoverer of the structure of DNA, has written: "Thus eventually one may hope to have the whole of biology 'explained' in terms of the level below it, and so on right down to the atomic level. . . . The knowledge we have already makes it highly unlikely that there is anything that cannot be explained by physics and chemistry."[24] The spectacular success of molecular biology has sometimes been taken as support for such reductionist claims. We will consider several forms of reductionism and then reply to them by defending a hierarchy of distinctive levels, both in evolutionary history and in the activity of organisms today. The discussion here is philosophical, but it involves the interpretation of biology. Theological issues are taken up in section III.

### 1. THREE FORMS OF REDUCTION

Three forms of reduction can be distinguished:[25] (1) methodological reduction as a research strategy; (2) epistemological reduction as a relation between theories; and (3) ontological reduction as a view of reality. They can be distinguished because they make different kinds of claims, though many authors shift uncritically from one to another.

## 1. Methodological Reduction: A Research Strategy

It is often a useful research strategy to study a complex whole by breaking it up into more manageable component units. In particular, the analysis of molecular structures and interactions has been a powerful tool in biological research. One could adopt reduction as a practical research strategy without claiming that all biological theories will be derived from chemical theories, or that nothing exists in the world except material particles.

If, however, methodological reduction is held to be the *only* valid research strategy, it can lead to the exclusion of synthetic or "compositionist" approaches, in which more inclusive wholes are studied. Some have feared that the bandwagon of interest in molecular biology would lead to the neglect of fields that deal with the whole organism, such as population genetics, embryology, ecology, and animal behavior. The biologist Clifford Grobstein makes a plea for multilevel analysis: "Sophisticated biological investigation thus involves a cross-feed of information between analyses proceeding at several levels."[26] Another biologist, Ernst Mayr says that dissection into components is helpful because processes at different levels are in some respects independent, but it is inadequate because these processes are also interdependent.[27] Alexander Rosenberg, a philosopher of science, holds that lower-level regularities are often too complex to allow the prediction of higher-level regularities. In practice, higher-level relationships must be investigated in their own terms. Biology is often organized around functions that can be identified only in relation to larger units and activities.[28] Methodological reduction may be accepted, then, as long as it does not lead to the neglect of research programs at a variety of levels, from molecules to ecosystems.

## 2. Epistemological Reduction: A Relation Between Theories

Here the claim is that the theories or laws of one level can be derived from those of another level. For example, the laws relating the volume, pressure, and temperature of a sample of gas can be derived from the mechanical laws governing the motion of molecules (if temperature is identified with the average kinetic energy of the molecules). According to the philosopher Ernest Nagel, there are two conditions for the reduction of one theory to another: (1) the *connectability* of all concepts in the two theories, and (2) the *derivability* of one set of theoretical statements from the other. Nagel shows that many biological concepts cannot be defined in chemical terms.[29] In the same vein, another philosopher, Morton Beckner, maintains that there are distinctive biological concepts, referring to the functioning of higher-level units, that cannot be translated into the concepts of physics and chemistry. Integrative functions are not specifiable by terms referring to the parts alone.[30]

Biologists have also upheld *the distinctiveness of biological concepts.* Francisco Ayala lists fitness, adaptation, predator, organ, heterozygosity, and sexuality among the biological concepts that cannot be translated into statements about molecules. Mayr claims that the uniqueness and unpredictability of evolutionary events can be described only by historical narrative, not by any set of lawful regularities. Genetic information can be accounted for only historically; particular sequences of DNA cannot be deduced from chemical laws. Moreover, the description and explanation of the behavior of organisms in terms of teleological categories (goals and purposes) will be useful when there are diverse means to reach a particular goal.[31]

Looking at the history of modern biology, Lindley Darden and Nancy Maull argue that *interlevel theories* were introduced as new hypotheses that could not have been derived from the theories of either field. They describe a field of inquiry as a set of distinctive theories, problems, techniques, and vocabularies. The connections between the vocabularies of differing fields were first advanced as imaginative hypotheses. For example, in 1904 it was postulated that genes (unobserved theoretical entities by which geneticists accounted for observed hereditary variations) are located in the chromosomes (dark-stained filaments observed by cytologists in the study of cell nuclei). In the 1950s, the genes of genetic theory were identified with DNA structures (molecular configurations studied by biochemists) through the hypothesis that DNA controls developmental growth. Jacob and Monod's operon theory of regulatory genes (1961) and subsequent research on the role of enzymes in protein synthesis elaborated on this hypothesis. The research was a response to questions that could not be answered in either genetics or molecular biology alone, and it led to concepts different from those in either field at the time. Darden and Maull suggest that the unity of science is an important goal, but it is not achieved by theory reduction:

An interfield theory, in explaining relations between two fields, does not eliminate a theory or field or domain. The fields retain their separate identities, even though new lines of research closely coordinate the fields. . . . It becomes natural to view the unity of science, not as a hierarchical series of reductions between theories, but rather as the bridging of fields by interfield theories.[32]

## 3. Ontological Reduction: A View of Reality

Here an assertion is made, not about research strategies or the relation between theories, but about the kinds of things that exist in the world. When it is stated that organisms consist of "nothing but atoms," a metaphysics of materialism and atomism is asserted. It is assumed that the true nature of an entity is manifest at its lowest level.

*Materialism* among modern biologists is partly a reaction to *vitalism,* in which life was held to be a special nonmaterial principle or agency. In the 1930s, Driesch interpreted experiments in embryology as evidence of a vital agent within the developing embryo, a purposeful "entelechy" which adjusts processes to achieve a future goal in spite of obstacles (for example, a newt can grow a new limb after an amputation). But the idea was vague and offered no testable hypotheses for particular cases, so it has been scientifically useless. Moreover, there is no clear line between living and nonliving forms (viruses, for instance, share characteristics with both). Vitalism has almost no advocates today, but the desire to avoid it has swayed many biologists toward a materialistic metaphysics.

*Organicism* seems to be a compromise between materialism and vitalism, but at crucial points it differs from both. Here life is understood as a type of organization and activity, not a separate nonmaterial entity or substance. There is no impassable gulf between the living and the nonliving (either in evolutionary history or among present forms), but rather a continuity of interdependent levels. Organicists oppose epistemological reductionism and defend the distinctiveness of biological concepts, but they go further in asserting that organismic concepts refer to aspects of the real world. If an organism is an integral whole with a hierarchy of levels of organization and activity, one can defend the distinctiveness of biological processes. Processes at one level are not fully determined by those at lower levels, and yet there is no violation of the laws governing processes at lower levels.

## 2. LEVELS, EMERGENCE, AND WHOLES

We must look further at the distinction between levels of analysis (an epistemological concept) and levels of organization and activity (ontological concepts).

### 1. Levels of Analysis

Every field of inquiry is limited by its conceptual tools. Any set of concepts is abstractive and selective, representing a particular way of simplifying complex phenomena. Complementary models may sometimes be helpful in analyzing phenomena at a given level. Diverse models are employed on differing levels, and none gives an exhaustive account. Higher-level theories are useful in correlating features of the integrated behavior of larger wholes, even when interlevel theories have been developed. Instrumentalists would uphold the value of theories at a variety of levels without making claims about the existence of levels in nature.

### 2. Levels of Organization and Activity

The philosopher William Wimsatt holds that nonreducible concepts with many links to observations should be given an ontological but revisable status as "candidates for reality." Differing levels of analysis reflect real structures in the world, though in a limited and partial way.[33] The critical realism that I defended in earlier chapters would allow for ontological as well as epistemological levels, that is, a multileveled view of reality. Organicism postulates significant differences among levels but without the sharp breaks and dualistic contrasts portrayed by vitalism. Nature consists of relatively stable strata within a continuous spectrum of complexity. *Levels of organization* specify structural relationships. *Levels of activity* specify events and processes.

A hierarchy of *functional processes* is always closely correlated and integrated with a hierarchy of *structural parts*. In a systems framework, the parts are identified, conceptualized, and related to one another through their roles in functionally construed processes. On the other hand, the functions are fulfilled through the interaction of the parts. These are complementary rather than competing ways of describing the same system. Stephen Toulmin writes, "Indeed, the very organization of organisms—the organization that is sometimes described as though it simply involved a 'hierarchy' of progressively larger structures—can better be viewed as involving a ladder of progressively more complex systems. All these systems, whatever their level of complexity, need to be analyzed and understood both in terms of the functions they serve and also of the mechanisms they call into play."[34]

Evolutionary history has seen the *emergence* of novel forms of order and activity that could not have been predicted from previous forms. The evolutionary account is inescapably historical rather than deductive in character because there is both chance and emergence in nature. When molecules, cells, and organisms appeared successively, they brought new properties and kinds of behavior. New forms of purposive behavior and mental life finally blossomed into consciousness and then self-consciousness.

A two-way interaction of *wholes and parts* occurs at many levels. We saw the importance of wholes already at the quantum level, as evident in the Pauli Exclusion Principle and the Bell's Theorem experiments. The atom must be viewed as a total vibratory system; the electron is more like a state of the system than a separate individual entity. In an ecological view of living things, every entity is considered within a hierarchy of more inclusive wholes. Inter-level theories often describe the behavior of parts in forming wholes.

In *process philosophy*, relationships are constitutive of every entity; relations are internal rather than external to its being. Wholes of diverse types are conveniently represented by the term *societies*. Charles Hartshorne calls an organism "a society of cells." In some societies (for example, a pile of sand grains) all members are of the same grade and there is almost no overall structure; the whole has less unity than each of its parts. Other societies consist of loose aggregates (for example, a sponge or even a tree) whose parts are relatively independent. An ant colony has some coordination and division of labor but no central agent. Other societies are well-unified wholes with radically dominant members and complex internal organization. Even in a human being, however, each cell has considerable independence; various organs and subsystems (heart, endocrine system, and so forth) function apart from any conscious control. Only with the growth of the nervous system is the unification of the experience of the whole organism achieved.[35]

The degree of *subordination of part to whole* thus varies widely. In the hierarchy of levels, the organism is the unit of reproduction and usually has a more complex integrative organization than levels above or below it. But there is great diversity in the kinds of integration that can occur at any of these levels. Consequently, there are variations in the extent to which a part preserves or loses its autonomy when it contributes to a larger whole. In general, an activity at any level is influenced by patterns of activity at both higher and lower levels. In this sense one can say that part and whole mutually influence each other, without implying that the whole is somehow an entity existing independently of the parts.

Michael Polanyi points out that a machine's design imposes *boundary conditions* on chemical and physical processes. The laws of physics and chemistry are not violated, but they are harnessed for organized functions. He suggests that the morphology and structure of an organism similarly constitutes boundary conditions that are not required by biochemical laws but are compatible with such laws.[36] In the case of the machine, of course, it is the human designer who "harnesses" the laws, and the behavior of the whole machine is similar in character to that of the parts, so the analogy is rather limited. Donald Campbell gives a more complex analysis of the *top-down causation* through which processes at lower levels are constrained by relationships at higher levels. For example, the huge jaws of the soldier termite are the developmental product of its DNA, but the DNA is itself the product of the selection of the whole organism in its dependence on the termite colony. (The jaws are so large, in fact, that it cannot feed itself and has to be fed by worker termites.)[37] In the world of organisms a complex interaction takes place among levels.

## 3. SENTIENCE AND PURPOSIVENESS

The sentience of simple organisms is a minimal responsiveness to the environment but sentience takes increasingly complex forms. *Perception* is the selective transmission of information about the environment. Even elementary sense organs can detect features of the environment relevant to the organism's life. Perception is an active process in which patterns important to its survival are picked out and organized. Responsive action is possible because sensations derive from an external environment and are taken to refer to it. A one-celled paramecium has a crude nervous system and a rudimentary form of memory. If it finds no food at one location it will not persist there but will use its coordinated oarlike hairs to move to another location. Short-term memory requires a new way of storing and recalling information, different from storage in the genes.

Sentience also seems to involve *an internal dimension,* a center of perception and action, some sort of elementary awareness and feeling. By the time a central nervous system appeared, there was a coordinating network and a new level of integration of experience, which developed eventually into consciousness and finally self-consciousness. We can try to imagine the awareness in higher animals and perhaps even that in lower vertebrates, but we can hardly imagine the rudimentary experience of invertebrates.

Sentience at even low levels seems to imply at least an elementary capacity for *pain* and *pleasure.* When a neural system is present, pain serves as an alarm system and an energizing force by which harm can be avoided. The capacities for both pain and pleasure were presumably selected for their high survival value. The behavior of animals gives evidence that they can suffer intensely. Even invertebrates under stress release endorphins and other pain-suppressant chemicals similar to those in human brains. It seems likely that there is suffering in lower creatures, but with much less intensity.[38]

Some forms of *goal-directedness* can occur in the inanimate world. A simple sensor and activator (such as a thermostat and furnace) can be connected as a control system, a self-regulating feedback mechanism that compensates for deviations from a steady state. A self-guiding missile "seeks its target" by mod-ifying its flight in response to reflected radar signals; it has a limited flexibil-ity of response to changing external conditions. But many organisms show much greater flexibility in actions to achieve a goal under varying condi-tions. This goes beyond the cybernetic model of a goal as a source of guiding signals. An animal may seek food when there is none and may do so in ways not previously attempted. Memory of past sequences and their outcomes leads to the anticipation of future occurrences, which serve as goals of pres-ent behavior. Animals and birds can devise novel and circuitous means of achieving an end, indicating an orientation toward the future and showing imagination in devising new ways of circumventing obstacles.[39]

Various forms of animal and insect behavior suggest the presence of *purpo-siveness* and *anticipation*. Some foresight is evident even amid largely instinc-tive actions. If a wasp encounters difficulties in building a nest, it will show limited ingenuity in devising new sequences of actions to complete the task. A rat deciding between two paths, in one of which it will receive an electric shock, hesitates as if imaginatively anticipating future consequences. Donald Griffin, Stephen Walker, and others have written about animal awareness. They have portrayed the evolutionary continuity of mental experience, the survival value of consciousness, and the development of higher levels of per-ception, memory, intelligence, and communication.[40]

How far down the scale of life can such concepts be extended? W. E. Agar and Bernhard Rensch suggest that all organisms should be considered as feeling, experiencing subjects, even at a rudimentary level.[41] The biologist Sewall Wright argues that in the spectrum of behavior from higher to lower organisms there is no discontinuity; since we cannot draw a line at any point, we must assume the universal presence of *something akin to mind*. There is no discontinuity in the development of minds from simpler structures in either the history of the world (evolution) or of the individual (embryology). "The emergence of even the simplest mind from no mind seems to me utterly incomprehensible." Wright concludes that at all organic levels an entity is mind to itself and matter as viewed by others. The unique creativity of each individual event and its essential nature as will or mind inevitably escapes the scientist, who deals only with regularities and sees only the external side of things.[42]

I am dubious about such attribution of mind to low-level organisms but I will argue for the attribution of elementary forms of experience. In dis-cussing process philosophy (chapter 11), I will suggest that unified entities at all levels should be considered as *experiencing subjects,* with at least rudimentary sentience, memory, and purposiveness. This will require reference to levels of experience as well as levels of activity. I will argue that we must recognize the emergence of distinctive forms of activity and experience at higher levels; mind and consciousness appear only at higher levels, and a developed self-consciousness only in human beings.

## III. THEOLOGICAL IMPLICATIONS

As we turn to the theological implications of evolution, we ask first about the relation of chance to design. Some models of continuing creation are then explored. Finally, several kinds of theological response are considered.

### 1. CHANCE AND DESIGN

Is evolution a *directional* process? History indeed shows a general trend toward greater complexity, responsiveness, and awareness. The capacity of organisms to gather, store, and process information has increased. However, when viewed locally and over shorter periods there seem to be many directions of change rather than a uniform stream. Short-term opportunism fills temporarily unoccupied ecological niches, which may turn out to be blind alleys when conditions change. There is no evidence of foresight in looking to future needs. Gould gives examples in which a structure originally filling one function was adapted for another function in a makeshift way. For instance, the panda's thumb developed from a bone and muscles in the wrist, a far from perfect design.[43] In some cases we see retrogression, as when a formerly independent organism becomes a parasite. And, of course, by far the majority of species have ended in extinction.

We have seen the *pervasive role of chance* in evolution, from mutation and genetic combination to unpredictable changes in environments. Evolutionary history is irreversible and unrepeatable. Potentialities that were present at one point were permanently excluded by particular lines of development. Most mutations are harmful to the organism, or even lethal. Monod believes that the prevalence of "blind chance" shows that the existence of all organisms is accidental and not the product of design. It is a meaningless universe in which we alone arbitrarily introduce any meaning in human life.[44]

Fred Hoyle and Chandra Wickramasinghe, on the other hand, argue that the origination of any particular protein molecule by chance is *inconceivably improbable.* If there are twenty different amino acids and one wants to construct a protein chain of one hundred amino acids, the number of possible combinations is enormous. If you shuffled them at random a billion times a second, it would take many times the history of the universe to run through all the combinations.[45] The argument is dubious, however, because there are specific attractive forces, and the various combinations are not equally probable or equally stable. As we said, the dice are loaded. As larger structures are formed, metastable states are likely to persist. Complexity comes into being by hierarchical stages, not in one gigantic lottery. Once there is reproduction, natural selection is an antichance agency, preserving highly improbable combinations through successive generations. Evolution shows a subtle interplay of chance and law.

In evolution we have to look at *chance, law,* and *history.* In a roulette wheel or a kaleidoscope, law and chance are both present in ever-changing patterns, but there is no historical memory, and the past is irrelevant to the future. But in natural history, earlier achievements get folded into the developmental levels of later organisms because they have left a record in the genes. Evolutionary historicity involves unpredictability and irreversibility. Even the general trends cannot be predicted from scientific laws but can only be described in historical narratives. John Maynard-Smith writes, "There is nothing in neo-Darwinism which enables us to predict a long-term increase in complexity."[46] Gould states, "Natural selection is a theory of *local* adaptation to changing environments. It proposes no perfecting principles, no guarantee of general improvement."[47]

Traditionally, *design* was equated with a detailed preexisting blueprint in the mind of God. Theologians since the church fathers were influenced by the Platonic view of an eternal order of ideas behind the material world. God was said to have a foreordained plan, which was carried out in creation. In this framework, chance is the antithesis of design. But evolution suggests another understanding of design in which there are general directions but no detailed plan. There could be a long-range strategy combined with short-range opportunism arising from feedback and adjustment. In this strategy, order grows by the use of chaos rather than by its elimination. There is improvement but not perfection. There is increasing order and information but no predictable final state.[48] Robert Russell urges us not to equate disorder (entropy) with evil, or order with the good, for disorder is sometimes a precondition for the emergence of new forms of order. He cites Prigogine's work on systems far from equilibrium as an example of disorder that leads to novel structures. More generally, new life is possible only because of the death of the old. Pain, suffering, and the challenge of crises can contribute to growth.[49]

D. J. Bartholomew points out that human beings can *use chance* to further their purposes. We toss a coin in the interest of fairness, and we seek random samples in making representative surveys. Many games combine skill and chance; by shuffling cards we generate variety, surprise, and excitement. In evolution, he says, variety is a source of flexibility and adaptability. Varied populations can respond to changing circumstances better than monocultures, and of course genetic variation is essential for evolutionary change. Chance and law are complementary rather than conflicting features of nature. Random events at one level may lead to statistical regularities at a higher level of aggregation. Redundancy and thresholds may limit the effects of random events on integrated systems. On this reading, chance would be part of the design and not incompatible with it.[50]

Thus three theological responses to chance are possible.

1. *God controls events that appear to be random.* Perhaps events are determined by God, though to us there seems to be an element of chance. This would be like Einstein's view that quantum uncertainties are merely a reflection of human ignorance; but here it would be a hidden divine action rather than hidden natural causes that exactly determines every event. We looked earlier at Pollard's suggestion that God controls all subatomic indeterminacies. Pollard extends the idea to the claim that apparently chance events in evolution are predestined by God. The "accidental" or "coincidental" intersection of two unrelated causal chains may also have been providentially arranged.[51] Donald MacKay and Peter Geach similarly maintain that every microevent is divinely directed, without violation of the long-run statistical laws that science has discerned.[52]

But this view seems vulnerable to the objections of Gould and others that it is hard to imagine that every detail of evolutionary history is the product of deliberate intelligent design. There have been too many blind alleys and extinct species and too much waste, suffering, and evil to attribute every event to God's specific will. Another objection to this view is that it is implicitly reductionistic in assuming that God enters mainly at the lowest level (in atomic or molecular uncertainties). In Pollard's view, God acts only indirectly on larger wholes and higher levels by starting "from the bottom up" rather than "from the top down." The model of "God as Determiner of Indeterminacies" is explored further in chapter 12.

2. *God designed a system of law and chance.* This was Darwin's view at the time he wrote *Origin*. Earlier in this century, several authors portrayed design, not in particular biological phenomena, but in the systematic conditions that made life and consciousness possible. L. J. Henderson described the many chemical and physical properties that are favorable for the existence of life. Carbon, for example, has a unique place in the organic world because of its variety of multiple bonds. Henderson combined a teleological view of nature as a whole with a mechanistic view of its processes.[53] F. R. Tennant elaborated a "wider teleological argument" based on the conditions of distinctively human existence and the interconnectedness of matter, life, and human personality.[54] The arguments here are like those of the Anthropic Principle in relation to the Big Bang, but they deal more specifically with organic and human life. We have seen that the structures of DNA and proteins are dependent on incredibly complex combinations of interatomic forces and bonding angles. There is no reason to think that just any combination of forces would have led to life and consciousness. Design is identified with the lawful structures of the world, which make higher-level activities possible.

Recent authors point to both chance and law as expressions of God's overall design of the universe. Thus Polkinghorne writes, "The actual balance between chance and necessity, contingency and potentiality which we perceive seems to me to be consistent with the will of a patient and subtle Creator, content to achieve his purposes through the unfolding of process and accepting thereby a measure of the vulnerability and precariousness which always characterize the gift of freedom by love."[55] Here the problems of waste, suffering, and human freedom are less acute, for only the general system and not the details of particular events are expressions of God's will. Insofar as chance is really present, the predestination of every event cannot be accepted. God designed a system whereby law and chance could lead to life and mind and the diverse dimensions of human experience. God does not interfere with the system. But the theologian may object that in this interpretation God's role is limited to originating and sustaining the natural process.

3. *God influences events without controlling them.* This resembles the second view in rejecting predestination and acknowledging genuine chance in the world. But it resembles the first view in giving God a continuing active role, though a limited one. Chance, lawful causes, and God enter the constitution of each event. God's purposes are expressed not only in the unchanging structural conditions of life, but more specifically in relation to changing situations and patterns. Continuing creation, in this view, is a trial-and-error experiment, always building on what is already there. Evolutionary history has involved suffering and waste throughout, but it has resulted in the appearance of varied and valuable forms of experience. There are risks that the experiment might fail on this planet. Human folly may yet lead to a nuclear holocaust in which civilization, and perhaps the human species itself, does not survive.

The zoologist Charles Birch maintains that evolutionary history resembles a vast experiment. It is an unfinished universe, a world in birth, a dynamic process of trial and error. Struggle and suffering, accident and chance, uncertainty and risk are never absent. He holds that we must imagine a continuous and flexible creativity in the process, not an omnipotent designer executing a preconceived plan. For Birch this suggests the Whiteheadian God of persuasive love rather than coercive power, a God who influences and is influenced by the world, who allows freedom in humanity and spontaneity in nature, and who is involved in the world and participates in its slow growth. Birch adopts Whitehead's view that all entities have an inner aspect; every entity is considered a center of at least rudimentary experience.[56]

## 2. MODELS OF CREATION

Before looking at some doctrines that theologians have discussed in relation to evolution, let us consider some theological models. Models, I suggested earlier, are less conceptually precise than doctrines but more powerful in personal religious life and communal liturgy.

The Bible itself includes a variety of models of God as Creator. Some of these were indicated in the previous chapter. In Genesis, God is a purposeful designer imposing order on chaos. God's command is powerful and the divine Word is effective. Other biblical images picture a potter forming an object (Jer. 18:6, Isa. 64:8) or an architect laying out the foundations of a building (Job 38:4). God is Lord and King, ruling the universe to bring about intended purposes. The world is a manifestation of God's Word and an expression of divine Wisdom, which communicates meaning. In the New Testament, God creates through the Word (John 1), a term that, we have seen, brings together the Hebrew concept of divine Word active in the world and the Greek concept of Word (*logos*) as rational principle. The purpose of creation is made known in Christ, the Word incarnate. Here is a rich diversity of models, each a partial and limited analogy, highlighting imaginatively a particular way of looking at God's relation to the world.

The potter and craftsman analogies assume the production of a completed, static product. They seem less helpful in thinking about an ongoing, dynamic process. The image of God as gardener is more promising, though it occurs rarely in the Bible (for example, Gen. 2:8), perhaps because the Israelites wanted to distance themselves from the nature gods of surrounding cultures. The analogies of God as King and Ruler were emphasized in medieval and Calvinist thought. But the doctrines of omnipotence and predestination to which they led are difficult to reconcile with the current scientific view of nature.

In the Bible, the model of father is used for God's relation to persons, but there is also a fatherly care for nature (for example, the birds and lilies of Matt. 6:26). God as mother was a rare image in a patriarchal society, but it appears occasionally (for example, Isa. 49:15 and 66:13). The parental analogy is usually drawn from a parent nurturing a growing child rather than from procreation and birth. This seems a particularly appropriate image of God's relation to the world; the wise parent allows for an increasing independence in the child while offering encouragement and love. Such an image can maintain a balance between what our culture thinks of as masculine and feminine qualities, in contrast to the heavily "masculine" monarchical model of omnipotence and sovereignty.

The biblical image of God as *Spirit* seems to me particularly helpful. Here the analogy is the distinctive vitality, creativity, and mystery of the human spirit. The human spirit is the active person as a rational, feeling, willing self responding to other persons and to God. In the previous chapter, I pointed out the reference to the Spirit in creation (Gen. 1:2) and in the continuing creation of the creatures: "When thou sendest forth thy Spirit, they are created" (Ps. 104:30). The Spirit also represents God's activity in the worshiping community and in the inspiration of the prophets. I will propose in the next chapter that we can think of Christ as having been inspired by the Spirit. The idea of the Spirit allows us to bring together our understanding of God as Creator and as Redeemer.

Among contemporary theologians, Conrad Hyers has asked what models of creation are compatible with a world of order and chance. He suggests that the combination of intention and unpredictability in an artist's interaction with a medium provides an apt analogy. Again, God is like a poet or dramatist in whose work there is both plan and surprise, or like the writer of a novel whose plot shows both coherent unity and the novelty of the unexpected.[57]

Arthur Peacocke has written extensively about models of God in an evolutionary world. Of classical models he find Spirit and *logos* most suitable for expressing immanent divine creativity. God is the communicator, conveying meaning through the patterns of nature as well as through the person of Christ. Peacocke also uses many striking new images, some of which are systematically developed as models. One is the mind/body relation as an analogy for God's relation to the world. The world might be thought of as God's body, he suggests, and God as the world's mind. We can look on cosmic history as the action of an agent expressing intentions.[58] This is indeed a promising model, but it raises several questions. Does the analogy presuppose a mind/body dualism? Does the world have as much unity and coordination as the body of an organism? If God is the cosmic mind, what room is there for human freedom?

Peacocke also mentions briefly the alternative model of a pregnant mother bringing a baby into being *within* her body.[59] This seems to represent a degree of unity intermediate between that of a mother's relation to her own body, on the one hand, and that of her relation to a growing child after birth, on the other. I am inclined to favor the growing child analogy. I will suggest that the social model of process thought is able to preserve the separate identity of both God and individual creatures, along with a recognition of their interdependence and relatedness.

Noting the unpredictability of evolutionary history, Peacocke says God is like the choreographer of an ongoing dance or the composer of a still-unfinished symphony, experimenting, improvising, and expanding on a theme and variations. Peacocke uses other analogies that assign a positive role to chance. Chance is God's radar beam sweeping through the diverse possibilities that are invisibly present in each configuration in the world. Chance is a way of exploring the range of potential forms of matter.[60] God has endowed the stuff of the world with creative potentialities, which are successively disclosed. The actualization of these potentialities can occur only when suitable conditions are present. Events occur not according to a predetermined plan but with unpredictable novelty. God is experimenting and improvising in an open-ended process of continuing creation. Peacocke rejects the idea of omnipotence and speaks of the self-limitation of a God who suffers with the world.

Peacocke writes that "the natural causal creative nexus of events *is* itself God's creative action." He holds that processes of nature are *inherently* creative. This might be interpreted as a version of the second option outlined above: God initially designed a system of law and chance, through which higher forms of life slowly came into being. This would be a sophisticated form of deism. But Peacocke also says that God is "at work continuously creating in and through the stuff of the world he had endowed with those very potentialities."[61] The images of an improvising choreographer or composer imply an active, continuing relationship with the world. Peacocke specifically defends the idea of continuing creation.

## 3. CONFLICT, INDEPENDENCE, AND DIALOGUE

We can make an interim assessment of some theological positions concerning creation and evolution, using my basic classification scheme of *Conflict,* *Independence,* and *Dialogue.* The fourth option, *Integration,* is discussed in the concluding section.

### 1. Conflict Between Creation and Evolution

The first version is *scientific materialism.* In chapter 4, I cited Monod, Wilson, and Dennett and criticized the reductionism and materialism of their metaphysics. Another example is Richard Dawkins's *The Blind Watchmaker,* which has the subtitle *Why the Evidence of Evolution Reveals a Universe without Design.* Much of the book is a clear and forceful presentation of current evolutionary theory and a defense of orthodox neo-Darwinism against its scientific critics. He also replies to the argument that the various parts of the eye could not be products of separate chance variations because one part would be useless without all the other parts. Dawkins shows how the eye and other organs could have arisen from many independent small improvements. A light-sensitive cell or a very simple eye is better than nothing. He provides a lucid discussion of the collaboration of genes in embryonic development.

But Dawkins also makes some rather dogmatic philosophical and religious statements without careful discussion. He accepts epistemological reductionism: "The hierarchical reductionist believes that carburettors are explained in terms of smaller units . . . which are explained in terms of smaller units . . . which are ultimately explained in terms of the smallest of fundamental particles. . . . My task is to explain elephants, and the world of complex things, in terms of the simple things that physicists either understand, or are working on."[62] Dawkins's wider claim is stated at the outset: "All appearance to the contrary, the only watchmaker in nature is the blind forces of physics, albeit deployed in a very special way."[63] He asserts that natural selection is the only conceivable source of complexity. This leads him in the conclusion to a "disproof" of the existence of God:

The whole book has been dominated by the idea of chance, by the astronomically long odds against the spontaneous arising of order, complexity and apparent design. . . . The same applies to the odds against the spontaneous existence of any fully fashioned perfect and whole beings, including—I see no way of avoiding the conclusion—deities.[64]

Since chance and natural selection are the only source of complexity, Dawkins says, a complex God could not exist. It would have been helpful if he had distinguished more clearly between scientific evidence and philosophical speculation.

*Biblical literalism* is the second version of *Conflict.* We have seen some of the overwhelming evidence from diverse disciplines for the occurrence of a long evolutionary history spanning millions of years. Scientists may disagree about some of the details of the Modern Synthesis, but they offer absolutely no support to those creationists who believe creation occurred in a few days or a few thousand years. On the other hand, creationists could rightly object if an atheistic philosophy, such as that of Dawkins, were taught in the biology classroom. Both the scientific materialist and the scientific creationist have failed to respect the proper boundaries of science. The former makes statements about religion as if they were part of science. The latter makes statements about science that are dictated by religious beliefs.

## 2. The Independence of Creation and Evolution.

*Neo-orthodoxy* has no difficulty accepting the findings of evolutionary biology because science and religion are assigned to separate spheres. God acts in human history, primarily in the person of Christ, and not in the natural world. The argument from design and all forms of natural theology are suspect because they rely on human reason rather than on divine revelation. The doctrine of creation is not a theory about beginnings or about subsequent natural processes; it is an affirmation of dependence on God and the essential goodness and orderliness of the world. In the previous chapter I indicated my sympathy with many aspects of neo-orthodoxy, particularly its conviction that scripture should be taken seriously but not literally and its characterization of the main theological content of the doctrine of creation *ex nihilo*. However, its strong emphasis on transcendence leads to a gulf between God and nature and a neglect of divine immanence. Moreover, the absolute dichotomy between humanity and nonhuman nature appears dubious today, along with the body/soul dualism often used to support such a dichotomy. Neo-orthodoxy can express the theological themes of the *ex nihilo* tradition, once it is divorced from a beginning of time, but it can do little with the continuing creation tradition.

The second version of the *Independence* thesis is *existentialism*, which also makes an absolute separation of spheres. God is encountered only in the immediacy of personal involvement, decision, and commitment. God acts only in personal life, not in the impersonal arena of nature. What matters religiously is the transformation of one's own life in a new understanding of authentic personal existence, which has no connection with theories about mutations and natural selection. The doctrine of creation is an acknowledgment of one's own dependence on God and gratitude for one's life as a gift. Existentialism offers important insights concerning the character of religious faith. But once again, God's relation to nonhuman nature gets short shrift. Nature is merely the impersonal setting for the drama of personal existence. The sharp separation of human and nonhuman life does not accord with the evolutionary view. If the ecological understanding of our participation in the wider web of life is ignored, the door to the exploitation of the environment is left wide open.

The third version of *Independence* is *linguistic analysis*. Human life encompasses various self-contained language systems, each with its distinctive rules and functions. Religious language expresses a way of life through the rituals, stories, and practices of a religious community. Creation stories, in particular, provide a cosmic framework of meaning and practical guidance for living. Science, on the other hand, asks strictly delimited questions in the interest of prediction and control. Toulmin's early writings suggest that it is an illegitimate mixing of languages when evolution is extrapolated to support either atheism or theism.[65] I acknowledge these functions of creation stories in human life, but I do not think that *religious beliefs* can be ignored. The linguists accept an instrumentalist account of both science and religion; there can be no conflict because neither makes truth claims. As a critical realist, I hold that both fields make statements about reality, though these statements are selective and partial and always revisable. We cannot exclude the possibility that particular statements about creation and about evolution could conflict or support each other. At some points we need to modify traditional religious doctrines in the light of biological evidence. Our goal is a coherent interpretation of all experience, not a collection of unrelated "language games."

## 3. Dialogue About Creation and Evolution

In the previous chapter I indicated that cosmology raises issues of *design, chance,* and *necessity,* and we have seen that the same issues arise in evolutionary biology. I suggested that *intelligibility* and *contingency* in cosmology were presuppositions or limit questions that can be topics of dialogue between scientists and theologians, even though they cannot be answered by the methods of science. I proposed that the contingency of laws and events is consistent with the idea of continuing creation in theology.

One way of encouraging a second-order dialogue between theologians and scientists, while maintaining the integrity of each enterprise, is to pursue the neo-Thomist distinction between *primary and secondary causality.* God as primary cause works through the secondary causes, which science describes. There are no gaps in the scientific account, which is complete on its own level. But God sustains the whole natural sequence. Primary causes represent a totally different order of explanation. As McMullin puts it, "He works equally in all parts of His creation."[66] Usually this position assumes the classical doctrines of divine omnipotence and predestination. This would require that God control the indeterminacies that appear to us as chance.

The neo-Thomist position is appealing because it shows great respect for science while maintaining many of the doctrines of classical theism. It tries to avoid deism by asserting that God has a continuing role in sustaining the natural order. It can be supplemented by the belief that occasional acts of miraculous divine intervention occur. But it is difficult to reconcile with the biblical idea that God has a more active continuing role in nature and history. In chapter 12, I will argue that the assumption of predestination encounters problems in dealing with freedom, chance, and evil in the world.

## 4. THE INTEGRATION OF CREATION AND EVOLUTION

In trying to relate creation and evolution, can we go further than a dialogue regarding limit questions? I have described three kinds of *Integration:* natural theology; a theology of nature; and systematic synthesis.

## 1. Natural Theology

Here the claim is that theistic conclusions can be drawn directly from the evolutionary evidence. Unlike the creationists, these authors are well read in contemporary biology and accept a long evolutionary history. However, they sometimes seem to misinterpret the scientific evidence in describing the alleged shortcomings of evolutionary theory. Leconte DuNouy writes, "Chance alone is radically incapable of explaining an irreversible evolutive phenomenon."[67] But we have seen that we are not dealing with "chance alone"; we have chance plus stable structures plus natural selection. Charles Raven argues that many coordinated changes would have to have occurred simultaneously for a complex organ like the eye to appear. An eye lens is useless, he says, without a retina, and vice versa.[68] But this is a dubious claim; there is in nature a wide diversity of organs of vision, some simple and some complex, some with lenses and some without.

Hugh Montefiore has recently argued that neo-Darwinian explanations of evolutionary change are inadequate and that a theistic explanation is far more probable. He accepts the claims of Raven and others that complex organs and behaviors would require the coordination of many mutations, and thus "some other force seems to be at work here." Chance and natural selection do not explain all these phenomena, so there must be a directive force, and God is "by far the most probable explanation."[69] Montefiore is cautious in his claims, but he bases his case on the inadequacies of current scientific explanations, which seems to be a sophisticated form of the "God of the gaps" position. It is vulnerable insofar as these gaps in the scientific account have been or will be filled in.

Such objections from the scientific side cannot be made against the wider teleological argument in which design is built into the laws and processes that science describes. Today God can be viewed as *the Designer of a self-organizing system*, a many-leveled creative process of law, chance, and emergence. In chapter 7 I cited the work of Prigogine and of Kauffman on self-organization in which new levels of order appear in systems far from equilibrium. In discussing evolution I referred to built-in constraints that limit the possibilities for stable molecular structures and developmental patterns. A world of hierarchical levels seems to have an inherent tendency to move toward emergent complexity, life, and consciousness. A patient God could have endowed matter with diverse potentialities and let it create more complex forms on its own. In this interpretation God respects the integrity of the world and lets it be itself, just as God respects human freedom and lets us be ourselves. An attractive feature of this option is that it provides at least partial answers to the problems of death and suffering that were such a challenge to the classical argument for design. Competition and death are intrinsic to an evolutionary process. Pain is an inescapable concomitant of greater sensitivity and awareness, and it provides a valuable warning against external dangers.

As I said in the case of the Anthropic Principle in the previous chapter, I do not believe that design arguments of this kind are conclusive when taken alone. However, they can play a supportive role as part of a theology of nature. Design is what one would expect with an intelligent and purposeful God—though I will suggest that the presence of chance, evil, and human freedom should lead us to modify traditional ideas of omnipotence. My main objection to such a reformulated deism is that we are left with a distant and inactive God, a far cry from the active God of the Bible who continues to be intimately involved with the world and human life.

## 2. A Theology of Nature

Instead of a natural theology, I advocate a theology of nature, which is based primarily on religious experience and the life of the religious community but which includes some reformulation of traditional doctrines in the light of science. Theological doctrines start as human interpretations of individual and communal experience and are therefore subject to revision. Our understanding of God's relation to nature always reflects our view of nature. In particular, articulation of the continuing creation theme today must take into account the new view of nature as a dynamic, interdependent, evolutionary process of which humanity is a part.

One form of theology of nature is the extension of new ideas from science to suggest possible ways in which God might interact with the world. Such suggestions must be consistent with the scientific evidence but need not be required by it. We have seen that *the communication of information* is an important concept in several areas of science such as communication theory, computer networks, and DNA in organisms. In each case communication requires selective response (decoding) and the interpretation of a message in a wider context. Several authors, including Polkinghorne, have proposed a model of God as communicator of information and have claimed that it does not require any violation of scientific laws. The proposal is not unlike the biblical idea of the divine Word or *logos,* which can be viewed as the communication of rational structure and meaning when interpreted in a wider context. Another proposal advanced by Peacocke and others starts from the idea of *top-down causality* within the hierarchy of levels in an organism and suggests that God acts from a still higher level. God could be thought of as a top-down cause acting on the world as a constraint or boundary condition without violating lawful relationships at lower levels. Peacocke also extends the idea of *whole-part relations* by considering God as the all-encompassing whole of which natural organisms are parts. We will examine these proposals in detail in the final chapter.

Some reviewers take Teilhard de Chardin's *The Phenomenon of Man* to be a form of natural theology. In the preface he says he will argue from scientific evidence alone (though he grants that consideration of the total human phenomenon goes beyond any of the sciences). But I maintain that the book, seen in the context of Teilhard's writings as a whole, is more appropriately viewed as a theology of nature. His unifying vision is indebted to both evolutionary biology and the Christian tradition, and this vision informs all his writing.[70]

On the scientific side, Teilhard describes in detail the historical evolution from matter to life, mind, and society. He discusses mutations and chance at several points and speaks of "the billion-fold trial-and-error of mechanical forces."[71] He rejects the Lamarckian idea that acquired characteristics can be inherited. But he agrees with Lamarck in assigning a major role to the organism's own efforts and interior life—the rudimentary forms of sentience and purposiveness that he calls "the within of things." These internal forces are said to use chance variations. Chance is "seized and used by a principle of internal self-organization."[72] There is slow progress toward greater complexity and consciousness, but not a simple straight-line development. Teilhard does not introduce divine intervention to account for particular gaps in the scientific account. Teleology is displayed in the whole process, not in the design of particular structures.

But the scientific side of the book is subject to several criticisms. He identifies chance with neo-Darwinism and identifies directionality with the operation of "the within." This neglects the extent to which natural selection itself exerts a directional influence. Many scientists object to the way that Teilhard extends scientific terms metaphorically without indicating that he is doing so (*radial energy* and *psychic temperature,* for example). He does not distinguish between accepted scientific ideas and more speculative philosophical proposals. In the last two chapters he pictures the "convergence of evolution" and introduces a concept of God as Omega, "the principle we needed to explain the persistent march of things toward greater consciousness." Some scientists dismiss Teilhard as a poet and mystic, but this neglects the seriousness with which he took the scientific data. However, let us grant that he was giving an interpretation of science, not a strictly scientific account.

Teilhard's Christian convictions undoubtedly influenced his portrayal of the directionality of cosmic history and the significance of human personality. These convictions are more explicitly stated in the epilogue of *The Phenomenon of Man* and are developed in his theological writings. But he does not simply draw on inherited traditional beliefs, for he proposes extensive doctrinal reformulation in the light of the idea of evolution, which he says is "a condition for all thought today." Teilhard defends a divine creativity immanent in the whole natural order. He objects to the separation of sacred and secular realms. Christ is presented not as an intrusion into the world but as the continuation and fulfillment of a long cosmic preparation. According to Teilhard, the purpose of the incarnation was not primarily the "remedial" work of atoning for human sin, but the "constructive" work of uniting all reality and bringing it to union with God. Redemption, then, is social and cosmic as well as individual; creation and redemption form a single process. Sin and evil, which in a static world are difficult to reconcile with the goodness of God, are now seen to be inescapable by-products of a slow creative process.[73] Teilhard's theological ideas, in short, are indebted to both evolutionary biology and the Christian tradition. He gives us an evolutionary theology of nature from which we can learn much, despite the problems in his style of writing.

## 3. Systematic Synthesis

A final version of *Integration* is the synthesis of evolution and creation within an inclusive metaphysical system. Metaphysics is the search for a coherent set of basic categories applicable to all types of human experience and all events in the world. As such, it must draw from other fields beside science and religion, but it must include the insights of these two areas of human life.

An evolutionary metaphysics will give an important place to temporality and change in its characterization of all entities. It will express the interdependence of all beings in an ecological understanding of the web of life. It will presuppose the continuity of human and nonhuman life, though it can also acknowledge unique characteristics of human existence. It will deal with the distinctive nature of mental life without assuming a mind/body dualism. One way of allowing for both continuity and discontinuity in evolution is the articulation of a metaphysics of levels, in which there are characteristics common to all levels, but novel kinds of organization and activity emerge at higher levels.

Teilhard de Chardin's writing incorporated a partially developed set of evolutionary metaphysical categories. Teilhard rejected much of the Thomistic metaphysics to which he had been exposed in his training as a Jesuit. In place of the Thomistic categories of being and substance, he took becoming and process as the basic characteristics of reality. Instead of identifying perfection with the timeless, he held that time, change, and relatedness are attributes of all beings, including God. Instead of a sharp line between human and nonhuman, or between mind and matter, he held that there is a mental side in all beings.[74] But Teilhard's competence and training were greater in science and in theology than in philosophy. He had greater gifts of poetic imagination and of spiritual intensity than of philosophical reasoning. So we must turn to others for the systematic metaphysical categories in which to express a unified evolutionary and religious vision.

The process philosophy of Whitehead and his followers is the most promising metaphysical system in which evolution and continuing creation can be integrated. We will examine it in chapter 11, after we have carried the evolutionary story a stage further in chapter 10 by considering the evolution of human life.

# Part Four

## PHILOSOPHICAL AND
## THEOLOGICAL REFLECTIONS

## CHAPTER 10

# Human Nature

The three previous chapters dealt with specific sciences—physics, astronomy, and biology—and their philosophical and theological implications. Part 4 presents some philosophical and theological reflections concerning human nature (chapter 10), process thought (chapter 11), and models of God's relationship to nature (chapter 12). The goal of the present chapter is to compare what biology and the biblical tradition have to say about human nature. I will also occasionally refer to anthropology, psychology, sociology, history, and philosophy, but I do not intend to deal systematically with these disciplines. The basic question is whether evolutionary biology and biblical religion are consistent in their views of human nature. The final section is a brief reflection on the human future in the light of earlier conclusions.

## I. BIOLOGY AND HUMAN NATURE

We begin with a summary of the scientific evidence concerning the relation of human to nonhuman species, both in evolutionary history and in comparing them today. Next, the claims of sociobiology about the genetic determinants of human behavior are examined, and some differences between cultural and biological evolution are set forth. The perennial mind/body problem is then discussed in an evolutionary context.

### 1. HUMAN ORIGINS

Evidence from molecular biology and from fossil discoveries indicates that human beings and modern African apes are descended from common ancestors. African chimpanzees and gorillas share more than 99 percent of their DNA with that of human beings (which would be comparable to the genetic kinship of horses and zebras or of dogs and foxes). *Australopithecus afarensis,* an apelike creature, was walking on two legs some 4 million years ago. In Tanzania, Mary Leakey found footprints of that age, consistent only with an upright posture. In Ethiopia, Donald Johanson found the bones of a short female, dubbed Lucy, who walked on two legs but had long arms and a brain size like that of the great apes, while her teeth show that she was a meat eater. It appears that the move from trees to grassland encouraged upright posture, free hands, and a shift to hunting, long before the development of a larger brain.[1]

*Homo habilis*, discovered by Louis Leakey and others, was present 2 million years ago, had a larger brain, and chipped stones to make primitive tools. *Homo erectus*, dating from 1.6 million years ago, had a much larger brain, lived in long-term group sites, made more complicated tools, and probably used fire. Archaic forms of *Homo sapiens* appeared 500,000 years ago, and the Neanderthals were in Europe 100,000 years ago. The Cro-Magnons made paintings on cave walls and performed burial rituals 30,000 years ago. Agriculture goes back only 10,000 years. The earliest known writing, Sumerian, is 6,000 years old. Techniques for melting metallic ores brought the Bronze Age and then, less than 3,000 years ago, the Iron Age. Here we have at least the broad outlines of the evolution of both physiology and behavior from nonhuman to human forms and the beginnings of human culture.[2]

Darwin himself stressed the similarities of animal and human abilities, but more recent interpreters point out both *similarities and differences*. Some differences of degree are so great that they add up to differences of kind, but without sharp discontinuities. Within a continuous evolutionary process, significant novelty has occurred. The brain has increased not only in size but in complexity and in the addition of new structures with distinctive functions. The human brain itself incorporates this long history. At the base of our brains are the oldest structures, which we share with reptiles and birds; they control respiration, the cardiovascular system, and instinctive behavior, which is rigidly programmed genetically. The midbrain or limbic system, which we share with animals, controls our hormones and emotional life (pleasure, fear, sex, hunger, and so forth). The outer layer or neocortex, which is prominent in higher mammals and humans, controls perceptual, cognitive, and communicative processes. The neocortex makes possible more complex forms of language, learning, and intelligence.[3]

Only human beings are fully capable of language, but chimpanzees can be taught limited forms of *symbolic communication*. Chimps lack the vocal organs (especially the larynx) necessary for articulated speech, but they can be taught to communicate in sign language or with geometric symbols on a computer keyboard. They can combine these symbols into simple sentences. D. M. Rumbaugh and others have found evidence of elementary abstract thought. From a few examples, chimps can form general concepts, such as food or tool, and then assign a new object to the correct conceptual category. They can express intentions, make requests, and communicate information to other chimps.[4] These results are impressive, though still far below the level of a two-year-old child. But they do suggest that language ability could have evolved gradually.

Higher animals seem to have a rudimentary *self-awareness*. If a chimp sees in a mirror a mark previously placed on its forehead, it will try to remove the mark. But in human beings there is a self-consciousness that seems to be unparalleled. The greater capacity to remember the past, to anticipate the future, and to use abstract symbols liberates us from our immediate time and place. We can imagine possibilities only distantly related to present experience, and we can reflect on goals going far beyond immediate needs. Humans are aware of their finitude and the inevitability of death, and they ask questions about the meaning of their lives. They construct symbolic worlds through language and the arts.[5]

Many species of insects and animals live in complex *social orders* with definite roles and patterns of cooperative behavior. In insects these patterns are for the most part genetically determined; in higher animals there is a greater capacity for learning and individuality. Primates have elaborate social structures and patterns of dominance and submission. Dolphins form close friendships and engage in playful activity. In such species information relevant to survival is transmitted socially, learned by the young from their parents rather than passed on through the genes. But in the case of humans, we have many more ways of transmitting information from generation to generation, including language, writing, the public media, education, and the institutions of society.

The discoveries of science, the inventions of technology, the imaginative literature and artistic work of the humanities all testify to human *intellectual power and creativity*. Despite the presence of unconscious impulses, which Freud has helped us to recognize, we are capable of rational reflection about ourselves. Despite the pressures of social conditioning, we are able to take responsibility for moral choices. Despite the constraints of both genes and culture, we are not completely determined but are agents with at least limited freedom.

In short, humanity is part of nature, but a unique part. We are the product of a long evolutionary history and retain a powerful legacy from the past. But we also have creative abilities and potentialities without parallel among the species of the earth. We are biological organisms, but we are also responsible selves. If research in recent decades has at some points found greater similarities with other life forms than had been previously suspected, these findings should lead us to greater respect for those forms, not to the denial of human dignity. At other points contemporary science offers ample testimony of the uniqueness of humanity among the creatures on planet earth.

## 2. SOCIOBIOLOGY AND CULTURAL EVOLUTION

The last two decades have seen the development of sociobiology, the biological study of social behavior in both nonhuman and human species. One interesting example concerns the origins of *altruistic behavior*. If evolution is the survival of the fittest, how can we explain behavior in which an organism repeatedly jeopardizes its own survival? Social insects such as ants will sacrifice themselves to protect the colony. Worker ants work for the colony; they are sterile and do not even have any descendants. Edward O. Wilson and others have shown that such behavior reduces the number of descendants an individual will have, but it enhances the survival of close relatives who have many of the same genes. If I share half of my genes with my brother or sister, it will help to perpetuate my genes if I am willing to protect their reproductive futures, even at some risk to my own life.[6] Richard Dawkins entitles his book *The Selfish Gene* because he holds that all apparent altruism can be explained by its contribution to genetic survival.[7]

Another example cited by sociobiologists is the almost universal *taboo against incest*. We know today that inbreeding leads to harmful recessive genes and to mentally and physically handicapped children. We can say, therefore, that groups with a taboo against incest were stronger genetically and had a selective advantage over those without such a taboo (even if they had no inkling that sexual relations with close relatives could have harmful consequences). Other examples deal with the genetic basis for differences between *male and female roles* in society. Sociobiologists cite the fact that in many species the males are larger, and they view primate society as male dominated. Studies also show that aggression is associated with the level of male hormones and can be increased or reduced by altering the hormone level.

Critics point out that although scientists normally examine alternative hypotheses, Wilson seldom even mentions the cultural explanations that anthropologists have advanced for many of these social phenomena. Anthropologists have asserted that few if any cultures are organized throughout according to the genetic kinship coefficients worked out by Wilson.[8] He has been accused of a *genetic determinism* that would open the door to justifying the status quo. If human behavior is determined by the genes, there would be little we could do to change it.[9] Wilson does acknowledge the plasticity of human behavior and the possibility of change. Yet there is no place for real freedom in his analysis. He suggests that a diversity of genetically programmed censors and motivators operates in the emotions of the limbic system, among which we can choose those we will favor and those we will suppress or redirect. But these choices are determined by our value systems, which are themselves under genetic control. Only biological knowledge can help us: "We must consciously choose among the emotional guides we have inherited. To chart our destiny means we must shift from automatic control based on our biological properties to precise steering based on biological knowledge."[10]

Evident here is the *reductionism* that runs through Wilson's writing. He is confident that genetics and biology will account for all aspects of human life. "The mind will be precisely explained as an epiphenomenon of the neural machinery of the brain."[11] Wilson asserts what I have called the *Conflict* model; both religion and ethics will be explained and eventually replaced by biological knowledge: "If religion, including the dogmatic secular ideologies, can be systematically analyzed and explained as a product of the brain's evolution, its power as an external source of morality will be gone forever."[12] It seems to me inconsistent that Wilson never says that science is similarly discredited by its evolutionary origins, although it, too, is obviously "a product of the brain's evolution." In the past, he says, morality has been an expression of emotions encoded in the genes. "The only demonstrated function of morality is to keep the genes intact." But now science can "search for the bedrock of ethics—by which I mean the material basis of natural law."[13] "Empirical knowledge of our biological nature will allow us to make optimum choices among the competing criteria of progress."[14]

Wilson embraces a sweeping epistemological reductionism that makes all the academic disciplines into branches of biology: "It may not be too much to say that sociology and the other social sciences, as well as the humanities, are the last branches of biology to be included in the Modern Synthesis."[15] He moves from detailed testable hypotheses to unsupported claims about how a particular social behavior "could have been selected," to broad generalizations about all human experience. Throughout is an implicit metaphysics of materialism and occasionally an explicit advocacy of what he calls *"scientific materialism."* All of his explanations are on one level only—the action of genes. But the historical origins or genetic preconditions of a trait do not provide the last word on its present status. Wilson states that "genes hold culture on a leash."[16] How long is that leash? And does not culture also constrain and redirect the effects of genes? Perhaps we should turn his metaphor around and say that culture holds the leash today.

Let us then compare *cultural evolution* and *biological evolution*. I suggest that the former is more significant today, and that while there are parallels between them, there are also important differences. First, cultural innovation replaces mutations and genetic recombination as the source of *variability*. Such innovations are to some extent deliberate and directional; they are certainly not random. New ideas, institutions, and forms of behavior are often creative and imaginative responses to social problems and crises. Here the uniqueness and unpredictability of events in human history are evident. The linguistic meanings and the ideas and reasons of agents are distinctive features of human history, as we saw in chapter 6. We are the product of particular cultural histories.

Next, in the competition between ideas, *selection* occurs through social experience and reinforcement. The most useful ideas are retained in a trial-and-error process, but many factors enter into social judgments of success. Here selection is less harsh than biological selection, because ideas can be rejected without the death of the individuals who hold them.

Finally, *the transmission of information* occurs through memory, language, tradition, education, and social institutions rather than through genes. At each of these stages, change is more rapid and can be more deliberate than in the case of biological evolution. Major changes can take place within a few generations or even within a generation. On the other hand, old ideas can surface again and be revived, so they are not permanently lost, as are the genes of extinct species.

*Science*, like other cultural activities, is in a general sense a product of evolution. Its methods are a refinement of the problem-solving ability and the inductive and deductive reasoning that in simple forms are evident in primates today. Such intellectual abilities undoubtedly had survival value, and selection favored them among our ancestors.[17] But does science today have a structure similar to that of biological evolution? There have been several recent proponents of *an evolutionary epistemology*. Stephen Toulmin says that in the scientific community various theories compete for recognition, and the most successful ones are selected and passed on to the next generation. He grants that sociological factors and metaphysical assumptions influence the acceptance of new ideas, but he argues that the broad pattern of variation and selection is like that in evolutionary history.[18]

Karl Popper also draws parallels between *science* and *evolution*. Scientists formulate a profusion of hypotheses and try to refute or falsify them by empirical evidence, nonviolently eliminating those that are unfit. There is no logic in formulating hypotheses, but there is a logic in testing and eliminating them.[19] Donald Campbell looks at the individual scientist rather than at the scientific community. Random trial-and-error exploration and selection of ideas take place in the scientist's mind before a theory is propounded in public.[20] I would reply that the parallel between science and evolution is rather limited because the search for new ideas in science is not random. The number of possible theories is too large to test them at random. Some empirical discoveries are fortuitous, like the discovery of penicillin, but the formulation of theories is not. It is deliberate and directed. I suggested earlier that it is often based on an imaginative analogy or model. The goal of science is to understand the world, not to propagate one's ideas. Here again the differences between cultural and biological evolution are more significant than their similarities.

## 3. THE STATUS OF MIND

*The human brain* is the most complex system that has been found in the natural world. It contains some 100 billion neurons, each connected with hundreds or thousands of other neurons through synaptic junctions (perhaps 100 trillion of them). Electrical signals are transmitted through this network in incredibly complex patterns. We have some understanding of how the input information from sensory organs is processed and how output signals control the motor activity of muscles.[21] But we know very little about what goes on in between: how input information is integrated with memory, emotional responses, and reflective deliberation. We do know that the *left hemisphere* of the brain is usually associated with analytical, systematic, abstract, and sequential thought (such as mathematical reasoning), while the *right hemisphere* plays a larger role in intuitive, imaginative, concrete, and holistic thought (such as pattern recognition and artistic creation).[22]

We know that *physical and chemical intervention* affects both consciousness and behavior. Electrical stimulation of particular brain areas by microelectrodes can evoke vivid memories and feelings (happiness, anxiety, anger, and so forth) or produce such motor effects as raising an arm. Drugs can powerfully influence both mood and behavior. All of these findings add to the evidence that mental life is strongly dependent on physical events in the brain. But they do not provide a final answer to the *mind/body problem*. Let us look at each of the four main alternatives within an evolutionary framework.[23] Philosophical issues are considered here and theological ones in subsequent sections.

## 1. Dualism

Dualism in the West goes back to Plato and Augustine, but the most influential modern formulation is that of Descartes, who said that mind and body are two distinct entities that interact causally. They differ radically in their characteristics. Mental events are inherently private rather than publicly observable and are nonspatial rather than spatially extended. Mental phenomena as directly experienced include ideas and sensations, thoughts and feelings, memories and expectations, and acts of deliberating and deciding. The relationships between mental events (such as the logical deduction of ideas or the coordination of means to ends) do not at all resemble forces between physical objects.

Several prominent neurophysiologists have defended a *mind/brain dualism*. Wilder Penfield points out that the patient whose brain is electrically stimulated is aware that it is not he or she who is raising the arm. Penfield postulates a center of decision radically distinct from the neural network, "a switchboard operator as well as a switchboard."[24] John Eccles holds that the mind searches and selects among brain modules, reads them out, integrates them, and then modifies other brain circuits: "The self-conscious mind is an independent entity that is actively engaged in reading out from the multitude of active centers in the modules of the liaison areas of the dominant cerebral hemisphere."[25] Eccles shows that impulses appear in the supplementary motor area before those in the motor area only when there is a deliberate, voluntary initiation of action. The philosopher Karl Popper, who with Eccles coauthored *The Self and Its Brain,* similarly defends the interaction of consciousness and brain and the causal efficacy of mental phenomena.[26]

Several *objections to dualism* may be raised. One objection is that the influence of mental events seems to violate the conservation of energy. However, mental events might only involve the redirection of energy or an action within the limits of quantum indeterminacies. A more serious difficulty is that the postulated mental and physical entities are so dissimilar that it is hard to imagine how they could interact. Of course we do accept interactions between quite dissimilar things—such as an invisible magnetic field and a compass needle—but only if we can find lawful relations between them. Does mind occur only in human beings? Descartes thought so (holding that animals are mindless machines), but more recent dualists usually hold that simpler mental phenomena occur in animals. However, by portraying mind as totally unlike matter, dualists have difficulty explaining how mind could have evolved from matter. By definition, dualism does not allow for anything intermediate between matter and mind; it assumes there is only one kind of mind, though it might be present to varying extents. Everything except mind is assumed to be totally devoid of sentience, subjectivity, or interiority, and it is difficult to see how such properties (as distinct from new objective properties) could ever arise.

## 2. Materialism

Among earlier materialists were the Greek atomists and the philosophers of the French Enlightenment. A recent version is the *behaviorism* of B. F. Skinner and his followers. This started as a methodological recommendation that psychologists should avoid any reference to subjective mental phenomena inaccessible to public observation. Science should deal only with objective events such as the correlation of a stimulus and a behavioral response.[27] However, if it is assumed that we can give a complete account without reference to mental events, we end with a metaphysics of materialism. The philosopher Gilbert Ryle claims that mental concepts are really statements of dispositions to behave in particular ways. Mental concepts, he says, can be translated into concepts referring to observable behavior.[28]

But surely I do not find out that I have a pain by observing my own behavior. In reporting on pains, ideas, emotions, or dreams, I am referring to immediate experiences, which can be correlated with an indefinite range of possible behaviors but are identical to none of them. Behaviorism has been the basis of significant psychological research in both rats and humans, but its limitations as an all-embracing explanatory framework have become apparent. Humanistic and cognitive psychology, both of which make use of mental terms, have tried to deal with some of the human phenomena that behaviorism neglected. I have considered the comparison of computers and the human brain and the proposals of cognitive psychology in my *Ethics in an Age of Technology*.

A modification of materialism is *epiphenomenalism,* which holds that mental phenomena exist but are not causally effective. Mental qualities accompany neural events without influencing them, as shadows accompany moving objects without influencing them. The causal connection is only in one direction, from physical to mental events (or to other physical events), never from mental to physical ones. The physical world is an autonomous system, it is said, and when we understand it we will be able to give a complete account of all events.[29] But how could consciousness have evolved if it had no biological function? How could it have been selected if it was irrelevant to survival? And are not relationships among mental concepts, such as ideas and motives, more useful than concepts of neural activity in understanding most of the actions of persons today?

A final version of materialism is the *neural identity theory* proposed by Herbert Feigl and J.J.C. Smart. They argue that mental and physical terms differ in significance or connotation but will turn out as a matter of empirical fact to refer to or denote the same things, namely neural events. A particular sensation, for example, simply is a particular kind of neural event, though we cannot yet specify it physiologically. The basic laws are all physical.[30] But as a scientific hypothesis this theory is a long way from confirmation in even the simplest cases. Moreover, it cannot account for the privileged position of the subject or the distinctive properties of mental experience. There are serious objections, then, to this as to other renditions of materialism.

## 3. Two-Aspect Theories

Leibniz, in his theory of *parallelism*, maintained that mental and physical events proceed on separate tracks, without any interaction or inherent connection, but perfectly synchronized in a harmony established by God at the outset. For Spinoza, on the other hand, the connections were inherent and universal. His monistic version of *panpsychism* presents one underlying substance, Nature, with at least two sets of attributes, mental and physical. Every event is at the same time mental and physical. Whitehead has often been understood to propose a form of pluralistic panpsychism: every actual occasion has a "physical pole" and a "mental pole." I will suggest, however, that these are technical terms referring to the receptive and self-creative phases of the momentary experience of all entities. Whitehead actually ascribes mind only to higher-level entities and therefore belongs with the fourth group below, Multilevel Theories.

P. F. Strawson relies on *ordinary language* and says that persons are a distinctive type of being to which we ascribe both mental and physical predicates.[31] Other authors have said that mental and physical concepts occur in *alternative languages* in which we describe the same set of events for different purposes. We can acknowledge that the logic of mental concepts is different from that of physical concepts without assuming a dualistic metaphysics. Physical language is no more reliable or useful than mental language, so we need not assume a materialistic metaphysics. Thus MacKay says that "observer-language" and "actor-language" are "two complementary descriptions," which should be taken with equal seriousness. We can explain human actions in terms of the intentions of agents without denying the power of biochemistry in explaining neurophysiological phenomena.[32]

Two-language theories thus avoid some of the problems of dualism and materialism, but they leave unresolved the question of the nature of the events to which both languages refer. Alternative languages may satisfy the instrumentalist, but not the critical realist.

## 4. Multilevel Theories

I agree with the two-language view that mental and physical concepts are abstractions from the primary reality of events, but I would go on to assert that reality itself is organized on a variety of levels, each with its characteristic types of activity. The mind/brain problem would then be a particular case of the more general problem of the relation between levels discussed in the previous chapter. Such a view is congenial to an evolutionary viewpoint and provides a framework for understanding both human and nonhuman life today.

Consider *the emergence of the self* in evolutionary history. In the early stages of life, there was sentience, purposiveness, exploratory behavior, and rudimentary forms of awareness and experience, all of which confer a selective advantage. Mental activity required a central nervous system; even a simple brain was a very complex system in which there occurred new forms of memory, anticipation, and consciousness. Only in human beings did self-consciousness arise.

In the *embryological development* of the human fetus under the guidance of the human genetic program, the neurological structures are formed that make possible these higher levels of integration, activity, and experience. The newborn baby has a very limited self-awareness, and the developmental process continues in the early years. Social interaction and language seem to be essential for the fulfillment of selfhood. Selfhood thus represents the highest level in which rational, emotional, social, and bodily capacities are integrated. Self is a broader concept than mind, which since Descartes has been identified mainly with rational capacities.

Roger Sperry, who received a Nobel Prize for his split-brain research, takes some limited steps toward a *multilevel* view. He maintains that in all organisms there is a hierarchy of levels, with distinctive irreducible laws at higher levels. Emergent, holistic properties arise from organizational relationships and configurational patterns in space and time. Causation and control operate from higher levels downward, making use of the laws of lower levels without violating them. Sperry writes: "Whole entities in nature are also governed by novel emergent properties of their own, and these holistic properties in turn exert downward control over the parts." "When a new entity is created the new properties of the entity, or system as a whole, thereafter overpower the causal forces of the component entities at all successively lower lowers in the multinested hierarchies of the new infrastructure."[33]

Sperry maintains that *mental states* are higher-level emergent properties of the brain. Against the materialists, he asserts that consciousness is causally effective. Consciousness must have contributed to survival for it was selected in evolutionary history. Mental activity supervenes on neural activity without violating physiological laws:

Causal control is thus shifted in brain dynamics from levels of pure physical, physiological or material determinacy to levels of mental, cognitive, conscious or subjective determinacy.... The mental forces do not violate, disturb, or intervene in neuronal activity but they do supervene. Interaction is mutually reciprocal between the neural and mental levels in the nested brain hierarchies. Multilevel and interlevel causation is emphasized in addition to the one-level sequential causation more traditionally dealt with.[34]

Sperry repeatedly insists that he is not a dualist; he takes dualism to mean that mental events can exist independently of physical events. But he shares with dualists the conviction that mental states and physical events are totally dissimilar kinds of things. "The subjective qualities are ... of very different quality from neural, molecular, and other material components of which they are built."[35] He does affirm human freedom and self-determination, though the latter turns out to be a higher-level causality in which thoughts, feelings, beliefs and ideals combine to determine behavior.

I will try to show in the next chapter that process thought departs further from dualism by proposing that *experience* and *subjectivity* are present in integrated entities at all levels. Interaction takes place between entities at diverse levels (for example, the mind and the cells of the brain), but this is interaction between entities that all have an inward side as moments of experience. Process thought holds that consciousness occurs only in complex neural systems, so this is not "panpsychism." But moments of experience are attributed to all unified entities; *panexperientialism* would be a more appropriate designation. We will return in the next chapter to the process understanding of levels of experience.

## II. RELIGION AND HUMAN NATURE

Can evolutionary and religious views of human nature be reconciled? We start by noting that religion itself has evolved from its roots in early human history to the development of the major world religions. We then examine the biblical view of human nature and compare it with the findings of evolutionary science. Last, the role of Christ in an evolutionary cosmos is considered.

### 1. THE EVOLUTION OF RELIGION

No one has contributed more to the discussion of religion and science during the last twenty-five years than Ralph Burhoe as founder and for many years editor of *Zygon: Journal of Religion and Science.* His own writing has been mainly on the relation of religion to *biocultural evolution.* He starts by describing the coevolution and coadaptation of genes and culture, giving more attention than does Wilson to the distinctive features of culture. Burhoe says that altruism toward individuals who are not close relatives (sharing common genes) cannot be explained by genetic selection. He holds that religion has been the major force in fostering altruism and social cooperation extending beyond genetic kin. The set of values transmitted by religious myths and rituals binds a society together. Religion has been selected because it contributed to the survival of the biocultural group.[36]

Burhoe points out that in the past *religion* has fostered both loyalty to one's own group and hostility to other groups that threatened it; both aspects aided group survival. As tribal religions gave way to more universal ones, the circle of loyalty expanded. Each of the major world religions represented "a well-winnowed wisdom" expressed in terms of the best understandings of the world available in its times. But to be credible today, Burhoe holds, religious beliefs must be reformulated along strictly scientific lines. This will encourage globally shared values, which are essential to survival in the nuclear age.[37]

Burhoe advocates an *evolutionary naturalism* as the religious philosophy best suited to a scientific culture. For him, nature is the functional equivalent of the traditional God, and it should be the object of our worship and obedience. We are totally dependent on the evolutionary process for our existence, our sustenance, and our destiny. Nature is omnipotent and sovereign, the power on which we are dependent; it is our creator and judge. We must adapt to the requirements of "the all-determining reality system. . . . Man's salvation comes in recognizing this fact and adapting to it or bowing down before the majesty and glory of the magnificent program of evolving life in which we live and move and have our being."[38]

Burhoe's writing draws heavily from research in biology and anthropology, and it is illuminating in its analysis of religious phenomena. But when he endorses evolutionary naturalism he is defending a *metaphysical system* and not a conclusion that is part of science itself. Such a metaphysics is appealing because of its respect for science and its universalism in a global age. But I do not believe that it can deal adequately with the problems of human freedom, evil and conflict in nature, religious experience, or historical revelation.[39] I would grant that adaptation and survival are preconditions of other human values, but I would maintain that they cannot supply the full content of our value judgments. There are significant choices within the constraints of survival. We have to ask: What kind of survival should we seek?

Let us consider the evolution of the three basic features of religion mentioned in chapter 5: ritual, story, and religious experience.

## 1. Ritual

Julian Huxley, Konrad Lorenz, and other ethologists have described animal rituals. Animals exhibit many formalized behavioral repertoires, such as the courtship or territorial rituals of animals and birds, which are genetically transmitted. One member of a species is programmed to respond to the ritual behavior of a second member, who can thus signal intentions and evoke appropriate responses. Some interpreters believe that human rituals may be supported by similar genetic and lower-brain structures, with strong emotional correlates, though the particular rituals are culturally learned higher-brain patterns.[40] Most anthropologists, by contrast, take ritual to be entirely transmitted by culture, with no specific genetic basis. They say that the most important human rituals help individuals and groups to cope with the major crises and transitions of life: birth, puberty, marriage, and death.[41] We find evidence of burial rituals, for example, as early as the Cro-Magnon caves thirty thousand years ago.

Some anthropologists hold that ritual is the primary religious phenomenon from which other features of religion arose. They take religious beliefs to be later rationalizations of rituals, whose social functions are all-important.[42] For example, almost every culture has initiation ceremonies in which the adolescent is brought into the adult world and the continuity of the social order is upheld. But other interpreters maintain that ritual has many dimensions, all of which are significant. Ritual is indeed community forming, but it often takes the form of a symbolic reenactment of an earlier story (myth).

Religious rituals can also be understood as symbolic representations of the holy, as is characteristic of sacrifices and sacraments. Rituals may be understood as vehicles for communicating with the divine, for expiating guilt, for celebrating and offering thanks, or for expressing grief and loss in a cosmic setting.[43]

## 2. Story

Unique to humans is the need to live in a meaningful world. We have said that myths or sacred stories are taken as manifesting some aspect of the cosmic order. They offer people a way of understanding themselves and of ordering their experience. They provide patterns for human actions and guidance for living in harmony with the cosmic order. These stories are often related to the experience of the sacred, and they point to a saving power in human life. Many stories are acted out in ritual, though in some cases the story may be a later explanation of the ritual. More often, story and ritual seem to have developed together.[44]

Some stories refer to primeval times, the origins of the world and humanity, or the sources of human alienation, suffering, and death. Creation stories, we have noted, are found in almost all cultures. Other myths tell about the end of time or patterns of cyclical return or death and rebirth in the seasons and in human life. Still others are built around particular events or persons in the community's memory. Levi-Strauss and the structuralists find a common pattern in myths: the partial resolution of one of the basic contradictions or polarities in life, for example, life/death, good/evil, male/female, or culture/nature. The symbolic mediation of such conflicts helps people respond to individual and social stress and crisis, thereby aiding adaptation and social stability.[45]

## 3. Religious Experience

As indicated earlier, the numinous experience of the holy is present in virtually all cultures. People around the world report a sense of awe and wonder in the presence of powers that seem to transcend the human. The mystical experience of union with all things also has roots in preliterate cultures, and the meditative practices that encourage it are found in many cultures.

The psychiatrist Eugene d'Aquili holds that religious experience is associated mainly with the *right brain*. Science and much of our daily understanding of the world (including causal and temporal ordering) are products of left-brain functioning, which is analytical, logical, and abstractive. We have said that right-brain functioning, by contrast is holistic, integrative, and inclusive. It plays a major role in spatial ordering and pattern recognition—and in religious experience, according to d'Aquili. In mystical experience, reality is perceived as a unity without a temporal dimension, and the self-other polarity is dissolved. In differing cultures, the experience may be interpreted as union with a personal God or as participation in an impersonal Absolute. In either case, the experience carries a strong conviction of the existence of a transcendent unity beyond ordinary experience. We believe in the reality of the external world as ordered mainly by the left brain, though we can't prove its existence. Similarly, says d'Aquili, we can believe in the reality of absolute unitary being, which is primarily grasped through the right brain, though we can't prove that it exists.[46]

These basic components—ritual, story, and religious experience—seem to have been present in the earliest periods of human history as well as in nonliterate cultures today. But there were important developments during what the philosopher Karl Jaspers has called *the axial period*, from 800 to 200 B.C.E., in five centers of civilization: China, India, Persia, Greece, and Israel.[47] In this period parallel movements arose, from which have come all of the main world religions. Significant leaders stood out as individuals: Confucius, Gautama the Buddha, Zoroaster, Plato and Aristotle, the Hebrew prophets. Influential documents were written: the Tao Te Ching, the Bhagavad Gita, the Hebrew Bible, and so forth. (Of course, there were important earlier figures, such as Moses, and subsequent ones, including Christ and Muhammad, but Judaism, Christianity, and Islam are all derived from Hebrew monotheism, which took its distinctive form in the axial period.)

The *world religions*, which have their roots in this period, share a number of features. Each tells of initial revelatory experiences that were interpreted and reinterpreted within particular historical contexts and cultural assumptions. All have sacred scriptures, which are extensively used in connection with worship, liturgy, and instruction. All have both specific moral teachings and more general ethical principles. They have faced common problems but sometimes responded to them in different ways. For example, in the earlier tribal period, religion had been strongly identified with the local community. The new traditions sought greater universality and the rational articulation of general principles, but they also allowed for more individuation. The self became problematic in a new way. The East frequently sought release from the self's bondage to suffering and anxiety through meditation and asceticism, while the West more often sought reorientation of the self through obedience to God.

The biblical scholar Gerd Theissen uses *an evolutionary model* to interpret the development of biblical religion, but he recognizes the limitations of the model. Religious innovations, he says, are novel ideas and practices that are subjected to subsequent trial-and-error testing. The universal monotheism of the Hebrew prophets, the radical commitment of Christ's life, and the inner transformation of the early Christians were all innovations that we can think of as mutations, though they were not random. But all three cases presented a protest against the kind of harshness typical of natural selection, a protest in the name of a God of love as well as judgment. In contrast to the process of evolution, the God of the Bible was said to have a special concern for the weak and disadvantaged. Biblical faith involves adaptation, not to the prevailing natural or cultural environment, but to the ultimate reality: God.[48] Theissen thus makes considerable use of evolutionary categories but often to show how biblical assumptions differ from those of biology.

Finally, anthropologists and sociologists have portrayed the functional role of religion in binding individuals in social groups and in *preserving the social order.* Early in the century, Emile Durkheim described the function of religion in legitimating prevailing values and institutions. Through religious practices, individuals are taught to internalize the group's expectations and restrain egotistical desires. Durkheim held that the gods are merely symbolic expressions of social values. Religion provides the central symbols and rituals by which societies interpret and validate themselves. In this view, religion has been a predominantly conservative force, contributing to social stability and reflecting prevailing norms.[49]

Max Weber, by contrast, saw religion as *a source of change* as well as of stability. Charismatic individuals have started new religious movements that altered the course of history. Religion is in part a reflection of social values, but it is also an influence upon social values. Weber's most famous case study traces the influence of Protestantism on the rise of capitalism. For him, religion is not simply the product of other social forces.[50]

We can grant that religion does serve important functions in human life, which contribute to both stability and change. But this does not mean that religion is just a survival mechanism or a purely human creation. At the same time it may have been a response to a transcendent reality. The social sciences provide important insights into the role of religion as a social institution, but they cannot provide the last word in evaluating religious claims. As Frederick Streng puts it: "Social scientists limit themselves to interpreting those aspects of religious life that can be defined and observed empirically and that can be understood in terms of human creative processes and patterns of experience. This position, for other scholars of religion, seems oversimplified because it tends to reduce 'religion' to something else, rather than considering religious phenomena in their own right."[51]

## 2. THE BIBLICAL VIEW OF HUMAN NATURE

Let us focus more specifically on Judaism and Christianity. The two central stories of Judaism are creation and the covenant. Christianity adds a third, the story of Christ. We have said that sacred stories show the nature of the cosmic order and our place in it. What understanding of human nature is implied by these biblical stories? Is the biblical view compatible with the findings of evolutionary biology?

We have seen (chapter 8) that the biblical creation story is somewhat complex because, according to most historical scholars, the seven-day narrative (Gen. 1:1 to 2:3) was written in the postexilic period, several centuries later than the Adam and Eve narrative (2:4 to 3:24). The creation of humanity occurs in both accounts. In addition, subsequent interpreters have emphasized the distinction between the perfect state of humanity as created (up to 2:24) and its subsequent sinful state after the fall. But if we take other portions of the Bible along with Genesis, we can trace four themes that describe human nature.[52]

## 1. A Creature, but Unique among Creatures

The Bible sees humanity as rooted in nature, sharing the finitude, creature-liness, and death of all living things. All creatures are part of a single system, an interdependent community of life, an inclusive order. The sixth day of creation is integral with the first five days. Adam is formed from the dust, enlivened by the breath of life: "You are dust, and to dust you shall return" (Gen. 3:19). Yet humans alone are made "in the image of God" (1:26). They alone are responsible selves who can be addressed by God. They alone are free moral agents who can respond to the demands of righteousness and justice.

The conclusion of the Adam and Eve story (3:16–19) implies that in the Garden of Eden there was no death and suffering for humanity (or for other creatures, according to later interpreters); death and suffering were a divine punishment for sin. Today we cannot accept the historicity of such a paradise. We know that death and suffering are necessary conditions of life in an evolutionary world. New life is possible only through the death of the old. Pain is the price of greater sentience, and it is often a signal of danger. The image of Adam and Eve in paradise can be retained only as a symbol of the goodness of creation and the conviction that finitude as such is not evil. Sin results from human choices, not from the structures of the world for which God is responsible.[53] (We will return to the problem of the existence of evil and suffering in the next chapter.)

The biblical authors pictured the separate creation of each kind of creature. They did not, of course, have any notion of the evolutionary continuity of nonhuman and human life. But they did portray both similarities and differences between nonhuman and human life, which would be broadly consistent with the scientific evidence presented above. Only in the early centuries of the Christian church were the differences accentuated and absolutized by the introduction of the Greek idea of an immortal soul, as we shall see. I will suggest that by drawing an absolute line between humanity and other creatures, later Christianity contributed to the attitudes that encouraged environmental destruction.

## 2. An Individual, but in Community

In the biblical tradition, we are inherently social beings. Men and women were made for each other, and Genesis 1 treats them identically. But the story of the creation of Eve from Adam's rib and her role in tempting Adam reflected the assumptions of a patriarchal society and, unfortunately, contributed to the subsequent subordination of women. But at least the social character of selfhood was acknowledged. Moreover, the covenant was with a people, not with a succession of individuals. Some of the psalms and later prophets focus on the individual (for example, Jeremiah speaks of a new covenant written in the heart of each person), but this was always within the context of persons-in-community. Judaism has preserved this emphasis on the community, whereas Christianity has sometimes been more individualistic (for example, some Protestants focus on saving individual souls). In the Bible, we are not self-contained individuals; we are constituted by our relationships. We are who we are as children, husbands and wives, parents, citizens, and members of a covenant people.

This view of *the social self* is consistent with scientific findings. Both genetic and cultural evolution are group processes. We evolved as social beings; language and symbolic thought would be impossible without others. Children have been discovered who had grown up in isolation from all human contact; they were unable to acquire language later and were permanently deprived of many aspects of normal human existence. We gain our sense of self in part by the ways our parents and others ascribe feelings and intentions to us and treat us as persons. The image of persons-in-community emphasizes our relatedness, without denying the value of the individual or absorbing the individual in the collective.

## 3. In God's Image, but Fallen

According to Genesis, humanity was created "in the image of God." The image has been variously interpreted as rationality, spiritual nature, responsibility, or personal existence. Others have understood the *Imago Dei* relationally: it refers to the relation of human beings to God, or to their dominion over all other creatures. There has been extended debate as to how much of the image was lost in the fall. The theologian Matthew Fox says that Genesis represents an "original blessing" of humanity, and that "original sin" was later given a central place only because Paul, Augustine, and their followers were pessimistic about human nature, leaving a powerful legacy of guilt among Christians.[54] Fox overstates his case, but it is clear that the Bible itself sees humanity as ambivalent, capable of both good and evil, rather than as fundamentally evil. "Thou hast made him little less than God, and dost crown him with glory and honor" (Ps. 81:5). We have remarkable capacities, which can be used creatively and compassionately. This basically positive appraisal of human nature has been characteristic of Judaism through the centuries.

But *Adam's fall* is also an important part of the story. In most of Christian history, Adam was assumed to be both an actual individual and a representative of humanity. In the light of evolutionary biology, we can retain the latter but not the former. Once again, we must take the story seriously but not literally. Adam's story is Everyman's journey from innocence to responsibility and sin. Sin is compounded of egocentricity and disobedience to God. Self-centeredness and turning from God are two sides of the same act. The story goes on to portray the experience of anxiety, evasiveness, and sense of guilt. To these facets of individual sin, other biblical passages, especially in the Prophets, add the communal dimension of social injustice (for example, Amos 1–4). Failure to love God and neighbor are seen as inseparable from inordinate self-love.

Modern theologians have tried to express these biblical ideas in contemporary terms. Reinhold Niebuhr rejects the idea that original sin is inherited from Adam, but he says that we do inherit sinful social structures that perpetuate themselves in injustice and oppression. Every group tends to absolutize itself, blind to the rationalization of its self-interest. Niebuhr also describes the anxiety and insecurity that lead individuals to try to deny their limitations.[55] Feminist theologians have pointed out, however, that women in a patriarchal culture often have too little self-esteem; the traditional concept of sin hinders their achievement of self-respect and empowerment.

Paul Tillich identifies sin with three dimensions of *estrangement*. Sin is estrangement from other persons in self-centeredness and lovelessness. It is estrangement from our true selves in pursuing fragmented and inauthentic goals. It is estrangement from God, the ground of our being, in attempted self-sufficiency. For Tillich, estrangement, brokenness, and division can be overcome only in reconciliation, healing, and wholeness.[56] To Tillich's three forms of sin I would add a fourth: estrangement from nonhuman nature by denying its intrinsic value and violating our interdependence. I suggest that sin, in all its forms, is *a violation of relatedness*.

Events of the twentieth century have supported *a more sober assessment* of human nature than was characteristic of the authors in the eighteenth and nineteenth centuries who wrote about the perfectibility of humanity in an Age of Reason and an Age of Progress. No event has more undermined such optimism than the depth of evil in the massacre of six million Jews in the Holocaust. Auschwitz occurred, not in a primitive society, but in a nation of outstanding scientific and cultural achievements. Moreover, twentieth-century science has provided evidence of inherited aggression from our animal past and of the power of the unconscious over our decisions and actions. I have argued that many of these accounts are overdrawn and do not absolve us from personal responsibility, but they do point to the presence of irrational forces in human nature. Animals rarely kill members of their own species; their combat is often ritualized and stops short of serious injury. Yet among the human species, this century has seen unprecedented violence, and a large fraction of the world's scientific and technological resources is devoted to improving the weapons of mass destruction. We threaten whole populations with nuclear annihilation. The concept of sin is not outdated.

On the other hand, there is some evidence from psychotherapy that *too negative a view* of human nature and too low an estimate of ourselves can be harmful. Guilt without forgiveness or self-hatred without self-acceptance seem to hinder rather than encourage love of others. Some theologians join psychologists in calling for a self-respect that is not self-absorption. Perhaps the goal is self-understanding and realism in recognizing both our creative and our destructive potentialities.

### 4. A Unitary Person, Not a Body-Soul Dualism

The Bible looks on body, mind, and spirit as aspects of a personal unity. The self is a unified activity of thinking, feeling, willing, and acting. H. W. Robinson writes, "Characteristic of the Old Testament, the idea of human nature implies a unity, not a dualism. There is no contrast between the body and the soul such as the terms instinctively suggest to us."[57] According to Oscar Cullmann, "the Jewish and Christian interpretation of creation excludes the whole Greek dualism of body and soul."[58] There is, then, no biblical dichotomy between matter and spirit. In particular, the body is not the source of evil or something to be disowned, escaped, or denied—though it may be misused. We find instead an affirmation of the body and a positive acceptance of the material order. The person is an integral being, an active bodily self. Lynn de Silva writes:

Biblical scholarship has established quite conclusively that there is no dichotomous concept of man in the Bible, such as is found in Greek and Hindu thought. The biblical view of man is holistic, not dualistic. The notion of the soul as an immortal entity which enters the body at birth and leaves it at death is quite foreign to the biblical view of man. The biblical view is that man is a unity; he is a unity of soul, body, flesh, mind, etc., all together constituting the whole man.[59]

When belief in a future life did develop in the intertestamental and New Testament periods, it was expressed in terms of the *resurrection of the total person* by God's act, not the inherent immortality of the soul. Cullmann shows that the future life was seen as a gift from God "in the last days," not an innate human attribute.[60] Paul speaks of the dead as sleeping until the day of judgment when they will be restored—not as physical bodies nor as disembodied souls, but in what he calls "the spiritual body" (1 Cor. 15:44). Such views of the future life may be problematic, but they do testify that our faith is in God and not in our own souls and that our whole being is the object of God's saving purpose.

Paul's contrast of *flesh* and *spirit* at first seems to support a dualistic view, but more careful analysis shows that this is not the case. He never portrays a body that is inherently evil and a soul that is inherently good. Sin is in the will, which governs our whole being; "spiritual" sins such as pride and self-righteousness are prominent in Paul's account (for example, Rom. 7–8). (To be sure, Paul does speak of an inherited impulse to evil and of the occasions of temptation presented by the body. But "the flesh" is a symbol of the weakness of human nature in all its dimensions, rather than of any intrinsic evil associated with matter or the body as such.)

Only in later gnostic and Manichaean movements did a strong *dualism* develop in which matter was understood to be evil. This trend was influenced by the Greek idea (evident already in Plato's *Phaedo* and prominent in the Hellenistic world) that the body is a prison from which death liberates the soul. Other forces in the declining Greco-Roman culture aided the growth of asceticism, monasticism, rejection of the world, and the search for individual salvation. Some of these negative attitudes toward the body are seen in Augustine's writing and in medieval Christianity, but they represent a departure from the biblical affirmation of the goodness of the material world as God's creation.[61]

The classical dualism of *soul* and *body* accentuated the distinction between humanity and other creatures. Even though the scheme was ultimately theocentric, the premise that only human beings had souls encouraged an anthropocentric view of our status within the world. In the Middle Ages this was counterbalanced by a sense of the organic unity of a world designed according to God's purposes. But the nonhuman world plays only a supporting role in the Medieval and Reformation dramas of human redemption, and it is not surprising that there was little resistance to the exploitation of nature for human purposes when industrial technology later developed.[62]

Some kinds of scientific evidence seem to support this biblical picture of a unitary person, *a psychosomatic unity*. We know that genes and drugs drastically influence human personality. There are genetic and biochemical as well as environmental factors in mental illness. If one imagined a soul immune to such influences, it would be an abstract and detached entity unrelated to the living person or to biological and evolutionary processes. A self, by contrast, is the highest level of a unified organic being. Moreover, the preponderance of evidence from psychology is that people are healthier if they accept their bodily existence, including their sexuality, as a potentially valuable part of their total being, rather than denying or suppressing it.

In sum, it would be consistent with both the scientific and the biblical outlook to understand the person as *a multileveled unity* who is both a biological organism and a responsible self. We can escape both dualism and materialism if we assume a holistic view of persons with a hierarchy of levels. Some of these levels we share with all matter, some we share with all living things, some with all animal life, while some seem to be uniquely human. The person can be represented by the concept of *the self*, conceived not as a separate entity but as the individual in the unified activity of thinking, willing, feeling, and acting. The self is best described, not in terms of static substances, but in terms of dynamic activities at various levels of organization and functioning. In the biblical view, it is this integral being whose whole life is of concern to God.

## 3. THE ROLE OF CHRIST

The person of Christ is relevant to the Christian understanding of human nature for two reasons. First, Christ has traditionally been viewed as *the realization of true humanity*. In him we see the character of God's purposes for human life, the fulfillment of human nature. Second, the Christian community has experienced through the story of Christ *the power of reconciliation* overcoming estrangement—or, in more traditional terms, redemption overcoming sin. The Christian account of humanity would be incomplete without the story of Christ. Our task is to understand how this story can be viewed in an evolutionary cosmos and a religiously pluralistic world.

We noted earlier that the Gospels were written a generation after Christ's death, and they reflect the experience and theological interpretations of the early Christian community. The resurrection experiences were clearly crucial for the disciples. Whatever happened at Easter and Pentecost convinced them that God had vindicated Christ's person and mission. The early Christians experienced a release from self-centeredness and fear of death. Their lives were transformed in joy and gratitude and they proclaimed the good news of what God had done in Christ.

The early Christians were convinced that in Christ *God had taken the initiative.* Through him they had come to a new experience of God. Preaching to Jewish listeners, they spoke of him as the Messiah ("the anointed one," *Christos* in Greek), the deliverer whom Israel awaited. Jesus had associated his own person with the coming of the Kingdom, though he evidently interpreted his messianic role as that of a suffering servant, rather than as political leader or supernatural ruler. Writing to Greek readers, Paul used a different terminology: "God was in Christ, reconciling the world to himself" (2 Cor. 5:18). John identified Christ with "the Word," the *logos* of Hellenistic thought, the principle of divine wisdom that was now "the Word made flesh" (John 1:14).[63]

For several centuries the church wrestled with ways of expressing its conviction concerning *the human* and *the divine* in Christ. The view of the Ebionites that Christ was a great teacher "adopted" by God for a special mission was rejected. Equally unacceptable was the opposite extreme, the Docetist claim that Christ was God incognito, merely disguised in the likeness of a man but not really human (and not really dying on the cross). The final formula agreed on at Chalcedon in 451 was "complete in Godhead and complete in manhood, two natures without division, confusion or separation, in one person." The Nicene creed said he was "of one substance with the Father."

These *creedal formulas* served the negative function of ruling out unacceptable views. But they said nothing about how the "two natures" were related to each other. Moreover, they have often been interpreted in such a way that Christ's humanity was compromised (as an impersonal human nature without a human personality, or a human body without a human consciousness). The static Greek categories in which the doctrines were expressed, such as nature and substance, were familiar in the early church and in the medieval world, but this wider framework of thought is both problematic and unfamiliar today.[64]

I submit that in reformulating Christology today we should keep in mind the intent of the classical doctrines but should make use of categories of *relationship* and *history* rather than of substance. On *the human side* of the relationship, we can speak of Christ as a person who in his freedom was perfectly obedient to God. Through his own openness to God, his life reveals God's purposes to us. He identified himself with God and did not obstruct or distort God's will. He was inspired and empowered by God. On *the divine side,* we can speak of God as acting in and through the person of Christ. Christ is thus God's revelation to us. What was unique about Christ, in other words, was his relationship to God, not his metaphysical "substance." We can speak of the unity between Christ and God and yet assert the presence of two wills.

For example, in Gethsemane he prayed (Luke 22:42), "Not my will but thine be done." We have to think of what God did and also of what Christ did as a free human being. Without freedom and personal responsibility there would be no true humanity.[65]

Geoffrey Lampe maintains that the most adequate Christology is a recovery of the idea that *God as Spirit* was present in the life of Christ. In the Old Testament, the Spirit was God active in creation and in human life, notably in the inspiration of the prophets. According to the Gospels, Christ received the Spirit at his baptism. The early church experienced at Pentecost an outpouring of joy and love, which they accepted as the gift of the Spirit. For them, the Spirit was closely associated with Christ, through whom they had come to a new experience of God. Lampe discusses Paul's many references to the Spirit and his description of the Christian virtues as "fruits of the Spirit."[66]

But Lampe points out that with the development of *trinitarian thought* in the patristic period, the Spirit was no longer thought of as God's presence but as a separate being mediating between God and the world. The Holy Spirit was subordinated to the eternal Son who was identified with the *logos* as agent of creation. In the revision of the Nicene Creed in 589, it was said that the Spirit proceeds from the Father "and the Son" (*filioque,* a term that the Eastern Orthodox church rejected). It was also said that the eternal Son assumed the general form of human nature—an idea that Lampe thinks compromised the historical individuality and the true humanity of Christ. He maintains that if we say that God's presence inspired the free human response of Christ, we can acknowledge his full humanity, while affirming that through Christ God acted decisively. Moreover, it is the same Spirit who inspires other persons and evokes their faith and love. There is one God who as indwelling Spirit was present in the life of the prophets, Christ, and the early church—and can be present in our lives today.

Lampe holds that such a view brings together *creation* and *redemption* as a single continuous activity of God. Through the long evolutionary process God formed responsive creatures. But Christ was a focal point of God's activity and self-revelation, and he is for us the key to understanding the whole creative and saving work:

The one continuous creative and saving work of God as Spirit begins with the origin and evolution of the cosmos itself, becomes personal communion with created persons when rational human beings come into existence, comes to be defined, so far as God's indwelling in man is concerned, in Christ as the pattern and archetype of personal union between God as Spirit and the spirit of man, and moves forward towards the goal of creation when humanity will be fully formed into the likeness of Christ, the model "Adam."[67]

I suggest, then, that in an *evolutionary perspective* we may view both the human and the divine activity in Christ as a continuation and intensification of what had been occurring previously. We can think of him as representing a new stage in evolution and a new stage in God's activity. Christ as a person (not just as a body) was part of the continuous process that runs back through *Australopithecus* and the early forms of life to those atoms formed in primeval stars. He was also in the line of cultural and religious evolution that we have traced, and he was deeply formed by the ethical monotheism of Israel. Yet in his person and life and ideas, and in the community's response to him, he represented something genuinely new. We have said that in the sphere of culture, novelty is not the result of random mutations, and selection is not mainly a matter of physical survival; both are results of human freedom and decision.

But we can also view Christ as the product of a *divine activity* that has a long history. For millions of years there was the continuing creation of the nonhuman world, and then of humanity and culture, at an accelerating rate. In the great religious traditions of the world, and especially in the history of Israel, God's immanent creativity was increasingly focused, and individual persons were increasingly responsive. In Christ, both divine intention and human response allowed a more powerful revelation of God's nature than had occurred previously. We have, then, a basic continuity of creation and redemption.

Writing in the Anglican tradition, Lionel Thornton presents a Christology in the framework of *emergent evolution*. Each new level in evolution brought greater complexity, freedom, and social interaction, and each incorporated all previous levels within a new unity. In humanity, at the level of spirit, there was a greater openness to the eternal order, but also a failure to respond to it. Thornton says that Christ as "the new creation" was both the fulfillment and the transformation of the previous cosmic series in a new order of reality. He was at once a culmination of the series and a new revelation of the eternal.[68] It appears, however, that by portraying Christ as a new species, Thornton has denied that he was fully human.

Teilhard de Chardin has also represented Christ as *the fulfillment of evolution*. In his view, Christ was not primarily an antidote to human sin but a new stage in evolution, organically related to the whole cosmic process. Grace is a creative force in all life, fulfilling nature rather than replacing it. Redemption is a continuation of creation on a new level, leading to the consummation of evolutionary convergence. In Christ we see the divine purpose: to unite all reality and bring it to union with God.[69] As noted earlier, redemption for Teilhard is social and cosmic as well as individual. I have found his writing helpful, but I will suggest in the next chapter that process theology offers a more adequate framework for articulating an evolutionary Christology.

What is the relevance of Christ to us today? The Christian community believes that it is through Christ that *reconciliation* may occur in our lives. If sin means estrangement from God, from ourselves, from other persons, and from the rest of nature, then reconciliation is also fourfold. Reconciliation with God takes place when repentance and forgiveness overcome guilt and when we know we are accepted despite our inadequacies. There is reconciliation with ourselves when healing and wholeness replace brokenness and fragmentation and when self-acceptance accompanies empowerment and renewal. There is reconciliation with other persons when we are released from self-centeredness, freed to love the neighbor and to take action for social justice.[70] Reconciliation with the rest of nature occurs when we recognize our common dependence on God and our continuing interdependence. If sin is indeed the violation of relationships, redemption is *the fulfillment of relationships*. For the Christian community the power of reconciliation and renewal is revealed most completely in the person of Christ.

The most important ritual in Christianity is the Eucharist or Lord's Supper, which directs the community's attention to *Christ's death*. There have been two main theological interpretations of this event.[71] In the *objective* interpretation, set forth by Anselm and dominant in Catholic thought and evangelical Protestantism, the cross is an expression of God's justice in relation to human sin. As a substitutionary atonement, "Christ died for our sins" by taking our place and undergoing the judgment we deserve. (This was an extension of the Old Testament idea of sacrifices to expiate human sins, but since it was held that in Christ God had provided the sacrifice, it was also seen as an expression of God's love.) In the *subjective* interpretation, set forth by Abelard and dominant among liberal Protestants, Christ's self-sacrifice was a moral example, which can inspire us to examine our own lives. Christ's teaching, life, and death are a revelation of God's love (more than of justice), and they can bring us to repentance. The transformation occurs in us as we ourselves accept God's forgiveness and love. The subjective view is more consistent with the understanding of Christ presented above, but at least some of the insights of the objective view can be combined with it.

With this interpretation, we can be loyal to the tradition in which revelation and renewal have occurred for us, without claiming that they cannot occur elsewhere. We can acknowledge divine initiative and human response *in other traditions*. We can respect the power of reconciliation wherever it occurs. This would lead to a path between absolutism or exclusivism, on the one hand, and relativism or skepticism, on the other. In a religiously pluralistic world, it would encourage genuine dialogue in which we can learn from each other without denying our indebtedness to our own tradition, as was proposed in chapter 6.

The classical view draws *an absolute line* between Christ and other humans, just as it draws an absolute line between human and nonhuman life. In both cases there is said to be a difference in metaphysical substance—Christ's divine substance, in the first instance, the human soul in the second. I am suggesting that in comparing Christ and other people, as in comparing human and nonhuman life, we should speak of *differences in degree*. These can add up to differences in kind, but with no absolute lines. In both cases the genuinely new emerges showing both continuity and discontinuity with the old. One might think of a spectrum of persons, starting with a typical religious believer, then the prophets and saints, the founders of other religious traditions, and finally Christ. In all of these lives there was divine initiative and committed human response, in varying degrees. God's mode of operation was the same throughout, but God's purposes and the human responses varied. For the Christian, Christ is the distinctive but not exclusive revelation of the power of God.

As in the previous chapter, we have in this chapter rejected both materialism (ontological reductionism) and dualism in favor of the idea of a hierarchy of levels. We can accept all that science tells us about our evolutionary history and biochemical functioning. We can at the same time acknowledge the unique features of human mental, cultural, and religious life. Beyond that, we can without inconsistency portray a special role for the person of Christ within this historical framework. In the next chapter we will explore the contribution of process thought to the systematic articulation of these claims.

## III. THE HUMAN FUTURE

Ideas about the future are inescapably speculative. Yet our expectations and hopes strongly influence our actions, which can affect the future. What can be said about the human future from the standpoint of science and from the standpoint of theology?

### 1. SCIENCE AND THE HUMAN FUTURE

In chapter 8 we looked at the speculations of cosmologists concerning the future of the cosmos. Their conclusions allow a very long time for *biological evolution* to continue on planet earth. Our sun will support life for at least five billion years—longer than there has been life on earth in the past, and ten thousand times the total span of *Homo sapiens*. We have seen that in the past the pace of biological evolution has increased as higher levels of complexity were achieved. Our genes represent the cumulative legacy of a long history of interaction of organisms and environments, stretching back to the dawn of life. The past is built into the present, and it shapes the future, providing the starting point for further evolutionary change but not determining it. Human nature is not static or complete, and there is no reason to think that we are the end of the line.

But we have seen that *cultural evolution,* while it is built on this genetic heritage, permits much more rapid and deliberate change. It, too, provides for the transmission of information from the past and for the introduction of novelty, but in culture there are distinctive forms of innovation and selection. In an earlier chapter we listed some of the special features of human history: the ideas and goals of agents, the social meanings of language, the possibility of imaginative new responses to social challenges and crises. Today humankind faces immediate crises, which require changes on a time scale far shorter than that of biological evolution. Richard Leakey, an expert on the early ancestors of humankind, was recently asked what he thought humankind would be like a million years from now. He replied that the important period to think about is the next one hundred years, for that is the time when human existence is imperiled.[72]

A major factor in the current human crisis is *technology*. Technology goes back to the early use of tools, the production of metals, and the medieval use of wind and water power, but it developed rapidly with the introduction of steam power in the Industrial Revolution. The technologies of the twentieth century are new in two ways: they are based on advances in science, and they exert power over nature and human destiny on an unprecedented scale. For example, ecological destruction is occurring at an unparalleled rate. Species have become extinct throughout evolutionary history, but now by some estimates ten thousand species are driven to extinction each year; their genetic libraries, built up over millions of years, are lost forever.

*Nuclear technology* is the most dramatic example of our new power. Knowledge of nuclear forces made it possible for us to split the atom—a striking example of Einstein's conclusion concerning the equivalence of energy and mass ($E = mc^2$). We try to suppress the memory of Hiroshima. We build up gigantic nuclear arsenals, hoping that their presence will prevent their use but courting disaster as more and more nations acquire nuclear weapons. A nuclear holocaust would destroy the fabric of human civilization and possibly threaten the survival of humanity. While this outcome does not appear probable, it is a sign of our arrogance and blindness that we would take even a small risk of destroying in a few days or months what God has evoked into being over the past millions of years.

*Genetic engineering* offers the prospect of the deliberate alteration of the genetic structure of organisms and even of human beings. Here again is an unprecedented power over the human future. We face promising possibilities for improving the agricultural productivity of crops in the midst of food scarcities and for lifting the burden of human suffering caused by genetically inherited diseases. But we also face risks of unintended repercussions and controversial ethical issues, especially if human genes are altered not just to cure diseases but to achieve improvements in human characteristics. *Information technologies*, communications, computers, and new forms of artificial intelligence will have major impacts on society and on our self-understanding.

Today we see new evidence of *global interdependence* and the need for a global viewpoint. Many environmental impacts, such as the greenhouse effect, are global. Natural resource use, international trade, communications networks, and economic policies connect us around the world. The astronauts' amazing photographs of the earth from the moon are images of our planet for the space age. Can we develop institutions that will encourage planetary survival without suppressing cultural diversity? We must act with urgency without ignoring the needs of future generations. Our economic and political institutions encourage us to adopt a very short time scale: this year's profit statement, next year's election. We must learn to view short-term national goals in the context of long-term global goals.

## 2. THEOLOGY AND THE HUMAN FUTURE

How does Christian theology view the future? We have seen that there were two strands in *biblical eschatology*. Prophetic eschatology saw God's judgment in times of crisis and possible disaster, but it also held out hope for the future if the nation changed its ways. Apocalyptic eschatology, on the other hand, despaired of human action and placed all its hope in a supernatural intervention that would destroy the present world and establish a totally new order. I indicated that the latter view undercuts human responsibility, and I expressed the conviction that our actions make a difference. In the prophetic view, the Kingdom of God will come through a combination of divine initiative and human response. The prophets' message included a strong call to social justice and a vision of *shalom* (peace and harmony). It presupposed that human beings are not totally sinful and can respond to God's call. Christ, in turn, carried further the call to love and reconciliation, and he exemplified it in his own life.

Theologian Philip Hefner has explored our role as *created cocreators* in an evolutionary context. He presents the whole evolutionary process as God's way of creating free creatures. As created, we are dependent on sources beyond ourselves, including a genetic past, which was dominant before humanity appeared. As cocreators, we have freedom and the capacity to seek new directions, possibilities that are novel and yet within the constraints set by our genetic inheritance. Hefner says that nature is "stretched" and "enabled" as it gives rise to the new zone of freedom. "*Homo sapiens* is God's created cocreator whose purpose is the stretching/enabling of the systems of nature so that they can participate in God's purposes in the mode of freedom."[73] God is immanent in the creativity and self-transcendence evidenced in evolutionary history and continuing into the future.

Hefner maintains that we can participate in *God's ongoing creative work:* "We humans created in the image of God are participants and co-creators in the ongoing work of God's creative activity. We are being drawn toward a shared destiny which will ultimately determine what it means to be a true human being."[74] Hefner holds that Christ is the prototype of true humanity and represents a radically new phase in cultural evolution. In Christ we come to know God's will as universal love. The eschatological hope is a confidence in God's purpose to perfect and fulfill the creation. Human beings can be conscious agents in a new level of creation, says Hefner, but they are also in a stage of great precariousness and vulnerability. Technology gives us immense powers over nature, and our decisions will affect all terrestrial life. We have a responsibility, not only for our own future, but also for the rest of the creatures on our planet.

The World Council of Churches has set forth some social goals for our times. At the WCC conference on Faith and Science held at MIT in 1979, those goals were summarized as "Justice, Participation, and Sustainability."[75] A revised version was adopted at the WCC Assembly in Vancouver in 1983: "Peace, Justice, and the Integrity of Creation."[76] I would myself stress three goals:

1. *Justice.* Today there is a grossly inequitable global distribution of resources. Four hundred years of Western military and economic domination have created and perpetuated gaps between rich and poor nations. Large-scale technologies are expensive and lead to a concentration of economic power, both within nations and between nations. The biblical concern for the oppressed and dedication to social justice are profoundly relevant to a technological world.

2. *Environmental Preservation.* The goal of preserving the environment includes sustaining natural resources, reducing pollution, and preserving species and ecosystems. The biblical themes of stewardship, the celebration of nature, and a sacramental view of nature can offset the one-sided emphasis on human dominion that contributed to the unbridled exploitation of the environment. This requires us to rethink our understanding of the relation of humanity to nonhuman nature and to develop a more adequate theology of nature for representing God's relation to the created order.

3. *Participation.* Many citizens feel either incompetent or unable to take part in policy decisions in a technological society. The concentration of economic power in large-scale technologies is reflected in the political power of industrial and governmental bureaucracies. The preservation of democracy and political freedom requires an examination of how citizens can participate with legislators and technical experts in the complex policy decisions of an age of technology.

Apart from such particular ethical goals, the biblical tradition can contribute significantly in its *images of the future.* In times of crisis, people are searching for new visions; changes in perceptions and in values can occur more rapidly than during more stable times. The Bible presents images of human fulfillment that do not ignore material welfare; we are called to concern for the hungry and the homeless. But it also describes other sources of fulfillment in interpersonal relationships, appreciation of the natural world, and spiritual growth. Above all, its vision of *shalom* includes social harmony and cooperation as well as peace and prosperity. These ethical goals and their relevance for an age of science-based technology are taken up in my *Ethics in an Age of Technology.*

## CHAPTER 11

# Process Thought

We have traced successive levels of reality in subatomic particles, atoms, molecules, lower forms of life, animals, and human beings. We have asked how these levels were related to each other historically and how they are related to each other in organisms today. At each stage the philosophical and theological implications were explored. At this point our conclusions can be summarized by indicating some general characteristics of nature, which are evident in all its forms. We then consider the distinctive metaphysical categories that process philosophy proposes for the coherent interpretation of these varied phenomena. Finally, process theology is explored, drawing from both process philosophy and biblical thought. After reading the first summary section, the reader seeking a briefer presentation of process themes will find it in the last section of chapter 12, which compares current theological options.

## I. SUMMARY: A MULTILEVELED COSMOS

The individual sciences encountered in previous chapters are diverse in the domains that they study and in the concepts and theories that they employ. Nevertheless, there has arisen a common evolutionary and ecological view that cuts across disciplinary lines. The change is so far-reaching that it can be considered a paradigm shift. The older paradigm is still prevalent; we are in a period of competing paradigms (in Kuhn's terms) or programs (in Lakatos's). The new outlook stands out more clearly if it is compared with dominant Western assumptions in previous periods. Chapter 1 presented the medieval and Newtonian views of nature in their historical contexts.[1] At the risk of oversimplification, I summarize them here in order to highlight the new features of contemporary thought.

### 1. MEDIEVAL AND NEWTONIAN VIEWS

*The medieval view of nature* combined Greek and biblical ideas, reflecting the continuing influence of Plato and Aristotle as well as scripture (see fig. 4).

1. Nature was seen as a fixed order; there was change within it, and there was directionality in human history, but the basic forms were thought to be immutable.

2. It was teleological (purposeful) in that every creature expressed both the divine purposes and its own built-in goals. Phenomena were explained in terms of purposes.

3. It was substantive; the components were separate mental and material substances. A substance was taken to be independent and externally related, requiring nothing but itself (and God) in order to be.

4. The cosmos was hierarchical, with each lower form serving the higher (God/man/woman/animal/plant). Nature was a single coherent whole, a graded but unified order, with all parts working together for God's purposes according to the divine plan. The institutions of church and society were also held to be fixed and hierarchical, integrated into the total cosmic order. The scheme was anthropocentric in holding that all creatures on earth were created for the benefit of humanity; an absolute distinction was assumed between humanity and other creatures. The earth was the center of the cosmos, surrounded by the celestial spheres and the eternal heavens.

5. The interpretive categories were dualistic, with fundamental contrasts between soul and body, between immaterial spirit and transitory matter, and between the perfect eternal forms and their imperfect embodiment in the material world. The purpose of the material was to serve the spiritual, and the goal of this life was to prepare for the next.

6. To summarize the medieval view, we might think of nature as a Kingdom, an ordered society with a sovereign Lord.

### Fig. 4  Changing Views of Nature

| MEDIEVAL | NEWTONIAN | TWENTIETH-CENTURY |
| --- | --- | --- |
| 1. Fixed order | Change as rearrangement | Evolutionary, historical, emergent |
| 2. Teleological | Deterministic | Law and chance, structure and openness |
| 3. Substantive | Atomistic | Relational, ecological, interdependent |
| 4. Hierarchical, anthropocentric | Reductionistic | Systems and wholes, organismic |
| 5. Dualistic (spirit/matter) | Dualistic (mind/body) | Multi-leveled |
| 6. Kingdom | Machine | Community |

*The Newtonian view* differed at each of these points.

1. It gave greater scope to change, but only to change as rearrangement of the unchanging components, the fundamental particles of nature. The basic forms were still thought to be fixed, with no genuine novelty or historical development in nature.

2. Nature was deterministic rather than teleological. Mechanical causes, not purposes, determined all natural events. Explanation consisted in the specification of such causes. It was asserted that the future could be predicted if we had complete knowledge of the past.
3. It was atomistic in taking separate particles rather than substances to be the basic reality of nature. The theory of knowledge (epistemology) was that of classical realism: the object can be known as it is in itself apart from the observer. The atomistic outlook was paralleled by an individualistic view of society (seen, for example, in ideas of economic competition and social contract theories of government).
4. The approach to nature was reductionistic and mechanistic rather than hierarchical, since the physical mechanisms and laws at the lowest levels were thought to determine all events (except those in the human mind).
5. It was dualistic, though the division differed from that of the Middle Ages. Newton accepted the Cartesian dualism of mind and body; God and human minds were the great exceptions in a mechanistic world. Human rationality was seen as the mark of our uniqueness, even if the earth was no longer at the center of the cosmic system. But the leaders of the eighteenth-century Enlightenment believed that humanity was also a part of the all-encompassing world machine, whose operation could be explained without reference to God. Such a materialistic world held no place for consciousness or inwardness except as subjective illusions. Moreover, if nature is a machine, it is an object that can appropriately be exploited for human uses.
6. The Newtonian view can be summarized in the image of nature as a machine.

## 2. THE NEW VIEW OF NATURE

Twentieth-century science, we have seen, departs significantly from the Newtonian conception of nature (see fig. 4, right column).

1. In place of immutable order, or change as rearrangement, nature is now understood to be evolutionary, dynamic, and emergent. Its basic forms have changed radically and new types of phenomena have appeared at successive levels in matter, life, mind, and culture. Historicity is a basic characteristic of nature, and science itself is historically conditioned.
2. In place of determinism, there is a complex combination of law and chance, in fields as diverse as quantum physics, thermodynamics, chaos theory, cosmology, and biological evolution. Nature is characterized by both structure and openness. The future cannot be predicted in detail from the past, either in principle or in practice.
3. Nature is understood to be relational, ecological, and interdependent.

Reality is constituted by events and relationships rather than by separate substances or separate particles. In epistemology, classical realism now appears untenable; some interpreters advocate instrumentalism, but I have defended critical realism.

4. Reduction continues to be fruitful in the analysis of the separate components of systems, but attention is also given to systems and wholes themselves. Distinctive holistic concepts are used to explain the higher-level activities of complex systems, from organisms to ecosystems. The interaction between systems or levels can often be described as the communication of information.

5. There is a hierarchy of levels within every organism (but not an extreme hierarchy of value among beings, as in the medieval view, which could be used to justify the exploitation of one group of beings by another). Mind/body dualism finds little support in science today. The contemporary scientific outlook is less anthropocentric; human beings have capacities not found elsewhere in nature, but they are products of evolution and parts of an interdependent natural order. Other creatures are valuable in themselves. Humanity is an integral part of nature. The human being is a psychosomatic unity—a biological organism but also a responsible self.

6. Here we might propose as a summary the image of nature as a community—a historical community of interdependent beings. I will suggest that process thought is particularly compatible with this view of nature.

## II. PROCESS PHILOSOPHY

Process philosophy has developed a systematic metaphysics that is consistent with the evolutionary, many-leveled view of nature presented in previous chapters and summarized above. We look first at Whitehead's basic metaphysical categories. The ways in which he applies these categories to diverse entities in the world, from particles to persons, are then examined. Finally, we will try to evaluate the adequacy of process philosophy from the viewpoint of science, postponing the theological issues until the subsequent section.

### 1. AN ECOLOGICAL METAPHYSICS

Whitehead tried to formulate an inclusive conceptual scheme that would be sufficiently general to be applicable to all entities in the world. His goal was a coherent set of concepts in terms of which every element of experience could be systematically interpreted and organized. He wanted to construct "a system of ideas which bring aesthetic, moral and religious interests into relation with those concepts of the world which have their origin in natural science."[2] The formulation of his basic categories was an imaginative generalization from human experience, but it was also indebted to twentieth-century science.[3]

1. *The Primacy of Time.* The starting point of process philosophy is becoming rather than being. To Whitehead, transition and activity are more fundamental than permanence and substance. He pictures the basic components of reality as interrelated dynamic events. He rejects the atomist's view of reality as unchanging particles that are merely externally rearranged. Whitehead was familiar with the new role of time in science, especially the replacement of material particles by vibratory patterns in quantum physics, and the unpredictable and historical character of evolution. The future is to some extent open and indeterminate; reality exhibits chance, creativity, and emergence. Genuine alternative possibilities exist, that is, potentialities that may or may not be actualized in time.

2. *The Interconnection of Events.* The world is a network of interactions. Events are interdependent; every event has an essential reference to other times and places. Every entity is initially constituted by its relationships. Nothing exists except by participation. Each occurrence in turn exerts an influence, which enters into the becoming of other occurrences. Whitehead points again to the new physics. Formerly we imagined independent, localized, self-contained particles bumping into each other externally and passively without themselves undergoing alteration. Today we talk about interpenetrating fields that extend throughout space and change continually. The biological world is a web of mutual dependencies. Whitehead extends these ideas into what may be called "an ecological view of reality."[4]

3. *Reality As Organic Process.* The word *process* implies temporal change and interconnected activity. Whitehead also calls his metaphysics "the philosophy of organism." The basic analogy for interpreting the world is not a machine but an organism, which is a highly integrated and dynamic pattern of interdependent events. The parts contribute to and are also modified by the unified activity of the whole. Each level of organization—atom, molecule, cell, organ, organism, community—receives from and in turn influences the patterns of activity at other levels. Every event occurs in a context, which affects it. This may also be called a "social view of reality," for in a society there is unity and interaction without loss of the individuality of the members. The world is a community of events.

4. *The Self-Creation of Every Entity.* Although Whitehead emphasizes the interdependence of events, he does not end with a monism in which the parts are swallowed up in the whole. An event is not just the intersection of lines of interaction; it is an entity in its own right with its own individuality. He maintains a genuine pluralism in which every entity is a unique synthesis of the influences upon it, a new unity formed from an initial diversity. Every entity takes account of other events and reacts and responds to them. During the moment when it is on its own, it is free to appropriate and integrate its relationships in its own way. Each entity is a center of spontaneity and self-creation, contributing distinctively to the world. Whitehead wants us to look at the world from the viewpoint of the entity itself, imagining it as an experiencing subject.

Reality thus consists of an interacting network of individual *moments of experience*. These integrated moments he calls "actual occasions" or "actual entities." We can call them "entities" (emphasizing their integration), or "events" (emphasizing their temporality), but we must always keep in mind both their wider relationships and their interiority as moments of experience.

Whitehead describes the *self-creation* of each new entity as an individual instant of experience under the guidance of its "subjective aim." Even the influence of the past on the present, which can be viewed externally as efficient causality, can also be considered the action of the present entity as a momentary subject conforming to the objectified past and reproducing or reenacting its pattern. Each such subject has at least a modicum of creative freedom in shaping the particular unity of experience into which its past inheritance is woven and integrated. During its brief existence it is autonomous, closed to any additional data, and on its own in making something of itself—even if its activity essentially repeats that of its predecessors in a routine and "mechanical" fashion.

Efficient causality characterizes the transition between entities, while final causality dominates the momentary internal growth of the entity itself as it progressively actualizes its own synthesis, embodying a particular pattern of forms. An example of this process would be the way in which memory, feeling, bodily data, and sensory data are integrated actively, selectively, and with anticipation, in *a moment of human experience.* But a similar synthesis, in much simpler forms, can be postulated for the experience of any unified entity, though not for inanimate objects such as stones or aggregates such as plants, which lack a center of unified experience.

Summarizing Whitehead's detailed discussion, we may say that *causality* is a complex process in which many strands are interwoven. (a) Every new entity is in part the product of *efficient causation,* which refers to the influence of previous entities on it. Objective "data" from the past are given to each present entity, to which it must conform, but it can do so in alternative ways. (b) There is thus an element of *self-causation* or self-creation, for an entity unifies its "data" in its own manner from its unique perspective on the universe. Every entity contributes something of its own in the way it appropriates its past, relates itself to various possibilities, and produces a novel synthesis that is not strictly deducible from the antecedents. (c) Thus a creative selection occurs from among alternative potentialities in terms of goals and aims, which is *final causation.* Causality thus includes many influences, none of which is coercive or strictly deterministic. The outcome is not predictable. In brief, every new occurrence can be looked on as a present response (self-cause) to past entities (efficient cause) in terms of potentialities grasped (final cause).

Whitehead ascribes the ordering of these potentialities to God. God as *the primordial ground of order* structures potential forms of relationship before they are actualized. In this function God seems to be an abstract and impersonal principle. But Whitehead's God also has specific purposes for the realization of maximum value, selecting particular possibilities for particular entities. God is *the ground of novelty* as well as of order, presenting new possibilities among which alternatives are left open. God elicits the self-creation of individual entities and thereby allows for novelty as well as structure. By valuing particular potentialities to which creatures can respond, God influences the world without determining it. God acts by being experienced by the world, affecting the development of successive moments. But God never determines the outcome of events or violates the self-creation of each being. Every entity is the joint product of past causes, divine purposes, and the new entity's own activity.

## 2. DIVERSE LEVELS OF EXPERIENCE

Whitehead wants his basic categories to apply to all entities, but he proposes radical differences in the way these categories are exemplified in entities at different levels. There are great differences in degree and in the relative importance of the categories, which amount to differences in kind, and yet there is a continuity in evolutionary history and in ontological structure. There are no absolute lines of the sort that dualists defend. In chapter 9 we talked about levels of analysis and levels of organization and activity. A Whiteheadian scheme would also have to consider levels of experience.

An *electron*, as understood in quantum physics, has an episodic, transitory, and unpredictable character. On the other hand, *an atom* is more stable and unified, acting as a whole vibratory pattern whose component electrons cannot be distinguished. The atom essentially repeats the same pattern, with negligible opportunity for novelty. It is dominated by efficient causation, in which the influence of the past is passed on with no significant modification. *Inanimate objects* such as stones have no higher level of integration, and the indeterminacy of the atoms simply averages out statistically. A stone has no unified activity beyond the physical cohesion of the parts.[5]

A *cell*, by contrast, has considerable integration at a new level. It can act as a unit with at least a rudimentary kind of responsiveness. There is an opportunity for novelty, though it is minimal. If the cell is in a *plant*, little overall organization or integration is present. There is some coordination among plant cells, but plants have no higher center of experience. But *invertebrates* have an elementary sentience as centers of perception and action. The development of a nervous system made possible a higher level of unification of experience, the evolutionary function of which was to synthesize sensory data and coordinate appropriate motor responses. We discussed earlier the new forms of memory, learning, anticipation, and purposiveness in *vertebrates*. Consciousness, like sentience, was selected and intensified because it guided behavior that contributed to survival.

In *human beings*, the self is the highest level in which all of the lower levels are integrated. The human self may hold conscious aims and consider distant goals. Final causation and novelty in individual and cultural life predominate over genetic and biological determinants, though the self is always

dependent on lower-level structures. Symbolic language, rational deliberation, creative imagination, and social interaction go beyond anything previously possible in evolutionary history. Humans enjoy a far greater intensity
and richness of experience than occurred previously.

In a complex organism, *downward causation* from higher to lower levels
can be present because, according to process philosophy, every entity is what
it is by virtue of its relationships. Reality consists of interrelated events rather
than unchanging particles. The atoms in a cell behave differently from the
atoms in a stone. The cells in a brain behave differently from the cells in a
plant. The sixteen cells in an animal embryo soon after conception will normally produce different parts of the animal; yet one of those cells alone, if
separated from the others, will produce a whole animal. Every entity is influenced by its participation in a larger whole. Emergence arises in the modification of lower-level constituents in a new context. But causal interaction
between levels is not total determination; there is some self-determination by
entities at all levels.

The process view of *the mind/body relation* is a version of what I called a
"multilevel theory." It can also be termed "nondualistic interactionism."[6]
Process thinkers agree with dualists that interaction takes place between the
mind and the cells of the brain, but they reject the dualists' claim that this is
an interaction between two totally dissimilar entities. Between the mind and
a brain cell there are enormous differences in characteristics, but not the
absolute dissimilarity that makes interaction so difficult to imagine in dualism. Moreover, the mind/body relation is only one example of the relation
between levels, not a problem unique to human and perhaps animal minds.
The process view has much in common with two-language theories or a parallelism that takes mental and neural phenomena to be two aspects of the
same events. But unlike these views, it can refer to interaction, downward
causality, and the constraints that higher-level events exert on events at lower
levels. At higher levels there are new events and entities and not just new
relationships among lower-level events and entities.

Looking at diverse types of individuals, Whitehead attributes *subjective experience* in progressively more attenuated forms to persons, animals, lower organisms, and cells (and even, in principle, to atoms, though at that level it is
effectively negligible), but not to stones or plants or other aggregates. David
Griffin proposes that this should be called *panexperientialism* rather than
*panpsychism,* since for Whitehead mind and consciousness are found only at
higher levels.[7] Consciousness occurs only when there is a central nervous system. (Griffin suggests that Whitehead's technical concepts of a "physical
pole" and a "mental pole" in all entities might better have been called the
"receptive" and "self-creative" phases of experience, since the latter is present
even when there is no mind.)[8] Every entity is a subject for itself and becomes
an object for others. But only in higher life forms is the data from brain cells
integrated in the high-level stream of experience we call mind. Consciousness and mind are thus radically new emergents in cosmic history.

Whitehead thus does not attribute mind or mentality (as ordinarily understood) to lower-level entities, but he does attribute at least *rudimentary forms of experience* to unified entities at all levels, which runs against the assumptions of many scientists. What are the reasons for such attribution?

1. *The Generality of Metaphysical Categories.* In Whitehead's view, a basic metaphysical category must be universally applicable to all entities. The diversity among the characteristics of entities must be accounted for by the diversity of the modes in which these basic categories are exemplified and by differences in their relative importance. The subjective aspects of atoms are vanishingly small and may for all practical purposes be considered absent, but they are postulated for the sake of metaphysical consistency and inclusiveness. Mechanical interactions can be viewed as very low-grade organismic events (since organisms always have mechanical features), whereas no extrapolation of mechanical concepts can yield the concepts needed to describe subjective experience. Starting with mechanical concepts, one either ends with materialism or one has to introduce a dualistic discontinuity. New phenomena and new properties can emerge historically, but not new basic categories.

2. *Evolutionary and Ontological Continuity.* There are no sharp lines between an amoeba and a human being, either in evolutionary history or among forms of life today. The universe is continuous and interrelated. Process thought is opposed to all forms of dualism: living and nonliving, human and nonhuman, mind and matter. Human experience is part of the order of nature. Mental events are a product of the evolutionary process and hence an important clue to the nature of reality. A single fertilized cell gradually develops into a human being with the capacity for thought. We cannot get mind from matter, either in evolutionary history or in embryological development, unless there are some intermediate stages or levels in between, and unless mind and matter share at least some characteristics in common.

3. *Immediate Access to Human Experience.* I know myself as an experiencing subject. Human experience, as an extreme case of an event in nature, is taken to exhibit the generic features of all events. We should then consider an organism as a center of experience, even though that interiority is not directly accessible to us. In order to give a unified account of the world, Whitehead employs categories (such as "self-creation" and "subjective aim") that in very attenuated forms can be said to characterize lower-level events, but that at the same time have at least some analogy to our awareness as experiencing subjects. Such a procedure might be defended on the ground that if we want to use a single set of categories, we should treat lower levels as simpler cases of complex experience, rather than trying to interpret our experience by concepts derived from the inanimate world or resorting to some form of dualism.

Whitehead's categories are readily applicable to organisms with *a middle range of complexity.* Even for simpler organisms it is reasonable to speak of elementary forms of perception, memory, sentience, anticipation, purpose, and novelty. The distinctiveness of higher forms is maintained by treating consciousness, mind, and self-consciousness as irreducible *emergents,* which are not present in even rudimentary form at lower levels. But Whitehead's analysis seems somewhat strained at the two ends of the spectrum.

At the upper end, his categories seem to me inadequate to express *the continuing identity of the human self.* Whitehead holds that every actual entity is a discrete moment of experience, which in its self-creative phase is on its own, cut off from the world. Here Whitehead was influenced by quantum physics, in which interactions are discrete and transitory. He was also influenced by relativity, in which a finite time interval is required for the transmission of any effect from one point to another. In process thought, endurance is represented by the repetition of a pattern, not by an enduring substance. For Whitehead, the self comes into being only at the end of the brief moment of unification, by which time it is already perishing. I would question whether human experience has such a fragmentary and episodic character. Perhaps reality at higher levels is more like a continually flowing process, from which temporal moments are abstractions. This might allow for a continuing self-identity without reverting to static or substantive or dualistic categories.[9]

In dealing with *the inanimate world,* the Whiteheadian analysis does not present any direct inconsistency with contemporary science. Creativity is said to be either totally absent (in the case of stones and inanimate objects, which are aggregates without integration or unified experience) or so attenuated that it would escape detection (in the case of atoms). A vanishingly small novelty and self-determination in atoms is postulated only for the sake of metaphysical consistency and continuity. But does process philosophy allow adequately for the radical diversity among levels of activity in the world and the emergence of genuine novelty at all stages of evolutionary history? Could greater emphasis be given to emergence and the contrasts between events at various levels, while preserving the basic postulate of metaphysical continuity? I have stressed the hierarchical character of a multiplicity of levels in organisms and persons, whereas many process writers refer to only two levels at a time (the mind and the cells of the brain, for example, without reference to intermediate levels of organization). Other authors have said that intermediate levels of organization in an organism can be included in the framework of process philosophy.[10] I believe that the Whiteheadian system could be modified in such directions without endangering its coherence.

## 3. SCIENCE AND METAPHYSICS

There is in general a two-way relationship between science and metaphysics. In the first direction, science is one of the fields of inquiry from which metaphysics must draw. A metaphysical system must offer a plausible interpretation of the natural sciences, along with the data of other academic disciplines (psychology, history, religion, and so forth) and diverse types of human experience. In the reverse direction, metaphysical assumptions will, over a period of time, affect the kinds of phenomena that scientists study and the kinds of concepts they employ. Metaphysics will influence the broad conceptual frameworks that we earlier referred to as scientific paradigms.

There are many features of *contemporary science* with which process metaphysics is very congenial. Temporality, indeterminacy, and holism are characteristics of the microworld as understood by contemporary physics, a world that can be known only through observational interaction. Process thought rejects determinism, allows for alternative potentialities, and accepts the presence of chance as well as lawful relationships among events. In biology, especially in molecular biology, reductionistic and mechanistic approaches remain fruitful, but I have argued that there are irreducible properties of higher-level wholes, as process philosophy asserts. We have seen that information is contextual in character, whether it is transmitted by genes, by memory in brains, by symbolic language, or by cultural artifacts and institutions. Information is an improbable configuration, which is a message only when it is read off in relation to a wider context.

Process thought shares with *evolutionary biology* the assumption of historical continuity, including the continuity of nonhuman and human life. The process understanding of the psychosomatic unity of the human being and the social character of selfhood is consonant with the evidence from many fields of science. Process thought shares with ecology the themes of relationality and mutual interdependence. To both, nature is a community and not a machine.

Process categories can make an important contribution to *environmental ethics*. Human and nonhuman life are not separated by any absolute line. If other creatures are centers of experience, they too are of intrinsic value and not just of instrumental value to humanity. Yet there is a great difference between the richness of experience of a person and that of a mosquito, so they are not of equal intrinsic value. Another process theme with environmental implications is the idea of interdependence. Moreover, process thought leads to an emphasis on divine immanence in nature rather than the traditional emphasis on transcendence; this also encourages respect for nature.

Strong parallels exist between *systems theory* and process philosophy. Whitehead's thought may be compared with Ludwig von Bertalanffy's general systems theory and Ervin Laszlo's systems philosophy.[11] A common theme is hierarchical ordering of levels of organization. The context and the larger whole constrain the parts. Wholes possess a degree of autonomy, especially at higher levels; freedom increases with complexity and organization. In systems theory, information is context-dependent and expresses a limitation of possibilities. James Huchingson suggests that a Whiteheadian "actual entity" is like an information processing system selecting from among possibilities. Moreover, he proposes, we could think of God and the world as a coupled system with rich feedback loops. It is an open system, not a predetermined order. Cybernetics leads to flexible, provisional action and continual relevant adjustment, not the effecting of a detailed preset plan.[12] These all seem to me to be legitimate parallels, providing that we acknowledge the importance of feelings and purposes as well as conceptual information in process thought. Systems theory has had only limited success in representing the personal characteristics of human life.

Several questions might be raised about process thought in relation to science. Is the *subjective experience* of an entity, which is postulated in process metaphysics, accessible to scientific investigation? Does not science have to start from objective data, excluding anything subjective in the object of inquiry? Whitehead sometimes stresses the selectivity of science and the abstractive character of its concepts. It is "the fallacy of misplaced concreteness" to take scientific concepts as an exhaustive description of the real world. "Science can find no individual enjoyment in nature; science can find no aim in nature; science can find no creativity in nature; it finds mere rules of succession. These negations are true of natural science; they are inherent in its methodology."[13] On this reading, we must accept the limitations of science and supplement it by including it in a wider metaphysical synthesis that integrates diverse kinds of experience. This would also limit the contribution that process metaphysics might make to science.

Griffin has pointed out other passages in which Whitehead says that more adequate metaphysical categories are *in the interest of science itself,* and that scientific concepts are reformable.[14] Griffin suggests that if every entity is for itself a moment of experience, one would expect this to be reflected in observable behavior. We have noted the inadequacy of psychological behaviorism, which tries to avoid all reference to mental events. Ethologists use explanatory concepts referring to the mental life of animals. In an earlier chapter we noted that a group of organisms may first adopt a novel and adaptive pattern of behavior; at a later time, mutations that facilitate this behavior may be selected (the Baldwin effect). In such a case, the initiative and creativity of the organisms, rather than a random mutation, was the primary factor in initiating an evolutionary change. As we consider lower levels, how can we draw a sharp line at any point? Conversely, scientists adopting a process metaphysics might sometimes redirect research to problems formerly neglected and might propose new concepts and hypotheses to be tested against observations.

Scientists have been understandably wary of *concepts of purpose.* The idea of divine purpose in nature, especially the assumption of a precise design or plan, has sometimes cut short the search for natural causes. Reference to the purposes held by natural agents has at times hindered the progress of science. Aristotle, for example, said that falling bodies seek their natural resting place and that an oak seed seeks to become an oak. But process thinkers avoid these pitfalls. They hold that the behavior of inanimate objects can be explained entirely by efficient causation. They do argue that concepts of anticipation and purposeful behavior can in attenuated form be extended far down the scale of life, but this does not exclude the presence of efficient causes. The resistance of some biologists to any reference to purposes may be partly a legacy of atomistic and materialistic assumptions of the past. There are, to be sure, dangers in the anthropomorphic extension of human qualities to the nonhuman sphere, but there are also dangers in "mechanomorphic" attempts to explain everything with the concepts of physics and chemistry. On balance, then, process philosophy seems to be a promising attempt to provide a coherent system of concepts for interpreting a wide variety of phenomena in the world.

## III. PROCESS THEOLOGY

In looking at the theological significance of process thought we must first consider the writings of its most influential exponents, Whitehead and Hartshorne. We will then consider some Christian theologians who have explicitly used process categories. Last, we will examine the treatment of the problem of evil and suffering by process theologians.

### 1. THE ROLE OF GOD

In Whitehead's metaphysics, God has a threefold role in the unfolding of every event.[15] First, God is *the primordial ground of order.* God envisages the potential forms of relationships that are not chaotic but orderly, even before they are actualized. This aspect of God is an answer to the question, Why does the world have the particular type of order it has rather than some other type? This function of God seems to be automatic, passive, and unchanging; God would only be an abstract metaphysical principle, the impersonal structure of the world, "the inevitable ordering of things conceptually realized in the nature of God." But Whitehead's God selects possibilities for the "initial subjective aims" of particular entities. Such relevance presupposes God's knowledge of and responsiveness to the world.

Second, God is *the ground of novelty.* Here the question is, Why do new kinds of things come into existence (in evolutionary history, for instance) rather than merely repeat the patterns of their predecessors? "Apart from God," Whitehead writes, "there would be nothing new in the world, and no order in the world."[16] God presents novel possibilities, but there are many of these, so alternatives are left open. God elicits the self-creation of individual entities and thus allows for freedom as well as structure and directionality. By valuing particular potentialities to which creatures respond, God influences the world without determining it. New possibilities are open even for inanimate atoms, as their evolution into animate beings has disclosed. On the level of humanity, God's influence is the lure of ideals to be actualized, the persuasive vision of the good. God's goal is the harmonious achievement of value.

A third characteristic is that God is *influenced by events in the world* (Whitehead calls this "the consequent nature of God"). The central categories of process philosophy (temporality, interaction, mutual relatedness) apply also to God. God is temporal in the sense that the divine experience changes in receiving from the world and contributing to it. God's purposes and character are eternal, but God's knowledge of events changes as those events occur. God influences the creatures by being part of the data to which they respond. God is supremely sensitive to the world, supplementing its accomplishments by seeing them in relation to the infinite resources of potential forms and reflecting back to the world a specific and relevant influence. Whitehead occasionally uses personal images as well as more abstract principles to portray this action:

But the principle of universal relativity is not to be stopped at the consequent nature of God. This nature itself passes into the temporal world according to its gradation of relevance to the various concrescent occasions. . . . For the perfected actuality passes back into the temporal world, and qualifies this world so that each temporal actuality includes it as an immediate fact of relevant experience. For the kingdom of heaven is with us today. The action of the fourth phase is the love of God for the world. It is the particular providence for particular occasions. What is done in the world is transformed into a reality in heaven, and the reality in heaven passes back into the world. By reason of this reciprocal relation, the love in the world passes into the love in heaven, and floods back again into the world. In this sense, God is the great companion—the fellow-sufferer who understands.[17]

Charles Hartshorne was strongly influenced by Whitehead, but he uses a more familiar terminology and occasionally differs in emphasis. He maintains that classical Christianity attributed a one-sided perfection to God in exalting permanence over change, being over becoming, eternity over temporality, necessity over contingency, self-sufficiency over relatedness. He advocates *dipolar theism,* the view that God is both eternal and temporal (but in differing ways, so there is no contradiction in asserting both). God is eternal in character and purpose but changing in the content of experience. God's essential nature is not dependent on any particular world. God will always exist and be perfect in love, goodness, and wisdom. God is omniscient in knowing all reality—though not the future, which is undecided and hence inherently unknowable. Even aspects of the divine that change have a perfection of their own. God is not merely influenced by the world; God is "infinitely sensitive" and "ideally responsive." Divine love is supremely sympathetic participation in the world process.[18]

As compared to traditional theologians, Hartshorne does indeed qualify *God's sovereignty over nature.* God participates in the self-creation of other beings, but they have effective power too. Yet God is adequate to all needs, including the need of the creatures to make their own decisions. God does all that it would be good for God to do, but not all that it would be good for us in our freedom to do. God has power sufficient to influence the universe in the best way consistent with the divine purposes. The risks of evil might have been reduced by eliminating freedom, but positive opportunities for creative value would have been lost. God accepts the risks that are inescapably linked to the opportunities. Hartshorne holds that the world is in God (*panentheism*), a view that neither identifies God with the world (*pantheism*) nor separates God from the world (*theism*). "God includes the world but is more than the world."[19]

## 2. GOD'S ACTION IN THE WORLD

Between God and the world there is interdependence and reciprocity, according to Whitehead, but the relationship is not symmetrical. God is affected by the world, but God alone is everlasting and does not perish. Though not self-sufficient or impassible, God is not totally within the temporal order, and God's basic purposes are unchanging. Divine immanence is thus more strongly emphasized than transcendence, yet God's freedom and relative independence are defended, along with priority in status. For nothing comes into being apart from God. Within the cosmic community, God has a unique and direct relationship to each member. God is omnipresent, a universal influence, one who experiences all actualities and preserves their achievements eternally.[20]

Whitehead portrays God's activity as more akin to *persuasion* than to compulsion. God does not determine the outcome of events or violate the self-creation of all beings. God is never the sole cause of an event but is one influence among others. Divine love, like love between human beings, is a significant influence that is causally effective, making a difference in the activity of other beings but not sacrificing their freedom. The power of love consists in its ability to evoke a response while yet respecting the integrity of the other. Thus causality within interpersonal relationships, rather than mechanical force, seems to provide the basic analogy for God's relation to the world. Whitehead strongly rejects the coercive element he finds in traditional theism. The rejection appears to be partly based on moral grounds (coercion is on a lower ethical plane than persuasion) and partly on metaphysical grounds (divine determination is incompatible with creaturely freedom).

For Whitehead, God's action is *the evocation of response.* Since human capacity for response far exceeds that of other beings, it is in human life that God's influence can be most effective. God's ability to engender creative change in lower beings seems to be limited. God is always one factor among others, and particularly with respect to low-level beings, in which experience is rudimentary and creativity is minimal, this power seems to be negligible. Insofar as natural agents exercise causal efficacy, God's ability to compel change is thereby restricted. But we must remember that God is not absent from events that monotonously repeat their past, for God is the ground of order as well as novelty. At low levels, God's novel action may be beyond detection, though signs of it may be present in the long sweep of cosmic history and emergent evolution. Even in contributing to novelty, God always acts along with other causes. The Whiteheadian analysis allows for the actions of a multiplicity of agents.

Whitehead modifies the traditional view of *God as creator,* but he does not totally repudiate it. He disavows creation out of nothing (*ex nihilo*) in an act of absolute origination but offers a version of continuous creation. No entity comes into being apart from God, and no materials are given to God from some other source. "He is not *before* all creation but *with* all creation."[21] Whitehead suggests that there may have been many cosmic epochs with differing forms of order. God always acts along with other causes, and yet everything depends on God for its existence. God provides all initial aims, and "in this sense he can be termed the creator of each temporal actual entity."[22] God evokes new subjects into being and preserves their achievements and is thus both the source and conserver of all finite values. While creativity is universally present in the self-creation of every entity, God is the primary instance of creativity and is active in all its instances.

In Whitehead's view, God has *priority of status* over all else, though not absolute temporal priority. God was never without a universe, and in every moment there is given to God a world that has to some extent determined itself. But this does not represent an ultimate dualism; this is not Plato's God struggling to impose form on recalcitrant matter. Whitehead attributes to God the all-decisive role in the creation of each new occasion, namely provision of its initial aim. Every occasion is dependent on God for its existence as well as for the order of possibilities it can actualize.

Does the role of God in process thought conflict with *the assumptions of science*? In the past, God has been invoked to explain a variety of phenomena for which no scientific explanation was available. "The God of the gaps" has, of course, been a losing proposition, as one gap after another was filled by new scientific advances. In the Whiteheadian view, however, God does not intervene at discrete points but is present in all events in a role different from that of natural causes. God is the source of order and novelty, an answer to a different sort of question than the questions that science answers. We can speak of God acting, but God always acts with and through other entities rather than by acting alone as a substitute for their actions.

Whereas some theologians identify God's role with order, and others with violations of order, for Whitehead God is involved in *both order and novelty*. Order arises from God's structuring of possibilities and from the entity's conformation to its past. Novelty arises from God's offering of alternative possibilities and from the entity's self-creation. This means that no event can be attributed solely to God. God's role in the world is not readily detectable. The process theologian Daniel Williams writes,

God's causality is exercised in, through, and with all other causes operating. There is no demand here to factor out what God is adding to the stream of events apart from those events. But there is the assignment of specific functions to God's causality. . . . Every "act of God" is presented to us in, through, and with the complex of human nature and life in which we are. When we say God elected Israel, or that he sends his rain on the just and the unjust, we must not ignore the complex analysis of assignable causes and factors in Israel's history or in the cosmic record of rainfall. We have no way of extricating the acts of God from their involvement in the activities of the world. To assign any particular historical event to God's specific action in the world is to risk ultimate judgment on our assertions. Faith leads us to take the risk.[23]

At *lower levels,* especially in the inanimate world, God's action is almost entirely confined to the maintenance of the order whose regularities are precisely those studied by the scientist. God's purpose for low-level beings is that they be orderly; God's gift is the structuredness of the possibilities they exemplify. At lower levels, where law predominates over creativity and efficient causes are more important than final causes, God's novel action is beyond detection. Moreover, even when there is novelty at higher levels, God always acts along with other causes, qualifying but not abrogating their operation. This seems to limit God's power severely, as compared to traditional ideas of omnipotence. But it is consistent with our understanding of evolution as a long, slow, gradual process over billions of years. Each stage is built on previous stages and supports the next stage. Complex forms presuppose simple ones. Life had to await appropriate conditions. Cosmic history resembles a long trial-and-error experiment more than a detailed predetermined plan. Process thought holds that God works patiently, gently, and unobtrusively.

If God does not act unilaterally but only through the responses of other beings, we would expect the divine influence to be more effective at *higher levels* where creativity and purposeful goals are more prominent. It is not surprising that the rate of evolutionary change accelerated in early human and then cultural history. In human life, in religious experience, and in the rise of the major religious traditions—especially in the biblical tradition and the person of Christ—God's influence and human response could occur in unprecedented ways. The Whiteheadian understanding of God, in short, is consistent with what we know about biological and human history. But is it consistent with the biblical tradition?

## 3. CHRISTIAN PROCESS THEOLOGY

Whitehead and Hartshorne were primarily philosophers, though both were influenced by Christian ideas. A number of theologians have used process categories in reformulating specifically Christian beliefs in the contemporary world. Cobb and Griffin express the dipolar character of process theism by speaking of God as *creative-responsive love.* God as creative is the primordial source of order and novelty, which can be identified with the biblical concept of *logos* as rational principle and divine Word. God as responsive is temporal and affected by the world. These qualities are particularly evident in the message and life of Christ and in the idea of the Holy Spirit as God's presence in nature and in the community.[24]

The process view does allow for *particular divine initiatives.* If God supplies distinctive initial aims to each new entity, no event is wholly an act of God, but every event is an act of God to some extent. There is thus a structural similarity between God's actions in nonhuman and human life, but there are also important differences. God's basic *modus operandi* is the same throughout, but the consequences will vary widely between levels of being.

In *the human sphere,* God builds on the past, including existing cultural traditions, and depends on the free responses of individuals and communities.

God loves all equally, yet that love may be revealed more decisively in one tradition or person than another. God calls all, but people respond in diverse ways. Some experiences of God's grace may be felt with exceptional power, and an individual may have an unusual commitment to the fulfillment of God's will. In process theology we can discuss God's action in nature, in religious experience, and in Christ, using a common set of concepts while recognizing the distinctive features of each. Continuing creation and redemption are brought within a single framework.

Cobb and Griffin can thus speak of *Christ as God's supreme act.* In Israel there was already a tradition of divine initiative and human response, which could be carried further. Christ's message and life were rooted in this past and in God's new aims for him, and he powerfully expressed God's purposes and love. Christ can be taken as incarnation of the *logos,* the universal source of order, novelty, and creative transformation wherever they occur. In Christ we see a specific and crucial instance of a more general divine action. But Christ's free decision and faithful response were also needed to actualize God's aims for him, so the full humanity of Christ was not compromised. Here the character of God as persuasive and vulnerable love is evident. Christ was subject to the same conditions and limitations as were other persons but was unique in the content of God's aims for him and in his actualization of those aims. This was not a discontinuous and coercive intrusion from outside, but the decisive instance of God's creative presence throughout the world; he is thus our clue to that wider presence. If we see Christ's life and his vision of God as revealing the nature of reality, we can be open to the power of creative transformation in our own lives.[25]

Here the importance of *revelation in history* is evident. Lewis Ford points out that in the process view God's action in the world is contingent on what happens in the world. If God has interacted historically, we can learn about this only from the particularities of history and not from the general structures of reality, which metaphysics studies.[26] Because historical events are unique and unpredictable, they cannot be deduced from universal principles, as we saw in chapter 6. But the particular work of God as Redeemer must be consistent with the broader work of God as Creator. As Paul Sponheim puts it, our metaphysics must "provide structural possibilities for the illumination of God's particular activity."[27]

I submit that it is in the biblical idea of *the Spirit* that we find the closest parallels to the process understanding of God's presence in the world and in Christ. We have seen that in the Bible the Spirit was associated with the initial creation and with the continuing creation of the creatures: "When thou sendest forth thy Spirit, they are created." The Spirit inspires the prophets (for example, Isa. 42:1) and is present in worship and prayer: "Take not thy holy Spirit from me" (Ps. 51:11). Christ received the Spirit at his baptism (Mark 1:10), and the early community received it at Pentecost (Acts 2). In the previous chapter, I cited Lampe's argument for understanding Christ as inspired by the Spirit. This would allow us to acknowledge God's particular activity in Christ within the context of God's activity in nature, in religious experience, and in other religious traditions. In each case grace operates through and within natural structures rather than by replacing or superseding them.

Let us look at some implications of process theology for *religious life*. Marjorie Suchocki has used process categories to understand and express the Christian experience of sin and redemption. After setting forth a social and relational view of reality, she defines sin as the violation of relationships. It is an absolutizing of the self and a denial of interdependence. Sin is experienced, not only in individual alienation from God and other people, but also in social structures of injustice and exploitation. Suchocki holds that redemption is release from the prison of the detached self. God's love is also a judgment on the structures that isolate us from each other. In Christ's life, God's love was embodied and expressed. In him we see at work a transformative power stronger than death, a power that can bring reconciliation into our lives.[28]

In the process framework, the goal of *prayer* is openness and responsiveness to the divine call. It involves conforming one's decisions to the possibilities offered by God, or, in traditional terms, "doing the will of God." God's will here is the achievement of value and harmony among all beings, the realization of inclusive love. Such love may sometimes be identified with traditional teachings and church authorities, but it may sometimes require us to question these teachings and authorities. The Spirit leads us in unexpected ways in healing our brokenness as individuals and as a society. Prayer can also be an occasion of wonder and gratitude for life as a gift and a time of self-examination and confession of our failure to respond to the call of inclusive love.[29]

The Jewish existentialist Martin Buber urges us to look on our lives as *a dialogue with God* in which we respond with our actions. In every event we are addressed by God. This does not mean that everything that happens is God's will or is a result of God's action alone. But we can ask ourselves what God might be saying to us in every event. Our response occurs in "the speech of our lives" and not just in our words. Buber seeks the sanctification of everyday life, through which we are in dialogue with the Eternal Thou.[30] It seems to me that this theme in Buber's writing is consistent with the process understanding of living in God's presence.

A significant contribution of process thought is a concept of *responsible selfhood,* which avoids a soul/body dualism. The previous chapter referred to the spirit/matter and soul/body dualisms in medieval Christianity, which seem to have been more indebted to Greek than to biblical sources. The Christian tradition has too often encouraged a negative asceticism, an alienation from the body, and a concern only for the salvation of the soul. More recently, many people in Western culture have reacted against the repression of the body and have sought an uncontrolled sensuality. The process view avoids both these extremes. It acknowledges our embodiment and asserts that bodily events enter into each moment of experience. Process writers encourage respect for the body but also assert human freedom, self-determination, and the power of personal and social goals beyond bodily gratification. Responsible selfhood is a holistic concept that includes but transcends the body.

Process thought makes common cause with *feminism* in rejecting the dualisms that have led to hierarchical domination. Feminists have pointed to the links between three forms of dualism: man/woman, mind/body, and humanity/nature. The first term of each pair has in the past been assumed to be superior to the second. The three dualisms support each other because the first terms (man, mind, humanity) have been associated together, as are the second set of terms (woman, body, nature). Feminists usually agree with process thinkers, not only in rejecting these dualisms, but in replacing them with a holistic relationality and an inclusive mutuality. They also agree in insisting on openness and creativity in human self-determination and in seeking freedom from the hierarchical roles of the past. Feminists bring an active commitment to social change and human liberation, which may be more influential than the abstract writings of some process theologians.[31]

Feminists and process writers also agree in criticizing the *patriarchal* and *monarchical* view of God expressed in traditional ideas of omnipotence. Feminists value the caring and nurturing aspects of both human nature and the divine. Whitehead explicitly rejected the image of God as an imperial ruler and spoke of God's "tender care that nothing be lost" and "the Galilean vision of humility." God's consequent nature is receptive and empathetic as well as active. One reason for developing a theology of the Holy Spirit today is that the Spirit has few associations with masculine imagery. Process thought thus has important implications for both theological formulation and religious life.

## 4. THE PROBLEM OF EVIL AND SUFFERING

The problem of evil and suffering is so important theologically that we should consider alternative responses to it before looking at the distinctive position of process theologians. The classical question of *theodicy* is, Why would an all-good and all-powerful God allow widespread evil and suffering? We have seen that pain, conflict, and death are pervasive in evolutionary history and in nonhuman nature today. Suffering, violence, and tragic evil have been present throughout human history. The suffering of innocent children is a particular challenge to religious faith, as seen in several poignant scenes in modern literature. Ivan in Dostoevski's *Brothers Karamazov*, Elie Wiesel in his autobiographical novel *Night*, and Dr. Rieux in Camus's *The Plague* all protest the agonizing death of an innocent child. Father Paneloux says to Rieux, "Perhaps we should love what we cannot understand," and Rieux replies, "No, Father. I've a very different idea of love. And until my dying day I shall refuse to love a scheme of things in which children are put to torture."[32] The death of six million Jews in Nazi extermination camps presents the starkest example of unmitigated evil and suffering, and it challenges the ideas of God's justice and providential care, which both the Jewish and Christian traditions have held.

The problem does not arise in *Buddhism* or *Hinduism,* for in those traditions all suffering is deserved. According to the impersonal law of *karma,* all souls are reborn (reincarnated) in human or animal forms according to their just deserts. Any suffering in this life is merited by actions in previous lives. There is no purposeful creator God on whom our suffering might be blamed. Moreover, in Hinduism suffering belongs to the phenomenal world of *maya* (illusion), which is not ultimately real. Suffering can be escaped when we realize the identity of the soul (atman) with the all-inclusive One (Brahman). In Buddhism, suffering is a product of our egocentric attachments and desires, and it is overcome in nonattachment and the dissolution of the self that occurs in enlightenment.[33]

The most influential Christian position was formulated by Augustine, who held that all evil and suffering are *the consequences of human sin* in Adam and his successors. Sin is misused freedom and cannot be blamed on God. Nature and humanity were created perfect but were corrupted by Adam's fall, through which death and disharmony entered the world. Human suffering is not unjust, according to Augustine, for we all deserve punishment for sin, even if some are by God's grace spared such punishment. Moreover, the righteous will be rewarded and the wicked punished in a future life, vindicating God's justice in the long run. Similar views can be found earlier in the writings of Paul and later (with some variations) in Aquinas, Luther, Calvin, and other classical theologians. I have suggested, however, that neither a primeval state of perfection nor a historical fall are credible today. I argued that the story of Adam should be taken as a symbolic statement of the estrangement of each of us from God, neighbor, self, and nature. Death and suffering were inescapable features of an evolutionary process long before the appearance of humanity.

Some theodicies minimize *the reality of evil* by interpreting it as a discipline or a test of faith. Evil would then be a temporary means to good ends. Other writers defend the reality of evil and the omnipotence of God, and they end by compromising *the goodness of God.* If everything that happens is God's will, then God is responsible for evil. In a more sophisticated version, if God is the source of all that is, then evil as well as good must in some sense be present in God. Hegel, Berdyaev, and Tillich are among the authors who have spoken of positivity and negativity within the Godhead. Still others have asserted all three components of the classical theodicy problem and have concluded that there is no rational solution. It is *a mystery* that we do not understand but that we should accept in faith and submission to God. Most Christian theodicies have continued to defend God's goodness and the reality of evil but have in some way qualified *God's power.* The most extreme limitation of God's power would be the existence of a cosmic principle of evil. Zoroastrianism and Manichaeism, for example, pictured a cosmic struggle between the forces of light and the forces of darkness, but the church fathers rejected such an ultimate dualism. (Satan was said to be a fallen angel who is no permanent threat to God.)

Many modern Christian theodicies have asserted God's *voluntary self-limitation* in order to effect three goals:

1. *Human Freedom.* Augustine said that sin in Adam and his successors was freely chosen. However, human freedom is difficult to reconcile with Augustinian ideas of original sin and predestination. Later interpreters held that freedom requires a genuine choice of good or evil, and therefore God had to allow the possibility that individuals would choose evil. In a world of mutual interdependence, those choices could hurt other individuals (even on the scale of the Holocaust). But could God not have created beings who were free to sin but would never do so? No, according to the "free-will defense," for virtues come into being only in the moral struggle of real decisions, not ready-made by divine fiat. Further, God wants our free response of love, not actions to which we have no alternatives.[34]

2. *Laws of Nature.* There must be dependable regularities in the world if we are to make responsible decisions about the consequences of our actions. An orderly world reflects God's rationality and dependability. Moreover, the growth of human knowledge would be impossible without the existence of such regularities. Neither moral character nor scientific knowledge would be possible if God intervened frequently to save us from suffering. Earthquake disasters and cancer are products of such natural laws, not the result of divine punishment. Animal pain was an inescapable concomitant of increased sentience, and it facilitated the avoidance of danger, which contributed to evolutionary survival.

3. *Moral Growth.* Suffering often has an educational value. The trials of ancient Israel were seen as "the furnace of affliction" in which, as with a precious metal, refinement could occur. Paul said that "suffering produces endurance, and endurance produces character, and character produces hope" (Rom. 5:3). Sometimes undeserved suffering can have a redemptive effect on others, as in the suffering servant passages of Isaiah and the Christian understanding of the cross. More generally, moral courage would be impossible without danger, temptation, and struggle. The suffering of others also calls forth our sympathy and love.

John Hick has developed this idea of *moral growth*. He traces his view back to Irenaeus in the second century, who said that humanity was not created perfect but imperfect with an opportunity for moral development. Irenaeus held that perfection could lie only in the future, not in the past. Hick sees this as consistent with an evolutionary view in which animal instinct develops into early human aggression and then into greater human maturity, moral insight, and capacity for love. The world is a place of "soul-making," an appropriate environment for moral action. In a pain-free world our decisions would have no harmful consequences. Moral virtues have to be acquired in the long hard struggle of life. Only in a world of challenge and response can the higher potentialities of personality be realized. Hick recognizes that growth is not completed in this life, and he holds that it will continue in the afterlife. In the end, all people will be won over by the infinite love of God. A limitless good beyond this world is adequate justification for the painful process of preparing for it.[35]

Hick's view qualifies God's power in practice but not in principle. God's power is infinite, but it is *voluntarily self-limited* for the sake of human growth. Hick's theodicy deals only with human suffering and says nothing about subhuman pain or the waste of billions of years preparing for humanity. Could these not have been avoided, if God is omnipotent? Again, does moral growth require the intensity and pervasiveness of evil and suffering we see around us? Some people may be strengthened by suffering, but others are broken and embittered by it. The world may be a moral gymnasium or a school for character, but some people seem to have little chance of succeeding in it. Hick has minimized the destructiveness of evil to justify its presence. He also has to invoke the afterlife to justify the injustices in this life.

Process theologians share many of Hick's ideas but go further in *the limitation of God's power.* Griffin rejects creation *ex nihilo* and speaks of the continuing creation of order out of chaos. Evolution is a long, slow, step-by-step process. Inescapable struggle and conflict have taken place because there has always been a multiplicity of beings with at least some power of their own. There were also inescapable correlations in evolutionary advance. With greater intensity of experience came a greater capacity for enjoyment, but at the same time a greater capacity for suffering. Greater power of self-determination goes hand-in-hand with greater power to be affected by others. Interdependence allows us to benefit from others but also to be harmed by them. These are metaphysically necessary correlations, which would obtain in any world. Even God could not escape them, though these are principles that belong to the divine essence and are not external conditions imposed on God.[36]

Griffin maintains that in relation to low-grade entities God's influence is very limited, and changes occur only over a long period of evolutionary history. God cannot stop the bullet speeding toward your head, because a bullet is an aggregate and not a unified occasion of experience susceptible to God's persuasion. Human beings can change more rapidly, but they can also deviate more dramatically from God's aims. Griffin argues that God is not morally blameworthy or directly responsible for particular evils, which arise from the powers of the creatures. The world never fully embodies God's will, which is for the good alone. But there is no ultimate dualism. Evil and suffering could have been avoided only by refraining from creating, which is contrary to the divine nature; in that sense, God is ultimately responsible for evil. The positive opportunities, however, were worth the risks that went with them.

Process thought can contribute not only to the theoretical explanation of the existence of suffering but also to the practical question of how we respond to it. One theme in traditional Christian thought is that *God shares in our suffering* and stands with us in it. One meaning of the cross is that God participates in human suffering. Many Christians have felt that God was especially near in times of suffering. Classical theology, however, has said that God is impassible, unaffected by us, and incapable of suffering. At this point the process understanding of God's consequent nature allows a stronger assertion that God suffers with us in our suffering. God is with us and for us, empowering us in our present lives.

But process thinkers also defend immortality in one of two forms. *Objective immortality* is our participation in God's consequent nature, whereby God's life is permanently enriched. Our lives are meaningful because they are preserved everlastingly in God's experience, in which evil is transmuted and the good is saved and woven into the harmony of the larger whole. God's goal is not the completed achievement of a static final realm, but rather a continuing advance toward richer and more harmonious relationships. Other process writers defend *subjective immortality,* in which the human self continues as a center of experience in a radically different environment but amid continuing change rather than a changeless eternity. (Whitehead said that this would be consistent with his metaphysics, though he himself accepted only objective immortality.) Cobb speculates that we might picture a future life, neither as absorption into God nor as the survival of individuals in isolation, but as a new kind of community transcending individuality.[37]

Process thought is consistent with recent themes in science. It also offers some distinctive insights to theology. A final evaluation of its theological adequacy must await a comparison with some current theological alternatives in the final chapter.

## CHAPTER 12

# God and Nature

How can God act if the world is governed by scientific laws? What is God's relation to the causal processes of nature? Any answer to such questions presupposes a view of nature as well as a view of God's activity. In this chapter we start from the theological side, examining some of the ways in which God's action in the natural order is currently portrayed and then evaluating these interpretations in the light of our previous conclusions. We will explore several answers to these questions within the Christian tradition.[1]

Our answers are crucial to the intellectual task of articulating a theology of nature. Our understanding of God's relation to nature also has practical implications for the way we treat the environment in the face of the crises that threaten it today. In the first section, classical theism is discussed. Then some alternatives are examined: God as determiner of indeterminacies, God as communicator of information, God's self-limitation, God as agent, and the world as God's body. In the final section, the strengths and weaknesses of process theism are analyzed. Each of these views, I argue, holds a dominant model of God's relation to the world, as summarized in figure 5.

Fig. 5 Models of God's Role in Nature

| THEOLOGY | DOMINANT MODEL | CONCEPTUAL ELABORATION |
|---|---|---|
| Classical | Ruler-Kingdom | Ommipotent, omniscient, unchanging sovereign |
| Deist | Clockmaker-Clock | Designer of a law-abiding world |
| Neo-Thomist | Workman-Tool | Primary cause working through secondary causes |
| Quantum | Determiner of Indeterminacies | Actualizer of potentialities |
| Word (*logos*) | Speaker-Hearer | Communicator of information |
| Kenotic | Parent-Child | Voluntary self-limitation and vulnerability |
| Linguistic | Agent-Action | Events in the world as God's action |
| Embodiment | Person-Body | The world as God's body |
| Process | Leader-Community | Creative participant in the cosmic community |

# I. CLASSICAL THEISM

In earlier chapters we saw that the Bible includes a great variety of models of God. In relation to nature, God is represented as a purposeful designer imposing order on chaos, a potter or craftsman making an artifact, and an architect setting out the foundations of a building. Again, God is a life-giving Spirit at work throughout nature and a communicator expressing meaning and rational structure through the divine Word. God is Lord and King, ruling both history and nature to effect intended purposes. In relation to Israel, God is the liberator delivering the community from bondage and the judge dedicated to righteousness and justice. In relation to individuals, God is the judge but also the careful shepherd, the forgiving father and (more rarely) the nurturing mother. God is also the redeemer who brings new wholeness to communities and individuals—and even to nature in the final fulfillment.

In subsequent history, some of these models were emphasized and developed in theological concepts and systematic doctrines, while others held only subordinate roles. We look first at the monarchical model of divine sovereignty in medieval and Reformation theology. We then consider recent neo-Thomist and neo-Reformation writers who hold that God as primary cause works through the lawful secondary causes, which science studies.

## 1. THE MONARCHICAL MODEL

In the Middle Ages, biblical and Aristotelian ideas were brought together, especially in the writings of Thomas Aquinas, which were so influential in later Catholic theology. The biblical model of God as king and ruler was elaborated into formal theological doctrines of divine omnipotence and omniscience. The dominant model was that of the absolute monarch ruling over his kingdom, though other models were also present. A similar view of God was prominent in the Reformation, particularly in Calvin's emphasis on divine sovereignty and predestination. These two themes are also prominent in Islamic thought.

In the classical doctrine of divine *omnipotence,* God governs and rules the world in providential wisdom. All events are totally subordinate to God's will and power. Foreordination was said to involve not only foreknowledge but also the predetermination of every event. Both medieval Thomism and Reformation Protestantism held that God intervenes miraculously as a direct cause of some events, in addition to a more usual action of working through secondary natural causes. There is a strictly asymmetrical, one-way relation: God affects the world, but the world does not affect a God who is eternal, unchanging, and impassible.

God's *eternity* was, of course, a biblical theme, and the human quest for the security of a permanence beyond change is a perennial one. But the exclusion of all temporality from God's nature seems to have been indebted mainly to Greek thought. Plato had pictured a realm of eternal forms and timeless truth, imperfectly reflected in the world; the perfect was the unchanging. Aristotle had spoken of God as the Unmoved Mover, the immutable Absolute.

Aquinas argued that God is *impassible,* unaffected by the world. God loves only in the sense of doing good things for us, but without passion or emotion. God's being is wholly self-sufficient and independent of the world and receives nothing from it. Since God knows all events in advance and controls every detail, divine knowledge is unchanging, and in God there is no element of responsiveness. In the last analysis, the passage of time is unreal to God, for whom all time is spread out simultaneously.[2] All of this seems to contrast with the dynamic God of the Bible who is intimately involved in Israel's history and responds passionately to its changing situations.

To be sure, other themes qualified this image of divine sovereignty. God's control was never sheer power, for it was always the power of love. Dante ends *The Divine Comedy* with a vision of God as "the Love that moves the Sun and other stars."[3] Classical theism indeed emphasized transcendence, and God was said to act occasionally by supernatural intervention from outside nature. But classical theism also defended divine immanence. God is preeminently present in the incarnation, the sacraments, and the life of the church, but the Holy Spirit animates nature as well as human life. The metaphysical dualism of spirit and matter was mitigated insofar as the spiritual realm permeates the material realm.

A number of authors in this century have defended the idea of God's *immutability* and *impassibility.* E. L. Mascall maintains that God is timeless and sees all time simultaneously. We cannot add anything, he says, to God's eternal perfection. The highest form of love is totally disinterested and uninvolved.[4] Similarly, H. P. Owen holds that God does not change in any way. God does respond to the needs of the world but without being changed internally by such a response.[5] Richard Creel argues that God is immutable in nature, in will, in feeling, and in knowledge of possibilities. God is self-sufficient, and the world is strictly unnecessary for the divine being. God's joy and inner life are unaffected by the world. God could not be grieved by our choices. Creel grants that God's knowledge of actualities must change as they occur, but God has decided in advance on appropriate responses to deal with all possible events; those responses can be implemented without any change on God's part.[6]

Clearly, much can be said in support of a monarchical model, which focuses on God's power. It is in accord with the awe and mystery that we earlier identified with numinous religious experience. Supreme power, if combined with supreme goodness, is an attribute that makes worship appropriate. It is also in accord with some (but not all) features of the biblical witness. The ideas of transcendence and sovereignty are indeed present in the creation story and other biblical passages (Isa. 6 and 40–48, or Job 38–41, for example). In the classical view, God's power was uniquely manifest in the resurrection (though sometimes this was articulated in ways that are difficult to reconcile with the message of Christ's teachings, life, and the cross). Some aspects of science may also accord well with the monarchical model, especially the power and mystery of the Big Bang, the immense sweep of cosmic history, and the marvel of biological and human life. But six problems with this model lead many theologians to qualify, modify, or reject it.

*1. Human Freedom.* Divine omnipotence and predestination appear incompatible with the existence of genuine alternatives in human choice. No subtleties in distinguishing foreknowledge from foreordination seem to be able to circumvent this basic contradiction. Humanity's total dependence on and submission to an authoritarian God is also in tension with human responsibility and maturity; these ideas too often have resulted in the repression rather than the fulfillment of human creativity. If all power is on God's side, what powers are assignable to humanity?

*2. Evil and Suffering.* In the previous chapter we explored the problem of theodicy: Why would a good and omnipotent God allow evil and suffering? We saw that solutions that minimize the reality of evil and suffering are inconsistent with human experience. Nor can evil and suffering be taken as the consequences of Adam's fall if we accept evolutionary science. But if omnipotence is defended, and everything that happens is God's will, then God is responsible for evil and suffering, and God's goodness is compromised. We saw that many current theodicies refer to God's voluntary self-limitation in the interest of human freedom, the lawfulness of nature, or a world suitable for moral growth. These solutions are considered again in section II below, but we can note here that they entail a major qualification of the monarchical model, if not a rejection of it.

*3. Patriarchy.* The characteristics of the monarchical God are those our culture identifies as "masculine" virtues: power, control, independence, rationality, and impassibility, rather than what are stereotyped as "feminine" virtues: nurturance, responsiveness, interdependence, and emotional sensitivity. The identification of God with "masculine" qualities seems to reflect the biases of a patriarchal culture, and this model of God has in turn been used to justify male dominance in society.

*4. Religious Intolerance.* The exaltation of God's power encouraged an exclusivist view of revelation. Taken with a hierarchical understanding of the authority of the church, it was used to support absolute claims to religious truth. When coupled with political and military power, it led to religious persecution, crusades, holy wars, and colonial imperialism, all in God's name. Such views are a continuing danger in a world of religious pluralism and nuclear weapons.

*5. An Evolutionary World.* During the centuries when the monarchical model was formulated, a static and hierarchical view of reality was assumed. The world was accepted as a fixed order whose basic forms were unchanging, given once for all. This tended to reinforce the idea of creation *ex nihilo* in an absolute beginning; the biblical idea of continuing creation was virtually ignored. Each lower form served the higher in the hierarchy: God/man/woman/animal/plant. This fixed order was unified by God's sovereign power and omniscient plan. These assumptions were, of course, challenged by evolution.

*6. Law and Chance in Nature.* With the rise of modern science, the idea of supernatural intervention in nature seemed increasingly dubious. By the eighteenth century, God's wisdom and power were seen only in the initial design of the universe, not in its continuing governance. Deism took seriously the lawfulness of nature at the price of relegating God's activity to the distant past. We have seen that more recently the role of chance has called into question both the determinism of predestination and the determinism of lawful causes.

## 2. PRIMARY AND SECONDARY CAUSES

In earlier chapters we saw that with the growth of science nature was increasingly viewed as a law-abiding machine. God was the clockmaker and the world was the clock—an autonomous and self-sufficient mechanism. The unfailing rule of law, not miraculous intervention, is the evidence of divine benevolence. Providence is expressed not by action in particular events but by the total cosmic design, the overall structure and order of the world.[7] This was the inactive God of deism, who started the mechanism and then let it run by itself. Nature was viewed as a self-contained system whose interactions are to be exhaustively accounted for in the purely natural terms of lawful cause and effect. And if nature apart from humanity is just a complicated machine, it has no rights or interests or intrinsic value over against us, and we can exploit it to our own advantage.

More recently, a number of neo-Thomist authors have tried to defend divine omnipotence and the lawful world of science without accepting the inactive God of deism. They do so by developing the Thomistic distinction between *primary* and *secondary causes,* which allows God a continuing role. God as primary cause works through the secondary causes that science describes. Étienne Gilson invokes the model of a worker and a tool. In God's hands "creatures are like a tool in the hands of the workman." One can say that an ax cuts the wood or that the man using the ax cuts the wood; each produces the whole effect. Unlike the woodsman, though, God has conferred on all things their forms and their distinctive powers.[8]

The first level of God's action in nature is *conservation.* If God ceased to sustain the world, it would lapse again into nothingness. Moreover, the powers of natural agents require a continual influx of divine power to be efficacious. Powers are only potentialities until they are actualized; every potency must be moved to act by God. Divine *concurrence* includes a more direct control over the actions of natural agents. God operates in the operation of created agents. God foresees and predetermines every detail in the world, ordering and governing every occurrence. This foreknowledge is itself the cause of all things.

Gilson also insists, however, on the reality of *secondary causes.* It is misguided to say that God is the only cause or that what appear to be natural causes are only the occasions on which God produces the effects. God delegates causal efficacy to the creatures. There are genuine centers of activity, interrelated and dependent on each other as well as on God. The conviction of the regularity of such cause-effect relationships provides a basis for science. Lawfulness obtains because each being has its essence, its natural way of behaving, and so it always produces the same effect.[9]

How then can the same effect be attributed to both *divine* and *natural* causality? The resolution must start by recognizing that these are not two actions doing essentially the same thing, not two causes on the same level, each contributing to part of the effect. Rather, the whole effect is produced by both divine and natural causes, but under completely different aspects. Two causes can both be operative if one is instrumental to the other. God is primary cause, in a different order from all instrumental secondary causes. God sometimes produces effects directly, as in the case of miracles, but usually works through natural causes.

Does such divine control preclude *contingency* and *human freedom*? As Garrigou-Lagrange puts it, God "infallibly moves the will to determine itself freely to act." The apparent inconsistency of a foreordained free choice, which will "infallibly come to be contingently," is resolved as follows. A contingent event is defined as one that is not uniquely determined by its natural causes. If God were merely to calculate the future from the present, as we would have to, God could not know the future. Since God is eternal, however, the future is present to God as it will actually be, a single definite outcome. God, being above time and having unchanging knowledge, does not know the future as potentially and indeterminately contained in its worldly causes, but determinately as specified in the eternal divine decree. Within the world, an act is uncertain before it takes place. But for God there is no "before"; for God it has taken place.[10]

In neo-Thomist thought, moreover, *divine causality* is rich and many-faceted, far from any simple mechanical coercion. God is the origin of form and matter but also has a role in final causation. Each being is given a natural inclination, which is genuinely its own but which also expresses God's purposes. God endows every creature with an intrinsic nature and a way of acting and leaves it free to follow the goal toward which it strives. Divine causality can occur at various levels. In the case of the human will, God moves it from within, inclining it toward the good, calling forth its own powers, so its free acts remain its own. Here God's influence is the final causality of attraction to the good, and God's action becomes the power of love. This seems to me a more apt analogy than "instrumental causes" (such as worker and tool) in which the instrument is totally subordinated to the user. These aspects of neo-Thomism have much in common with process thought.

As another example, consider the discussion of *double agency* by the Anglican theologian Austin Farrer. "God's agency must actually be such as to work omnipotently on, in and through creaturely agencies, without either forcing them or competing with them." God acts through the matrix of secondary causes and is manifest only in the overall resulting pattern. "He does not impose an order against the grain of things, but makes them follow their own bent and work out the world by being themselves. . . . He makes the multitude of created forces make the world in the process of making or being themselves."[11] Primary and secondary causes operate at totally different levels, according to Farrer. We can't say anything about *how* God acts; there are no "causal joints" between infinite and finite action and no gaps in the scientific account. So, too, the free act of a person can at the same time be ascribed to the person and to the grace of God acting in human life.

Neo-Reformation (neo-orthodox) writers have also used the idea of primary and secondary causes to defend *divine sovereignty over nature*. Karl Barth asserts that God "rules unconditionally and irresistibly in all occurrence." Nature is God's "servant," the "instrument of his purposes." God controls, orders, and determines, for "nothing can be done except the will of God." God foreknows and also predetermines and foreordains. "The operation of this God," Barth writes, "is as sovereign as Calvinist teaching describes it. In the strictest sense it is predestinating."[12]

Barth insists, however, that divine omnipotence must always be considered in the light of God's action in Christ. He feels that both Aquinas and Calvin represented sovereignty as absolute power in the abstract, which tended toward metaphysical necessity or arbitrary despotism. Our concern should be, not omnipotence as such, but the power revealed in Christ, which is *the power of love*. God's power is simply the freedom to carry out purposes centering in the covenant of grace. Moreover, Barth defends both human freedom and the lawfulness of the created order. God respects the degree of independence given to the creatures, preserving them in being and allowing creaturely activity to coexist with divine activity. The divine work is not just a higher potency supervening on a lower, but an activity "within a completely different order." God's governance is on another plane distinct from all natural causes.

Barth thus affirms both *divine sovereignty* and *creaturely autonomy*. God controls, and all creaturely determination is "wholly and utterly at the disposal of his power." The creature "goes its own way, but in fact it always finds itself on God's way." All causality in the world is completely subordinate to God. When a human hand writes with a pen, the whole action is performed by both— not part by the hand and part by the pen; Barth declares that creaturely causes, like the pen, are real but "have the part only of submission" to the divine hand that guides them.[13]

The idea of primary and secondary causality among these writers has the great merit of respecting the integrity of the natural causal nexus, which science studies. They avoid deism by insisting that the natural order does not stand on its own but requires the continued concurrence of God. Of course, such general, uniform concurrence, working equally in all events, does not fully represent the biblical God who acts. Most defenders of double agency claim that God has also intervened directly at a few points in history, perhaps in miracles, or at least in the particularity of incarnation in Christ. But it is more difficult to allow here for any forms of divine action intermediate between general concurrence and miraculous intervention. Moreover, the "paradox of double agency" employs ideas of causality that remain problematic. The woodsman causes the motion of the ax, which is his instrument, but primary causes do not cause secondary causes in a similar way. Finally, by retaining classical conceptions of God's omnipotence, foreknowledge, and eternity, the interpretation is in the end deterministic, despite protracted efforts to allow for human freedom. If in God's view there is only one outcome, no genuine alternatives exist, though we may think they do. Chance and evil in the world are also difficult to reconcile with such divine determination.

## II. SOME ALTERNATIVES

Let us consider five recent alternatives to classical theism. In the first, God is the determiner of indeterminacies. In the second, God is communicator of information. In the third, omnipotence is qualified by God's self-limitation. In the fourth, God's action is said to be like that of a human agent, which can be described in the language of intentions rather than in the language of causes. In the fifth, the world is viewed as God's body.

Proponents of all five models insist that *God does not intervene* in violation of the laws of nature or fill gaps in the natural order that might be filled by natural causes (the "God of the gaps"). In each case, God fills a role distinct from that of interactions within nature. None of these authors is proposing a proof of God's existence as a form of natural theology. All are proposing models of ways in which a God who is accepted on other grounds (such as religious experience in a historic interpretive tradition) might be reconceived today as acting in nature—an approach that I have referred to as a *theology of nature* rather than a *natural theology*. Each of these proposals is consistent with the scientific evidence but is not required by it.

### 1. GOD AS DETERMINER OF INDETERMINACIES

In chapter 7 I defended the view that uncertainties in the predictions made by quantum theory reflect indeterminacy in nature itself rather than the inadequacy of current theory. In that interpretation, *a range of possibilities* is present in the world. Quantum events have necessary but not sufficient physical causes. If they are not completely determined by the relationships described by the laws of physics, their final determination might be made directly by God. What appears to be chance, which atheists take as an argument against theism, may be the very point at which God acts. Divine sovereignty would be maintained if God *providentially controls* the events that appear to us as chance. No energy input would be needed, since the alternative potentialities in a quantum state have identical energy. God does not have to intervene as a physical force pushing electrons around but instead actualizes one of the many potentialities already present—determining, for example, the instant at which a particular radioactive atom decays.[14]

We have seen that under some conditions the effects of very small differences at the microlevel are greatly amplified in *large-scale phenomena*. In nonlinear thermodynamics and chaos theory, an infinitesimal initial change can produce dramatic changes in the larger system. Similar trigger effects occur in evolutionary mutations and in genetic and neural systems today. Scientific research finds only law and chance, but perhaps in God's knowledge all events are foreseen and predetermined through a combination of law and particular divine action. Since God's action would be scientifically undetectable, it could be neither proved nor refuted by science. This would exclude any proof of God's action of the kind sought in natural theology, but it would not exclude the possibility of God's action affirmed on other grounds in a wider theology of nature.

If we assume that *God controls all indeterminacies,* we could preserve the traditional idea of predestination. This would be theological determinism rather than physical determinism, since nothing happens by chance. But then the problems of waste, suffering, and human freedom would remain acute. Nancey Murphy has proposed that God determines all quantum indeterminacies but arranges that lawlike regularities usually result, in order to make stable structures and scientific investigation possible and to ensure that human actions have dependable consequences so that moral choices are possible. Orderly relationships do not constrain God, since they are included in God's purposes. God grants causal powers to created entities. Murphy holds that in human life God acts both at the quantum level and at higher levels of mental activity but does it in such a way that human freedom is not violated.[15]

An alternative would be to say that most quantum events occur by chance but that *God influences some of them* without violating the statistical laws of quantum physics. This view has been defended by Robert Russell, George Ellis, and Thomas Tracy, and it is consistent with the scientific evidence.[16] One objection to this model is that it assumes *bottom-up causality* within nature once God's action has occurred, and thus it seems to concede the reductionist's claim that the behavior of all entities is determined by their smallest parts (or lowest levels). The action would be bottom up even if one assumed that God's intentions were directed to the larger wholes (or higher levels) affected by these quantum events. However, most of these authors also allow for God's action at higher levels, which then results in a top-down influence on lower levels, in addition to quantum effects from the bottom up. The model thus can be combined with one of the models discussed below.

## 2. GOD AS COMMUNICATOR OF INFORMATION

We have encountered the concept of *information* at many points in previous chapters. In closed thermodynamic systems, entropy is a measure of disorder, which increases with time, accompanied by a loss of order and information. In living things, DNA encodes the information needed for the construction of particular proteins in developing and functioning organisms. Evolutionary history shows a trend toward an increasing capacity of organisms to gather, process, and respond to information from the environment. In human life, information can be transmitted between generations not only by genes but by speech, literature, art, music, and other cultural forms. In computers, information is encoded in binary or digital form as instructions for electronic circuits, which carry out information processing.

We said that information is *an ordered pattern* (of DNA bases, alphabetical letters, auditory sounds, binary digits, or any other combinable elements) that is one among many possible sequences or states of a system. Information is *communicated* when another system (a living cell, reader, listener, or computer, for example) responds selectively—that is, when information is coded, transmitted, and decoded. The meaning of the message is dependent on a wider context of interpretation. It must be understood dynamically and relationally rather than in purely static terms as if the message were contained in the pattern itself.

In radio transmissions, computers, and biological systems, the *communication of information* between two points requires a physical input and an expenditure of energy (the Brillouin-Szilard relationship). But if God is omnipresent (including presence everywhere at the microlevel), no energy would be required for the communication of information. Moreover, the realization of alternative potentialities already present in the quantum world would convey differing information without any physical input or expenditure of energy.

John Polkinghorne proposes that God's action is *"an input of pure information."* In chaos theory an infinitesimally small energy input produces a very large change in the system. Polkinghorne suggests that in imagining God's action we might extrapolate chaos theory to the limiting case of zero energy. (This differs from quantum theory in which there actually is *zero* energy difference between alternative potentialities so no extrapolation is needed.) He holds that God's action is a nonenergetic input of information expressing holistic patterns. God's selection among the envelope of possibilities present in chaotic processes could bring about novel structures and types of order exemplifying systemic higher-level organizing principles.[17]

Arthur Peacocke has used a rich variety of analogies for God's relation to the world, most of which involve *the communication of information*. God is like the choreographer of a dance in which many decisions are left up to the dancers or like the composer of a still unfinished symphony who is experimenting, improvising, and expanding on a theme and variations. Peacocke also suggests that the purposes of God are communicated through the pattern of events in the world. We can look on evolutionary history as the communication of an agent who expresses intentions but does not follow an exact predetermined plan. Moreover, an input of information from God could influence the relationships among our memories, images, and concepts, just as our thoughts influence the activity of neurons in our brains. Peacocke maintains that Christ was a powerfully God-informed person who was a uniquely effective vehicle for God's self-expression; in Christ, God's purposes are more clearly revealed than elsewhere in nature or history.[18]

Peacocke proposes that God exerts a *top-down causality* on the world. Peacocke extends the idea of levels within nature to include another level. God's action from the highest level would be a boundary condition or constraint on relationships at lower levels, without violating lower-level laws. Boundary conditions may be introduced not just at spatial or temporal boundaries but also internally as information that provides additional specification allowed by but not determined by lower-level laws. In human beings, God influences their highest evolutionary level, that of mental activity, which would affect neural networks and neurons. Within human life, divine action would be effected down the hierarchy of natural levels; we have at least some understanding of relationships between these adjacent levels.[19] Peacocke's use of top-down causality seems to me more problematic in the case of divine action on inanimate matter. We would have to assume direct influence between God (the highest level) and matter (the lowest level), in the absence of the intermediate levels that we find in living things. But I welcome the suggestion of top-down causality as an alternative to the bottom-up causality of action at the quantum level or at the turning points in chaotic systems.

The divine Word *(logos)* in biblical thought resembles the concept of information. In Greek thought, the *logos* was a universal rational principle, but biblical usage also expressed the Hebrew understanding of Word as creative power. The Word in both creation and redemption can indeed be thought of as the communication of information from God to the world. As in the case of genetic information and human language, the meaning of the message must be discerned within a wider context of interpretation. God's Word to human beings preserves their freedom because it requires their response.[20]

But the divine *logos* is not simply the communication of an impersonal message because it is inseparable from an ongoing personal relationship. If we believe that one of God's purposes was the creation of loving and responsible persons, not simply intelligent information processors, we will have to draw our analogies concerning the communication of information primarily from human life rather than from the genetic code or computers programs. The value of the concept of information is that it is applicable at many different levels.

## 3. GOD'S SELF-LIMITATION

In discussing the problem of evil (theodicy) in the previous chapter, I described the view of Hick and others that God's power is voluntarily self-limited in order to allow for human freedom, moral growth, and the lawfulness of nature. Several biblical scholars have explored the theme of God's suffering in the Bible,[21] but I will confine myself to the writings of recent British theologians. A statement by the Doctrine Commission of the Church of England criticizes both the monarchical model and the clockmaker model and rejects immutability and impassibility. Two alternative models are proposed. The first is that of *the artist and the work of art*. The artist's vision changes and is reformulated as the work proceeds. Moreover, the medium (the sculptor's wood or stone, for instance) always imposes constraints on the artist. God has similarly chosen a medium that imposes inescapable constraints; God exercises a limited control and redeems imperfections rather than preventing them.[22]

The second model proposed in the Anglican statement is that of *the parent and the growing child*. As the child matures, the parent exercises persuasion and holds up moral standards rather than acting coercively. Some forms of intervention would defeat the parent's goals. So, too, in the face of Israel's rebelliousness, God is patient and faithful and will not abandon the covenant people. God loves like a father who suffers when a son fails to respond. In a section on "the suffering of God," the statement insists that the cross and the resurrection always go together and that new life is given amid suffering and death. God does not promise that we will be protected from life's ills. The promise is that God will be faithful and will empower us with endurance and insight if we are open to them.

W. H. Vanstone says that authentic love is always accompanied by *vulnerability*. In human life, inauthentic love seeks control, as when a possessive parent holds onto a child. Authentic love is precarious and brings the risk of rejection. It requires involvement rather than detachment, and this also makes a person vulnerable. The biblical God is affected by the creation, delighting in its beauty but grieved by its tragic aspects. Vanstone holds that there is no predetermined plan or assured program. There is, rather, "a vision which is discovered in its own realization."

The creation is "safe," not because it moves by program towards a predetermined goal, but because the same loving creativity is ever exercised upon it. . . . It implies only that that which is created is other than he who creates; that its possibility must be discovered; that its possibility must be "worked out" in the creative process itself; and that the working out must include the correction of the step which proved a false step, the redemption of the move which, unredeemed, would be tragedy. . . . Our faith in the Creator is that He leaves no problem abandoned and no evil unredeemed.[23]

Vanstone says that evil is inescapable in the long process of creation. God must wait on the responses of nature and humanity. Nature is not just the stage for the human drama; it is the result of a labor of love and as such is worthy of our celebration and care. Here Vanstone extends the ancient theme of *kenosis* or self-emptying: in the incarnation God set aside omnipotence, "taking the form of a servant" (Phil 2:7). He concludes his book with a "Hymn to the Creator," ending with this stanza:

Thou art God; no monarch Thou
Thron'd in easy state to reign;
Thou art God, Whose arms of love
Aching, spent, the world sustain.[24]

Brian Hebblethwaite suggests that though God has an unchanging goal, many paths lead to it. The future is *open and unpredictable,* awaiting the creatures' choices. There can be no detailed foreknowledge, and God changes in response to what the creatures do. Hebblethwaite defends human freedom and also indeterminacy and chance at lower levels. He rejects the idea that God determines what appear to us as chance atomic events; he insists that there is real randomness, which even God cannot know in advance. Evolution reflects millions of years of chance; God respects the structures of creation but somehow weaves these events into unforeseeable providential patterns. In this framework, he says, the problems of evil and suffering are more tractable than under the assumption that every detail is predestined.[25]

Keith Ward ascribes *reciprocity* and *temporality* to God. He rejects divine omnipotence and self-sufficiency. Creativity is inherently temporal, responsive, and contingent. God's power, knowledge, and beatitude are limited by the creatures' power, freedom, and suffering, respectively. But these are voluntary self-limitations, since God could at any time destroy or modify the world. Chance, law, and plurality in the world produce the possibility of conflict and evil; sentience makes pain and suffering as well as pleasure and joy possible. God chooses good and accepts evil as its concomitant.

Ward says that God is *neither omnipotent nor helpless* but guides an evolutionary process that includes law, chance, and the emergence of novelty. God's nature and purposes are eternal and unchanging, but divine knowledge and creativity are changing. Ward acknowledges indebtedness to the dipolar theism of process thought but claims that Whitehead's God is helpless and passive, a "cosmic sponge" (which seems to me to be a misreading of Whitehead). Ward accepts only God's voluntary self-limitation, whereas for Whitehead the limitations of divine power are metaphysical and inescapable.[26]

Another Anglican who appreciates but also criticizes Whitehead is John Macquarrie. He finds the traditional emphasis on transcendence, eternity, and impassibility one-sided and wants to balance these characteristics by *immanence, temporality,* and *vulnerability.* He calls his view "Dialectical Theism." God is "above time" in the constancy of a purpose that suffering does not defeat or overwhelm. Macquarrie draws heavily from such exponents of mysticism as Plotinus and Eckhart, who emphasized immanence and the inward unity of all things in God. He says that evil is inescapable in such a creation, and it can be more readily accepted if we know that God participates in the world's suffering.[27]

A final example is Paul Fiddes's *The Creative Suffering of God.* Of all these authors, Fiddes is the most sympathetic to process thought, and he draws extensively from it, though in the end he departs from it. He gives detailed critiques of ideas of God's immutability, self-sufficiency, and timelessness, and he accepts the process position concerning God's relatedness and temporality. God is with us in our suffering but is not overwhelmed or defeated by it. But Fiddes does not agree with process thought that God's involvement with the world is necessary or that God needs the world in order to be fully actualized. He maintains that God has freely chosen and accepted self-limitation for the sake of human freedom. Here he is indebted to Barth's theme that God loves in freedom and chooses to be in relation to the world. Fiddes says that relatedness, fellowship, and community are already present *within* the life of the trinitarian God and do not require a world to be actualized.[28]

Fiddes is impressed with the process understanding of how *God's suffering affects us.* We feel another person's sympathy with our feelings. In Christ's death we experience judgment but also an acceptance that enables us to accept the truth about ourselves. Costly forgiveness can have a transforming effect. But Fiddes holds that this can be better expressed through trinitarian ideas: "Process thought, then, points in a valuable way to the powerful effect which an exchange of feelings between us and a suffering God can have upon us, but I believe this insight can be carried through better with the more thoroughgoing personal analogy for God which is offered in Trinitarianism."[29]

Compared to the monarchical model, these views seem to accord better with the biblical understanding and also with evolutionary history and human experience. The models of artistic creativity and parental love appear particularly appropriate. These views go far toward answering the objections raised against the monarchical model: the problems of freedom, evil, evolution, and chance. They could also be developed to answer the classical tendencies toward patriarchy and religious intolerance. Many feminists are sympathetic to the kenotic model, but with the caveat that the idea of vulnerability and suffering love must not be used to justify the continuing submission or self-abnegation of women. I will suggest that process theology expresses many of the same insights but develops them further in a coherent metaphysical system.

## 4. GOD AS AGENT

Another model of God's relation to the world is drawn from the relation of agents to their actions. Many proponents of this model have been influenced by *linguistic analysis,* which holds that diverse types of language serve radically differing functions. (This was one version of the *Independence* thesis in chapter 4.) Writings in the philosophy of action contend that the explanation of actions by *intentions* is very different from the explanation of effects by *causes.* An action of a human agent is a succession of activities ordered toward an end. Its unity consists in an intention to realize a goal. An action differs from a bodily movement. A given bodily movement (for example, moving my arm outward in a particular way) may represent a variety of actions (such as mailing a letter, sowing seeds, or waving to someone). Conversely, a given action may be carried out through a variety of sequences of bodily movements. An action cannot be specified, then, by any set of bodily movements, but only by its purpose or intent.[30]

Analysis in terms of *intentions* does not preclude analysis in terms of *scientific laws.* The physiologist need not refer to my purposes in explaining my arm movement. In addition, intentions are never directly observable. Calling it an action involves an interpretation of its meaning and often requires observation over a considerable temporal span; it may, of course, be misinterpreted and wrongly identified. The agents of actions are embodied subjects acting through their bodies. Instead of a mind/body dualism of two distinct substances, we have two ways of talking about a single set of events. An agent is a living body in action, not an invisible mind interacting with a visible body. Yet the agent transcends any single action and is never fully expressed in any series of actions.

Similarly, we can say that cosmic history is an action of *God as agent.* Reference to divine intentions does not exclude a scientific account of causal sequences. John Compton writes,

We can distinguish the causal development of events from the meaning of these events viewed as God's action. Scientific analysis of physical nature and of human history has no more need of God as an explanatory factor than the physiologist needs my conscious intent to explain my bodily movements. Nor does God need to find a "gap" in nature in order to act, any more than you or I need a similar interstice in our body chemistry. Each story has a complete cast of characters, without the need for interaction with the other story, but quite compatible with it. What happens is that the evolution of things is seen or read, in religious life—as my arm's movement is read in individual life—as part of an action, as an expression of divine purpose, in addition to its being viewed as a naturalistic process.[31]

The *intentions of an agent* are never directly observable and may be difficult to guess from events in a limited span of time. In the case of God's intentions, a paradigm tradition provides a vision of a wider context within which the pattern is interpreted. There is indeed a strong biblical precedent for talking about God in terms of purposes in history. Today the linguistic approach would encourage us to treat the language of divine action as an alternative to scientific language, not as a competitor with it. The cosmic drama can be interpreted as an expression of the divine purpose. God is understood to act in and through the structure and movement of nature and history.

The theologian Gordon Kaufman suggests that the whole course of evolutionary development can be considered as *one all-encompassing action,* unified by God's intentions. Within this master action are various subactions—the emergence of life, the advent of humanity, the growth of culture—which are phases of a total action moving toward greater consciousness, freedom, and community. Kaufman sees the history of Israel and the life of Christ as special subactions decisively expressing the divine intention. He maintains that the evolutionary process is at the same time an unbroken causal nexus, which the scientist can study without reference to God's purposes.[32]

Maurice Wiles has elaborated the thesis that cosmic history is *one overarching action.* He rejects the traditional understanding of particular divine actions in the providential guidance of individual events:

Think of the whole continuing creation of the world as God's one act, an act in which he allows radical freedom to his human creation. The nature of such a creation, I have suggested, is incompatible with the assertion of further particular divinely initiated acts within the developing history of the world. God's act, like many human acts, is complex. I have argued that particular parts of it can rightly be spoken of as specially significant aspects of the divine activity, but not as specific, identifiable acts of God.[33]

Wiles proposes that God's intention is unvarying and God's action is uniform, but our responses will vary in differing contexts:

God's fundamental act, the intentional fruit of the divine initiative, is the bringing into existence of the world. That is a continuous process, and every part of it is therefore in the broadest sense an expression of divine activity. Differences within the process, leading us to regard some happenings as more properly to be spoken of in such terms than others, are dependent not on differing divine initiatives but on differing degrees of human responsiveness. The players in the improvised drama of the world's creation, through whom the agency of the author finds truest expressions, are not ones to whom he has given some special information or advice, but those who have best grasped his intention and developed it.[34]

Wiles differs from deism by holding that God acts in the whole of cosmic history, not just in its initial design. But he agrees with deism in holding that God does not act with particular intentions at particular points in that history. It seems to me that by abandoning the idea of particular divine initiatives in history, Kaufman and Wiles have departed significantly from the biblical witness. Moreover, in their interpretation Christ seems to be special only because of the way we respond to him, not because of any special divine action in his life.

## 5. THE WORLD AS GOD'S BODY

Several theologians have developed the model of the world as God's body. Sallie McFague's use of this model was mentioned in chapter 5. Grace Jantzen, in *God's World, God's Body*, starts by defending a holistic understanding of the human person as a psychosomatic unity, citing support from the Old Testament and recent psychology and philosophy. She rejects the classical mind/body dualism with its devaluation of matter and the body. The God/world relation is analogous to that of person/body, rather than mind/body or soul/body. Jantzen thinks that the classical view of God as disembodied spirit is a product of the Christian Platonism that contrasted eternal forms with a lower realm of temporal matter; this view held that God is immutable and therefore immaterial. But a few church fathers, such as Tertullian, accepted the Stoic assertion that God is embodied, though they rejected the determinism and pantheism of Stoicism.

Jantzen acknowledges that there are significant differences between God and human persons but suggests that these can be described in terms of *God's perfect embodiment*, rather than disembodiment. We have direct awareness of our thoughts, feelings, and many events in our bodies, but much is going on in our bodies of which we are not aware (for example, the processes in our internal organs). God, by contrast, has direct and immediate knowledge of all events in the cosmos. God as omnipresent perceives from every point of view, not from a limited viewpoint as we do. With such directness, God needs no analogue of a nervous system. Again, we can directly and intentionally affect a limited range of actions of our bodies; much that goes on, such as the beating of our hearts, is unintentional. God, however, is the universal agent for whom all events are basic actions, though some events may be more significant and revelatory than others. Instead of treating all of cosmic history as one action, as Wiles does, Jantzen holds that there are particular actions arising from God's response to changing situations.[35]

Though God is free of many of the limitations that the human body imposes, the presence of any body does impose limitations, but Jantzen maintains that in the case of God these are voluntary *self-limitations*. God is always embodied but has a choice about the details of embodiment, which we do not have. A universe has always existed, but its present form is a voluntary self-expression. God could eradicate the present universe and actualize something different; God could exist without this world, but not without any world. God is always in complete control and the world is ontologically dependent. Yet God has voluntarily given the creatures considerable independence and autonomy. At this point Jantzen resembles the proponents of God's self-limitation discussed earlier, though she departs from them when she says that God and the world are "one reality." But she maintains that God transcends the world, just as we can say that a person transcends physical processes if we reject a mechanistic reductionism. She also suggests that the idea of the world as God's body would lead us to respect nature and would encourage ecological responsibility.[36]

Thomas Tracy, on the other hand, argues that God is a *nonbodily* agent. In the human case, he says, embodiment means (1) existence as a unified organic process, and (2) limitation by subintentional, automatic processes. But the world, says Tracy, does not resemble a unified organism. Instead, there seems to be a looser pluralism, a society of distinct agents. Moreover, God is not inherently limited by involuntary processes, though some self-imposed limitations accompanied the choice to create other agents and to respect their integrity. Tracy accepts the more traditional position that God could exist without any world. God's vulnerability is the result of love and not necessity. Tracy describes his position as intermediate between classical theism (in which God's being is independent of the world) and process theism (in which God and the world affect each other). He concludes that God is a nonbodily agent with unrestricted intentionality who interacts temporally with the world in mutually affecting relations.[37]

I would agree with Tracy that the world does not have the kind of unity that a human body possesses. To be sure, the mystical tradition has testified to an underlying unity and has sometimes referred to God as the world-soul; but mystics speak of an undifferentiated identity wherein distinctions are obliterated, which is very different from the organized integration of cooperatively interacting parts that characterizes the unity of a body. Every body we have encountered also has an external environment, whereas with a cosmic body all interactions would be internal. The most serious objection to the model is that it does not allow sufficiently for the independence of God and the world. God's relation to other agents seems to require a social or interpersonal analogy in which a plurality of centers of initiative is present.

## III. PROCESS THEISM

In process thought reality is envisaged as a society in which one member is preeminent but not totally controlling. The world is a community of interacting beings rather than a monarchy, a machine, the action of an agent, or the body of an agent. We look first at the advantages of process theism in comparison with the options considered above and then analyze some of the problems it entails.

### 1. GOD AS CREATIVE PARTICIPANT

In the previous chapter I suggested that the process view is *social* in that it portrays a plurality of centers of activity. It can also be called *ecological* in that it starts from a network of relationships between interdependent beings, rather than from essentially separate beings. We can think of God as *the leader of a cosmic community*. It is neither a monarchy nor a democracy, since one member is preeminent but not all-powerful. God is like a wise teacher, who desires that students learn to choose for themselves and interact harmoniously, or a loving parent who does not try to do everything for the members of a family. God's role is creative participation and persuasion in inspiring the community of beings toward new possibilities of a richer life together.

Like the proponents of *God as determiner of indeterminacies,* process thinkers acknowledge quantum indeterminacy, but they portray both openness and order at all levels and not primarily at the lowest level; moreover, they hold that God does not unilaterally determine events at any level. Like *God as communicator of information,* the God of process thought brings new forms of order in the encouragement of creative possibilities interpreted in a wider context. The concept of top-down causality between levels of reality is also congenial to process thought, which is holistic in portraying interconnected events at a variety of levels. The theme of *God's self-limitation* is clearly present and is carried even further in process thought.

The analogy of *the world as God's body* is used by some process thinkers. Hartshorne points out that a person's character can remain unchanged amid major bodily changes and that God's essence is uniquely independent of the particulars of the universe. Like Jantzen, he observes that we have only dim awareness of some portions of our bodies and our past, whereas God knows the world completely at every point and forgets nothing. Hartshorne proposes that the mind-body analogy, if appropriately extended, provides an image of God's infinitely sympathetic and all-embracing participation in the world process, a mode of influence that is internal rather than external. He says that the relationship between human persons is indirect and is mediated by language or physical objects, so that a human society is a less apt analogy for God's relation to the world.[38] Hartshorne's development of the mind-body model is helpful, but I believe that *interpersonal social models* best represent the combination of independence and interdependence that characterizes individual entities in relation to each other and in relation to God. We have more independence than cells in a cosmic organism. Here Whitehead's more pluralistic model allows a larger role for both human and divine freedom, intention, and action.

Drawing on the discussion in the previous chapter, we can see that the process model offers distinctive answers to each of the six problems in the monarchical model.

*1. Human Freedom.* Human experience is the starting point from which process thought generalizes and extrapolates to develop a set of metaphysical categories that are exemplified by all entities. Self-creativity is part of the momentary present of every entity. It is not surprising, then, that process thought has no difficulty in representing human freedom in relation to both God and causes from the past. In particular, omnipotence and predestination are repudiated in favor of a God of persuasion, whose achievements in the world always depend on the response of other entities. Process theism strongly endorses our responsibility to work creatively to further God's purposes while recognizing human frailty and the constraints imposed by the biological and social structures inherited from the past. We are participants in an unfinished universe and in God's continuing work. God calls us to love, freedom, and justice. Time, history, and nature are to be affirmed, for it is here that God's purposes can be carried forward.

*2. Evil and Suffering.* Human sin can be understood as a product of human freedom and insecurity. Suffering in the human and nonhuman world is no longer a divine punishment for sin or an inexplicable anomaly. The capacity for pain is an inescapable concomitant of greater awareness and intensity of experience. Greater capacity to hurt others is a concomitant of the new forms of interdependence present at higher levels of life. In an evolutionary world, struggle and conflicting goals are integral to the realization of greater value. By accepting the limitations of divine power we avoid blaming God for particular forms of evil and suffering; we can acknowledge that they are contrary to the divine purposes in that situation. Instead of God the judge meting out retributive punishment, we have God the friend, with us in our suffering and working with us to redeem it.

*3. "Masculine" and "Feminine" Attributes.* The classical view of God was heavily weighted toward what our culture thinks of as "masculine" virtues: power, rationality, independence, and impassibility. By contrast, process thinkers also ascribe to God what our culture takes to be "feminine" virtues: nurturance, sensitivity, interdependence, and responsiveness. These authors refer to God's tenderness, patience, and responsive love. The typical male image of control and self-sufficiency is rejected in favor of images of participation, education, and cooperation. In reacting against the monarchical model of God's power, process thinkers may sometimes seem to make God powerless, but in fact they are pointing to alternative forms of power in both God and human life. Power as control is a zero-sum game: the more one party has, the less the other can have. Power as empowerment is a positive-sum game. The goal in picturing both divine and human virtues is to integrate masculine/feminine attributes within a new wholeness, like the wider unity within which the Taoists held that the contrasting qualities of yin and yang are embraced.

4. *Interreligious Dialogue.* In contrast to the exclusivist claims of revelation in classical theism, process thought allows us to acknowledge that God's creative presence is at work at all points in nature and history. But it also allows us to speak of the particularity of divine initiatives in specific traditions and in the lives and experience of specific persons. Unlike deism, it defends the idea of God's continuing action in the world—including actions under special conditions that reveal God's purposes with exceptional depth and clarity. Such a framework would offer encouragement to the path of dialogue among world religions as an alternative to both the militancy of absolutism and the vagueness of relativism (chapter 6). We can accept our rootedness in a particular community and yet remain open to the experience of other communities.

5. *An Evolutionary and Ecological World.* We have seen that process thought is in tune with the contemporary view of nature as a dynamic process of becoming, always changing and developing, radically temporal in character. This is an incomplete cosmos still coming into being. Evolution is a creative process whose outcome is not predictable. Reality is multileveled, with more complex levels built on simpler ones, so we can understand why it had to be a very long, slow process if God's role was evocation and not control. Also fundamental to process thought is a recognition of the ecological interdependence of all entities. Here there is no dualism of soul and body and no sharp separation between the human and the nonhuman. Anthropocentrism is avoided because humanity is seen as part of the community of life and similar to other entities, despite distinctive human characteristics. All creatures are intrinsically valuable because each is a center of experience, though there are enormous gradations in the complexity and intensity of experience. In addition, by balancing immanence and transcendence, process thought encourages respect for nature.

6. *Chance and Law.* Within the monarchical model, any element of chance is a threat to divine control (unless God controls what to us appears to be chance). Within deism it is assumed that all events in nature are objectively determined. Process thought is distinctive in holding indeterminacy among its basic postulates. It affirms both order and openness in nature. Here divine purpose is understood to have unchanging goals but not a detailed

eternal plan; God responds to the unpredictable. Process thought recognizes alternative possibilities, potentialities that may or may not be realized. There are many influences on the outcome of an event, none of them absolutely determining it.

## 2. PROBLEMS IN PROCESS THEOLOGY

I take seriously three criticisms of process theology, though I believe that there are answers to each.

### 1. Christianity and Metaphysics

The context of religious discourse is the worshiping community. Writings in process theology, by contrast, often seem abstract and speculative. God is described in philosophical categories rather than through stories and images. But we must remember that differing types of discourse can have the same referent. A husband can refer to his wife in the personal language of endearment or in the objective language of a medical report. Moreover, process metaphysics is not proposed as a substitute for the language of worship but as a substitute for alternative metaphysical systems. Metaphysics is inescapable as soon as one moves from the primary language of worship (story, liturgy, and ritual) to theological reflection and doctrinal formulation.

The use of *philosophical categories* in theology is not new. Augustine was indebted to Plato, Aquinas to Aristotle, nineteenth-century Protestantism to Kant. In each case the theologian had to adapt the philosopher's ideas to the theological task. In turn, the theologian's philosophical commitments led to greater sensitivity to some aspects of the biblical witness than to others. The components of any creative synthesis are themselves altered by being brought together. Whitehead, like Kant, was a philosopher already deeply influenced by the Christian vision of reality. Whitehead recognized the tentative and partial character of his attempt at synthesis; he held that every philosophical system illuminates some types of experience more adequately than other types, and none attains to final truth.

At certain times in the past the imposition of a rigid *philosophical system* has hindered both scientific and theological development. The dominance of the Aristotelian framework from the thirteenth to the seventeenth centuries was in some ways detrimental to both science and theology. In the search for unity and coherence, we must avoid any premature or externally imposed synthesis. We can expect no complete and final system; our endeavors must be tentative, exploratory, and open, allowing a measure of pluralism in recognition of the variety of experience. Christianity cannot be identified with any metaphysical system. The theologian must adapt, not adopt, a metaphysics. Many process insights may be accepted without accepting the total Whiteheadian scheme. These insights can lead to the modification of classical religious models so that they more accurately reflect the experience of the Christian community as well as contemporary scientific understanding.

## 2. God's Transcendence and Power

It has been said that the God of process philosophy lacks the transcendence and power characteristic of the biblical God. One critic says that such a weak God would evoke our pity rather than our worship.[39] Transcendence is indeed less emphasized in process theology than in classical Christianity, but it is still strongly represented. God is distinct from the world and not identified with it, as in pantheism. Every entity is radically dependent on God for its existence and the order of possibilities that it can actualize. God's freedom and priority in status are upheld; God alone is everlasting, omniscient, and omnipresent. God is perfect in love and wisdom. God's unchanging purposes for good are not contingent on events in the world.

The process God does have power, but it is the *evocative power* of love and inspiration, not controlling, unilateral power. It is power that is also creative empowerment, not the abrogation of creaturely powers. The power of love and goodness is indeed worthy of worship, commitment, and also gratitude for what God has done, whereas sheer power would only be cause for awe and fear. God's love is not irresistible in the short run, but it is inexhaustible in the long run.

Several themes in Christian thought support the portrayal of *a God of persuasion*. Christ's life and death reveal the transformative power of love. We have freedom to respond or not, for grace is not irresistible. In the last analysis, I suggest, the central Christian model for God is the person of Christ himself. In Christ it is love, even more than justice or sheer power, that is manifest. The resurrection represents the vindication rather than the denial of the way of the cross, the power of a love stronger than death. Process theology reiterates on a cosmic scale the motif of the cross, a love that accepts suffering. By rejecting omnipotence, process thought says that God is not directly responsible for evil. Whereas exponents of kenotic self-limitation hold that the qualifications of divine omnipotence are voluntary and temporary, for Whiteheadians the limitations are metaphysical and necessary, though they are integral to God's essential nature and not something antecedent or external to it.

Process theology does call into question the traditional expectation of an *absolute victory over evil*. In chapter 8 we traced the historical development from the prophetic eschatology of God's Kingdom on earth to the apocalyptic eschatology of a final supernatural victory. Process thought is more sympathetic to the former. It holds that God does not abolish evil but seeks to turn it to good account by transmuting it and envisaging the larger pattern into which it can be integrated. This is a God of wisdom and compassion who shares in the world's suffering and is a transforming influence on it, and who also preserves its accomplishments forever within the divine life. Process thought does not look to a static completion of history but to a continued journey toward greater harmony and enrichment. We have seen that subjective immortality is affirmed by some process theologians, while others defend only the objective immortality of contributing to God's everlasting experience.

In process thought, *God's power over nature* is indeed limited. Lower-level events are essentially repetitive and mechanical, though this in itself accords with God's intentions. Yet even the inanimate included an infinitesimal element of new potentiality, which only the long ages of cosmic history could disclose. Continuing creation has been a long, slow travail, building always on what was already present. Evolutionary history seems to point to a God who acts not by controlling but by evoking the response of the creatures. It is in *human life*, then, that the greatest opportunities for God's influence exist. In religious experience and historical revelation, rather than in nature apart from humanity, the divine initiative is most clearly manifest. Here our earlier methodological assertion that theology should be based on religious experience and historical revelation is supported by our understanding of God's mode of action.

## 3. Criteria for Theological Reformulation

Process theology has been criticized for departing too far from classical theology. Can its reformulation of the earlier tradition be justified? The answer must make use of all four of the criteria presented in chapter 5.

The first criterion is *agreement with data*. This refers to the continued intersubjective testing of beliefs against the experience of the religious community. Since all data are theory-laden, and religious experience is influenced by theological interpretation, this criterion cannot be decisive, but it is nevertheless important. The process view of God as creative love accords well with what I described as the Christian experience of reconciliation. I have suggested that the numinous experience of the holy can also be adequately accounted for in the process understanding of God's transcendence and moral purpose, despite its emphasis on immanence. The experience of moral obligation has often been mentioned in process writings. And, of course, the experience of order and creativity is given a central place in all process thought.

Mystical experience of the unity of all things has been less prominent in the West than in the East, and process thought agrees with the Christian tradition in rejecting monism. But process theologians have often been sympathetic to meditative practices and more open to God's presence in nature than many forms of Western theology. They have appreciated the contribution of the Franciscan tradition to environmental awareness and welcomed the combination of mysticism and concern for nature in Teilhard's writing and in some of the classical Christian mystics.

I suggested earlier that the stories and rituals of a tradition are part of the data that must be interpreted. This would mean that process insights should be tested against the biblical record and the subsequent life of the religious community, rather than against previous theological formulations alone. The Bible itself is a diverse document, and process thought seems more in tune with some of its themes than with others. We have said, for example, that it finds prophetic eschatology more consistent with the overall biblical message than apocalyptic eschatology. Process theology directs attention to Christ's life and the suffering love of the cross, and it sees the resurrection as evidence of the transforming power of that love rather than as an independent manifestation of God's power.

The second criterion is *coherence*. Any reformulation must be consistent with the central core of the Christian tradition. We saw that, according to Lakatos, the "hard core" of a tradition may be protected by making modifications in "auxiliary hypotheses" in order to accommodate discordant data. I take the central core of Christianity to be belief in God as creative love, revealed in Christ. Omnipotence is then treated as an auxiliary hypothesis, which can be modified to accommodate the data of human freedom, evil and suffering, and an evolutionary cosmos. I have suggested that the new view of nature requires reformulating our understanding of God's relation to nature, but this can be done without abandoning the tradition's core. Process theology deserves high marks for internal coherence. It brings together within a single set of basic categories the divine initiatives in nature, history, religious experience, and the person of Christ. I maintained that this coherence is also expressed in the biblical idea of the Holy Spirit at work in all of these spheres. This can in turn help us to integrate the personal, social, and ecological dimensions of our lives.

*Scope* is the third criterion. Process thought seeks comprehensiveness in offering a coherent account of diverse types of experience—scientific, religious, moral, and aesthetic. It tries to articulate an inclusive world view. It pays a price in the abstractness of its concepts, but its basic categories allow for a greater diversity of types of experience than most metaphysical systems. In particular, the idea of levels of experience and evolutionary emergence provide a better balance between continuity and discontinuity (both in history and in ontology) than do either materialist or dualist alternatives. Process theology is responsive to the experience of women as well as men. Its scope is also broad in its openness to other religious traditions. It can accept the occurrence of divine initiative in other religious communities, while maintaining fidelity to the central core of the Christian tradition, in accordance with the path of dialogue in a pluralistic world.

*Fertility* is the fourth criterion. Lakatos says that a program is progressive only if it leads to new hypotheses and experiments over a period of time. Process thought has stimulated creative theological reflection, and it has been extended to new domains and disciplines in recent decades. But the fertility of religious ideas has many dimensions. Is ethical action encouraged and sustained? Process theologians have given distinctive analyses of some of the most urgent problems of our times, such as the ecological crisis and social injustice. Process theology has the capacity to nourish religious experience and personal transformation. It must be expressed in individual religious life, communal worship, and social action, as well as in theological reflection. I believe that by these four criteria the reformulations of classical tradition proposed in process theology are indeed justified.

## IV. CONCLUSIONS

If theology is critical reflection on the life and thought of the religious community, the context of theology is always the worshiping community. Religious experience, story, and ritual are the starting points for articulating doctrines and beliefs.

The biblical tradition starts with response to *God as Redeemer*. For the Christian community, renewal and wholeness have been found through confrontation with historical events. Here people have known release from insecurity and guilt, from anxiety and despair; here they have discovered, at least in a fragmentary way, the power of reconciliation that can overcome estrangement. Here they have come to know the meaning of repentance and forgiveness and of the new self-understanding and release from self-centeredness that are the beginning of the capacity for love. They can only confess what has occurred in their lives: that in Christ something happened that opens up new possibilities in human existence. The purpose of creation is made known in Christ, "the new creation," who is at the same time the full flowering of the created order and the manifestation of continuing creation. The power of God is revealed as the power of love. God is thus encountered in historical events, in the creative renewal of personal and social life, in grace that redeems alienation. These aspects of the biblical witness are well represented in neo-orthodoxy and linguistic analysis.

But I have urged that while theology must start from historical revelation and personal experience, it must also include *a theology of nature* that does not disparage or neglect the natural order. In neo-orthodoxy, nature remains the unredeemed stage for the drama of human redemption. In linguistic analysis, discourse about phenomena in the natural order has no functions in common with discourse about God. These positions minimize the continuity between nature and grace, between impersonal and personal realms, and between language about nature and language about God. But the Bible itself takes a predominantly affirmative attitude toward the natural world; God is Lord of all of life, not of a separate religious realm. The biblical God is Creator as well as Redeemer.

Each of the models of God examined in this chapter has its strengths and its shortcomings. The *monarchical model* dwells on the transcendence, power, and sovereignty of God. These attributes correspond to the numinous experience of the holy. This model was already present in the biblical view of God as Lord and King. It is appropriate for many aspects of the three main biblical stories: the grandeur of the creation narrative, the liberating events of the exodus and covenant, and the transforming experience of the resurrection of Christ. Some parts of science are in keeping with this model: the awesome power of the Big Bang, the contingency of the universe, the immense sweep of space and time, and the intricate order of nature. But the elaboration of this model in the classic doctrines of omnipotence and predestination conflicts with the evidence of human freedom, evil and suffering, and the presence of chance and novelty in an evolutionary world.

The *neo-Thomist model* of worker and tool (or double agency) shares many of the strengths of the monarchical model. It is expressed in the idea of primary and secondary causes, which operate on totally different planes. Some scientists welcome this idea, since it upholds the integrity of the natural causal nexus. God's normal role is to maintain and concur with the natural order, yet all events are indirectly predetermined in the divine plan. Thus all the problems inherent in the concept of omnipotence are still present. Furthermore, any particular divine initiatives (in Christ, or in grace in human life) are supernatural interventions of a totally different kind. Creation and redemption are contrasting rather than similar modes of divine action.

God as *determiner of indeterminacies* is consistent with the most common interpretation of quantum theory. Here God does not intervene to overrule the laws of nature but actualizes one among the range of potentialities already present in nature. This action at the microlevel could in turn affect large-scale events (through mutations, neural events, or chaotic systems, for example). If God controls all indeterminacies, this would imply a divine determinism with the same problems as the classical models above. Alternatively, God might resolve only some of the indeterminacies at crucial turning points in the history of the cosmos. My chief objection to the use of this model alone is that it assumes a bottom-up causality within the world of nature, which has usually been associated with reductionism.

God as *communicator of information* seems to be a promising model. It builds on the importance of information in many fields of science, including thermodynamics, the genetic code, computer science, and human communication. The message carried in any communication is dependent on the wider context of interpretation and response. The theological use of this model is supported by the biblical concept of the divine Word, or *logos*. God's action would occur as a top-down cause from higher to lower levels rather than as a bottom-up cause.

The *kenotic model* of God's voluntary self-limitation answers many of the objections to the monarchical model. Here the proposed analogies are artistic creativity and parental love. Love always entails vulnerability, reciprocity, and temporality rather than impassibility, unilateral power, and unchanging self-sufficiency. God's self-limitation allows for human freedom and the laws of nature, and it thereby renders the problems of evil and suffering more tractable. Yet because the self-limitation is voluntary it does not imply any inherent limitation in God's ultimate power. Such a view accords with the Christian experience of reconciliation and with many features of the biblical witness, such as Israel's free choice in accepting the covenant and Christ's acceptance of the cross. It also seems to fit the pattern of evolutionary history as a long and costly process. I find it a very valuable contribution to theological reflection. It shares many of the assumptions of process theology. When its metaphysical implications are systematically developed, I expect that it will move even closer to process views.

The model of *God as agent* is in keeping with the biblical identification of God by actions and intentions. The linguistic analysts who use this model have made helpful distinctions between the functions of scientific and religious language, but they have ended by isolating them in completely separate spheres. Causes and intentions should be distinguished, but they cannot remain totally unrelated, in either human or divine action. When Wiles and Kaufman speak of cosmic history as one divine action, they have given up the biblical understanding of particular divine initiatives, and they have jeopardized both divine and human freedom.

The model of *the world as God's body* emphasizes divine immanence, which was a somewhat neglected theme in traditional theology. Advocates of this model say that the relation of God to the world is even closer than that of the human mind to the body, since God is aware of all that is and acts immediately and directly. This model would indeed give strong encouragement to ecological responsibility. As developed by Hartshorne, the mind-body analogy can be considered one form of social analogy, since in process thought a human being is a society of entities at many levels, with one dominant entity, the mind. I have argued, however, that the cosmic organism image does not allow sufficiently for the freedom either of God or of human agents in relation to each other. It also has difficulty in adequately representing God's transcendence.

In the *process model,* God is a creative participant in the cosmic community. God is like a teacher, leader, or parent. But God also provides the basic structures and the novel possibilities for all other members of the community. God alone is omniscient and everlasting, perfect in wisdom and love, and thus very different from all other participants. Such an understanding of God, I have suggested, expresses many features of religious experience and the biblical record, especially the life of Christ and the motif of the cross. Process thought is consonant with an ecological and evolutionary understanding of nature as a dynamic and open system, characterized by emergent levels of organization, activity, and experience. It avoids the dualisms of mind/body, humanity/nature, and man/woman. Of all the views considered here, it gives the strongest endorsement of environmental responsibility.

Process thought represents God's action as Creator and Redeemer within a single conceptual scheme. God's action in the nonhuman and human spheres is considered within a common framework of ideas. The biblical stories can be taken as a single story of continuing creation and renewal, the story of life and new life. The *logos,* the divine Word, is the communication of rational structure and personal meaning. The Spirit is God's presence in nature, the community, religious experience, and Christ. Creation and redemption are two aspects of a single continuing divine activity. We can therefore tell an overarching story that includes within it the story of the creation of the cosmos, from elementary particles to the evolution of life and human beings, continuing in the stories of covenant and Christ—with a place in it for the stories of other religious traditions.

The process model thus seems to have fewer weaknesses than the other models considered here. But according to critical realism, all models are limited and partial, and none gives a complete or adequate picture of reality. The world is diverse, and differing aspects of it may be better represented by one model than by another. God's relation to persons will differ from God's relation to impersonal objects like stars and rocks. The pursuit of coherence must not lead us to neglect such differences. We need diverse models to remind us of these differences. In addition, the use of diverse models can keep us from the idolatry that occurs when we take any one model of God too literally. Only in worship can we acknowledge the mystery of God and the pretensions of any system of thought claiming to have mapped out God's ways.

Perhaps, after all, we should return to the biblical concept of the Holy Spirit. The Spirit is said to indwell, renew, empower, inspire, guide, and reconcile. Reference to the Spirit can help us to avoid the separation of creation and redemption that occurred in much of classical Christianity. It is free of the male imagery so prominent elsewhere in Christian history. It will help us recover a sense of the sacred in nature that can motivate a strong concern for the environment today. The Spirit is God working from within in both human life and the natural world, which is consistent with process thought but can also be expressed through other models. The theme of the 1991 assembly of the World Council of Churches was a prayer in which we can join: "Come, Holy Spirit, renew thy whole creation."

# Notes

## Chapter 1

1. A. Rupert Hall, *The Scientific Revolution, 1500–1800* (London: Longmans Green, 1954); Herbert Butterfield, *The Origins of Modern Science* (New York: Macmillan, 1951); Alexandre Koyré, *Metaphysics and Measurement: Essays in Scientific Revolution* (London: Chapman and Hall, 1968).

2. John Murdoch and Edith Sylla, "The Science of Motion," in *Science in the Middle Ages,* ed. David Lindberg (Chicago: Univ. of Chicago Press, 1978); Robert Westman and David Lindberg, eds., *Reappraisals of the Scientific Revolution* (Cambridge: Cambridge Univ. Press, 1990).

3. William Wallace, "The Philosophical Setting of Medieval Science," in *Science in the Middle Ages,* ed. Lindberg; Edward Grant, "Science and Theology in the Middle Ages," in *God and Nature: Historical Essays on the Encounter between Christianity and Science,* ed. David C. Lindberg and Ronald L. Numbers (Berkeley and Los Angeles: Univ. of California Press, 1986).

4. See William C. Dampier, *A History of Science and Its Relations with Philosophy and Religion,* 4th ed. (Cambridge: Cambridge Univ. Press, 1948), chap. 2; also A. C. Crombie, *Medieval and Early Modern Science,* 2 vols. (Cambridge: Harvard Univ. Press, 1961); R. G. Collingwood, *The Idea of Nature* (Oxford: Clarendon Press, 1945).

5. Thomas Aquinas, *Summa Theologia,* pt. I, qq. 2 and 12; Étienne Gilson, *The Christian Philosophy of Thomas Aquinas* (New York: Random House, 1956).

6. Anthony J. P. Kenny, *The Five Ways of St. Thomas Aquinas' Proofs of God's Existence* (New York: Schocken Books, 1969); Brian Davies, *The Thought of Thomas Aquinas* (Oxford: Oxford Univ. Press, 1992).

7. In addition to Copernicus's *De Revolutionibus* (1543), see Robert S. Westman, ed., *The Copernican Achievement* (Berkeley and Los Angeles: Univ. of California Press, 1975); Edward Rosen, *Copernicus and the Scientific Revolution* (New York: Krieger, 1984).

8. See Gerald Holton, "Johannes Kepler's Universe: Its Physics and Metaphysics," *American Journal of* Physics 24 (1956): 340; Judith V. Field, *Kepler's Geometrical Cosmology* (Chicago: Univ. of Chicago Press, 1988).

9. Galileo, *Dialogue on the Two Chief World Systems* (1632), trans. T. Salusbury (Chicago: Univ. of Chicago Press, 1953); see also Charles C. Gillispie, *The Edge of Objectivity* (Princeton: Princeton Univ. Press, 1960), chap. 1.

10. Alfred North Whitehead, *Science and the Modern World* (New York: Macmillan, 1925); Edwin A. Burtt, *The Metaphysical Foundations of Modern Science,* rev. ed. (New York: Humanities Press, 1951); Koyré, *Metaphysics and Measurement.*

11. Arnold Thackray, "History of Science," in *A Guide to the Culture of Science, Technology and Medicine,* ed. Paul T. Durbin (New York: Free Press, 1980); John R. R. Christie, "The Development of the Historiography of Science," in *Companion to the History of Science,* ed. R. C. Olby et al. (London: Routledge, 1990).

12. Galileo, *The Assayer,* reprinted in A. C. Danto and S. Morgenbesser, eds., *Philosophy of Science* (New York: Meridian, 1960), p. 30.

13. René Descartes, *Discourse on Method* and *Meditation* (New York: Liberal Arts Press, 1976).

14. Robert Westman, "The Copernicans and the Churches," in *God and Nature,* ed. Lindberg and Numbers; John Dillenberger, *Protestant Thought and Natural Science* (New York: Doubleday, 1960).

15. Galileo, "Letter to the Grand Duchesss Christina" (1615), trans. Stillman Drake, in *Discoveries and Opinions of Galileo* (New York: Doubleday, 1957), p. 185.

16. Galileo, in *Discoveries and Opinions of Galileo*, p. 197. See discussion in Ernan McMullin, "How Should Cosmology Relate to Theology?" in *The Sciences and Theology in the Twentieth Century*, ed. Arthur Peacocke (Notre Dame: Univ. of Notre Dame Press, 1981).

17. Jerome J. Langford, *Galileo, Science and the Church*, rev. ed. (Ann Arbor: Univ. of Michigan Press, 1971); William R. Shea, "Galileo and the Church," in *God and Nature*, ed. Lindberg and Numbers; Stillman Drake, *Galileo* (New York: Hill and Wang, 1980).

18. Cardinal Paul Poupard, ed., *Galileo Galilei: Toward a Resolution of 350 Years of Debate, 1633–1983* (Pittsburgh: Duquesne Univ. Press, 1987); Pope John Paul II, "Lessons of the Galileo Case," *Origins* 22 (Nov. 12, 1992): 372.

19. Benedict Spinoza, *Ethics*, pt. I, in *The Chief Works of Benedict de Spinoza*, trans. R. H. M. Elwes (London: G. Bell and Sons, 1889).

20. Isaac Newton, *Mathematical Principles of Natural Philosophy*, trans. A. Motte (Berkeley: Univ. of California Press, 1934); see especially the Preface and General Scholium.

21. John Fauvel et al., eds., *Let Newton Be! A New Perspective on His Life and Works* (Oxford: Oxford Univ. Press, 1988).

22. Burtt, *Metaphysical Foundations*, p. 239.

23. Isaac Newton, *Optics* (New York: Dover, 1952), p. 344.

24. Robert Boyle, "The Christian Virtuoso," in *The Works of the Hon. Robert Boyle*, ed. T. Birch (London: A. Millar, 1744).

25. Richard S. Westfall, *Science and Religion in Seventeenth Century England* (New Haven: Yale Univ. Press, 1958).

26. Boyle, "The Usefulness of Experimental Philosophy," in *Robert Boyle*, ed. Birch; James R. Jacob, *Robert Boyle and the English Revolution* (New York: Burt Franklin, 1977).

27. John Hedley Brooke, *Science and Religion: Some Historical Perspectives* (Cambridge: Cambridge Univ. Press, 1991), chap. 4; John Brooke, "The God of Isaac Newton," in *Let Newton Be!*, ed. Fauvel; William Austin, "Isaac Newton on Science and Religion," *Journal of History of Ideas* 31 (1970): 521–42.

28. Frank Manuel, *The Religion of Isaac Newton* (Oxford: Clarendon Press, 1974); Richard S. Westfall, *Never at Rest: A Biography of Isaac Newton* (Cambridge: Cambridge Univ. Press, 1984); Richard Westfall, "The Rise of Science and the Decline of Orthodox Christianity: A Study of Kepler, Descartes, and Newton," in *God and Nature*, ed. Lindberg and Numbers.

29. John W. Draper, *History of the Conflict between Religion and Science* (New York: D. Appleton, 1874); Andrew Dickson White, *A History of the Warfare of Science with Theology*, 2 vols. (New York: D. Appleton, 1896).

30. Roy Porter and Mikulas Teich, eds., *The Scientific Revolution in National Context* (Cambridge: Cambridge Univ. Press, 1992).

31. Robert Merton, *Science and Technology in Seventeenth-Century England* (New York: H. Fertig, 1970); first published in *Osiris*, vol. 4, part 2 (1938).

32. Bernard Barber, *Science and the Social Order* (New York: Free Press, 1952), p. 58.

33. I. Bernard Cohen, *Puritanism and the Rise of Modern Science: The Merton Thesis* (New Brunswick: Rutgers Univ. Press, 1990).

34. Charles Webster, *The Great Instauration: Science, Medicine, and Reform, 1626–1660* (London: Duckworth, 1975); also Charles Webster, "Puritanism, Separatism, and Science," in *God and Nature*, ed. Lindberg and Numbers; Brooke, *Science and Religion*, chap. 3.

35. Cohen, ed., *Puritanism and the Rise of Modern Science*, p.75.

36. Gary Deason, "Reformation Theology and the Mechanistic Conception of Nature," in *God and Nature*, ed. Lindberg and Numbers; Charles Webster, *From Paracelsus to Newton: Magic and the Making of Modern Science* (Cambridge: Cambridge Univ. Press, 1982); Eugene Klaaren, *Religious Origins of Modern Science: Belief in Creation in Seventeenth Century Thought* (Grand Rapids: Eerdmans, 1977).

37. Margaret Jacob, "Christianity and the Newtonian Worldview," in *God and Nature*, ed. Lindberg and Numbers; Margaret Jacob, *The Newtonians and the English Revolution, 1689–1720* (Ithaca: Cornell Univ. Press, 1976); Margaret Jacob, *The Cultural Meaning of the Scientific Revolution* (New York: McGraw-Hill, 1988); Betty Jo Teeter Dobbs and Margaret Jacob, *Newton and the Culture of Newtonianism* (Atlantic Highlands, NJ: Humanities Press, 1995).

38. Toby E. Huff, *The Rise of Early Modern Science: Islam, China, and the West* (Cambridge: Cambridge Univ. Press, 1993).

39. See Butterfield, *Origins of Modern Science*; also Westman and Lindberg, eds., *Reappraisals of the Scientific Revolution*.

40. M. B. Foster, "The Christian Doctrine of Creation and the Rise of Modern Science," in *Creation: The Impact of an Idea*, ed. Daniel O'Connor and Francis Oakley (New York: Charles Scribner's Sons, 1969), originally a series of articles in *Mind* (1934–36); Reijer Hooykaas, *Religion and the Rise of Modern Science* (Grand Rapids: Eerdmans, 1972); Christopher Kaiser, *Creation and the History of Science* (Grand Rapids: Eerdmans, 1991).

## Chapter 2

1. Alexander Pope, "Epitaph on Newton," *The Works of Alexander Pope*, Elwin edition (London, 1882), 4:390.

2. Roger Hahn, "Laplace and the Mechanistic Universe," in *God and Nature*, ed. David Lindberg and Ronald Numbers (Berkeley and Los Angeles: Univ. of California Press, 1986).

3. Pierre Simon Laplace, *A Philosophical Essay on Probabilities*, 6th ed., trans. F. W. Truscott and F. L. Emory (New York: Dover, 1961), p. 4.

4. William C. Dampier, *A History of Science and Its Relation with Philosophy and Religion*, 4th ed. (Cambridge: Cambridge Univ. Press, 1948), p. 196.

5. Margaret Jacob, "Christianity and the Newtonian Worldview," in *God and Nature*, ed. Lindberg and Numbers; John Hedley Brooke, *Science and Religion: Some Historical Perspectives* (Cambridge: Cambridge Univ. Press), chaps. 5 and 6.

6. A. O. Lovejoy, *The Great Chain of Being* (Cambridge: Harvard Univ. Press, 1936), chaps. 6–8.

7. Basil Willey, *Eighteenth-Century Background* (London: Chatto & Windus, 1940), chap. 3; John Gascoigne, *Cambridge in the Age of Enlightenment: Science, Religion, and Politics from the Restoration to the French Revolution* (Cambridge: Cambridge Univ. Press, 1989).

8. See Gerald R. Cragg, *Reason and Authority in the Eighteenth Century* (Cambridge: Cambridge Univ. Press, 1964), and *The Church and the Age of Reason* (London: Penguin, 1960), chaps. 5, 11, 15.

9. Michael Buckley, S.J., *At the Origins of Modern Atheism* (New Haven: Yale Univ. Press, 1987).

10. Roy Porter and Mikulas Teich, eds., *The Enlightenment in National Context* (Cambridge: Cambridge Univ. Press, 1981).

11. Baron d'Holbach, *Systeme de la Nature*, quoted in Franklin Baumer, *Religion and the Rise of Scepticism* (New York: Harcourt, Brace, 1960), p. 64.

12. See Ernst Cassirer, *The Philosophy of the Enlightenment* (Princeton: Princeton Univ. Press, 1951); Crane Brinton, *The Shaping of the Modern Mind* (New York: Mentor, 1953), chap. 4; Thomas L. Hankins, *Science and the Enlightenment* (Cambridge: Cambridge Univ. Press, 1985), chap. 6.

13. Marquis de Condorcet, *The History of the Progress of the Human Spirit*, quoted in John H. Randall, *The Making of the Modern Mind* (Boston: Houghton Mifflin, 1940), p. 383. See also Robert Nisbet, *History of the Idea of Progress* (New York: Basic Books, 1980), chaps. 6 and 7.

14. Carl Becker, *The Heavenly City of the Eighteenth-Century Philosophers* (New Haven: Yale Univ. Press, 1932), chap. 4.

15. Randall, *Making of the Modern Mind*, p. 396.

16. See also Basil Willey, *Nineteenth-Century Studies* (London: Chatto & Windus, 1949), chap. 1.

17. Samuel Taylor Coleridge, *Aids to Reflection* (New York: N. Tibbals and Son, 1872 ).

18. William Wordsworth, "The Tables Turned," in *An Oxford Anthology of English Poetry*, ed. H. F. Lowry and W. Thorp (New York: Oxford Univ. Press, 1940), p. 589.

19. Wordsworth, "Tintern Abbey," in *Oxford Anthology of English Poetry*, p. 590.

20. Robert E. Schofield, "John Wesley and Science in Eighteenth Century England," *Isis* 44 (1953): 331–40; Brooke, *Science and Religion*, pp. 189–91.

21. David Hume, *An Enquiry Concerning Human Understanding* (Chicago: Open Court, 1927), p. 19; see John J. Jenkins, *Understanding Hume* (Lanham, MD: Barnes & Noble, 1992).

22. See David Hume, *Treatise on Human Nature* (Oxford: Clarendon Press, 1958), bk. 1, pt. 3; also *Enquiry Concerning Human Understanding*, secs. 4–7.

23. David Hume, *Dialogues Concerning Natural Religion* (New York: Social Science Publishers, 1948).

24. Hume, *Enquiry*, pp. 171f.

25. On the balance between an attenuated theism, an implicit naturalism, and a philosophical agnosticism in Hume's writings, see Stuart Hampshire in *David Hume: A Symposium*, ed. D. Pears (New York: St. Martin's Press, 1963); Antony Flew, *Hume's Philosophy of Belief* (London: Routledge & Kegan Paul, 1961), pp. 272–73; J. C. A. Gaskin, *Hume's Philosophy of Religion*, 2d ed. (Atlantic Highlands, NJ: Humanities Press, 1988).

26. Immanuel Kant, *Critique of Pure Reason*, trans. N. K. Smith (New York: Humanities Press, 1950), pp. 41–62.

27. Kant, *Critique*, pp. 507ff.

28. *Kant's Critique of Practical Reason and Other Works on the Theory of Ethics*, trans. T. K. Abbott (London: Longmans Green, 1923), pp. 38ff.

29. *Kant's Critique*, pp. 219f. See Philip Rossi and Michael Wreen, eds., *Kant's Philosophy of Religion Reconsidered* (Bloomington: Univ. of Indiana Press, 1991).

30. See chapters by Michael Friedman, Thomas Wartenberg, and Allen Wood in *The Cambridge Companion to Kant*, ed. Paul Guyer (Cambridge: Cambridge Univ. Press, 1992).

31. E. A. Burtt, *Types of Religious Philosophy*, rev. ed. (New York: Harper and Brothers, 1951), p. 266.

## Chapter 3

1. Martin J. S. Rudwick, "The Shape and Meaning of Earth History," and James R. Moore, "Geologists and Interpreters of Genesis," in *God and Nature*, ed. David Lindberg and Ronald Numbers (Berkeley and Los Angeles: Univ. of California Press, 1986).

2. See Bentley Glass, ed., *Forerunners of Darwin* (Baltimore: Johns Hopkins Press, 1959).

3. Charles C. Gillispie, *Genesis and Geology* (Cambridge: Harvard Univ. Press, 1951).

4. William Paley, *Natural Theology* (Boston: Gould, Kendall and Lincoln, 1850).

5. Loren Eiseley, *Darwin's Century* (New York: Doubleday, 1958), chap 1.

6. Francis Darwin, ed., *Life and Letters of Charles Darwin* (New York: D. Appleton, 1887) (cited hereafter as *LLD*), 1:68.

7. *The Origin of Species by Charles Darwin: A Variorum Text*, ed. Morse Peckham (Philadelphia: Univ. of Pennsylvania Press, 1959), pp. 747–48.

8. Edward Pfeifer, "The United States," in *The Comparative Reception of Darwin*, ed. Thomas F. Glick (Austin: Univ. of Texas Press, 1971).

9. David Hull, *Darwin and his Critics: The Reception of Darwin's Theory of Evolution by the Scientific Community* (Chicago: Univ. of Chicago Press, 1973); John Hedley Brooke, *Science and Religion: Some Historical Perspectives* (Cambridge: Cambridge Univ. Press, 1991), chap. 8.

10. Peter Bowler, *The Eclipse of Darwinism: Anti-Darwinian Evolution Theories in the Decades around 1900* (Baltimore: Johns Hopkins Univ. Press, 1983); Peter Bowler, *The Non-Darwinian Revolution: Reinterpreting a Historical Myth* (Baltimore: Johns Hopkins Univ. Press, 1988).

11. Huxley's account of the debate with Wilberforce is included in Tess Cosslett, ed., *Science and Religion in the Nineteenth Century* (Cambridge: Cambridge Univ. Press, 1984). It is challenged in J. R. Lucas, "Wilberforce and Huxley: A Legendary Encounter," *The Historical Journal* 22 (1979): 313–30.

12. Frank Burch Brown, "The Evolution of Darwin's Theism," *Journal of the History of Biology* 19 (1986): 1–45; Dov Ospovat, *The Development of Darwin's Theory: Natural History, Natural Theology, and Natural Selection, 1838–1859* (Cambridge: Cambridge Univ. Press, 1981); John Hedley Brooke, "The Relations Between Darwin's Science and his Religion," in *Darwinism and Divinity*, ed. John Durant (Oxford: Basil Blackwell, 1985).

13. *LLD*, 2:105.

14. *LLD*, 1:274.

15. *LLD*, 1:282; see also Janet Browne, *Voyaging: Charles Darwin*, vol. 1 (New York: Alfred Knopf, 1995).

16. *LLD*, 2:273.

17. A. Hunter Dupree, "Christianity and the Scientific Community in the Age of Darwin," in *God and Nature*, ed. Lindberg and Numbers.

18. A. R. Wallace, *Contributions to the Theory of Natural Selection*, 2d ed. (New York: Macmillan, 1871), p. 356.

19. John C. Greene, *The Death of Adam* (Ames: Iowa State Univ. Press), p. 301.

20. Greene, *Death of Adam*, p. 81.

21. See Richard Hofstadter, *Social Darwinism in American Thought*, rev. ed. (Boston: Beacon Press, 1955); Gretta Jones, *Social Darwinism and English Thought: The Interaction between Biological Thought and Social Theory* (Atlantic Highlands, NJ: Humanities Press, 1980).

22. Thomas H. Huxley, *Evolution and Ethics* (New York: D. Appleton, 1896), p. 83.

23. Huxley, *Evolution and Ethics*, p. 81.

24. The history of the metaphor of the "warfare between science and religion" is traced in detail in James R. Moore, *Post-Darwinian Controversies, 1870–1900* (Cambridge: Cambridge Univ. Press, 1979), part 1.

25. Charles Hodge, *Systematic Theology* (New York: Scribner, Armstrong, 1872), p. 165; also Charles Hodge, *What Is Darwinism?* (New York: Scribner, Armstrong, 1874 ); see Frederick Gregory, "The Impact of Darwinian Evolution on Protestant Theology in the Nineteenth Century," in *God and Nature*, ed. Lindberg and Numbers.

26. Among general treatments of the influence of evolution on nineteenth-century theology are: Gail Kennedy, ed., *Evolution and Religion* (Boston: D. C. Heath, 1957); John C. Greene, *Darwin and the Modern World-View* (Baton Rouge: Louisiana State Univ. Press, 1961); John Dillenberger, *Protestant Thought and Natural Science* (New York: Doubleday, 1960), chap. 8.

27. Moore, *Post-Darwinian Controversies*, part 3.

28. George Marsden, *Fundamentalism and American Culture: The Shaping of Twentieth Century Evangelicalism* (New York: Oxford Univ. Press, 1980); Ronald Numbers, *The Creationists* (New York: Alfred A. Knopf, 1992).

29. Pius XII, *Divino Afflante Spiritu* (1943).

30. Pius XII, *Humani Generis* (1950); Raymond Nogar in *New Catholic Encyclopedia* (New York: McGraw-Hill, 1967–89), 5:682–94; Walter Ong, ed., *Darwin's Vision and Christian Perspectives* (New York: Macmillan, 1960); Dianne Bergant, C.P., "Creation According to the Old Testament," in *Evolution and Creation*, ed. Ernan McMullin (Notre Dame: Univ. of Notre Dame Press, 1985).

31. John Paul II, "Message to Pontifical Academy of Sciences on Evolution," *Origins* 26 (Dec. 5, 1996): 414–16.

32. Moore, *Post-Darwinian Controversies;* James Moore, "Herbert Spencer's Henchmen: The Evolution of Protestant Liberals in Late Nineteenth Century America," in *Darwinism and Divinity*, ed. Durant.

33. Henry Ward Beecher, "The Two Revelations," included in *Evolution and Religion*, ed. Kennedy.

34. Lyman Abbott, *The Theology of an Evolutionist* (Boston: Houghton Mifflin, 1897).

35. Claude Welch, *Protestant Thought in the Nineteenth Century*, vol. 2, *1870–1914* (New Haven: Yale Univ. Press, 1985), chap. 6.

36. Robert M. Grant, *A Short History of the Interpretation of the Bible* (New York: Macmillan, 1963); Edgar Krantz, *The Historical Critical Method* (Philadelphia: Fortress Press, 1975).

37. Friedrich Schleiermacher, *On Religion: Speeches to its Cultured Despisers,* trans. and ed. Richard Crouter (Cambridge: Cambridge Univ. Press, 1996).

38. Albrecht Ritschl, *The Christian Doctrine of Justification and Reconciliation* (Edinburgh: T. & T. Clark, 1902).

39. Frederick Gregory, *Nature Lost? Natural Science and the German Theological Traditions of the Nineteenth Century* (Cambridge: Harvard Univ. Press, 1992), chap. 6.

40. Herbert Spencer, *First Principles*, 6th ed. (Akron, OH: Werner, 1900).

41. Chauncey Wright, *Philosophical Discussions* (New York: Henry Holt, 1878).

42. Ernst Haeckel, quoted in Eiseley, *Darwin's Century*, p. 346.

43. Frank Turner, *Between Science and Religion: The Reaction to Scientific Naturalism in Late Victorian England* (New Haven: Yale Univ. Press, 1974); Frederick Gregory, *Scientific Materialism in Nineteenth Century Germany* (Dordrecht, Holland: Reidel, 1977).

44. Bertrand Russell, *Mysticism and Logic* (New York: Doubleday, 1957), pp. 45, 54.

45. Friedrich Nietzsche, *The Genealogy of Morals* (New York: Doubleday, 1956).

46. Greene, *Darwin and the Modern World-View*, p. 132.

47. John H. Randall, *The Making of the Modern Mind* (Boston: Houghton Mifflin, 1940), p. 554.

48. Eiseley, *Darwin's Century*, p. 238.

## Chapter 4

1. John Haught in *Science and Religion: From Conflict to Conversation* (Mahwah, NJ: Paulist Press, 1995) rearranges themes in my last two categories and uses the terms *Conflict, Constrast, Contact,* and *Confirmation.*

2. Carl Sagan, *Cosmos* (New York: Random House, 1980), p. 4. See also Thomas W. Ross, "The Implicit Theology of Carl Sagan," *Pacific Theological Review* 18 (Spring 1985): 24–32.

3. Francis Crick, *Of Molecules and Men* (Seattle: Univ. of Washington Press, 1966), p. 10. See also *The Astonishing Hypothesis: The Scientific Search for the Soul* (New York: Charles Scribner's Sons, 1994).

4. Jacques Monod, *Chance and Necessity* (New York: Vintage Books, 1972), p. 180.

5. Monod, BBC lecture, quoted in *Beyond Chance and Necessity*, ed. John Lewis (London: Garnstone Press, 1974), p. ix.

6. Arthur Peacocke, *Creation and the World of Science* (Oxford: Clarendon Press, 1979), chap. 3.

7. Edward O. Wilson, *Sociobiology: The New Synthesis* (Cambridge: Harvard Univ. Press, 1975), p. 4.

8. Edward O. Wilson, *On Human Nature* (Cambridge: Harvard Univ. Press, 1978), chaps. 8, 9.

9. See the essays by Marshall Sahlins, Ruth Mattern, Richard Burian, and others in *The Sociobiology Debate,* ed. Arthur Caplan (New York: Harper & Row, 1978).

10. Daniel Dennett, *Consciousness Explained* (New York: Little Brown, 1991), p. 33; Dennett, *Darwin's Dangerous Idea: Evolution and the Meanings of Life* (New York: Simon & Schuster, 1995).

11. See Haught, *Science and Religion,* chap. 4.

12. Henry Morris, ed., *Scientific Creationism,* 2d ed. (El Cajun, CA: Master Books, 1985). The text of the ruling, McLean v. Arkansas, together with articles by several of the participants in the trial, is printed in *Science, Technology & Human Values* 7 (Summer 1982).

13. See Langdon Gilkey, *Creationism on Trial* (Minneapolis: Winston Press, 1985); Roland Frye, ed., *Is God a Creationist: The Religious Case Against Creation-Science* (New York: Charles Scribner's Sons, 1983).

14. See Philip Kitcher, *Abusing Science: The Case Against Creationism* (Cambridge: MIT Press, 1982); Michael Ruse, *Darwinism Defended: A Guide to the Evolution Controversies* (Reading, MA: Addison-Wesley, 1982).

15. Phillip Johnson, *Darwinism on Trial* (Downer's Grove, IL: Intervarsity Press, 1991), and *Reason in the Balance: The Case Against Naturalism in Science, Law and Education* (Downer's Grove, IL: Intervarsity Press, 1995).

16. Richard H. Bube, *Putting It All Together: Seven Patterns for Relating Science and the Christian Faith* (Lanham, NY: University Press of America, 1995); Howard van Til, *The Fourth Day: What the Bible and the Heavens Are Telling Us About the Creation* (Grand Rapids: Eerdmans, 1986).

17. A good introduction is Karl Barth, *Dogmatics in Outline* (New York: Harper & Row, 1949). See also W. A. Whitehouse, *Christian Faith and the Scientific Attitude* (New York: Philosophical Library, 1952).

18. Rudolf Bultmann, *Jesus Christ and Mythology* (New York: Charles Scribner's Sons, 1958).

19. Gilkey, *Creationism on Trial,* pp. 108–16. See also his *Maker of Heaven and Earth* (Garden City, NY: Doubleday, 1959).

20. Langdon Gilkey, *Religion and the Scientific Future* (New York: Harper & Row, 1970), chap. 2; *Nature, Reality and the Sacred: The Nexus of Science and Religion* (Minneapolis: Fortress Press, 1993).

21. Thomas Torrance, *Theological Science* (Oxford: Oxford Univ. Press, 1969), p. 281.

22. Useful summaries are given in Frederick Ferré, *Language, Logic, and God* (New York: Harper and Brothers, 1961), and William H. Austin, *The Relevance of Natural Science to Theology* (London: Macmillan, 1976). See also Stephen Toulmin, *The Return to Cosmology* (Berkeley and Los Angeles: Univ. of California Press, 1982), part 1.

23. Frederick Streng, *Understanding Religious Life,* 3d ed. (Belmont, CA: Wadsworth, 1985).

24. George Lindbeck, *The Nature of Doctrine: Religion and Theology in a Postliberal Age* (Philadelphia: Westminster Press, 1984), p. 22.

25. Arthur Eddington, *The Nature of the Physical World* (Cambridge: Cambridge Univ. Press, 1928), p. 16.

26. Alfred North Whitehead, *Science and the Modern World* (New York: Macmillan, 1925), chap. 1; Stanley L. Jaki, *The Road of Science and the Ways to God* (Chicago: Univ. of Chicago Press, 1978).

27. Christopher Kaiser, *Creation and the History of Science* (Grand Rapids: Eerdmans, 1991); "Scientific Work in its Theological Dimensions: Toward a Theology of Natural Science," in *Facets of Faith and Science*, vol. 1, ed. Jitse van der Meer (Lanham, MD: University Press of America, 1996).

28. Thomas Torrance, "God and the Contingent World," *Zygon* 14 (1979): 347. See also his *Divine and Contingent Order* (Oxford: Oxford Univ. Press, 1981).

29. Wolfhart Pannenberg, *Theology and the Philosophy of Science* (Philadelphia: Westminster Press, 1976).

30. Ernan McMullin, "Natural Science and Christian Theology," in *Religion, Science, and the Search for Wisdom,* ed. David Byers (Washington, DC: National Conference of Catholic Bishops, 1987). See also his "Introduction: Evolution and Creation," in *Evolution and Creation,* ed. Ernan McMullin (Notre Dame: Univ. of Notre Dame Press, 1985).

31. Ernan McMullin, "How Should Cosmology Relate to Theology?" in *The Sciences and Theology in the Twentieth Century,* ed. Arthur Peacocke (Notre Dame: Univ. of Notre Dame Press, 1981), p. 39.

32. Karl Rahner, *Foundations of Christian Faith* (New York: Seabury, 1978); Gerald McCool, ed., *A Rahner Reader* (New York: Seabury, 1975); Leo O'Donovan, ed., *A World of Grace: An Introduction to the Themes and Foundations of Karl Rahner's Theology* (New York: Seabury, 1980).

33. Karl Rahner, "Christology within an Evolutionary View of the World," *Theological Investigations,* vol. 5 (Baltimore: Helicon Press, 1966); also *Hominization: The Evolutionary Origin of Man as a Theological Problem* (New York: Herder and Herder, 1965).

34. David Tracy, *Blessed Rage for Order* (New York: Seabury, 1975); also *Plurality and Ambiguity* (San Francisco: Harper & Row, 1987).

35. Ian G. Barbour, *Myths, Models, and Paradigms* (New York: Harper & Row, 1974); Sallie McFague, *Metaphorical Theology: Models of God in Religious Language* (Philadelphia: Fortress Press, 1982); Janet Soskice, *Metaphor and Religious Language* (Oxford: Clarendon Press, 1985); Mary Gerhart and Allan Russell, *Metaphorical Process* (Fort Worth: Texas Christian Univ. Press, 1984).

36. Thomas S. Kuhn, *The Structure of Scientific Revolutions,* 2d ed. (Chicago: Univ. of Chicago Press, 1970).

37. Toulmin, *Return to Cosmology,* part III.

38. Michael Polanyi, *Personal Knowledge* (Chicago: Univ. of Chicago Press, 1958).

39. Polanyi, "Faith and Reason," *Journal of Religion* 41 (1961): 244.

40. John Polkinghorne, *One World: The Interaction of Science and Theology* (Princeton: Princeton Univ. Press, 1987), p. 64. See also his *Science and Creation* (London: SPCK, 1988).

41. Holmes Rolston, *Science and Religion: A Critical Survey* (New York: Random House, 1987).

42. Loren Eiseley, *The Immense Journey* (New York: Random House, 1946), p. 210.

43. Aldo Leopold, *A Sand County Almanac* (New York: Oxford Univ. Press, 1949).

44. Annie Dillard, *Pilgrim at Tinker Creek* (New York: Harper & Row, 1974), p. 146.

45. Matthew Fox, *Original Blessing* (Sante Fe: Bear & Co., 1983), and *Creation Spirituality* (San Francisco: HarperSanFrancisco, 1991).

46. Brian Swimme and Thomas Berry, *The Universe Story* (San Francisco: HarperSanFrancisco, 1990).

47. Charlene Spretnak, "Ecofeminism: Our Roots and Flowering," and Starhawk, "Power, Authority, and Mystery: Ecofeminism and Earth-based Spirituality," in *Reweaving the World: The Emergence of Ecofeminism,* ed. Irene Diamond and Gloria Feman Orenstein (San Francisco: Sierra Club Books, 1990); Judith Plant, ed., *Healing the Wounds: The Promise of Ecofeminism* (Philadelphia: New Society Publishers, 1989); Carol Adams, ed., *Ecofeminism and the Sacred* (New York: Continuum, 1993).

48. David Bohm, *Wholeness and the Implicate Order* (Boston: Routledge & Kegan Paul, 1980).

49. Fritjof Capra, *The Tao of Physics* (New York: Bantam Books, 1977).

50. Marilyn Ferguson, *The Aquarian Conspiracy* (Los Angeles: J. P. Tarcher, 1980); Ted Peters, *The Cosmic Self: A Penetrating Look at Today's New Age Movements* (San Francisco: HarperSanFrancisco, 1991); Ted Schultz, ed., *The Fringes of Reason: A Whole Earth Catalog* (New York: Harmony Books, 1989).

51. F. R. Tennant, *Philosophical Theology,* vol. 2 (Cambridge: Cambridge Univ. Press, 1930).

52. See, for example, W. N. Clarke, S.J., "Is Natural Theology Still Possible Today?" in *Physics, Philosophy, and Theology: A Common Quest for Understanding,* ed. Robert J. Russell, William R. Stoeger, S.J., and George V. Coyne, S.J. (The Vatican: Vatican Observatory, and Notre Dame: Univ. of Notre Dame Press, 1988).

53. Richard Swinburne, *The Existence of God* (Oxford: Clarendon Press, 1979), p. 291.

54. Stephen W. Hawking, *A Brief History of Time* (New York: Bantam Books, 1988), p. 291.

55. Freeman Dyson, *Disturbing the Universe* (New York: Harper & Row, 1979); see also Paul Davies, *The Mind of God: The Scientific Basis for a Rational World* (New York: Simon & Schuster, 1992).

56. John Barrow and Frank Tipler, *The Anthropic Cosmological Principle* (Oxford and New York: Oxford Univ. Press, 1986).

57. John Leslie, *Universes* (London and New York: Routledge, 1989).

58. Hugh Montefiore, *The Probability of God* (London: SCM Press, 1985).

59. Arthur Peacocke, *Theology for a Scientific Age,* enlarged edition (Minneapolis: Fortress Press, 1993).

60. Pierre Teilhard de Chardin, *The Phenomenon of Man* (New York: Harper & Row, 1959). I have discussed Teilhard in "Five Ways of Reading Teilhard," *Soundings* 51 (1968): 115–45, and in "Teilhard's Process Metaphysics," *Journal of Religion* 49 (1969): 136–59.

61. For example, James A. Nash, *Loving Nature: Ecological Integrity and Christian Responsibility* (Nashville: Abingdon Press, 1991).

62. Ian G. Barbour, ed., *Earth Might Be Fair: Reflections on Ethics, Religion and Ecology* (Englewood Cliffs, NJ: Prentice-Hall, 1972); *Technology, Environment and Human Values* (New York: Praeger, 1980), chap. 3; *Ethics in an Age of Technology* (San Francisco: HarperSanFrancisco, 1993), chap. 3; "The Church in an Environmental Age," in *Creation as Beloved of God,* ed. Rodney Petersen and Donald Conroy (Atlantic Highlands, NJ: Humanities Press, 1997).

63. Charles Hartshorne, *The Divine Relativity* (New Haven: Yale Univ. Press, 1948).

64. Charles Birch and John B. Cobb, Jr., *The Liberation of Life* (Cambridge: Cambridge Univ. Press, 1981).

65. John B. Cobb, Jr. and David Ray Griffin, *Process Theology: An Introduction* (Philadelphia: Westminster Press, 1976), p. 94. See also L. Charles Birch, *Nature and God* (London: SCM Press, 1965).

## Chapter 5

1. Several sections of this chapter are revisions or summaries of portions of two earlier books: Ian G. Barbour, *Issues in Science and Religion* (Englewood Cliffs, NJ: Prentice-Hall, 1966) and *Myths, Models, and Paradigms* (New York: Harper & Row, 1974). The original passages are identified in the notes below.

2. Carl G. Hempel, *Philosophy of Natural Science* (Englewood Cliffs, NJ: Prentice-Hall, 1966); Karl R. Popper, *The Logic of Scientific Discovery* (London: Hutchinson's Univ. Library, 1956).

3. W. V. Quine, "Two Dogmas of Empiricism," in his *From a Logical Point of View,* 2d ed. (New York: Harper Torchbooks, 1963).

4. N. R. Hanson, *Patterns of Discovery* (Cambridge: Cambridge Univ. Press, 1958); Michael Polanyi, *Personal Knowledge* (Chicago: Univ. of Chicago Press, 1958).

5. Thomas S. Kuhn, *The Structure of Scientific Revolutions,* 2d ed. (Chicago: Univ. of Chicago Press, 1970).

6. See, for example, Frederick J. Streng, *Understanding Religious Life* (Belmont, CA: Dickenson, 1976); Ninian Smart, *Worldviews* (New York: Charles Scribner's Sons, 1983).

7. Mircea Eliade, *The Sacred and the Profane,* trans. W. Trask (New York: Harcourt, Brace & World, 1959).

8. *Bhagavad Gita,* trans. Swami Prabhavananda and Christopher Isherwood (New York: New American Library, 1972); David Kinsley, *Hinduism* (Englewood Cliffs, NJ: Prentice-Hall, 1982).

9. In *Myths, Models, and Paradigms,* chap. 3, I discuss writings on scientific models by Mary Hesse, Max Black, Richard Braithwaite, Peter Achinstein, and others. See also W. H. Leatherdale, *The Role of Analogy, Model and Metaphor in Science* (New York: American Elsevier, 1974).

10. Niels Bohr, *Atomic Theory and the Description of Nature* (Cambridge: Cambridge Univ. Press, 1934), p. 96.

11. See Barbour, *Issues in Science and Religion,* pp. 162–74; also *Myths, Models, and Paradigms,* pp. 34–38.

12. Larry Laudan, "A Confutation of Convergent Realism," in *Scientific Realism,* ed. Jarret Leplin (Berkeley and Los Angeles: Univ. of California Press, 1984).

13. Ian Hacking, *Representing and Intervening* (Cambridge: Cambridge Univ. Press, 1983); Michael Devitt, *Realism and Truth* (Princeton: Princeton Univ. Press, 1984); James T. Cushing, C. F. Delaney, and Gary Gutting, eds., *Science and Reality* (Notre Dame: Univ. of Notre Dame Press, 1984); Ron Harré, *Varieties of Realism* (Oxford: Basil Blackwell, 1986); and Hilary Putnam, *The Many Faces of Realism* (LaSalle, IL: Open Court, 1987).

14. Ernan McMullin, "A Case for Scientific Realism," in *Scientific Realism,* ed. Leplin, p. 39.

15. In *Myths, Models, and Paradigms,* chap. 4, I discuss the writings of Ian Ramsey and Frederick Ferré on models in religion, and I develop a theory of religious models. There is some discussion of models in Earl MacCormac, *Metaphor and Myth in Science and Religion* (Durham, NC: Duke Univ. Press, 1976).

16. Richard Braithwaite, *An Empiricist's View of the Nature of Religious Belief* (Cambridge: Cambridge Univ. Press, 1955); see William H. Austin, *The Relevance of Natural Science to Theology* (London: Macmillan, 1976), chap. 3.

17. Janet Soskice, *Metaphor and Religious Language* (Oxford: Clarendon Press, 1985).

18. Frank Brown, "Transfiguration: Poetic Metaphor and Theological Reflection," *Journal of Religion* 62 (1982): 39–56; also his *Transfiguration: Poetic Metaphor and the Language of Religious Belief* (Chapel Hill: Univ. of North Carolina Press, 1983).

19. Barbour, *Myths, Models, and Paradigms,* pp. 56–60.

20. Ninian Smart, *The Concept of Worship* (London: Macmillan, 1972), and *Worldviews,* chap. 3.

21. Winston King, *Introduction to Religion: A Phenomenological Approach* (New York: Harper & Row, 1968), p. 165.

22. Ninian Smart, *Reasons and Faiths* (London: Routledge & Kegan Paul, 1958).

23. Sallie McFague, *Metaphorical Theology: Models of God in Religious Language* (Philadelphia: Fortress Press, 1982).

24. Sallie McFague, *Models of God: Theology for an Ecological, Nuclear Age* (Philadelphia: Fortress Press, 1987).

25. Kuhn, *Structure of Scientific Revolutions,* p. 147.

26. See Barbour, *Myths, Models, and Paradigms,* chap. 6.

27. See also Polanyi, *Personal Knowledge.*

28. Harold Brown, *Perception, Theory and Commitment: The New Philosophy of Science* (Chicago: Univ. of Chicago Press, 1977).

29. Brown, *Perception, Theory and Commitment,* p. 167.

30. Brown, *Perception, Theory and Commitment,* p. 167.

31. Frederick Streng, "Lens and Insight: Paradigm Changes and Different Kinds of Religious Consciousness" (Plenary address to Second Conference on East-West Religions in Encounter, "Paradigm Shifts in Buddhism and Christianity," Hawaii Loa College, Oahu, Hawaii, Jan. 4, 1984).

32. Hans Küng, "Paradigm Change in Theology," in *Paradigm Change in Theology,* ed. Hans Küng and David Tracy (Edinburgh: T. & T. Clark, 1989).

33. Stephan Pfürtner, "The Paradigms of Thomas Aquinas and Martin Luther: Did Luther's Message of Justification Mean a Paradigm Shift?" in *Paradigm Change in Theology,* ed. Küng and Tracy.

34. Kuhn, *Structure of Scientific Revolutions;* Polanyi, *Personal Knowledge;* W. D. King, "Reason, Tradition, and the Progressiveness of Science," in *Paradigms and Revolutions,* ed. Gary Gutting (Notre Dame: Univ. of Notre Dame Press, 1980).

35. Mark Blaug, "Kuhn versus Lakatos, or Paradigms versus Research Programs in the History of Economics," in *Paradigms and Revolutions,* ed. Gutting.

36. Richard Vernon, "Politics as Metaphor: Cardinal Newman and Professor Kuhn," in *Paradigms and Revolutions,* ed. Gutting.

37. Imre Lakatos, "Falsification and the Methodology of Scientific Research Programmes," in *Criticism and the Growth of Knowledge,* ed. I. Lakatos and A. Musgrave (Cambridge: Cambridge Univ. Press, 1970). Also Lakatos, *Philosophical Papers,* vol. 1, ed. John Worall and Gregory Currie (Cambridge: Cambridge Univ. Press, 1978).

38. See William Austin, "Religious Commitment and the Logical Status of Doctrines," *Religious Studies* 9 (1973): 39–48.

39. Nancey Murphy, *Theology in the Age of Scientific Reasoning* (Ithaca: Cornell Univ. Press, 1990); "Acceptability Criteria for Work in Theology and Science," *Zygon* 22 (1987): 279–97.

40. Gary Gutting, *Religious Belief and Religious Skepticism* (Notre Dame: Univ. of Notre Dame Press, 1982), chap. 5.

41. Basil Mitchell, *The Justification of Religious Belief* (London: Macmillan, 1973), chaps. 5–8.

42. H. Richard Niebuhr, *The Meaning of Revelation* (New York: Macmillan, 1941).

43. Paul Tillich, *Systematic Theology* (Chicago: Univ. of Chicago Press, 1957), 2:165–68.

## Chapter 6

1. Carl Becker, "What Are Historical Facts?" in *The Philosophy of History in Our Time,* ed. H. Meyerhoff (New York: Doubleday, 1959), p. 132.

2. William Dray, *Laws and Explanation in History* (Oxford: Oxford Univ. Press, 1957), p. 150.

3. R. G. Collingwood, *The Idea of History* (London: Oxford Univ. Press, 1946), part V.

4. Peter Winch, *The Idea of a Social Science* (London: Routledge & Kegan Paul, 1958).

5. C. G. Hempel, "The Function of General Laws in History," in *Readings in Philosophical Analysis,* ed. H. Feigl and W. Sellars (New York: Appleton-Century-Crofts, 1949), p. 459.

6. William Dray, *Philosophy of History* (Englewood Cliffs, NJ: Prentice-Hall, 1964); Patrick Gardiner, ed., *Theories of History* (Glencoe, IL: Free Press, 1959).

7. Terence Bell, "On Historical Explanation," *Philosophy of Social Science* 2 (1972): 182ff.

8. Holmes Rolston, *Science and Religion: A Critical Survey* (New York: Random House, 1987), chap. 6.

9. Gordon Graham, *Historical Explanation Reconsidered* (Aberdeen, Scotland: Aberdeen Univ. Press, 1983).

10. Stephen Toulmin, *Human Understanding: The Collective Use and Evolution of Concepts* (Princeton: Princeton Univ. Press, 1972), chaps. 2 and 6.

11. Phillip Clayton, *Explanation from Physics to Theology* (New Haven: Yale Univ. Press, 1989).

12. Paul Ricoeur, *Time and Narrative,* vol. 1 (Chicago: Univ. of Chicago Press, 1984).

13. See James B. Wiggins, ed., *Religion as Story* (New York: Harper & Row, 1975); Michael Goldberg, *Theology and Narrative: A Critical Introduction* (Nashville: Abingdon Press, 1982); Gary Comstock, "Two Types of Narrative Theology," *Journal of the American Academy of Religion* 55 (1987): 687–720.

14. David Tracy, *The Analogical Imagination: Christian Theology and the Culture of Pluralism* (New York: Crossroad Press, 1981).

15. Hans Frei, *The Eclipse of Biblical Narrative* (New Haven: Yale Univ. Press, 1974).

16. Sallie McFague TeSelle, *Speaking in Parables: A Study in Metaphor and Theology* (Philadelphia: Fortress Press, 1975); John Dominic Crossan, *In Parables: The Challenge of the Historical Jesus* (New York: Harper & Row, 1973).

17. H. Richard Niebuhr, *The Meaning of Revelation* (New York: Macmillan, 1941).

18. James McClendon, *Biography as Theology: How Life Stories Can Remake Today's Theology* (Nashville: Abingdon, 1974).

19. Stanley Hauerwas, *A Community of Character* (Notre Dame: Univ. of Notre Dame Press, 1981).

20. Van Harvey, *The Historian and the Believer* (New York: Macmillan, 1966).

21. Goldberg, *Theology and Narrative*, p. 240.

22. Roy MacLeod, "Changing Perspectives in the Social History of Science," in *Science, Technology, and Society*, ed. Ina Spiegel-Rossing and Derek Price (Beverly Hills: Sage Publications, 1977); Sal Restivo, "Some Perspectives in Contemporary Sociology of Science," *Science, Technology & Human Values* 35 (Spring 1981): 22–30.

23. J. R. Ravetz, *Science and Its Social Problems* (Oxford: Oxford Univ. Press, 1971).

24. Barry Barnes, *Interests and the Growth of Knowledge* (London: Routledge & Kegan Paul, 1977); David Bloor, *Knowledge and Social Imagery* (London: Routledge & Kegan Paul, 1966); Karin Knorr-Cetina, *The Manufacture of Knowledge* (Oxford: Pergamon, 1981); Karin Knorr-Cetina and Michael Mulkay, eds., *Science Observed* (Beverly Hills: Sage, 1983).

25. Mary Hesse, "Cosmology as Myth," in *Cosmology and Theology*, ed. David Tracy and Nicholas Lash (New York: Seabury, 1983); also her *Revolutions and Reconstructions in the Philosophy of Science* (Bloomington: Indiana Univ. Press, 1980), chap. 2.

26. Paul Forman, "Weimar Culture, Causality and Quantum Theory, 1918–1927," *Historical Studies in Physical Science* 3 (1971): 1.

27. Andrew Pickering, *Constructing Quarks* (Chicago: Univ. of Chicago Press, 1984).

28. Rubem Alves, "On the Eating Habits of Science" and "Biblical Faith and the Poor of the World," in *Faith and Science in an Unjust World*, ed. Roger Shinn (Geneva: World Council of Churches, 1980).

29. Gustavo Gutiérrez, *A Theology of Liberation* (Maryknoll, NY: Orbis Books, 1973); José Miguez-Bonino, *Doing Theology in a Revolutionary Situation* (Philadelphia: Fortress Press, 1975).

30. See Robert McAfee Brown, *Theology in a New Key* (Philadelphia: Westminster Press, 1978).

31. For example, James H. Cone, *God of the Oppressed* (New York: Seabury, 1975).

32. Ruth Bleier, *Science and Gender: A Critique of Biology and Its Theories of Women* (New York: Pergamon Press, 1984).

33. Helen Longino, "Scientific Objectivity and Feminist Theorizing," *Liberal Education* 67 (1981): 187–95. See also Ruth Hubbard, "Have Only Men Evolved?" in *Biological Woman: The Convenient Myth*, ed. R. Hubbard, M. Henifin, and B. Fried (Cambridge, MA: Schenkman, 1982).

34. Evelyn Fox Keller, *A Feeling for the Organism* (San Francisco: Freeman, 1983) and *Reflections on Gender and Science* (New Haven: Yale Univ. Press, 1984).

35. Sandra Harding, *The Science Question in Feminism* (Ithaca: Cornell Univ. Press, 1986), p. 250.

36. Carolyn Merchant, *The Death of Nature: Women, Ecology, and the Scientific Revolution* (New York: Harper & Row, 1980).

37. Nancy Chodorow, *The Reproduction of Mothering* (Berkeley and Los Angeles: Univ. of California Press, 1978); see also Keller, *Reflections on Gender and Science*, chaps. 4, 5, and 6.

38. For example, Letty Russell, *Feminist Interpretations of the Bible* (Philadelphia: Westminster, 1985).

39. Rosemary Radford Ruether, *New Woman/New Earth* (New York: Seabury Press, 1975) and *Sexism and God-Talk* (Boston: Beacon Press, 1983).

40. Mary Daly, *Beyond God the Father* (Boston: Beacon Press, 1973); Carol Christ and Judith Plaskow, eds., *Womanspirit Rising* (San Francisco: Harper & Row, 1979).

41. Richard Swinburne, "The Evidential Value of Religious Experience," in *The Sciences and*

*Theology in the Twentieth Century*, ed. Arthur Peacocke (Notre Dame: Univ. of Notre Dame Press, 1981), p. 190. See also his *The Existence of God* (Oxford: Oxford Univ. Press, 1979), chap. 13.

42. William Alston, "Christian Experience and Christian Belief," in *Faith and Rationality*, ed. A. Plantinga and N. Wolsterhoff (Notre Dame: Univ. of Notre Dame Press, 1983).

43. Steven Katz, "Language, Epistemology, and Mysticism," in *Mysticism and Philosophical Analysis*, ed. S. Katz (Oxford: Oxford Univ. Press, 1978), p. 46. See also Richard Jones, "Experience and Conceptualization in Mystical Knowledge," *Zygon* 18 (1983): 139-65.

44. Peter Donovan, *Interpreting Religious Experience* (London: Sheldon Press, 1979), p. 35.

45. Donovan, *Interpreting Religious Experience*, p. 72.

46. Ninian Smart, "Interpretation and Mystical Experience," *Religious Studies* 1 (1965): 75 and 79. See also his "Understanding Religious Experience," in *Mysticism and Philosophical Analysis*, ed. Katz.

47. Barbour, *Myths, Models, and Paradigms*, chap. 7.

48. For a critique, see William Rottschaefer, "Religious Cognition as Interpreted Experience: An Examination of Ian Barbour's Comparison of Epistemic Structures of Science and Religion," *Zygon* 20 (1985): 265-82.

49. John E. Smith, *Experience and God* (Oxford: Oxford Univ. Press, 1969), pp. 52, 84.

50. On religious pluralism, see Owen Thomas, ed., *Attitudes Toward Other Religions* (New York: University Press of America, 1986); John Hick and Brian Hebblethwaite, eds., *Christianity and Other Religions* (Philadelphia: Fortress Press, 1980).

51. John Hick, *God Has Many Names* (Philadelphia: Westminster Press, 1982), p. 52.

52. Hick, *God Has Many Names*, p. 75.

53. John Hick, *Problems of Religious Pluralism* (New York: St. Martin's Press, 1985), chap. 3.

54. John Cobb, *Beyond Dialogue* (Philadelphia: Fortress Press, 1982), explores ways in which Christianity and Buddhism can learn from and modify each other.

55. Paul F. Knitter, *No Other Name? A Critical Survey of Christian Attitudes Toward the World Religions* (Maryknoll, NY: Orbis Books, 1986); John Hick and Paul F. Knitter, eds., *The Myth of Christian Uniqueness: Toward a Pluralistic Theology of Religions* (Maryknoll, NY: Orbis Books, 1987).

56. The metaphor of chain and cable appears in Charles Sanders Peirce, *Collected Papers of Charles Sanders Peirce*, ed. Charles Hartshorne and Paul Weiss (Cambridge: Harvard Univ. Press, 1931-1935), 5:264.

57. Ninian Smart, *Worldviews* (New York: Charles Scribner's Sons, 1983), p. 170.

58. See Hick, *Problems of Religious Pluralism*, chap. 5.

59. On confessionalism and the dangers of trying to prove superiority, see H. R. Niebuhr, *The Meaning of Revelation*, chap. 1.

## Chapter 7

1. Readable accounts of quantum theory are given in Heinz Pagels, *The Cosmic Code* (New York: Bantam Books, 1982), part 1; J. C. Polkinghorne, *The Quantum World* (London: Penguin Books, 1986).

2. See, for example, James Trefil, *The Moment of Creation* (New York: Collier Books, 1983), part 2.

3. Niels Bohr, *Atomic Theory and the Description of Nature* (Cambridge: Cambridge Univ. Press, 1934), pp. 96-101; *Atomic Physics and Human Knowledge* (New York: John Wiley & Sons, 1958), pp. 39-41, 59-61.

4. Henry Folse, *The Philosophy of Niels Bohr: The Framework of Complementarity* (New York: North Holland, 1985), p. 237.

5. Folse, *Philosophy of Niels Bohr*, pp. 209 and 255.

6. Folse, *Philosophy of Niels Bohr*, p. 259.

7. C. A. Coulson, *Science and Christian Belief* (Chapel Hill: Univ. of North Carolina Press, 1955), chap. 3. See also D. M. MacKay, "Complementarity in Scientific and Theological Thinking," *Zygon* 9 (1974): 225-44.

8. See Barbour, *Issues in Science and Religion*, pp. 292-94, and Barbour, *Myths, Models, and Paradigms*, pp. 77-78.

9. Peter Alexander, "Complementary Descriptions," *Mind* 65 (1956): 145.

10. See Barbour, *Issues in Science and Religion*, pp. 298–305; also Robert Russell, "Theology and Quantum Theory," in *Physics, Philosophy, and Theology: A Common Quest for Understanding*, ed. R. J. Russell, W. R. Stoeger, S.J., and G. V. Coyne, S.J. (The Vatican: Vatican Observatory, and Notre Dame: Univ. of Notre Dame Press, 1988). A more technical elaboration is M. Jammer, *The Philosophy of Quantum Mechanics* (New York: John Wiley & Sons, 1974).

11. Albert Einstein letter quoted in M. Born, *Natural Philosophy of Cause and Chance* (Oxford: Oxford Univ. Press, 1949), p. 122. See also A. Pais, *Subtle Is the Lord* (Oxford: Oxford Univ. Press, 1982).

12. David Bohm, *Causality and Chance in Modern Physics* (Princeton: D. Van Nostrand, 1957).

13. Werner Heisenberg, *Physics and Philosophy* (New York: Harper & Row, 1958), and *Physics and Beyond* (New York: Harper & Row, 1971).

14. See Paul Davies, *God and the New Physics* (New York: Simon & Schuster, 1983), chaps. 8, 12; also *Other Worlds* (London: Abacus, 1982), chap. 7.

15. See Trefil, *Moment of Creation*, pp. 111–18.

16. Louis de Broglie, *Physics and Microphysics*, trans. M. Davidson (New York: Pantheon Books, 1955), pp. 114–15.

17. Jonathan Powers, *Philosophy and the New Physics* (New York: Methuen, 1982), chap. 4.

18. On the Bell's Theorem experiments, see Pagels, *Cosmic Code*, chap. 12; Polkinghorne, *Quantum World*, chap. 7; Davies, *Other Worlds*, chap. 6, and *God and the New Physics*, chap. 8.

19. Arthur Robinson, "Loophole Closed in Quantum Mechanics Test," *Science* 219 (1983): 40–41.

20. Davies, *Other Worlds*, p. 125. See also Henry Folse, "Complementarity, Bell's Theorem, and the Framework of Process Metaphysics," *Process Studies* 11 (1981): 259–73.

21. Polkinghorne, *Quantum World*, pp. 79, 80.

22. David Bohm, *Wholeness and the Implicate Order* (Boston: Routledge & Kegan Paul, 1980); David Ray Griffin, ed., *Physics and the Ultimate Significance of Time* (Albany: State Univ. of New York, 1985); Robert John Russell, "The Physics of David Bohm and Its Relevance to Philosophy and Theology," *Zygon* 20 (1985): 135–58 (this whole issue is devoted to Bohm).

23. See chapters by John Bell, David Bohm, and Basil Haley in *The Ghost in the Atom*, ed. Davies and Brown. See also James T. Cushing and Ernan McMullin, eds., *Philosophical Consequences of Quantum Theory: Reflections on Bell's Theorem* (Notre Dame: Univ. of Notre Dame Press, 1989).

24. Among popular accounts of relativity are Lincoln Barnett, *The Universe and Dr. Einstein* (New York: New American Library, 1952); Davies, *Other Worlds*, chap. 2; and William Kaufman, *Relativity and Cosmology*, 2d ed. (New York: Harper & Row, 1977). A more technical exposition is Lawrence Sklar, *Space, Time, and Spacetime* (Berkeley and Los Angeles: Univ. of California Press, 1974).

25. Quoted in Davies, *Other Worlds*, p. 50.

26. Milič Čapek, "Relativity and the Status of Becoming," *Foundations of Physics* 5 (1975): 607–17. See also Lawrence Fagg, *The Becoming of Time: Integrating Physical and Religious Time* (Atlanta: Scholars Press, 1995).

27. Andrew Dufner and Robert John Russell, "Foundations in Physics for Revising the Creation Tradition," in *Cry of the Environment*, ed. Philip Joranson and Ken Butigan (Santa Fe: Bear & Co., 1984).

28. Karl Heim, *Christian Faith and Natural Science* (New York: Harper and Brothers, 1953), pp. 133–34.

29. John Wilcox, "A Question from Physics for Certain Theists," *Journal of Religion* 41 (1961): 293–300; Lewis Ford, "Is Process Theism Compatible with Relativity Theory?" *Journal of Religion* 48 (1968): 124–35; Paul Fitzgerald, "Relativity Physics and the God of Process Philosophy," *Process Studies* 2 (1972): 251–76.

30. Davies, *God and the New Physics*, chap. 5.

31. Ilya Prigogine and Isabelle Stengers, *Order out of Chaos* (New York: Bantam Books, 1984).

32. James Gliek, *Chaos: Making a New Science* (New York: Viking, 1987); M. Mitchell Waldrop, *Complexity: The Emerging Science at the Edge of Order and Chaos* (New York: Simon & Schuster, 1992); John Holte, ed., *Chaos: The New Science* (Lanham, MD: University Press of America, 1993).

33. John Polkinghorne, "The Metaphysics of Divine Action," in *Chaos and Complexity: Scientific Perspectives on Divine Action*, ed. Robert John Russell, Nancey Murphy, and Arthur R. Peacocke (Rome: Vatican Observatory, and Berkeley: Center for Theology and the Natural Sciences, 1995).

34. Stephen Kellert, *In the Wake of Chaos: Unpredictable Order in Dynamic Systems* (Chicago: Univ. of Chicago Press, 1993).

35. James Gliek in closing address, 1990 Nobel Conference at Gustavus Adolphus College, quoted by Steven Weinberg in *Dreams of a Final Theory* (New York: Random House, 1992), p. 60.

36. Stuart Kauffman, *The Origins of Order: Self-Organization and Selection in Evolution* (New York: Oxford Univ. Press, 1993) and *At Home in the Universe: The Search for Laws of Self-Organization and Complexity* (New York: Oxford Univ. Press, 1995).

37. James Jeans, *The Mysterious Universe* (Cambridge: Cambridge Univ. Press, 1930), p. 186.

38. Arthur Eddington, *The Nature of the Physical World* (Cambridge: Cambridge Univ. Press, 1928), p. 244.

39. Eugene Wigner, *Symmetries and Reflections* (Bloomington: Indiana Univ. Press, 1967), p. 172.

40. John A. Wheeler, "Bohr, Einstein, and the Strange Lesson of the Quantum," in *Mind and Nature*, ed. Richard Elvee (San Francisco: Harper & Row, 1982); "The Universe as Home for Man," *American Scientist* 62 (1974): 683–91; "Beyond the Black Hole," in *Some Strangeness in the Proportion*, ed. Harry Woolf (Reading, MA: Addison-Wesley, 1980).

41. Holmes Rolston, *Science and Religion: A Critical Survey* (New York: Random House, 1987), p. 53.

42. Rolston, *Science and Religion*, p. 52.

43. William Pollard, *Chance and Providence* (New York: Charles Scribner's Sons, 1958).

44. Gary Zukav, *The Dancing Wu Li Masters* (New York: William Morrow, 1979); William Talbot, *Mysticism and the New Physics* (New York: Bantam Books, 1981); Amaury de Riencourt, *The Eye of Shiva* (New York: William Morrow, 1981); Ken Wilber, ed., *Quantum Questions: Mystical Writings of the World's Greatest Physicists* (Boulder, CO: Shambhala, 1984).

45. Fritjof Capra, *The Tao of Physics* (New York: Bantam Books, 1977), p. 266.

46. Sal Restivo, "Parallels and Paradoxes in Modern Physics and Eastern Mysticism," *Social Studies of Science* 8 (1978): 143–81 and 12 (1982): 37–71.

47. David Bohm, *Wholeness and the Implicate Order,* chap. 7; "Religion as Wholeness and the Problem of Fragmentation," *Zygon* 20 (1985): 124–33.

48. Richard Jones, *Science and Mysticism* (Lewisburg, PA: Bucknell Univ. Press, 1986).

49. Charles Hartshorne, *The Divine Relativity* (New Haven: Yale Univ. Press, 1948).

50. T. S. Eliot, *Burnt Norton* (London: Faber & Faber, 1941), p. 9. Used by permission of Faber & Faber.

**Chapter 8**

1. Readable general accounts of recent work in physical cosmology can be found in James Trefil, *The Moment of Creation* (New York: Collier Books, 1983), and John Barrow and Joseph Silk, *The Left Hand of Creation* (New York: Basic Books, 1983).

2. Michael Green, "Superstrings," *Scientific American* 255 (Sept. 1986): 48–60; Mitchell Waldrop, "Strings as a Theory of Everything," *Science* 229 (1985): 226–28.

3. For data in Figure 3, see Trefil, *Moment of Creation*, p. 34; Barrow and Silk, *Left Hand of Creation*, pp. 86 and 156.

4. Steven Weinberg, *The First Three Minutes* (New York: Basic Books, 1977).

5. Pope Pius XII, "Modern Science and the Existence of God," *The Catholic Mind* (Mar. 1952): 182–92.

6. Robert Jastrow, *God and the Astronomers* (New York: W. W. Norton, 1978), p. 116.

7. "Cosmic God Squad Under Fire," *Science* 257 (July 3, 1992): 29.

8. Fred Hoyle, *Ten Faces of the Universe* (San Francisco: W. H. Freeman, 1977).

9. For example, Isa. 51:9, Pss. 74:14, 89:10.

10. Jon D. Levinson, *Creation and the Persistence of Evil* (San Francisco: Harper & Row, 1988).

11. Joan O'Brien and Wilfred Major, *In the Beginning: Creation Myths from Ancient Mesopotamia, Israel, and Greece* (Chico, CA: Scholars Press, 1982).

12. Gerard von Rad, *The Problem of the Hexateuch* (New York: McGraw-Hill, 1966), pp. 131–43.

13. Claus Westermann, *Creation* (Philadelphia: Fortress Press, 1974); Bernhard Anderson, ed., *Creation in the Old Testament* (Philadelphia: Fortress Press, 1984).

14. See Ernan McMullin, "How Should Cosmology Relate to Theology?" in *The Sciences and Theology in the Twentieth Century,* ed. Arthur Peacocke (Notre Dame: Univ. of Notre Dame Press, 1981), pp. 19–21.

15. Edmund Jacob, *Theology of the Old Testament* (New York: Harper and Brothers, 1958), p. 139.

16. Jaroslav Pelikan, "Creation and Causality in the History of Christian Thought," *Journal of Religion* 40 (1960): 250. See also John Reumann, *Creation and New Creation* (Minneapolis: Augsburg, 1973), chap. 3.

17. Langdon Gilkey, *Maker of Heaven and Earth* (Garden City, NY: Doubleday, 1959); also *Creationism on Trial* (Minneapolis: Winston Press, 1985), chap. 8.

18. Barbour, *Issues in Science and Religion,* chap. 12.

19. David Kelsey, "Creatio Ex Nihilo," in *Evolution and Creation,* ed. Ernan McMullin (Notre Dame: Univ. of Notre Dame Press, 1985).

20. Frederick Streng, *Understanding Religious Life,* 3d ed. (Belmont, CA: Wadsworth, 1985); Mircea Eliade, *Myth and Reality* (New York: Harper & Row, 1963).

21. *Weekday Prayer Book* (New York: Rabbinical Assembly, 1962), p. 42.

22. B. J. Carr and M. J. Rees, "The Anthropic Principle and the Structure of the Physical World," *Nature* 278 (1979): 605–12. See also John Barrow and Frank Tipler, *The Anthropic Cosmological Principle* (Oxford and New York: Oxford Univ. Press, 1986).

23. Stephen W. Hawking, *A Brief History of Time* (New York: Bantam Books, 1988), p. 121; also his "The Anisotropy of the Universe at Large Times," in *Confrontation of Cosmological Theories with Observational Data;* ed. M. S. Longair (Dordrecht, Holland: Reidel, 1974).

24. Carr and Rees, "Anthropic Principle."

25. Barrow and Silk, *Left Hand of Creation,* p. 91; Paul Davies, *God and the New Physics* (New York: Simon & Schuster, 1983), p. 30.

26. B. Carter, "Large Number Coincidences and the Anthropic Principle in Cosmology," in *Cosmological Theories,* ed. Longair. See also Davies, *God and the New Physics,* chap. 12.

27. Stephen Hawking, quoted in John Boslough, *Stephen Hawking's Universe* (New York: William Morrow, 1985), p. 121.

28. Freeman Dyson, *Disturbing the Universe* (New York: Harper & Row, 1979), p. 250.

29. Weinberg, *The First Three Minutes,* chap. 8; John Gribbin, *In the Beginning: After COBE and Before the Big Bang* (Boston: Little Brown, 1993).

30. See P.C.W. Davies, *The Accidental Universe* (Cambridge: Cambridge Univ. Press, 1982).

31. Peter Atkins, *Creation Revisited* (Oxford and New York: W. H. Freeman, 1992), chap. 6.

32. John Leslie, *Universes* (London and New York: Routledge, 1989).

33. Alan Guth and Paul Steinhardt, "The Inflationary Universe," *Scientific American* 250 (May 1984): 116–28; Andre Linde, "The Self-Reproducing Inflationary Universe," *Scientific American* 271 (Nov. 1994): 48–55.

34. Hawking, *A Brief History of Time,* p. 174. A technical presentation of his theory is given in J. B. Hartle and S. W. Hawking, "Wave Function of the Universe," *Physical Review D* 28 (1983): 2960–75. See also C. J. Isham, "Creation of the Universe as a Quantum Process," in *Physics, Philosophy, and Theology,* ed. Russell et al.

35. Hawking, *Brief History of Time,* p. 175.

36. See Michael Foster, "The Christian Doctrine of Creation and the Rise of Modern Science," in *Creation: The Impact of an Idea,* ed. Daniel O'Connor and Francis Oakley (New York: Charles Scribner's Sons, 1969).

37. Thomas F. Torrance, *Divine and Contingent Order* (Oxford: Oxford Univ. Press, 1981). See also Stanley L. Jaki, *The Road to Science and the Ways to God* (Chicago: Univ. of Chicago Press, 1978).

38. Albert Einstein, *Ideas and Opinions* (London: Souvenir Press, 1973), p. 262; See Frederick Ferré, "Einstein on Religion and Science," *American Journal of Theology and Philosophy* 1 (1980): 21–28.

39. Quoted in Robert Jastrow, *God and the Astronomers*, p. 28.
40. Geoffrey F. Chew, "Bootstrap: A Scientific Idea?" *Science* 161 (1968): 762–65.
41. Trefil, *Moment of Creation*, p. 223.
42. John Polkinghorne, *One World: The Interaction of Science and Theology* (Princeton: Princeton Univ. Press, 1987), pp. 45, 63, and 98.
43. Robert John Russell, "Contingency in Physics and Cosmology: A Critique of the Theology of Wolfhart Pannenberg," *Zygon* 23 (1988): 23–43.
44. W. Norris Clarke, "Is Natural Theology Possible Today?" in *Physics, Philosophy, and Theology,* ed. Russell et al.
45. David Tracy, *Blessed Rage for Order* (New York: Seabury, 1975), chap. 5.
46. Pierre Teilhard de Chardin, *The Phenomenon of Man* (New York: Harper & Row, 1959), pp. 226–28.
47. Roger Schmidt, *Exploring Religion* (Belmont, CA: Wadsworth, 1980), chap. 7; Mircea Eliade, *The Sacred and the Profane*, trans. W. Trask (New York: Harcourt, Brace & World, 1959), chap. 4.
48. Claus Westermann, *Beginning and End in the Bible* (Philadelphia: Fortress Press, 1972); Ted Peters, *Futures—Human and Divine* (Atlanta: John Knox Press, 1978), chaps. 1, 2; Brian Hebblethwaite, *The Christian Hope* (Grand Rapids: Eerdmans, 1985).
49. Carl Braaten, "The Kingdom of God and Life Everlasting," in *Christian Theology*, 2d ed., ed. Peter Hodgson and Robert King (Philadelphia: Fortress Press, 1985); Zachary Hayes, O.F.M., *What Are They Saying About the End of the World?* (New York: Paulist Press, 1983).
50. Weinberg, *The First Three Minutes*, p. 144.
51. Steven Weinberg, *Dreams of a Final Theory* (New York: Pantheon, 1992), p. 255.
52. Freeman Dyson, *Infinite in All Directions* (New York: Harper & Row, 1988), p. 114.
53. Barrow and Tipler, *The Anthropic Cosmological Principle*, chap. 10; Frank Tipler, *The Physics of Immortality* (London: Macmillan, 1995).
54. See Peacocke, *Creation and the World of Science*, p. 330.

## Chapter 9

1. Julian Huxley, *Evolution: The Modern Synthesis* (London: Allen & Unwin, 1942).
2. For example, Gaylord G. Simpson, *The Meaning of Evolution* (New Haven: Yale Univ. Press, 1949). A good summary of the Modern Synthesis is given in Michael Ruse, *Darwinism Defended: A Guide to the Evolution Controversies* (Reading, MA: Addison-Wesley, 1982).
3. Hoimar von Ditfurth, *The Origins of Life: Evolution as Creation* (San Francisco: Harper & Row, 1982).
4. C. H. Waddington, *The Strategy of the Genes* (New York: Macmillan, 1957).
5. Alister Hardy, *The Living Stream* (London: Collins, 1965), chap. 6.
6. R. Goldschmidt, *Theoretical Genetics* (Berkeley: Univ. of California Press, 1955).
7. S. J. Gould and N. Eldredge, "Punctuated Equilibria," *Paleobiology* 3 (1977): 115–51.
8. G. Ledyard Stebbins and Francisco Ayala, "The Evolution of Darwinism," *Scientific American* 253 (July 1985): 72–85; F. Ayala, "The Theory of Evolution: Recent Successes and Challenges," in *Evolution and Creation*, ed. Ernan McMullin (Notre Dame: Univ. of Notre Dame Press, 1985).
9. Stephen Jay Gould, "Darwinism and the Expansion of Evolutionary Theory," *Science* 216 (1982): 384.
10. J. L. King and T. L. Jukes, "Non-Darwinian Evolution," *Science* 164 (1969): 788–98; Motoo Kimura, "The Neutral Theory of Molecular Evolution," *Scientific American* 241 (Nov. 1979): 98–126.
11. David L. Hull, "A Matter of Individuality," *Philosophy of Science* 45 (1978): 355–60; Anthony Arnold and Kurt Fristrup, "A Theory of Natural Selection: A Hierarchical Expansion," in *Genes, Organisms, Populations: Controversies over the Units of Selection*, ed. R. N. Brandon and R. Burian (Cambridge: MIT Press, 1984).
12. John Campbell, "An Organizational Interpretation of Evolution," in *Evolution at the Crossroads*, ed. David Depew and Bruce Weber (Cambridge: MIT Press, 1985); "Autonomy in Evolution," in *Perspectives on Evolution*, ed. Roger Milkman (Sunderland, MA: Sinauer Associates,

1982). See also David P. Depew and Bruce H. Weber, *Darwinism Evolving* (Cambridge: MIT Press, 1995), part III.

13. Stuart Kauffman, "Self-Organization, Selective Adaptation, and Its Limits: A New Pattern of Inference in Evolution and Development," in *Evolution at the Crossroads*, ed. Depew and Weber. See also Marjorie Grene, ed., *Dimensions of Darwinism* (Cambridge: Cambridge Univ. Press, 1984).

14. Mae-Wah Hoh and P. T. Saunders, eds., *Beyond Neo-Darwinism: An Introduction to the New Evolutionary Paradigm* (New York: Harcourt, Brace, Jovanovich, 1984).

15. S. Miller and L. Orgel, *The Origins of Life on the Earth* (Englewood Cliffs, NJ: Prentice-Hall, 1974); C. Folsome, *The Origin of Life* (San Francisco: W. H. Freeman, 1979).

16. A. G. Cairns-Smith, *Seven Clues to the Origin of Life* (Cambridge: Cambridge Univ. Press, 1985), and "The First Organisms," *Scientific American* 252 (June 1985): 90.

17. Manfred Eigen et al., "The Origin of Genetic Material," *Scientific American* 244 (April 1981): 88–118.

18. Jeffrey Wicken, *Evolution, Thermodynamics, and Information* (New York and Oxford: Oxford Univ. Press, 1987).

19. Jeremy Campbell, *Grammatical Man: Information, Entropy, Language, and Life* (London: Penguin Books, 1982), p. 265.

20. David Wilcox, "Of Messages and Molecules" (Paper presented at Princeton Center for Theological Inquiry, Oct. 23, 1988).

21. Wicken, *Evolution*, p. 177.

22. Herbert Simon, "The Organization of Complex Systems," in *Hierarchy Theory*, ed. Howard Patee (New York: George Braziller, 1973).

23. Niles Eldredge and Stanley Salthe, "Hierarchy and Evolution," in *Oxford Surveys of Evolutionary Biology 1984*, ed. Richard Dawkins (Oxford: Oxford Univ. Press, 1985); Stanley Salthe, *Evolving Hierarchical Systems* (New York: Columbia Univ. Press, 1985); F. H. Allen and Thomas B. Starr, *Hierarchy: Perspectives on Biological Complexity* (Chicago: Univ. of Chicago Press, 1982). See also Marjorie Grene, "Hierarchies in Biology," *American Scientist* 75 (1987): 504–10.

24. Francis Crick, *Of Molecules and Men* (Seattle: Univ. of Washington Press, 1966), pp. 14 and 98.

25. See Ian G. Barbour, *Issues in Science and Religion* (Englewood Cliffs, NJ: Prentice-Hall, 1966), pp. 327–37; Francisco Ayala, "Introduction," in *The Problem of Reduction*, ed. F. Ayala and T. Dobzhansky (Berkeley and Los Angeles: Univ. of California Press, 1974); Arthur Peacocke, *God and the New Biology* (London: J. M. Dent and Sons, 1986), chaps. 1 and 2.

26. Clifford Grobstein, "Levels and Ontogeny," *American Scientist* 50 (1962): 52.

27. Ernst Mayr, *The Growth of Biological Thought* (Cambridge: Harvard Univ. Press, 1982), chap. 2.

28. Alexander Rosenberg, *The Structure of Biological Science* (Cambridge: Cambridge Univ. Press, 1985), chaps. 2, 4, and 8.

29. Ernest Nagel, *The Structure of Science* (New York: Harcourt Brace, 1961), chap. 11.

30. Morton Beckner, *The Biological Way of Thought* (New York: Columbia Univ. Press, 1959), chap. 6; also "Reduction, Hierarchies and Organicism," in *The Problem of Reduction*, ed. Ayala and Dobzhansky.

31. Francisco Ayala, "Reduction in Biology: A Recent Challenge," and Ernst Mayr, "How Biology Differs from the Physical Sciences," in *Evolution at the Crossroads*, ed. Depew and Weber.

32. Lindley Darden and Nancy Maull, "Interfield Theories," *Philosophy of Science* 44 (1977): 60 and 61.

33. William Wimsatt, "Reductionism, Levels of Organization, and the Mind-Body Problem," in *Consciousness and the Brain*, ed. G. Globus, G. Maxwell, and I. Savodnik (New York: Plenum, 1976); also "Reduction and Reductionism," in *Current Issues in Philosophy of Science*, ed. P. D. Asquith and H. Kyberg (New York: Philosophy of Science Association, 1978).

34. Stephen Toulmin, "Concepts of Function and Mechanism in Medicine and Medical Science," in *Evaluation and Explanation in the Biomedical Sciences*, ed. H. T. Engelhardt and S. Spicker (Boston: D. Reidel, 1975), p. 53.

35. Charles Hartshorne, *Reality as Social Process* (Glencoe, IL: Free Press, 1953), chap. 1; *The Logic of Perfection* (LaSalle, IL: Open Court, 1962), chap. 7.

36. Michael Polanyi, "Life's Irreducible Structures," *Science* 160 (1968): 1308–12.

37. Donald Campbell, " 'Downward Causation' in Hierarchically Organized Biological Systems," in *The Problem of Reduction*, ed. Ayala and Dobzhansky.

38. Holmes Rolston, *Science and Religion: A Critical Survey* (New York: Random House, 1987), pp. 286–89.

39. Barbour, *Issues in Science and Religion*, pp. 337–44.

40. Stephen Walker, *Animal Thought* (London: Routledge & Kegan Paul, 1983); Donald R. Griffin, *Animal Thinking* (Cambridge: Harvard Univ. Press, 1984).

41. W. E. Agar, *A Contribution to the Theory of the Living Organism*, 2d ed. (Melbourne: Melbourne Univ. Press, 1951); Bernhard Rensch, "Arguments for Panpsychistic Identism," in *Mind in Nature*, ed. J. B. Cobb, Jr., and D. Griffin (Washington, DC: University Press of America, 1977).

42. Sewall Wright, "Gene and Organism," *American Naturalist* 87 (1953): 14; also "Panpsychism and Science," in *Mind and Nature*, ed. Cobb and Griffin.

43. Stephen Jay Gould, *The Panda's Thumb* (New York: Penguin Books, 1980), chap. 1.

44. Jacques Monod, *Chance and Necessity* (New York: Vintage Books, 1972).

45. Fred Hoyle and Chandra Wickramasinghe, *Evolution from Space* (London: Dent, 1981).

46. John Maynard-Smith, *On Evolution* (Edinburgh: Univ. of Edinburgh Press, 1972), p. 89.

47. Stephen Jay Gould, *Ever Since Darwin* (New York: W. W. Norton, 1977), p. 45.

48. John Bowker, "Did God Create This Universe?" in *The Sciences and Theology in the Twentieth Century*, ed. Arthur Peacocke (Notre Dame: Univ. of Notre Dame Press, 1981).

49. Robert John Russell, "Entropy and Evil," *Zygon* 19 (1984): 449–68.

50. D. J. Bartholomew, *God and Chance* (London: SCM Press, 1984).

51. William Pollard, *Chance and Providence* (New York: Charles Scribner's Sons, 1958), chap. 3.

52. Donald MacKay, *Science, Chance, and Providence* (Oxford: Oxford Univ. Press, 1978); Peter T. Geach, *Providence and Evil* (Cambridge: Cambridge Univ. Press, 1977). See also Barrie Britten, "Evolution by Blind Chance," *Scottish Journal of Theology* 39 (1986): 341–60.

53. L. J. Henderson, *The Fitness of the Environment*, (New York: Macmillan, 1913).

54. F. R. Tennant, *Philosophical Theology*, vol. 2 (Cambridge: Cambridge Univ. Press, 1930).

55. John Polkinghorne, *One World: The Interaction of Science and Theology* (Princeton: Princeton Univ. Press, 1987), p. 69.

56. L. Charles Birch, "Creation and Creator," *Journal of Religion* 37 (1957): 85, and *Nature and God* (London: SCM Press, 1965).

57. Conrad Hyers, *The Meaning of Creation* (Atlanta: John Knox, 1984), chap. 8.

58. Arthur Peacocke, *Creation and the World of Science* (Oxford: Clarendon Press, 1979), pp. 131–38; Peacocke, *Intimations of Reality* (Notre Dame: Univ. of Notre Dame Press, 1984), p. 76.

59. Peacocke, *Creation*, pp. 142–43; *Intimations*, p. 64.

60. Peacocke, *Creation*, p. 95.

61. Peacocke, *Intimations*, p. 66.

62. Richard Dawkins, *The Blind Watchmaker: Why the Evidence of Evolution Reveals a Universe without Design* (New York: W. W. Norton, 1987), pp. 13 and 15.

63. Dawkins, *Blind Watchmaker*, p. 5.

64. Dawkins, *Blind Watchmaker*, p. 317. See also Richard Dawkins, *River Out of Eden* (New York: Basic Books, 1995), and *Climbing Mount Improbable* (New York: W. W. Norton, 1996).

65. Stephen Toulmin, "Metaphysical Beliefs," in *Metaphysical Beliefs*, ed. A. Macintyre (London: SCM Press, 1957).

66. Ernan McMullin, "Natural Science and Belief in a Creator," in *Physics, Philosophy, and Theology: A Common Quest for Understanding*, ed. R. J. Russell, W. R. Stoeger, S.J., and G. V. Coyne, S.J. (The Vatican: Vatican Observatory, and Notre Dame: Univ. of Notre Dame Press, 1988).

67. Leconte DuNouy, *Human Destiny* (New York: Longman's, Green, 1947), p. 82.

68. Charles E. Raven, *Natural Religion and Christian Theology* (Cambridge: Cambridge Univ. Press, 1953), 2:183.

69. Hugh Montefiore, *The Probability of God* (London: SCM Press, 1985), chap. 10.
70. Ian G. Barbour, "Five Ways of Reading Teilhard," *Soundings* 51 (1968): 115–45.
71. Pierre Teilhard de Chardin, *The Phenomenon of Man* (New York: Harper & Row, 1959), p. 302.
72. Teilhard, *Man's Place in Nature* (New York: Harper & Brothers, 1966), p. 108.
73. Teilhard, *Christianity and Evolution* (New York: Harcourt Brace Jovanovich, 1971).
74. Ian G. Barbour, "Teilhard's Process Metaphysics," *Journal of Religion* 59 (1969): 136–59.

## Chapter 10

1. Sherwood Washburn, "The Evolution of Man," *Scientific American* 239 (Sept. 1978): 194–207; D. C. Johanson and M. Edey, *Lucy: The Beginnings of Humankind* (New York: Simon & Schuster, 1981).
2. David Pilbeam, "The Descent of Hominoids and Hominids," *Scientific American* 250 (Mar. 1984): 84–96.
3. Paul D. MacLean, "Evolution of the Psychencephalon," *Zygon* 17 (1982): 187–211.
4. D. M. Rumbaugh et al., "The Relationship between Language in Apes and Human Beings," in *Primate Behavior,* ed. J. L. Forbes and J. E. King (New York: Academic Press, 1982); J. deLuce and H. T. Wilder, eds., *Language in Primates* (New York: Springer-Verlag, 1983); Stephen Walker, *Animal Thought* (London: Routledge & Kegan Paul, 1983).
5. Theodosius Dobzhansky, *The Biological Basis of Human Freedom* (New York: Columbia Univ. Press, 1956), and *The Biology of Ultimate Concern* (New York: New American Library, 1967).
6. Edward O. Wilson, *Sociobiology: The New Synthesis* (Cambridge: Harvard Univ. Press, 1975).
7. Richard Dawkins, *The Selfish Gene* (Oxford: Oxford Univ. Press, 1976).
8. Marshall Sahlins, "The Use and Abuse of Biology," in *The Sociobiology Debate,* ed. Arthur Caplan (New York: Harper & Row, 1978). See also George Barbow and James Silverberg, eds., *Sociobiology: Beyond Nature/Nurture?* (Boulder, CO: Westview Press, 1980).
9. Sociobiology Study Group of Science for the People, "Sociobiology—Another Biological Determinism," *BioScience* 26 (Mar. 1976): 182–90.
10. Edward O. Wilson, *On Human Nature* (Cambridge: Harvard Univ. Press, 1978), p. 6.
11. Wilson, *On Human Nature,* p. 195.
12. Wilson, *On Human Nature,* p. 201.
13. Edward O. Wilson, "Religion and Evolutionary Theory," in *Religion, Science, and the Search for Wisdom,* ed. David Byers (Washington, DC: National Conference of Catholic Bishops, 1987), p. 90.
14. Wilson, *On Human Nature,* p. 167.
15. Wilson, *Sociobiology,* p. 4.
16. Wilson, *On Human Nature,* p. 176.
17. Michael Ruse, *Taking Darwin Seriously: A Naturalistic Approach to Philosophy* (New York and Oxford: Basil Blackwell, 1986), chap. 5.
18. Stephen Toulmin, *Human Understanding* (Princeton: Princeton Univ. Press, 1972).
19. Karl Popper, *Objective Knowledge: An Evolutionary Approach* (Oxford: Clarendon Press, 1972). See also Gerard Radnitzky and W. W. Bartley III, eds., *Evolutionary Epistemology: Rationality and the Sociology of Knowledge* (LaSalle, IL: Open Court, 1987).
20. Donald T. Campbell, "Evolutionary Epistemology," in *The Philosophy of Karl Popper,* ed. P. A. Schilpp (LaSalle, IL: Open Court, 1974).
21. David H. Hubel, "The Brain," *Scientific American* 241 (Sept. 1979): 45–52.
22. Sally Springer and Georg Deutsch, *Left Brain, Right Brain,* rev. ed. (San Francisco: W. H. Freeman, 1985).
23. A good overview is Jerome Shaffer, "The Mind-Body Problem," in *Encyclopedia of Philosophy,* ed. Paul Edwards (New York: Macmillan, 1967).
24. Wilder Penfield, *The Mystery of Mind* (Princeton: Princeton Univ. Press, 1975).
25. Karl Popper and John Eccles, *The Self and Its Brain* (New York and Berlin: Springer International, 1977), p. 355.
26. Popper and Eccles, *Self and Its Brain,* part 1.

27. B. F. Skinner, *Science and Human Behavior* (New York: Macmillan, 1956).
28. Gilbert Ryle, *The Concept of Mind* (London: Hutchinson's Univ. Library, 1949).
29. George Santayana, *The Realm of Essence* (New York: Charles Scribner's Sons, 1927); Francis Crick, *The Astonishing Hypothesis: The Scientific Search for the Soul* (New York: Charles Scribner's Sons, 1994).
30. Herbert Feigl, "The 'Mental' and the 'Physical,'" in *Minnesota Studies in the Philosophy of Science,* ed. H. Feigl et al., vol. 2 (Minneapolis: Univ. of Minnesota Press, 1958); J. J. C. Smart, "Materialism," *The Journal of Philosophy* 60 (1963): 651–62.
31. P. F. Strawson, *Individuals: An Essay in Descriptive Metaphysics* (London: Methuen, 1959).
32. Donald M. MacKay, *Brains, Machines, and Persons* (London: Collins, 1980).
33. Roger W. Sperry, "The New Mentalist Paradigm," *Perspectives in Biology and Medicine* 29 (Spring 1986): 417, and "Science, Values, and Survival," *Journal of Humanistic Psychology* 26 (Spring 1986): 21.
34. Sperry, "Science, Values, and Survival," p. 22, and *Science and Moral Priority* (New York: Columbia Univ. Press, 1983), p. 92.
35. Sperry, *Science and Moral Priority,* p. 100.
36. Ralph Wendell Burhoe, "The Human Prospect and 'The Lord of History,'" *Zygon* 10 (1975): 299–375.
37. Ralph Wendell Burhoe, "War, Peace, and Religion's Biocultural Evolution," *Zygon* 21 (1986): 439–72.
38. Burhoe, "The Human Prospect," p. 367. See also "Natural Selection and God," *Zygon* 7 (1972): 30–63.
39. See responses to Burhoe by Philip Hefner, Donald Musser, W. Widick Schroeder, and Arnold W. Raven in *Zygon* 12 (1977): 4–103. Burhoe's reply appears in *Zygon* 12 (1977): 336–89.
40. Eugene G. d'Aquili, "The Myth-Ritual Complex: A Biogenetic Structural Analysis," *Zygon* 18 (1983): 247–69.
41. Victor Turner, "Body, Brain, and Culture," *Zygon* 18 (1983): 221–45; Turner tries to integrate genetic and cultural factors. A purely cultural view is Arnold van Gennep, *The Rites of Passage* (London: Routledge & Kegan Paul, 1963).
42. A.F.C. Wallace, *Religion: An Anthropological View* (New York: Random House, 1966). See also chapters by Stanley Hyman and Lord Raglan in *Myth: A Symposium,* ed. Thomas A. Sebeok (Bloomington: Univ. of Indiana Press, 1958).
43. A good summary of the functions of ritual is given in Roger Schmidt, *Exploring Religion* (Belmont, CA: Wadsworth, 1980), chap. 8.
44. Mircea Eliade, *The Sacred and the Profane,* trans. W. Trask (New York: Harcourt, Brace & World, 1959), chap. 2; G. van der Leeuw, *Religion in Essence and Manifestation,* trans. J. E. Turner (London: Allen & Unwin, 1938), chap. 60.
45. Claude Levi-Strauss, *Structural Anthropology,* trans. C. Jacobson and B. G. Schoepf (New York: Basic Books, 1963).
46. Eugene d'Aquili, "Senses of Reality in Science and Religion: A Neuroepistemological Perspective," *Zygon* 17 (1982): 361–84; "Neuroepistemology," in *The Encyclopedia of Religion,* ed. Mircea Eliade (New York: Macmillan, 1987).
47. Karl Jaspers, *The Origin and Goal of History* (New Haven: Yale Univ. Press, 1953).
48. Gerd Theissen, *Biblical Faith: An Evolutionary Approach,* trans. J. Bowden (Philadelphia: Fortress Press, 1985).
49. Emile Durkheim, *Elementary Forms of Religious Life* (1912; reprint, New York: Collier, 1961).
50. Max Weber, *The Sociology of Religion* (1922; reprint, Boston: Beacon Press, 1963).
51. Frederick J. Streng, *Understanding Religious Life,* 2d ed. (Belmont, CA: Belmont Publishing, 1976), p. 50.
52. See, for example, Walther Eichrodt, *Man in the Old Testament,* trans. K. and R. Gregor Smith (London: SCM Press, 1951); Frederick C. Grant, *An Introduction to New Testament Thought* (Nashville: Abingdon Press, 1950), pp. 160–70.
53. See Reinhold Niebuhr, *The Nature and Destiny of Man* (New York: Charles Scribner's Sons, 1943), 1:173–77.

54. Matthew Fox, *Original Blessing* (Sante Fe: Bear, 1983).
55. Niebuhr, *Nature and Destiny*, vol. 1, chaps. 7 and 8.
56. Paul Tillich, *The Shaking of the Foundations* (New York: Charles Scribner's Sons, 1948), pp. 153–63; *Systematic Theology* (Chicago: Univ. of Chicago Press, 1957), 2:44–78.
57. H. Wheeler Robinson, *Religious Ideas of the Old Testament* (London: Gerald Duckworth, 1913).
58. Oscar Cullmann, *Immortality of the Soul or Resurrection of the Dead?* (New York: Macmillan, 1958), p. 30.
59. Lynn de Silva, *The Problem of Self in Buddhism and Christianity* (London: Macmillan, 1979), p. 75.
60. Cullmann, *Immortality*.
61. David Kelsey, "Human Being," and Robert Williams, "Sin and Evil," in *Christian Theology*, 2d ed., ed. Peter Hodgson and Robert King (Philadelphia: Fortress Press, 1985).
62. See Ian G. Barbour, *Technology, Environment and Human Values* (New York: Praeger, 1980), chap. 2.
63. Reginald Fuller, *The Foundations of New Testament Christology* (New York: Charles Scribner's Sons, 1965).
64. Sydney Cave, *The Doctrine of the Person of Christ* (London: Gerald Duckworth, 1925), chaps. 1–4; John McIntyre, *The Shape of Christology* (Philadelphia: Westminster Press, 1966), chap. 4; Walter Lowe, "Christ and Salvation," in *Christian Theology*, ed. Hodgson and King.
65. See D. M. Baillie, *God Was in Christ* (New York: Charles Scribner's Sons, 1948), especially chap. 5 on the paradox of grace.
66. G. W. H. Lampe, *God as Spirit* (Oxford: Clarendon Press, 1977).
67. Lampe, *God as Spirit*, p. 115.
68. Lionel Thornton, *The Incarnate Lord* (London: Longman's, Green, 1928). See also W. Norman Pittenger, *The Word Incarnate* (New York: Harper and Brothers, 1959).
69. Pierre Teilhard de Chardin, *Christianity and Evolution* (New York: Harcourt Brace Jovanovich, 1971).
70. Tillich, *Systematic Theology*, 2:165–80.
71. Baillie, *God Was in Christ*, chaps. 7 and 8; Robert S. Franks, *The Work of Christ* (London and New York: Nelson, 1962).
72. Richard Leakey was quoted on the National Public Radio program *All Things Considered*, Dec. 19, 1988.
73. Philip Hefner, "Theology's Truth and Scientific Formulation," *Zygon* 23 (1988): 270; *The Human Factor: Evolution, Culture and Religion* (Minneapolis: Fortress Press, 1993).
74. Philip Hefner, "The Evolution of the Created Co-Creator" in *Cosmos as Creation: Science and Theology in Consonance*, ed. Ted Peters (Nashville: Abingdon Press, 1989), p. 232. See also Hefner, "Can a Theology of Nature be Coherent with Scientific Cosmology," in *Evolution and Creation*, ed. S. Anderson and A. Peacocke (Aarhus, Denmark: Aarhus Univ. Press, 1987).
75. Roger Shinn, ed. *Faith and Science in an Unjust World* (Geneva: World Council of Churches, 1980).
76. World Council of Churches, *Gathered for Life* (Geneva: WCC, 1983).

## Chapter 11

1. See also N. Max Wildiers, *The Theologian and His Universe* (New York: Seabury, 1982).
2. Alfred North Whitehead, *Process and Reality* (New York: Macmillan, 1929), p. vi.
3. An introduction to process metaphysics is given in John B. Cobb, Jr., and David Ray Griffin, *Process Theology: An Introduction* (Philadelphia: Westminster Press, 1976), chap. 1. The basic sources are Alfred North Whitehead, *Science and the Modern World* (New York: Macmillan, 1925) and *Process and Reality*. Systematic expositions are given in William Christian, *An Interpretation of Whitehead's Metaphysics* (New Haven: Yale Univ. Press, 1959), and Ivor Leclerc, *Whitehead's Metaphysics* (New York: Macmillan, 1958). See Ian G. Barbour, *Issues in Science and Religion* (Englewood Cliffs, NJ: Prentice-Hall, 1966), pp. 128–31, 344–47. I have tried to present Whitehead's ideas with a minimal use of his technical terms.

4. Charles Birch and John B. Cobb, Jr., *The Liberation of Life* (Cambridge: Cambridge Univ. Press, 1981).
5. Charles Hartshorne, *Reality as Social Process* (Glencoe, IL: Free Press, 1953), chap. 1, and *The Logic of Perfection* (LaSalle, IL: Open Court, 1962), chap. 7.
6. I am indebted here to David Ray Griffin, "On Ian Barbour's *Issues in Science and Religion*," *Zygon* 23 (1988): 57–81.
7. David Ray Griffin, "Some Whiteheadian Comments," in *Mind in Nature: Essays on the Interface of Science and Philosophy*, ed. John Cobb, Jr., and David Ray Griffin (Washington, DC: University Press of America, 1977).
8. David Ray Griffin, "Of Minds and Molecules: Postmodern Medicine in a Psychosomatic Universe," in *The Reenchantment of Science*, ed. D. Griffin (Albany: State Univ. of New York Press, 1988), p. 154.
9. See David Pailin, "God as Creator in a Whiteheadian Understanding," in *Whitehead and the Idea of Process*, ed. H. Holz and E. Wolf-Gazo (Freiburg and München: Karl Alber Verlag, 1984); Frank Kirkpatrick, "Process or Agent: Two Models for Self and God," in *Philosophy of Religion and Theology*, ed. David Ray Griffin (Chambersburg, PA: American Academy of Religion, 1971); Paul Sponheim, *Faith and Process: The Significance of Process Thought for Christian Thought* (Minneapolis: Augsburg, 1979), pp. 90–98.
10. William Gallagher, "Whitehead's Psychological Physiology: A Third View," *Process Studies* 4 (1974): 263–74; Joseph Earley, "Self-Organization and Agency in Chemistry and in Process Philosophy," *Process Studies* 11 (1981): 242–58.
11. Mark Davidson, *Uncommon Sense: The Life and Thought of Ludwig von Bertalanffy, Father of General Systems Theory* (Los Angeles: J. P. Tarcher, 1983); Ervin Laszlo, *An Introduction to Systems Philosophy* (New York: Gordon & Breach, 1972).
12. James Huchingson, "Organization and Process: Systems Philosophy and Whiteheadian Metaphysics," *Zygon* 11 (1981): 226–41.
13. Alfred North Whitehead, *Modes of Thought* (Cambridge: Cambridge Univ. Press, 1938), p. 211.
14. Griffin, "On Ian Barbour's *Issues*," p. 57.
15. See Barbour, *Issues in Science and Religion*, pp. 440–42.
16. Whitehead, *Process and Reality*, p. 377.
17. Whitehead, *Process and Reality*, p. 532.
18. Charles Hartshorne, *The Divine Relativity* (New Haven: Yale Univ. Press, 1948), and *Reality as Social Process;* Charles Hartshorne and William L. Reese, *Philosophers Speak of God* (Chicago: Univ. of Chicago Press, 1953).
19. Hartshorne, *Divine Relativity*, p. 90.
20. See Christian, *Interpretation of Whitehead's Metaphysics;* Ivor Leclerc, *Whitehead's Metaphysics.*
21. Whitehead, *Process and Reality*, p. 521.
22. Whitehead, *Process and Reality*, p. 343.
23. Daniel Williams, "How Does God Act? An Essay in Whitehead's Metaphysics," in *Process and Divinity*, ed. W. L. Reese and E. Freeman (LaSalle, IL: Open Court, 1964).
24. Cobb and Griffin, *Process Theology*, chap. 3.
25. Cobb and Griffin, *Process Theology*, chap. 6; David Ray Griffin, *A Process Christology* (Philadelphia: Westminster Press, 1973); John B. Cobb, Jr., "A Whiteheadian Christology," in *Process Philosophy and Christian Thought*, ed. D. Brown, R. E. James, and G. Reeves (Indianapolis: Bobbs-Merrill Company, 1971). A more recent version is his "Christ Beyond Creative Transformation," in *Encountering Jesus: A Debate on Christology*, ed. Stephen Davis (Atlanta: John Knox Press, 1988).
26. Lewis Ford, "The Power of God and the Christ," in *Religious Experience and Process Theology*, ed. Harry James Cargas and Bernard Lee (New York: Paulist Press, 1976).
27. Sponheim, *Faith and Process*, p. 49.
28. Marjorie Hewitt Suchocki, *God, Christ, Church: A Practical Guide to Process Theology* (New York: Crossroad, 1982).
29. John B. Cobb, Jr., "Spiritual Discernment in a Whiteheadian Perspective," in *Religious Experience and Process Theology*, ed. Cargas and Lee.

30. Martin Buber, *Between Man and Man* (London: Macmillan, 1947), pp. 10–11, 15–16.

31. Suchocki, "Openness and Mutuality," in *Feminism and Process Thought*, ed. Sheila Greeve Davaney (New York and Toronto: Edwin Mellen Press, 1978).

32. Albert Camus, *The Plague*, trans. Stuart Gilbert (New York: Modern Library, 1948), p. 196.

33. See Ronald Green, "Theodicy," in *The Encyclopedia of Religion*, ed. Mircea Eliade (New York: Macmillan, 1987).

34. See Alvin Plantinga, *God and Other Minds* (Ithaca: Cornell Univ. Press, 1967), chaps. 5 and 6; also *God, Freedom, and Evil* (New York: Harper & Row, 1974).

35. John Hick, *Evil and the God of Love*, 2d ed. (New York: Harper & Row, 1977); "An Irenaean Theodicy," in *Encountering Evil: Live Options in Theodicy*, ed. Stephen T. Davis (Atlanta: John Knox Press, 1981).

36. David Ray Griffin, *God, Power, and Evil: A Process Theodicy* (Philadelphia: Westminster Press, 1976); "Creation Out of Chaos and the Problem of Evil," in *Encountering Evil*, ed. Davis. Hartshorne's theodicy is discussed in Barry L. Whitney, *Evil and the Process God* (Toronto: Edwin Mellen Press, 1985).

37. John B. Cobb, Jr., "What is the Future? A Process Perspective," in *Hope and the Future of Man*, ed. Ewert Cousins (Philadelphia: Fortress Press, 1972). See also Robert Mellert, "A Pastoral on Death and Immortality," in *Religious Experience and Process Theology*, ed. Cargas and Lee.

## Chapter 12

1. For an overview of some of these options, see Owen Thomas, ed., *God's Activity in the World* (Chico, CA: Scholars Press, 1983). See also Ian G. Barbour, *Issues in Science and Religion* (Englewood Cliffs, NJ: Prentice-Hall, 1966), chap. 13.

2. Thomas Aquinas, *Summa Theologica* I, q. 22, art. 4; q. 19, art. 4; q. 105, art. 5, etc. See also Étienne Gilson, *The Christian Philosophy of Thomas Aquinas* (New York: Random House, 1956).

3. Dante Alighieri, *The Paradiso*, trans. John Ciardi (New York: New American Library, 1970), canto 33.

4. E. L. Mascall, *He Who Is: A Study in Traditional Theism* (London: Longman's, Green, 1945).

5. H. P. Owen, *Concepts of Deity* (London: Macmillan, 1971).

6. Richard Creel, *Divine Impassibility: An Essay in Philosophical Theology* (Cambridge: Cambridge Univ. Press, 1986).

7. Richard S. Westfall, *Science and Religion in Seventeenth-Century England* (New Haven: Yale Univ. Press, 1958).

8. Étienne Gilson, "The Corporeal World and the Efficacy of Second Causes," in *God's Activity in the World*, ed. Thomas.

9. Gilson, "Corporeal World," in *God's Activity in the World*, ed. Thomas; also Gilson's *The Spirit of Medieval Philosophy* (New York: Charles Scribner's Sons, 1940), chap. 7; Brother Benignus Gerrity, *Nature, Knowledge, and God* (Milwaukee: Bruce Publishing, 1947).

10. Reginald Garrigou-Lagrange, *God: His Existence and His Nature* (St. Louis: Herder, 1934).

11. Austin Farrer, *A Science of God?* (London: Geoffrey Bles, 1966), pp. 76 and 90. See also his *Faith and Speculation* (London: Adam & Charles Black, 1967), chaps. 4 and 10.

12. Karl Barth, *Church Dogmatics*, vol. 3, pt. 3 (Edinburgh, Scotland: T & T Clark, 1958), p. 148.

13. Barth, *Church Dogmatics*, vol. 3, pt. 3, pp. 42, 94, 106, and 133.

14. William Pollard, *Chance and Providence* (New York: Charles Scribner's Sons, 1958); Donald MacKay, *Science, Chance, and Providence* (Oxford: Oxford Univ. Press, 1978).

15. Nancey Murphy, "Divine Action in the Natural Order: Buridan's Ass and Schrödinger's Cat," in *Chaos and Complexity*, ed. Robert John Russell, Nancey Murphy, and Arthur R. Peacocke (Rome: Vatican Observatory, and Berkeley: Center for Theology and the Natural Sciences, 1995); Nancey Murphy and George F. R. Ellis, *On the Moral Nature of the Universe: Theology, Cosmology and Ethics* (Minneapolis: Fortress Press, 1996).

16. Thomas F. Tracy, "Particular Providence and the God of the Gaps," and George F. R. Ellis, "Ordinary and Extraordinary Divine Action: The Nexus of Interaction," in *Chaos and Complexity*, ed. Russell et al.; Robert John Russell, "Theistic Evolution and Special Providence: Does God Really Act in Nature?" in *Evolutionary and Molecular Biology: Scientific Perspectives on*

*Divine Action,* ed. R. J. Russell, W. R. Stoeger, and F. J Ayala (Vatican Observatory, and Berkeley: Center for Theology and the Natural Sciences, 1997).

17. John Polkinghorne, *Reason and Reality* (Philadelphia: Trinity International Press, 1991), chap. 3, and *The Faith of a Physicist* (Princeton: Princeton Univ. Press, 1994), pp. 77–78; "The Metaphysics of Divine Action," in *Chaos and Complexity,* ed. Russell et al.

18. Arthur R. Peacocke, *Creation and the World of Science* (Oxford: Clarendon Press, 1979), chap. 3, and *Theology for a Scientific Age,* enl. ed. (Minneapolis: Fortress Press, 1993), chap. 9.

19. Arthur R. Peacocke, "God's Interaction with the World," in *Chaos and Complexity,* ed. Russell et al.

20. John Puddefoot, "Information Theory, Biology, and Christology," in *Religion and Science: History, Method, Dialogue,* ed. W. Mark Richardson and Wesley J. Wildman (New York: Routledge, 1996).

21. H. Wheeler Robinson, *The Cross in the Old Testament* (London: SCM Press, 1955); Terence E. Fretheim, *The Suffering of God: An Old Testament Perspective* (Philadelphia: Fortress Press, 1984). "The divine pathos" is discussed by the Jewish scholar Abraham Heschel in *The Prophets* (San Francisco: Harper & Row, 1965), pp. 24, 237, and 483. A Christian rendition is given in Jürgen Moltmann, *The Crucified God,* trans. R. A. Wilson and J. Bowden (London: SCM Press, 1974).

22. Doctrine Commission of the General Synod of the Church of England, *We Believe in God* (London: Church Publishing House, 1987), chap. 9.

23. W. H. Vanstone, *Love's Endeavor, Love's Expense* (London: Dartmon, Longman and Todd, 1977), pp. 63 and 64.

24. Vanstone, *Love's Endeavor,* p. 120.

25. Brian Hebblethwaite, "Providence and Divine Action," *Religious Studies* 14 (1978): 223–36, and "Some Reflections on Predestination, Providence, and Divine Foreknowledge," *Religious Studies* 15 (1979): 433–48.

26. Keith Ward, *Rational Theology and the Creativity of God* (Oxford: Basil Blackwell, 1982); also Ward, *God, Chance, and Necessity* (Oxford: One World Publications, 1996).

27. John Macquarrie, *In Search of Deity: An Essay in Dialectical Theism* (London: SCM Press, 1984).

28. Paul S. Fiddes, *The Creative Suffering of God* (Oxford: Clarendon Press, 1988).

29. Fiddes, *Creative Suffering of God,* p. 157. A kenotic view of God is also presented in Nancey Murphy and George Ellis, *On the Moral Nature of the Universe: Theology, Cosmology, and Ethics* (Minneapolis: Fortress Press, 1996).

30. Alan White, ed., *The Philosophy of Action* (Oxford: Oxford Univ. Press, 1968).

31. John J. Compton, "Science and God's Action in Nature," in *Earth Might be Fair,* ed. Ian G. Barbour (Englewood Cliffs, NJ: Prentice-Hall, 1972), p. 39.

32. Gordon Kaufman, "On the Meaning of 'Act of God,'" *Harvard Theological Review* 61 (1968): 175.

33. Maurice Wiles, *God's Action in the World* (London: SCM Press, 1986), p. 93.

34. Wiles, *God's Action in the World,* p. 107.

35. Grace Jantzen, *God's World, God's Body* (Philadelphia: Westminster Press, 1984).

36. Jantzen, *God's World, God's Body,* p. 156.

37. Thomas Tracy, *God's Action and Embodiment* (Grand Rapids: Eerdmans, 1984).

38. Charles Hartshorne, *Man's Vision of God* (Chicago: Willet Clark, 1941), chap. 5, and *The Logic of Perfection* (LaSalle, IL: Open Court, 1962), chap. 7.

39. Colin Gunton, *Becoming and Being: The Doctrine of God in Charles Hartshorne and Karl Barth* (Oxford: Oxford Univ. Press, 1978).

# Glossary

This glossary identifies briefly some crucial terms as they are used in this volume (some of the terms have other meanings in other contexts). A more extensive elaboration of each entry may be found on the page cited. Those marked with an asterisk may be pursued further on the pages listed in the Index of Selected Topics. Related terms are cross-referenced by the instruction "see"; contrasted terms are indicated by "compare."

AGNOSTICISM: The claim that there are insufficient grounds for either belief or disbelief in any ultimate reality. The agnostic does not deny the existence of God but denies the possibility of knowledge of God (compare THEISM). 43

AMINO ACID: One of twenty organic compounds containing an amino group ($NH_2$) and a carboxylic group (COOH), which are assembled to form the proteins found in all organisms (see DNA). 226

ANTHROPIC PRINCIPLE: The assertion that the physical constants of the early universe were delicately balanced or "fine-tuned": if they had had even slightly different values, carbon-based life and our presence as intelligent observers would not have been possible. 204

ANTHROPOCENTRISM: A view of the world in which humanity is central and all other creatures serve human interests. 8

*CHAOS THEORY: The theory of nonlinear dynamic systems in which infinitesimal changes in initial conditions can result in very large changes in subsequent behavior. 182

*COMPLEMENTARITY: The relationship between contrasting models and concepts, such as wave and particle, used to describe the same entity in quantum theory—and by extension in other disciplines (see QUANTUM THEORY). 167

*COMPLEXITY: The emergence of higher levels of order in the self-organization of systems with many components (see LEVEL, THERMODYNAMICS). 182

CONTINGENT: An event or relationship is contingent if it is not necessary or if it is dependent on particular conditions that may or may not occur. 209

COSMOLOGY: Religious, philosophical, or scientific beliefs about the origin, structure, and nature of the universe. 16

*DEISM: The belief that God created a law-abiding world and left it to run on its own (compare PANTHEISM, THEISM). 36

*DETERMINISM: (1) *Natural Determinism,* the claim that every event is the lawful consequence of antecedent events and is in principle predictable from knowledge of scientific laws and antecedent conditions; (2) *Theological Determinism,* the claim that God determines everything that happens, usually combined with belief that God foresees all events. 34, 306

*DNA: Deoxyribonucleic Acid, a helical molecule with two strands composed of sequences of nucleotide bases in triplets, each of which specifies a particular amino acid in the assembly of a protein chain (see AMINO ACID, GENE, INFORMATION). 225

*DUALISM: The claim that there are two distinct types of basic entity in the world, such as soul and body or mind and matter (compare IDEALISM, MATERIALISM). 259

*EMPIRICISM: The claim, first systematically articulated by Locke and Hume, that sensory experience is the primary source of knowledge and the justification for the truth of propositions. 43

ENTROPY: A measure of the disorder of a system. In closed systems, entropy tends to increase, accompanied by the loss of useful energy and loss of the information present in ordered patterns (see INFORMATION, THERMODYNAMICS). 181

EPISTEMOLOGY: Philosophical analysis of theories of knowledge and accounts of how knowledge is possible (includes EMPIRICISM, INSTRUMENTALISM, LINGUISTIC ANALYSIS, REALISM). 3

*ESCHATOLOGY: Beliefs concerning the end of history and the ultimate destiny of humanity and the world. 216

*EXISTENTIALISM: A twentieth-century movement that stresses human freedom, authenticity in facing finitude and death, and the distinctive character of personal existence (in contrast to the world of impersonal objects studied in science and the abstractions of philosophical systems). 85

GENE: A unit of the germ plasm that transmits specific hereditary characteristics; currently identified as a segment of DNA inherited by an organism from one of its parents (see DNA, SPECIES). 221

GRAND UNIFIED THEORY: A theory encompassing electromagnetic, weak nuclear, and strong nuclear forces, which would have been unified in the very early universe at temperatures and energies higher than those in any existing laboratory accelerator (see SUPERSYMMETRY). 196

*IDEALISM: A philosophical position asserting that mind or ideas are more fundamental than matter. Variant versions claim that archetypal forms, plans of biological organization, or eternal mathematical relationships underlie the structures in the world, or that the mind of the observer plays a central role in observations in quantum physics (compare DUALISM, MATERIALISM). 184

*INDETERMINACY: A property of nature if uncertainty in the prediction of quantum events is ascribed to the presence of a range of potentialities and the absence of exact laws in nature itself, rather than to the limitations of our knowledge of nature (see QUANTUM THEORY). 170

*INFORMATION: An ordered pattern (of alphabetical letters, binary digits, DNA bases, or any other distinguishable elements) that is one among many possible states of a system. Information is communicated when another system (a reader, computer, organic process, and so forth) responds to the pattern selectively—that is, when information is coded, transmitted, and decoded (see ENTROPY, DNA). 228

*INSTRUMENTALISM: The claim that ideas are instruments of action that can be judged only by their usefulness rather than as propositions that might be true or false. This includes the claims: (1) that scientific models and theories are only calculating devices for predicting and controlling observable phenomena, and (2) that religious beliefs can be judged only by their functions in individual and social life (compare REALISM). 168

*KENOTIC: A theology emphasizing God's voluntary self-limitation and vulnerability to suffering (rather than omnipotence and immutability). 315

LAMARCKISM: The theory (following Lamarck) that evolutionary changes in a species are primarily the product of changes in individual organisms acquired during their lifetime by habitual use and inherited by their descendants (compare NATURAL SELECTION). 54

*LEVEL: A part or aspect of a system that is relatively integrated and stable even when it interacts with other systems or subsystems in a hierarchy of levels. According to critical realism, epistemological *levels of analysis* reflect ontological *levels of organization* and *levels of activity* in the world (see COMPLEXITY; compare REDUCTIONISM). 233

*LINGUISTIC ANALYSIS: A philosophical movement initiated in England in the 1950s holding that differing types of language (scientific, religious, moral, and so forth) serve differing functions in human life not reducible to one another (see INSTRUMENTALISM). 87

*MATERIALISM: The belief that matter is the fundamental reality in the universe and that all phenomena can in principle be explained by the laws of matter (compare DUALISM, IDEALISM). 78

METAPHYSICS: Philosophical analysis of the most general characteristics and components of reality (includes DUALISM, IDEALISM, MATERIALISM, NEO-THOMISM, PROCESS PHILOSOPHY). 3

*MODEL: An imaginative representation of characteristics of an entity that is not directly observable and that is postulated by analogy with entities in a more familiar domain. Models contribute to the formulation of scientific theories that can be tested against data and to religious concepts used to interpret historical events and religious experience (see REALISM: CRITICAL REALISM). 115

NATURAL SELECTION: The theory formulated by Darwin and Wallace that some heritable variations among members of a species confer a slight advantage in the competitive struggle for survival, resulting in a gradual modification of the characteristics of the species and the formation of new species (compare LAMARCKISM; see SOCIOBIOLOGY, SPECIES). 52

*NATURAL THEOLOGY: Arguments for the existence of God based on human reason and observation, including arguments starting from evidence of design in nature or in the processes of nature (rather than from religious experience or revelation, as in a THEOLOGY OF NATURE). 98

*NEO-ORTHODOXY: A theological movement (initiated by Karl Barth in the 1920s in response to Protestant liberalism) that reclaims the Reformation's emphasis on the centrality of Christ and the sovereignty of God while remaining open to modern biblical scholarship. 85

*NEO-THOMISM: A twentieth-century movement, primarily among Roman Catholic and Anglican authors, that reformulates the thought of Thomas Aquinas in dealing with contemporary philosophical and theological problems. 309

ONTOLOGICAL: Referring to characteristics of reality (in contrast to epistemological, which means referring to characteristics of knowledge; see EPISTEMOLOGY). 232

*PANTHEISM: The view that God is identical with the totality of nature or the laws of nature or a world soul immanent in nature and not in any way transcending it (compare DEISM, THEISM). 16

*PARADIGM: Thomas Kuhn's term for a cluster of conceptual, methodological, and metaphysical presuppositions embodied in a tradition of scientific research. In a paradigm shift (such as that from classical physics to quantum theory and relativity), basic concepts are reformulated and familiar data are reinterpreted in radically new ways. 125

*PROCESS PHILOSOPHY: A systematic metaphysics, developed by Whitehead and others, emphasizing temporal becoming and the interdependence of events; the basic components of reality are portrayed as processes of becoming, which can also be viewed as moments of experience rather than as passive objects externally related to each other. 284

*QUANTUM THEORY: A theory first formulated in the 1920s in which the properties of atoms and subatomic particles are represented by wave functions and mathematical operators that allow prediction of the probability but not the exact value of observable events (see COMPLEMENTARITY, INDETERMINACY). 166

*REALISM: (1) *Classical Realism,* the view that objects have properties independent of our experience or knowledge of them; in science, the view that valid models and theories provide a representation of the world as it is in itself apart from the observer (compare IDEALISM); (2) *Critical Realism,* the view that models and theories inadequately and selectively represent particular aspects of the world for specific purposes (a position intermediate between CLASSICAL REALISM and INSTRUMENTALISM). 168

*REDUCTIONISM: Advocacy of: (1) *methodological reduction,* a useful research strategy in which the behavior of complex wholes is approached by analyzing their component parts, or (2) *epistemological reduction,* the claim that theories or laws at any level of analysis are derivable from theories or laws at lower levels, or (3) *ontological reduction,* the metaphysical claim that reality consists only of the simplest components organized in particular ways (see MATERIALISM). The second and third forms are criticized in this volume. 230

*RELATIVITY: (1) *Special Relativity,* Einstein's theory relating measurements of space, time, and mass for objects moving uniformly with respect to the observer (a theory implying a space-time continuum and the equivalence of mass and energy); (2) *General Relativity,* his theory relating accelerated motion, gravitational force, and the curvature of space (leading to equations of which an expanding universe is one solution). 177

RELIGION: A tradition of shared rituals, stories, experiences, beliefs, and ethical norms in which life is viewed in a wider context of meaning; most (but not all) religious traditions have sacred texts or scriptures, and most express belief in a higher power transcending human life (see RELIGIOUS EXPERIENCE, THEOLOGY). 110

*RELIGIOUS EXPERIENCE: The personal experiences characteristic of members of a religious community, including: numinous experience of the holy, mystical experience of unity, transformative experience of reorientation, courage in facing suffering and death, moral experience of obligation, and awe in response to order and creativity in the world (see RELIGION). 111

*REVELATION: God's self-disclosure (1) in *the natural world,* or (2) in the *scriptures* of a religious tradition, or (3) in *historical events* and in *the lives of persons* in a religious tradition (such as the Hebrew prophets and the person of Christ in the Christian tradition). The third view, which is defended in this volume, sees scripture as a human interpretation of revelatory events rather than as itself directly revealed by God (see THEOLOGY). 135

SOCIOBIOLOGY: The study of the evolutionary and genetic origins of social behavior in non-human and human species (see GENE, NATURAL SELECTION). 255

SPECIES: (1) in taxonomy, the lowest subdivision in the classification of types of organism according to the physiological characteristics that they share in common; (2) in current evolutionary theory, a population of potentially interbreeding organisms sharing a common gene pool (see GENE, NATURAL SELECTION). 222

SUPERSYMMETRY THEORY (or THEORY OF EVERYTHING): A theory unifying the four fundamental physical forces, applicable at the enormously high temperatures in the earliest instant of the universe before gravitational forces separated from electromagnetic, weak nuclear, and strong nuclear forces (see GRAND UNIFIED THEORY). 196

TELEOLOGICAL: Directed toward an end, goal, or purpose. The teleological argument claims that evidence of design in the natural world or in the processes of nature implies the presence of an intelligent Designer (see NATURAL THEOLOGY). 99

*THEISM: The view that God is a personal and purposeful eternal being transcending the world but also immanent in it (compare AGNOSTICISM, DEISM, PANTHEISM). 7

THEOLOGY: Critical reflection on the beliefs of a religious community in the context of its rituals, stories, experiences, and ethical norms, especially (in this volume) beliefs about God, nature, and human nature in various strands of the Christian tradition (see RELIGION, RELIGIOUS EXPERIENCE). 113

*THEOLOGY OF NATURE: Critical reflection, within a tradition based on historical revelation and religious experience, in which theological beliefs concerning nature are reformulated in the light of contemporary science. Traditional ideas of creation, providence, and human nature are modified to ensure consistency with well-supported scientific theories but are not derived primarily from science (compare NATURAL THEOLOGY). 100

THERMODYNAMICS: The study of heat flow and changes in energy and order in closed and open systems (see ENTROPY, COMPLEXITY). 181

# Index of Names

*Page numbers in italics refer to notes.*

# Index of Selected Topics